D1201675

St. Louis Community College

Forest Park
Florissant Valley
Meramec

Instructional Resources
St. Louis, Missouri

Theory and Research
on Small Groups

St. Louis Community College
at Meramec
Library

SOCIAL PSYCHOLOGICAL APPLICATIONS TO SOCIAL ISSUES

Published under the auspices of the
Society for the Psychological Study of Social Issues

A Continuation Order Plan is available for this series. A continuation order will bring delivery of each new volume
immediately upon publication. Volumes are billed only upon actual shipment. For further information please contact
the publisher.

Theory and Research on Small Groups

Edited by

R. Scott Tindale, Linda Heath, John Edwards, Emil J. Posavac, Fred B. Bryant, Yolanda Suarez-Balcazar, Eaaron Henderson-King, and Judith Myers

Loyola University of Chicago
Chicago, Illinois

A project of the faculty and students
in the Applied Social Psychology Graduate Program
at Loyola University of Chicago and
published under the auspices of the
Society for the Psychological Study of Social Issues

PLENUM PRESS • NEW YORK AND LONDON

Library of Congress Cataloging-in-Publication Data

Theory and research on small groups / edited by R. Scott Tindale ...
[et al.].
       p.   cm. -- (Social psychological applications to social issues
  ; v. 4)
       "A project of the faculty and students in the Applied Social
Psychology Graduate Program at Loyola University of Chicago and
published under the auspices of the Society for the Psychological
Study of Social Issues."
    Includes bibliographical references and index.
    ISBN 0-306-45679-6
    1. Small groups. 2. Small groups--Psychological aspects.
3. Small groups--Research.   I. Tindale, R. Scott. II. Loyola
University of Chicago. Applied Social Psychology Graduate Program.
III. Society for the Psychological Study of Social Issues.
IV. Series.
HM133.T47 1998
302.3'4--dc21   97-40977
                                                         CIP

ISBN 0-306-45679-6

© 1998 Plenum Press, New York
A Division of Plenum Publishing Corporation
233 Spring Street, New York, N.Y. 10013

http://www.plenum.com

All rights reserved

10 9 8 7 6 5 4 3 2 1

No part of this book may be reproduced, stored in a retrieval system, or transmitted in any form
or by any means, electronic, mechanical, photocopying, microfilming, recording, or otherwise,
without written permission from the Publisher

Printed in the United States of America

Editorial Advisory Board

Daniel Bar-Tal, *Tel Aviv University*
Andrew S. Baum, *University of Pittsburgh Medical Center*
Sharon S. Brehm, *University of Kansas*
Marilynn B. Brewer, *The Ohio State University*
Robert Cialdini, *Arizona State University*
James H. Davis, *University of Illinois at Urbana–Champaign*
Christine Dunkel-Schetter, *University of California, Los Angeles*
Ronald J. Fisher, *University of Saskatchewan*
Susan K. Green, *University of Oregon*
Christine Iijima Hall, *Arizona State University*
Sara B. Kiesler, *Carnegie-Mellon University*
Barbara J. Loken, *University of Minnesota*
Geoffrey Maruyama, *University of Minnesota*
Joseph E. McGrath, *University of Illinois at Urbana–Champaign*
Stuart Oskamp, *Claremont Graduate School*
Amado Padilla, *Stanford University*
Michael S. Pallak, *American Biodyne Research Corporation*
Daniel Perlman, *University of British Columbia*
Linda Perloff, *Behavioral Measurement Database Services*
Dennis P. Rosenbaum, *University of Illinois at Chicago*
Michael J. Saks, *University of Iowa*
Althea Smith, *Boston University*
Claude M. Steele, *Stanford University*
Geoffrey Stephenson, *University of Kent at Canterbury*
Tom Tyler, *University of California, Berkeley*
Carol M. Werner, *University of Utah*

Contributors

Elizabeth M. Anderson, Department of Psychology, Loyola University Chicago, Chicago, Illinois 60626

Linda Argote, Graduate School of Industrial Administration, Carnegie Mellon University, Pittsburgh, Pennsylvania 15213

Margaret Bagby, Developing Communities Project, University of Illinois at Chicago, Chicago, Illinois 60607-7137

Andrew Baum, University of Pittsburgh Cancer Institute, University of Pittsburgh, Pittsburgh, Pennsylvania 15213-3412

Jennifer L. Berdahl, Department of Psychology, University of Illinois, Urbana–Champaign, Illinois 61820

Anna Dickerson, Developing Communities Project, University of Illinois at Chicago, Chicago, Illinois 60607-7137

Joseph Filkins, Office of Institutional Planning and Research, DePaul University, Chicago, Illinois 60604

Ronald J. Fisher, Department of Psychology, University of Saskatchewan, Saskatoon, Canada, S7N 5A5

John C. Glidewell, Peabody College of Vanderbilt University, Nashville, Tennessee 37212

J. Richard Hackman, Department of Psychology, Harvard University, Cambridge, Massachusetts 02138

Larry Heuer, Department of Psychology, Barnard College, New York, New York 10027

Kelly B. Hyman, University of Pittsburgh Cancer Institute, University of Pittsburgh, Pittsburgh, Pennsylvania 15213-3412

David W. Johnson, Cooperative Learning Center, University of Minnesota, Minneapolis, Minnesota 55435

Roger T. Johnson, Cooperative Learning Center, University of Minnesota, Minneapolis, Minnesota 55435

James G. Kelly, Department of Psychology, University of Illinois at Chicago, Chicago, Illinois 60607-7137

Ranjani Krishnan, Katz Graduate School of Business, University of Pittsburgh, Pittsburgh, Pennsylvania 15260

Joseph E. McGrath, Department of Psychology, University of Illinois, Urbana–Champaign, Illinois 61820

Richard L. Moreland, Department of Psychology, University of Pittsburgh, Pittsburgh, Pennsylvania 15260

Steven Penrod, Law/Psychology Program, University of Nebraska–Lincoln, Lincoln, Nebraska 68588

Donna M. Posluszny, University of Pittsburgh Cancer Institute, University of Pittsburgh, Pittsburgh, Pennsylvania 15213-3412

Ernest J. Savoie, College of Urban, Labor, and Metropolitan Affairs, Wayne State University, Detroit, Michigan 48202

Christine M. Smith, Department of Psychology, Grand Valley State University, Allendale, Michigan 49401

Garold Stasser, Department of Psychology, Miami University of Ohio, Oxford, Ohio 45056

R. Scott Tindale, Department of Psychology, Loyola University of Chicago, Chicago, Illinois 60626

Sandra I. Vaughan, Department of Psychology, Miami University of Ohio, Oxford, Ohio 45056

Gwen M. Wittenbaum, Department of Communication, Michigan State University, East Lansing, Michigan 48824

Preface

Most social behavior occurs in groups. We live with families, travel in car pools, shop with friends, work as teams, worship in congregations, are entertained as audiences, learn in classes, and decide as juries. Thus, it is not surprising that much of the early work in social psychology focused on groups. Some of the earliest reported studies in social psychology concerned performance in groups (Ringelmann, 1913; Triplett, 1898). Later work by Sherif (1936) and Asch (1956) focused on conformity in groups. Probably the most famous social psychologist, Kurt Lewin, spent the majority of his later years studying behavior in groups and is considered the founder of the "group dynamics" movement (Lewin, 1951).

Given the importance of small groups in the early formulation of social psychology, it is interesting to note that published research on small groups declined strongly during the 1970s and 1980s (Moreland, Hogg, & Hains, 1994; Steiner, 1974). A number of explanations for the decline have been proposed (see Levine & Moreland, 1990; McGrath & Kravitz, 1982). However, potentially the most compelling explanation is that research on small groups has not declined, but that the focus of the research—and thus the publication outlets—have changed. Early work on small groups tended to focus on basic social psychological processes in an attempt to generate general theories. In addition, most of this research involved groups that already existed or ad hoc laboratory groups. The more recent work on small groups has tended to focus on how groups can be made better and the advantages (and disadvantages) of using groups in new and interesting ways. Much of this research involves newly formed groups, or follows trends in the use of groups in such domains as industry, education, community relations, and so on. Rather than addressing basic issues, this research focuses on applied questions and attempts to show how the use of groups can help address current issues such as global competitiveness, improved education, and empowered communities. Because of the issue-oriented nature of the research, more recent studies tend to be published in journals relevant to the issues rather than to basic social psychological phenomena.

The present volume attempts to bring some of this new research on small groups back into the domain of social psychology. The issues-oriented approach has not only discovered a number of interesting findings but has also led to new theoretical developments that have not received the attention they deserve in social psychology proper. In addition, this work has applied basic social psychological theories in new and interesting ways. We hope that by bringing together a number of top small-group researchers dealing with applied issues, we can both help to integrate the applied ideas into mainstream social psychology and make current researchers more aware of the theories and findings in domains other than their own.

The framework we used for early volumes in this series seemed well suited for the aforementioned goals and was adopted for this volume as well. Rather than focusing on a single applied issue, we have tried to show how small-group theory and research have addressed problems and issues across a wide variety of domains. The first chapter provides a brief history of small-group research and an overview of the rest of the volume. Johnson and Johnson (Chapter 2) and Moreland, Argote, and Krishnan (Chapter 3) focus on the benefits of learning in groups, both for classroom education and training in industry. Johnson and Johnson base their work on social interdependence theory (Deutsch, 1949), whereas Moreland, Argote, and Krishnan use the theory of transactive memory (Wegner, 1987). Glidewell, Kelly, Bagby, and Dickerson (Chapter 4) discuss community activism and the natural development of community leaders. Posluszny, Hyman, and Baum (Chapter 5) identify the benefits of small groups in health-care settings in relation to both patient education and social support. Fisher (Chapter 6) discusses the long history of cooperation and conflict in small groups to develop a model of interactive conflict resolution applicable to international negotiation and conflict management.

The last six chapters of the volume deal with the two areas most noted for research on groups: jury behavior and work-group performance. Penrod and Heuer (Chapter 7) evaluate two recent innovations related to juries—notetaking and question asking by jurors—using real jurors in actual trial settings. Filkins, Smith, and Tindale (Chapter 8) address the controversy surrounding "death-qualified" juries in capital cases, taking advantage of meta-analytic and computer simulation methodologies. Wittenbaum, Vaughan, and Stasser (Chapter 9) use a variety of theoretical perspectives to develop a model "tacit coordination" and discuss the implications for group process and performance. McGrath and Berdahl (Chapter 10) begin to address the changes in what we mean by a group due to technological advances. As computers and the Internet become more conducive to multiperson interaction, the typical constraints on group interaction may soon be obsolete as "virtual" groups become the norm. Savoie (Chapter 11) uses a case study approach to describe the "power" of teams to lead industry to new levels of quality and innovation. Finally, Hackman (Chapter 12), using theoretical constructs derived from applied research on groups, points out the many potential pitfalls of trying to use groups in organizations and lays the foundation for a prescriptive theory of successful work group performance.

Groups have always been a major part of human existence, and recent trends in many of the areas mentioned show that they will play even greater roles in people's lives in the future. It is our hope that the research and ideas presented in this volume will both help to make groups more effective and further stimulate new research and theorizing within social psychology on group processes and performance.

References

Asch, S. E. (1956). Studies of independence and conformity: A minority of one against a unanimous majority. *Psychological Monographs, 70* (9, Whole No. 416).

Deutsch, M. (1949). The effects of cooperation and competition upon group process. *Human Relations, 2,* 129–152.

Levine, J. M., & Moreland, R. L. (1990). Progress in small group research. *Annual Review of Psychology, 41,* 585–634.

Lewin, K. (1951). *Field theory in social science.* New York: Harper.

McGrath, J. E., & Kravitz, D. A. (1982). Group research. *Annual Review of Psychology, 33,* 195–230.

Moreland, R. L., Hogg, M. A., & Hains, S. C. (1994). Back to the future: Social psychological research on groups. *Journal of Experimental Social Psychology, 30,* 527–555.

Ringelmann, M. (1913). Recherches sur les moteurs animes: Travail de l'homme [Research on animate sources of power: The work of man]. *Annales de l'Institut National Agronomique, XII,* 1–40.

Sherif, M. (1936). *The psychology of social norms.* New York: Harper.

Steiner, I. D. (1974). Whatever happened to the group in social psychology. *Journal of Experimental Social Psychology, 10,* 94–108.

Triplett, N. (1898). The dynamogenic factors in pacemaking and competition. *American Journal of Psychology, 9,* 507–533.

Wegner, D. M. (1987). Transactive memory: A contemporary analysis of the group mind. In B. Mullen & G. Goethals (Eds.), *Theories of group behavior* (pp. 185–208). New York: Springer-Verlag.

Acknowledgments

This volume on the applications of theory and research on small groups to social issues is the result of extensive collaboration among many individuals and organizations. This is the fourth volume in the series on Social Psychological Applications to Social Issues, and it represents the efforts of the Society for the Psychological Study of Social Issues (SPSSI), Plenum Press, and Loyola University Chicago's Graduate Program faculty and students in Applied Social Psychology.

We thank the officers and Publications Committee of SPSSI for giving us the opportunity to produce not only this volume but also the entire series. We would also like to thank the editorial and production staff of Plenum Press, especially Eliot Werner, for their help on this project.

Our Editorial Board has played an important role throughout this endeavor, and we acknowledge their help on all aspects of the series. In particular, we would like to thank Daniel Bar-Tal, Andrew Baum, Marilynn Brewer, Ronald Fisher, Joseph McGrath, Daniel Perlman, Dennis Rosenbaum, Michael Saks, and Carol Werner for their advice and editorial assistance on this volume. Our thanks go out to Homer Johnson and Vicki Helgeson for their editing efforts as well.

A number of people at Loyola were helpful on various aspects of the preparation of this volume. Specifically, we would like to thank Elizabeth Anderson, Jennifer Brockway, Sigurlina Davidsdottir, Joseph Filkins, Kristienne Kattapong, Mark Lusnar, Pauline Morgan, and Linda Thomas for their help in editing the chapters, and the Department of Psychology secretarial staff for their help with the final preparations.

Finally, we thank our 26 authors whose research and ideas have kept the field of small-group research alive and well in social psychology, and whose efforts herein hopefully will lead the way for new insights and progress in our understanding of small groups and the social contexts in which they are embedded.

R. SCOTT TINDALE
LINDA HEATH
JOHN EDWARDS
EMIL J. POSAVAC
FRED B. BRYANT
YOLANDA SUAREZ-BALCAZAR
EAARON HENDERSON-KING
JUDITH MYERS

Contents

Theory and Research
on Small Groups

1

Small Group Research and Applied Social Psychology
An Introduction

R. Scott Tindale and Elizabeth M. Anderson

Background and History

Research on small groups has played a central role in social psychology virtually since its beginnings. Perhaps the earliest reported social psychological experiment focused on the performance-enhancing characteristics of working in groups, later termed *social facilitation* (Triplett, 1898). This work was soon followed by numerous studies on the effects of social context on individual performance (e.g., Allport, 1920; Kohler, 1926, 1927; Ringelmann, 1913; Travis, 1925). One of the first text books in social psychology (LeBon, 1895/1960) attempted to explain crowd behavior from the perspective of the "group mind." In 1932, Shaw demonstrated that groups were considerably better problem solvers than were individuals. She attributed this superiority to the ability of groups to locate and correct errors made by individuals. Throughout the 1940s and early 1950s, the work by Kurt Lewin and his associates (Lewin, 1947, 1951; Lewin, Lippitt, & White, 1939) brought the "group dynamics" movement into social psychology. Studying topics from attitude/behavior change to leadership style, this research continued to show the potential benefits of using groups for a variety of purposes.

During the 1950s and 1960s, small group research remained a dominant forces in social psychology. However, research methods and topics of interest began to change. As the cognitive revolution began to take shape in psychology as a whole, similar influences began to appear in research on small groups. Group creativity became a

R. Scott Tindale and Elizabeth M. Anderson • Department of Psychology, Loyola University of Chicago, Chicago, Illinois 60626.

Theory and Research on Small Groups, edited by R. Scott Tindale et al. Plenum Press, New York, 1998.

major interest, particularly in relation to the "brainstorming" technique (Osborn, 1953). In addition, rather than having groups work on the applied issues used by Lewin and his associates, group research became more lab oriented, following the lead of the "verbal learning" work in experimental psychology. Thus, researchers began studying groups in terms of their ability to remember lists of non-sense syllables or solve simple word problems or analogies (e.g., Davis & Restle, 1963; Lorge & Solomon, 1962; Perlmutter, 1955). Conformity research also became popular during this time, stemming mainly from the seminal work of Asch (1956). In the early 1960s, Stoner (1961) discovered that groups, rather than moderating extreme individual positions as many people supposed, often are more extreme in their judgments than are individuals. This became known as the "group polarization" effect (Myers & Lamm, 1976) and became the dominant topic of small group research for the next decade. Work in this area also tended to be laboratory based and used fairly simple choice and judgment problems.

It is not surprising that behavior in and by groups was a central topic in social psychology. In a sense, groups provided the essential "social" nature of the behaviors that defined the field. In addition, most of this early research showed groups in a very positive light. However, by the late 1960s, groups research began to wane. Although there are many potential explanations for this, two seem worthy of mention. First, some of the initially positive findings concerning groups could be explained without resorting to group-level phenomena. For example, Lorge and Solomon (1955) demonstrated that group superiority in problem solving was really nothing more than an increase in the number of people working on the problem. Later research on idea generation showed that multiple individuals working alone were both more productive and more creative than individuals working in interacting groups (Taylor, Berry, & Block, 1958). Thus, the positive "aura" assigned to groups began to fade. Second, the trend in the field toward more controlled, laboratory-based research addressing cognitive issues, such as cognitive dissonance and causal attribution, led to group-level questions being addressed by individual-level research designs. Topics such as group polarization and conformity remained popular research targets, but in order to control or hold constant as many factors as possible, researchers began addressing these questions with "fake" groups (i.e., individuals in rooms supposedly interacting with other group members). In addition, because many of the theoretical explanations for group phenomena were being formulated at the individual level, interacting group designs were no longer necessary for isolating the supposedly key features underlying a particular finding. There is also a practical reality to the shift in emphasis from the group to the individual. Group research tends to be costly, both in terms of time and research participants. As money for research began to become scarce during the 1970s and 1980s, individual-level research was far easier to run, with much less cost and a quicker turnaround time. Groups research did not totally vanish during this period of time. Due to a number of legal and political issues, research on juries remained viable well into the 1980s (see Tindale & Davis, 1983), although even here, much of the research was done with individual jurors (or mock jurors), and the results were generalized (often inappropriately) to juries. However, the place of prominence that small group research had held in the field was waning.

Groups research had become so scarce in social psychology by the mid-1970s that Steiner felt compelled to write a now-famous article that asked, "Whatever happened to the group in social psychology?" (Steiner, 1974). Steiner offered a "social issues" explanation (i.e., no important social movements in the 1970s) and predicted a resurgence by the late 1970s. His prediction, however, was found not to be accurate (Moreland, Hogg, & Hains, 1994). In addition to those reasons for the decline in groups research that we mentioned above, Levine and Moreland (1990), in their *Annual Review of Psychology* chapter, offered an additional explanation. They concluded that groups research was still alive and well but residing in other, mainly applied, disciplines, a conclusion that remains generally valid today. The emphasis on basic social psychological research on groups has been replaced by an applications-oriented approach. Unfortunately, much of the research on groups being conducted today does not appear in standard social psychological journals. It is much more likely to appear in journals emphasizing organizational behavior, military training, marketing, speech communication, or education.

The lack of a common domain for groups research has been both good and bad for the field. Many new and interesting ideas, theories, methods, and findings have been generated by attempting to study how groups work in a variety of settings. However, the fragmented nature of the field has inhibited the sharing of ideas and methods across disciplines. This, at times, has led to one discipline rediscovering phenomena well documented in another (see the exchange by Tindale & Larson, 1992a, 1992b; Michaelsen, Watson, Schwartzkopf, & Black, 1992). Thus, we felt the time was ripe to provide a source for groups researchers from many disciplines to share and exchange the knowledge that has been gained over the last 20 years about the benefits and pitfalls of behaving in groups for various purposes.

Overview of What Is to Come: Some General Themes

Based on the philosophy underlying the earlier volumes in this series (particularly Volumes 1 and 3), we asked groups researchers from a variety of disciplines and topic areas to provide chapters discussing the major trends in groups research in their domains while focusing on recent developments in their own work. Unfortunately, due to space limitations, we could not cover comprehensively all of the domains involved in small group research. However, the chapters included encompass many of the major areas and represent what we feel is some of the best work currently available on applications of small groups. There are five major domains or applied settings covered in the volume: learning and education settings (Johnson & Johnson, Chapter 2; Moreland, Argote, & Krishnan, Chapter 3); community/health-care settings (Glidewell, Kelly, Bagby, & Dickerson, Chapter 4; Posluszny, Hyman, & Baum, Chapter 5); international relations (Fisher, Chapter 6); legal/jury (Penrod & Heuer,

Chapter 7; Filkins, Smith, & Tindale, Chapter 8); and organization/performance settings (Wittenbaum, Vaughn, & Stasser, Chapter 9; McGrath & Berdahl, Chapter 10; Savoie, Chapter 11; Hackman, Chapter 12). Chapters 2 and 3 deal with learning in groups, both in educational and organizational settings. Chapters 4 and 5 concern support and empowerment in community and health-care settings. Chapter 6 focuses on conflict resolution and the use of third-party groups in international negotiations. Chapters 7 and 8 assess the implications of trial procedures on juror/jury behavior and courtroom functioning. Chapter 9 describes the notion of "tacit coordination" and its implications for task-performing groups. Chapter 10 addresses the implications of technology (e.g., computers) on how groups function and what groups may be like in the future. Chapter 11 provides a detailed description of how teams were used in a single organization. Finally, Chapter 12 discusses the potential pitfalls of using groups in performance settings and provides some guidelines for effective group perfor-mance. Although the chapters span a fairly wide range of settings and types of groups, there are two prominent areas of applied group research not represented: military teams and focus groups. However, these types of groups have been thoroughly discussed elsewhere (see Krueger, 1994; Swezey & Salas, 1992), and no single volume can really do justice to a content area as diversely defined as "groups."

Each chapter deals with its own set of theories, issues, and problems. However, there are a number of common themes that present themselves in multiple chapters. Some of these themes have surfaced in basic research on groups, but others are the direct outcome of studying natural groups in the actual settings in which they exist. Below, we attempt to elucidate some of the major themes than span across the chapters, though this is not an exhaustive list.

Leadership has been an important concern in group research for many years (e.g., Lewin, Lippitt, & White, 1939), and the importance of leadership is represented in a number of chapters in the present volume. It is a central theme in the chapter by Glidewell et al. (Chapter 4), where the dynamic aspects of leadership are strongly apparent in community groups. Different tasks require different leaders, and roles shift over time in groups depending upon the interests of the members and the skills that they bring to the group. Hackman (Chapter 12) and Savoie (Chapter 11) both point out the importance of managerial leadership when using groups in work settings, not only in terms of providing resources and support, but also for coaching and educa-tional purposes. McGrath and Berdahl (Chapter 10) discuss the importance of the facilitator for aiding groups in using performance-enhancement technology, even while the technology can substitute for certain leadership roles. Fisher (Chapter 6) points out the leadership role that third parties can play in conflict resolution and how that role should change over time. Finally, Penrod and Heuer (Chapter 7) show that fears about note taking on juries affecting leadership roles on the jury were un-founded.

Another theme that emerges from the volume is the *educational role of groups*. The chapters by Moreland et al. (Chapter 3) and Johnson and Johnson (Chapter 2) are composed around learning in groups, but other chapters touch on the educational value of groups as well. Posluszny et al. (Chapter 5) argue that support groups for cancer patients help the patients to understand their disease better and learn better coping skills. Hackman also points out that group members learn to work in groups over time and that such learning is important for group functioning. Savoie describes the learning process both within groups and the organization as a whole, in terms of discovering how best to use groups.

A third theme prevalent throughout the volume is *interdependence*. Although interdependence is not a new concept in the study of groups, its power is often limited in ad hoc laboratory groups, where the interdependence among the members is short-lived and usually experimentally created. But for groups in natural environments, it is often the interdependence that defines the group and gives it its purpose. Virtually every chapter in this volume in some way, shape, or form uses this theme to help explain how groups either do or should function. Fisher argues that effective intervention in conflicts requires an increased perception of interdependence among all three parties. Glidewell et al. discuss the interdependencies among community members and how these change over time. The chapters by Wittenbaum et al. and Moreland et al. show that coordination among group members is central to group performance. They both use the concept of transactive memory (Wegner, 1987) as a key example of how members depend on each other for information and defer to others who have more expertise or information for a particular subtask. Both Hackman and Savoie discuss the importance of realizing the presence of, and need for, interdependence, for both group members and the organization as a whole, for appropriate group functioning. Finally, Posluszny et al. point out the positive effects of mutual support and interdependence in groups of cancer patients.

A fourth theme that permeates the volume is *time*—and the *dynamic nature* of groups over time. Until recently, time was not paid much attention in small-group research and in fact was not an important variable for social psychology in general (McGrath & Kelly, 1986). However, as the current chapters demonstrate, time is a crucial variable for understanding natural groups that form, grow, develop, change, and dissolve in the context of a changing environment. Probably the clearest example of the importance of time is presented in the chapter by McGrath and Berdahl. The JEMCO project discussed in their chapter shows how groups change over time, and how changes that happen to groups over time are compensated for. It is also interesting to note that technology is changing the meaning of time in relation to groups, and society as a whole. Where group interaction used to happen face-to-face, and all members had to be present at the same time, computers (and other technologies) now allow group interaction to flow over time and distance, with members joining into the discussion as time permits. Obviously, this will remain an interesting area of research for many years to come. Many of the other chapters also discuss the implications of time and the dynamic nature of groups. Glidewell et al. emphasize the changes that occur in leadership and leadership roles in community action groups. Moreland et al. demonstrate how training people in groups may reduce the time it takes for groups to reach their optimal level of performance by creating transactive memory systems during training. Wittenbaum et al. discuss how tacit coordination builds over time, and how groups using tacit coordination differ from those in which time is designated to create coordination. Savoie's description of how the team concept developed at Ford shows both the time it takes to make such changes and the changes in perception that were necessary to integrate the "team" concept into organizations designed at the individual level. Fisher argues that international conflict resolution requires certain changes over time for both the parties in conflict and the intervention team. Finally, Penrod and Heuer demonstrate that note taking by jurors does not affect the amount of time it takes for a jury to deliberate and reach a final verdict.

This last point brings us to the final theme to be discussed here. Rather than being about groups per se, the final theme concerns what people generally believe about groups, or what might be called *groups myths*. A number of findings presented in this volume can be seen as debunking some of the myths that managers, people in general, and even some experts hold about groups. The chapters by Hackman, Penrod and Heuer, and Filkins et al. are probably the best examples of how applied research on groups can be useful for changing people's beliefs about groups. Hackman discusses the disproportionate number of failed attempts at using groups in organizations and points out six mistakes that are often made. Each of the mistakes can be interpreted as a misperception about how groups function. Beliefs such as "Groups are always better than individuals," or "Full group autonomy is necessary for groups to work at optimal levels" are two of the myths that Hackman argues can cause failures. Penrod and Heuer empirically evaluate a number of beliefs about the pros and cons of allowing jurors to take notes and ask questions during a trial. Their results debunk an amazing number of both the predicted positive and negative outcomes of such a practice. Finally, Filkins et al. address the potential jury verdict and composition biases caused by the use of "death qualification procedures." Although the meta-analytic results support some of the arguments made by critics of the procedures, the computer simulation results question the degree to which such procedures impact on the outcomes of capital trials.

A number of other standard group concepts repeatedly appear in these chapters, such as social comparison, social influence, faction size, norms and roles, and so on. However, each chapter also deals with distinct issues and concepts related to the specific task domains that they address. This, we feel, is one of the major contributions of this volume. By demonstrating both the similarities and the differences concerning how groups function in different settings, we hope to help instigate new theoretical integrations across domains as well as inform applied researchers as to the specific problems that arise from using groups in different domains. Groups are, and will remain, important components of our lives, and the better we understand how they function and when they are useful, the easier it will be to design both groups and the setting in which they are used for societal benefit.

References

Allport, F. H. (1920). The influence of the group upon association and thought. *Journal of Experimental Psychology, 3*, 159–182.

Asch, S. E. (1956). Studies of independence and conformity: A minority of one against a unanimous majority. *Psychological Monographs, 70* (9, Whole No. 416).

Davis, J. H., & Restle, F. (1963). The analysis of problems and the prediction of group problem solving. *Journal of Abnormal and Social Psychology, 66,* 103–116.

Kohler, O. (1926). Kraftleistungen bei Einzel- und Gruppenarbeit [Physical performance in individual and group situations]. *Industrielle Psychotechnik, 3,* 274–282.

Kohler, O. (1927). Uber den Gruppenwirkungsgrad der menschlichen Koperarbeit und die Bedingugn optimaler Kollektivkraftreaktion [On group efficiency of physical labor and the conditions of optimal collective performance]. *Industrielle Psychotechnik, 4,* 209–226.

Krueger, R. A. (1994). *Focus groups: A practical guide for applied research.* Thousand Oaks, CA: Sage.

LeBon, G. (1960). *The crowd* (translation of *Psychologie des foules*). New York: Viking Press. (Original published in 1895)

Levine, J. M., & Moreland, R. L. (1990). Progress in small group research. In M. R. Rosenwig & L. W. Porter (Eds.), *Annual review of psychology* (Vol. 41, pp. 585–634). Palo Alto, CA: Annual Reviews, Inc.

Lewin, K. (1947). Group decision and social change. In T. M. Newcomb & E. L. Hartley (Eds.), *Readings in social psychology* (pp. 330–344). New York: McGraw-Hill.

Lewin, K. (1951). *Field theory in social science.* New York: Harper.

Lewin, K., Lippitt, R., & White, R. (1939). Patterns of aggressive behavior in experimentally created "social climates." *Journal of Social Psychology, 10,* 271–299.

Lorge, I., & Solomon, H. (1955). To models of group behavior in the solution of eureka-type problems. *Pschometrica, 20,* 139–148.

Lorge, I., & Solomon, H. (1962). Group and individual behavior in free-recall verbal learning. In J. H. Criswell, H. Solomon, & P. Suppes (Eds.), *Mathematical methods in small group processes* (pp. 221–231). Stanford, CA: Stanford University Press.

McGrath, J. E., & Kelly, J. R. (1986). *Time and human interaction: Toward a social psychology of time.* New York: Guilford Press.

Michaelsen, L. K., Watson, W. E., Schwartzkopf, A., & Black, R. H. (1992). Group decision-making: How you frame the question determines what you find. *Journal of Applied Psychology, 77,* 106–108.

Moreland, R. L., Hogg, M. A., & Hains, S. C. (1994). Back to the future: Social psychological research on groups. *Journal of Experimental Social Psychology, 30,* 527–555.

Myers, D. G., & Lamm, H. (1976). The group polarization phenomenon. *Psychological Bulletin, 83,* 602–627.

Osborn, A. F. (1953). *Applied imagination.* New York: Scribners.

Perlmutter, H. V. (1955). Group memory of meaningful material. *Journal of Psychology, 35,* 361–370.

Ringelmann, M. (1913). Recherches sur les moteurs animes: Travail de l'homme [Research on animate sources of power: The work of man]. *Annales de l'Institut National Agronomique, XII,* 1–40.

Shaw, M. E. (1932). Comparison of individuals and small groups in the rational solution of complex problems. *American Journal of Psychology, 44,* 491–504.

Sherif, M., Harvey, O. J., White, B. J., Hood, W. R., & Sherif, C. W. (1961). *Intergroup conflict and cooperation: The Robbers Cave experiment.* Norman: Institute of Group Relations, University of Oklahoma.

Steiner, I. (1974). Whatever happened to the group in social psychology? *Journal of Experimental Social Psychology, 10,* 94–108.

Stoner, J. A. F. (1961). *A comparison of individual and group decisions involving risk.* Master's thesis, Massachusetts Institute of Technology, Cambridge, MA.

Swezey, R. W., & Salas, E. (1992). *Teams: Their training and performance.* Norwood, NJ: Ablex.

Taylor, D. W., Berry, P. C., & Block, C. H. (1958). Does group participation when using brainstorming facilitate or inhibit creative thinking? *Administrative Science Quarterly, 3,* 23–47.

Tindale, R. S., & Davis, J. H. (1983). Group decision making and jury verdicts. In H. Blumberg, P. Hare, V. Kent, & M. Davies (Eds.), *Small groups and social interaction* (Vol. 2, pp. 9–37). Chichester, UK: Wiley.

Tindale, R. S., & Larson, J. R., Jr. (1992a). Assembly bonus effect or typical group performance: A comment on Michaelsen, Watson, & Black (1989). *Journal of Applied Psychology, 77,* 102–105.

Tindale, R. S., & Larson, J. R., Jr. (1992b). It's not how you frame the question, it's how you interpret the results. *Journal of Applied Psychology, 77,* 109–110.

Travis, L. E. (1925). The effect of a small audience upon eye–hand coordination. *Journal of Abnormal and Social Psychology, 20,* 142–146.

Triplett, N. (1898). The dynamogenic factors in pacemaking and competition. *American Journal of Psychology, 9,* 507–533.

Wegner, D. M. (1987). Transactive memory: A contemporary analysis of the group mind. In B. Mullen & G. Goethals (Eds.), *Theories of group behavior* (pp. 185–208). New York: Springer-Verlag.

2

Cooperative Learning and Social Interdependence Theory

David W. Johnson and Roger T. Johnson

Cooperative Learning

> *Together we stand, divided we fall.*
> —Watchword of the American Revolution

One of social psychology's great success stories is the widespread use of cooperative learning. From being virtually unknown 30 years ago, cooperative learning is now a standard educational practice in almost every elementary and secondary school, and many colleges and universities in the United States, Canada, and a variety of other countries. To understand how social psychological theory and research has revolutionized teaching practices, it is first necessary to understand what cooperative learning is.

Cooperative learning exists when students work together to achieve joint learning groups (Johnson, Johnson, & Holubec, 1992, 1993). Any assignment in any curriculum for any age student can be done cooperatively. There are three ways that cooperative learning may be used. *Formal cooperative learning groups* may last for one class period to several weeks to complete any course requirement (such as solving problems, reading complex text material, writing an essay or report, conducting a survey or experiment, learning vocabulary, or answering questions at the end of a chapter). The teacher introduces the lesson, assigns students to groups (two to five members), gives students the materials they need to complete the assignment, and assigns students roles. The teacher explains the task, teaches any concepts or procedures the students need in order to complete the assignment, and structures the

David W. Johnson and Roger T. Johnson • Cooperative Learning Center, University of Minnesota, Minneapolis, Minnesota 55435.

Theory and Research on Small Groups, edited by R. Scott Tindale et al. Plenum Press, New York, 1998.

cooperation among students. Students work on the assignment until all group members have successfully understood and completed it. While the students work together, the teacher moves from group to group, systematically monitoring their interaction. The teacher intervenes when students do not understand the academic task, or when there are problems in working together. After the assignment is completed, the teacher evaluates the academic success of each student and has the groups process how well they functioned as a team. In working cooperatively, students realize that they (1) are mutually responsible for each other's learning and (2) have a stake in each other's success.

Informal cooperative learning groups are temporary, ad hoc groups that last from a few minutes to one class period that are used during a lecture, demonstration, or film to focus student attention on the material to be learned, set a mood conducive to learning, help set expectations as to what will be covered in a class session, ensure that students cognitively process the material being taught, and provide closure to an instructional session. *Cooperative base groups* are long-term cooperative learning groups (lasting for one semester or year) with stable membership that give each member the support, help, encouragement, and assistance he or she needs to make academic progress (attend class, complete all assignments, learn) and develop cognitively and socially in healthy ways.

What makes cooperative learning different from most instructional methods is that it is based on social interdependence theory and the related research. Social interdependence theory provides educators with a conceptual framework for understanding how cooperative learning may be (1) most fruitfully structured, (2) adapted to a wide variety of instructional situations, and (3) applied to a wide range of issues (such as achievement, ethnic integration, and prevention of drug abuse). In this chapter, we shall review the theory of social interdependence, the research that has been conducted on social interdependence, the conditions under which the theory is valid, and the variables that enhance its effectiveness. We will then return to its relevance and application to education.

Theory of Social Interdependence

There are at least three general theoretical perspectives that have guided research on cooperation—cognitive-developmental, behavioral, and social interdependence. The *cognitive-developmental perspective* is largely based on the theories of Piaget and Vygotsky. The work of Piaget and related theorists is based on the premise that when individuals cooperate on the environment, sociocognitive conflict occurs that creates cognitive disequilibrium, which in turn stimulates perspective-taking ability and cognitive development. The work of Vygotsky and related theorists is based on the premise that knowledge is social, constructed from cooperative efforts to learn, understand, and solve problems. The *behavioral theory perspective* focuses on the impact of group reinforcers and rewards on learning. Skinner focused on group contingencies, Bandura focused on imitation, and Homans, as well as Thibaut and

Kelley, focused on the balance of rewards and costs in social exchange among interdependent individuals. Although the cognitive-developmental and behavioral theoretical orientations have their followings, by far the most important theory dealing with cooperation is *social interdependence theory*.

Theorizing on *social interdependence* began in the early 1900s, when one of the founders of the Gestalt School of Psychology, Kurt Koffka, proposed that groups were dynamic wholes in which the interdependence among members could vary. One of his colleagues, Kurt Lewin, refined Koffka's notions in the 1920s and 1930s while stating that (1) the essence of a group is the interdependence among members (created by common goals), which results in the group being a "dynamic whole," so that a change in the state of any member or subgroup changes the state of any other member or subgroup; and (2) an intrinsic state of tension within group members motivates movement toward the accomplishment of the desired common goals. Lewin's students and colleagues, such as Ovisankian, Lissner, Mahler, and Lewis, contributed further research indicating that it is the drive for goal accomplishment that motivates cooperative and competitive behavior.

In the late 1940s, one of Lewin's graduate students, Morton Deutsch, extended Lewin's reasoning about social interdependence and formulated a theory of cooperation and competition (Deutsch, 1949, 1962). Deutsch's theory has served as a major conceptual structure for this area of inquiry for the past 45 years. Deutsch's theory was extended and applied to education by the authors at the University of Minnesota (Johnson, 1970; Johnson & Johnson, 1974, 1989). Our work has been extended and applied to business and industry (Tjosvold, 1986).

Social interdependence exists when individuals share common goals and each individual's outcomes are affected by the actions of the others (Deutsch, 1949, 1962; Johnson & Johnson, 1989). It may be differentiated from *social dependence* (i.e., the outcomes of one person are affected by the actions of a second person but not vice versa) and *social independence* (i.e., individuals' outcomes are unaffected by each other's actions). There are two types of social interdependence: cooperative and competitive. The absence of social interdependence and dependence results in individualistic efforts.

When individuals take action, there are three ways that what they do may be related to the actions of others. One's actions may promote the success of others, obstruct the success of others, or not have any effect at all on the success or failure of others. In other words, individuals may be (Deutsch, 1949, 1962; Johnson & Johnson, 1989):

1. Working together cooperatively to accomplish shared learning goals. When a situation is structured *cooperatively*, individuals' goal achievements are positively correlated; individuals perceive that they can reach their goals if and only if the others in the group also reach their goals. Thus, individuals seek outcomes that are beneficial to all those with whom they are cooperatively linked.
2. Working against each other to achieve a goal that only one or a few can attain.

When a situation is structured *competitively*, individuals work against each other to achieve a goal that only one or a few can attain. Individuals' goal achievements are negatively correlated; each individual perceives that when one person achieves his or her goal, all others with whom he or she is competitively linked fail to achieve their goals. Thus, individuals seek an outcome that is personally beneficial but detrimental to all others in the situation.

3. Working by oneself to accomplish goals unrelated to the goals of others. When a situation is structured *individualistically*, there is no correlation among participants' goal attainments. Each individual perceives that he or she can reach his or her goal, regardless of whether other individuals attain or do not attain their goals. Thus, individuals seek an outcome that is personally beneficial without concern for the outcomes of others.

The basic premise of social interdependence theory is that the type of interdependence structured in a situation determines how individuals interact with each other, which, in turn, determines outcomes (see Table 1). Positive interdependence tends to result in promotive interaction, negative interdependence tends to result in oppositional or contrient interaction, and no interdependence results in an absence of interaction. Depending on whether individuals promote or obstruct each other's goal accomplishments, there is *substitutability* (i.e., the actions of one person substitute for the actions of another), *cathexis* (i.e., the investment of psychological energy in objects and events outside of oneself), and *inducibility* (i.e., openness to influence). Essentially, in cooperative situations, the actions of participants substitute for each other, participants positively cathect to each other's effective actions, and there is high inducibility among participants. In competitive situations, the actions of participants do not substitute for each other, participants negatively cathect to each other's effective actions, and inducibility is low. When there is no interaction, there is no substitutability, cathexis, or inducibility. The relationship between the type of social interdependence and the interaction pattern it elicits is assumed to be bidirectional. Each may cause the other.

Promotive interaction tends to result in a wide variety of outcomes that may be subsumed into the categories of high effort to achieve, positive relationships, and psychological health. Oppositional interaction tends to result in low effort to achieve by most students, negative relationships, and low psychological health, and no interaction tends to result in low effort to achieve, an absence of relationships, and

Table 1. Social Interdependence Theory

Process	Cooperative	Competitive	Individualistic
Interdependence	Positive	Negative	None
Interaction pattern	Promotive	Oppositional	None
Outcome 1	High effort to achieve	Low effort to achieve	Low effort to achieve
Outcome 2	Positive relationships	Negative relationships	No relationships
Outcome 3	Psychological health	Psychological illness	Psychological pathology

psychological pathology. To discuss these outcomes in some depth, the history of the research on social interdependence needs to be reviewed.

Interaction Patterns

Between 1898 and 1989, over 575 experimental and 100 correlational studies were conducted by a wide variety of researchers in different decades with different age subjects, in different subject areas, and in different settings (see Johnson & Johnson, 1989, for a complete listing of these studies). One of the issues addressed by this research is the type of interaction patterns found within cooperative, competitive, and individualistic situations.

Positive interdependence creates promotive interaction. *Promotive interaction* occurs as individuals encourage and facilitate each other's efforts to reach the group's goals (such as maximizing each member's learning). Group members promote each other's success by (Johnson & Johnson, 1989):

1. Giving and receiving help and assistance (both task-related and personal).
2. Exchanging resources and information. Group members seek information and other resources from each other, comprehend information accurately and without bias, and make optimal use of the information provided. There are a number of beneficial results from (a) orally explaining, elaborating, and summarizing information and (b) teaching one's knowledge to others. Explaining and teaching increase the degree to which group members cognitively process and organize information, engage in higher-level reasoning, attain insights, and become personally committed to achieving. Listening critically to the explanations of groupmates provides the opportunity to utilize others' resources.
3. Giving and receiving feedback on taskwork and teamwork behaviors. In cooperative groups, members monitor each other's efforts, give immediate feedback on performance, and, when needed, give each other help and assistance.
4. Challenging each other's reasoning. Intellectual controversy promotes curiosity, motivation to learn, reconceptualization of what one knows, higher quality decision making, greater insight into the problem being considered, and many other important benefits (Johnson & Johnson, 1979, 1995b).
5. Advocating increased efforts to achieve. Encouraging others to achieve increases one's own commitment to do so.
6. Mutually influencing each other's reasoning and behavior. Group members actively seek to influence and be influenced by each other. If a member has a better way to complete the task, groupmates usually quickly adopt it.
7. Engaging in the interpersonal and small-group skills needed for effective teamwork.
8. Processing how effectively group members are working together and how the group's effectiveness can be continuously improved.

Negative interdependence typically results in oppositional interaction. *Oppositional interaction* occurs as individuals discourage and obstruct each other's efforts to achieve. Individuals focus both on increasing their own success and on preventing anyone else from being more successful than they are. *No interaction* exists when individuals work independently, without any interaction or interchange with each other. Individuals focus only on increasing their own success and ignore as irrelevant the efforts of others. Each of these interaction patterns creates different outcomes.

Outcomes of Social Interdependence

Social interdependence is a generic human phenomenon that has impact on many different outcomes simultaneously. Over the past 95 years, researchers have focused on such diverse dependent variables as individual achievement and retention, group and organizational productivity, higher-level reasoning, moral reasoning, achievement motivation, intrinsic motivation, transfer of training and learning, job satisfaction, interpersonal attraction, social support, interpersonal affection and love, attitudes toward diversity, prejudice, self-esteem, personal causation and locus of control, attributions concerning success and failure, psychological health, social competencies, and many others. These numerous outcomes may be subsumed within three broad categories (Johnson & Johnson, 1989): (1) effort to achieve, (2) positive relationships, and (3) psychological health (see Figure 1).

If research is to have impact on theory and practice, it must be summarized and communicated in a complete, objective, impartial, and unbiased way. In an age of information explosion, there is considerable danger that theories will be formulated on small and nonrepresentative samples of available knowledge, thereby resulting in fallacious conclusions that in turn lead to mistaken practices. A quantitative reviewing procedure, such as meta-analysis, allows for more definitive and robust conclusions. A *meta-analysis* is a method of statistically combining the results of a set of independent studies that test the same hypothesis and using inferential statistics to draw conclusions about the overall result of the studies. The essential purpose of a meta-analysis is to summarize a set of related research studies, so that the size of the effect of the independent variable on the dependent variable is known.

Effort to Achieve

To ensure that the graduates from our school system perform as well or better than any 18-year-old student in the world, schools must continuously improve the instructional program, so that students are knowledgeable (especially in math and science), have the ability to think critically and use higher-level reasoning, and are committed to lifelong learning. The research comparing the impact of cooperative, competitive, and individualistic efforts on achievement and productivity provides educators with a direction on how to do so.

Figure 1. Outcomes of cooperative learning. *Source*: Johnson and Johnson (1989).

The investigation of the relative impact of the three types of social interdependence on achievement is the longest standing research tradition within American social psychology. Between 1898 and 1989, researchers conducted over 375 experimental studies with over 1,700 findings on social interdependence and productivity and achievement (Johnson & Johnson, 1989). And that does not count the research on social facilitation and other related areas in which implicit competition may be found. Because research participants have varied widely as to sex, economic class, age, and cultural background, and a wide variety of research tasks and measures of the dependent variables have been used, and the research has been conducted by many different researchers with markedly different orientations, working in different settings and in different decades, the overall body of research on social interdependence has considerable generalizability.

A meta-analysis of all studies (Johnson & Johnson, 1989) found that the average person cooperating performed at about two-third standard deviation above the average person learning within a competitive (effect size = 0.67) or individualistic situation (effect size = 0.64) (see Table 2). Not all the research, however, has been carefully conducted. The methodological shortcomings found within many research studies may significantly reduce the certainty of the conclusion that cooperative efforts produce higher achievement than do competitive or individualistic efforts. When only studies with high internal validity were included in the analysis, the effect sizes were 0.88 and 0.61, respectively. Further analyses revealed that the results held constant when group measures of productivity were included as well as individual measures, for short-term as well as long-term studies, and when symbolic as well as tangible rewards were used.

A number of the studies conducted operationally defined cooperation in a way that included elements of competition and individualistic work. The original jigsaw studies, for example, operationalized cooperative learning as a combination of positive resource interdependence and an individualistic reward structure (Aronson, 1978). Teams–Games–Tournaments (TGT; DeVries & Edwards, 1974) and Student–Team–Achievement Divisions (STAD; Slavin, 1986) operationalized cooperative learning as a combination of ingroup cooperation and intergroup competition, and Team–Assisted–Individualization (TAI; Salvin, 1986) is a mixture of cooperative and individualistic learning. When such "mixed" operationalizations were compared with "pure" operationalizations, the effect sizes for the cooperative versus competitive comparison were 0.45 and 0.74, respectively, $t(37) = 1.60$, $p < .06$ (Johnson &

Table 2. Mean Effect Sizes for Impact of Social Interdependence on Dependent Variables[a]

Conditions	Achievement	Interpersonal attraction	Social support	Self-esteem
Total studies				
Coop vs. Comp	0.67	0.67	0.62	0.58
Coop vs. Ind	0.64	0.60	0.70	0.44
Comp vs. Ind	0.30	0.08	−0.13	−0.23
High-quality studies				
Coop vs. Comp	0.88	0.82	0.83	0.67
Coop vs. Ind	0.61	0.62	0.72	0.72
Comp vs. Ind	0.07	0.27	−0.13	−0.25
Mixed operationalizations				
Coop vs. Comp	0.40	0.46	0.45	0.33
Coop vs. Ind	0.42	0.36	0.02	0.22
Pure operationalizations				
Coop vs. Comp	0.71	0.79	0.73	0.74
Coop vs. Ind	0.65	0.66	0.77	0.51

Note: Coop = Cooperation, Comp = Competition, Ind = Individualistic
[a]From Johnson and Johnson (1989).

Johnson, 1989). The effect sizes for the cooperative versus individualistic comparisons were 0.13 and 0.61, respectively, $t(10) = 1.64$, $p < .07$.

Achievement in cooperative learning groups involves more than the level of learning of its members. It is also important to understand (1) the extent to which members of cooperative learning groups influence each other's achievement and (2) the direction of the influence (students could uniformly achieve higher or lower within a learning group). If group members do influence each other's achievement, their test scores should be quite similar. If little influence occurs, the level of achievement among group members could be dissimilar due to some members doing all the work while other members loaf. Few studies have examined this issue. The current evidence implies that even when students are quite diverse, with one member of each group being academically gifted and at least one member of each group being academically handicapped, (1) academic ability is a better predictor of achievement in individualistic than in cooperative learning situations; (2) within cooperative learning groups, members influence each other's learning to such an extent that initial differences in achievement level (whether a student is a low, medium, or high achiever) do not determine what the student learns; and (3) because achievement was significantly higher in the cooperative than in the individualistic condition, it may be assumed that members influence each other in ways that raise achievement (Archer-Kath, Johnson, & Johnson, 1994; Smith, Johnson, & Johnson, 1981).

Besides higher achievement and greater retention, cooperation, compared with competitive or individualistic efforts, tends to result in more (Johnson & Johnson, 1989):

1. Willingness to take on difficult tasks and persist, despite difficulties, in working toward goal accomplishment. In addition, there is intrinsic motivation, high expectations for success, high incentive to achieve based on mutual benefit, high epistemic curiosity and continuing interest in learning, and high commitment to achieve.
2. Long-term retention of what is learned.
3. Higher-level reasoning, critical thinking, and metacognitive thought. The aims of education include developing individuals "who can sort sense from nonsense," or who have the critical thinking abilities of grasping information, examining it, evaluating it for soundness, and applying it appropriately. Cooperative learning promotes a greater use of higher-level-reasoning strategies and critical thinking than do competitive or individualistic learning strategies. Cooperative learning experiences promote more frequent insight into and use of higher-level cognitive and moral reasoning strategies than do competitive or individualistic learning experiences (effect sizes = 0.93 and 0.97, respectively). Even on writing assignments, students working cooperatively show more higher-level thought.
4. Creative thinking (process gain). *Process gain* occurs when new ideas, solutions, or efforts are generated through group interaction that are not generated when persons work individually. In cooperative groups, members more

frequently generate new ideas, strategies, and solutions that they would think of on their own.

5. Transfer of learning from one situation to another (group to individual transfer). *Group-to-individual transfer* occurs when individuals who learned within a cooperative group demonstrate mastery on a subsequent test taken individually. What individuals learn in a group today, they are able to do alone tomorrow.

6. Positive attitudes toward the tasks being completed. Cooperative efforts result in more positive attitudes toward the tasks being completed and greater continuing motivation to complete them. The positive attitudes extend to the work experience and the organization as a whole.

7. Time on task. Over 30 studies did in fact measure time on task. They found that cooperators spent more time on task than did competitors (effect size = 0.76) or students working individualistically (effect size = 1.17). Competitors spent more time on task than did students working individualistically (effect size = 0.64). These effect sizes are quite large, indicating that members of cooperative learning groups do seem to spend considerably more time on task than do students working competitively or individualistically.

Because the most credible studies (due to their high quality methodologically) and the "pure" operationalizations of cooperative learning produced stronger effects, considerable confidence can be placed in the conclusion that cooperative efforts promote more positive cross-ethnic relationships than do competitive or individualistic efforts.

Kurt Lewin often stated, "I always found myself unable to think as a single person." Most efforts to achieve are a personal but social process that requires individuals to cooperate and to construct shared understandings and knowledge. Both competitive and individualistic structures, by isolating individuals from each other, tend to depress achievement.

Positive Interpersonal Relationships

A faithful friend is a strong defense, and he that hath found him, hath found a treasure.
—Ecclesiastes 6:14

The second set of issues facing schools involves relationships among students. Schools increasingly have students who are isolated and unattached to family or peers and students from a variety of ethic, historical, and cultural backgrounds. In response, schools have to focus on building (1) a learning community, (2) positive relationships among heterogeneous students, and (3) positive relationships between classmates and lonely, isolated, alienated, at-risk students. There is considerable evidence comparing the impact of cooperative, competitive, and individualistic efforts on interpersonal attraction and social support.

Since 1940, over 180 studies have compared the impact of cooperative, competitive, and individualistic efforts on interpersonal attraction (Johnson & Johnson, 1989). Cooperative efforts, compared with competitive and individualistic experiences, promoted considerably more liking among individuals (effect sizes = 0.66 and 0.62, respectively, see Table 2.2). The effects sizes were higher for (1) high quality studies and (2) the studies using pure operationalizations of cooperative learning than for studies using mixed operationalizations. The weighted effect sizes for cooperation versus competition and cooperation versus individualistic efforts are 0.65 and 0.64, respectively. When only the methodologically high-quality studies are examined, the effect sizes go up to 0.77 and 0.67, respectively. "Pure" cooperation results in greater effects than do mixtures of cooperative, competitive, and individualistic efforts (cooperative vs. competitive, pure = 0.75 and mixed = 0.48; cooperative vs. individualistic, pure = 0.67 and mixed = 0.36).

Much of the research on interpersonal relationships has been conducted on relationships between white and minority students and between nonhandicapped and handicapped students (Johnson & Johnson, 1989). There have been over 40 experimental studies comparing some combination of cooperative, competitive, and individualistic experiences on cross-ethnic relationships and over 40 similar studies on mainstreaming of handicapped students (Johnson & Johnson, 1989). Their results are consistent. Working cooperatively creates far more positive relationships among diverse and heterogeneous students than does learning competitively or individualistically.

An extension of social interdependence theory is *social judgment theory*, which focuses on relationships among diverse individuals (Johnson & Johnson, 1989). The social judgments that individuals make about each other increase or decrease the liking they feel toward each other. Such social judgments are the result of either a process of acceptance or a process of rejection (Johnson & Johnson, 1989). *The process of acceptance* is based on the individuals promoting mutual goal accomplishments as a result of their perceived positive interdependence. The promotive interaction tends to result in frequent, accurate, and open communication; accurate understanding of each other's perspective; inducibility; differentiated, dynamic, and realistic views of each other; high self-esteem; success and productivity; and expectations for positive and productive future interaction. *The process of rejection* results from oppositional or no interaction, based on perceptions of negative or no interdependence. Both lead to no or inaccurate communication; egocentrism; resistance to influence; monopolistic, stereotyped, and static views of others; low self-esteem; failure; and expectations of distasteful and unpleasant interaction with others. The processes of acceptance and rejection are self-perpetuating. Any part of the process tends to elicit all the other parts of the process.

The positive relationships among members promoted by cooperative efforts have considerable impact on a wide variety of variables. Generally, the more positive the relationships among group members (i.e., the more cohesive the group), the lower the absenteeism, the fewer the members who drop out of the group, and the more likely students will commit effort to achieve educational goals, feel personal responsibility for learning, take on difficult tasks, be motivated to learn, persist in working toward goal achievement, have high morale, be willing to endure pain and frustration on behalf of learning, listen to and be influenced by classmates and teachers, commit to each other's learning and success, and achieve and produce (Johnson & Johnson, 1994).

Positive peer relationships influence the social and cognitive development of students and such attitudes and behaviors as educational aspirations and staying in school (Johnson & Johnson, 1989). Relationships with peers influence what attitudes and values students adopt, whether students become prosocially or antisocially oriented, whether students learn to see situations from a variety of perspectives, develop autonomy, and aspirations for postsecondary education, and whether students learn how to cope with adversity and stress.

Besides liking each other, cooperators give and receive considerable social support, both personally and academically (Johnson & Johnson, 1989). Since the 1940s, over 106 studies comparing the relative impact of cooperative, competitive, and individualistic efforts on social support have been conducted. Social support may be aimed at enhancing another person's success (task-related social support) or at providing support on a more personal level (personal social support). Cooperative experience promoted greater task-oriented and personal social support than did competitive (effect size = 0.62) or individualistic (effect size = 0.70) experiences. Social support tends to promote achievement and productivity, physical health, psychological health, and successful coping with stress and adversity.

Interpersonal relationships are at the heart of communities of practice. Learning communities, for example, are based as much on relationships as they are on intellectual discourse. The more students care about each other, and the more committed they are to each other's success, the harder each student will work and the more productive students will be.

Psychological Adjustment and Social Competence

The third set of educational issues involves promoting students' psychological health, self-esteem, and social competencies. *Psychological health* is the ability to develop, maintain, and appropriately modify interdependent relationships with others to succeed in achieving goals (Johnson & Johnson, 1989). To manage social interdependence, individuals must correctly perceive whether interdependence exists, and whether it is positive or negative, be motivated accordingly, and act in ways consistent with normative expectations for appropriate behavior within the situation. Four studies have directly measured the relationship between social interdependence and psychological health. The samples studied included suburban high-school seniors (Johnson & Norem-Heibeisen, 1977), juvenile and adult prisoners (James & Johnson, 1983), step-couples (James & Johnson, 1988), and Olympic hockey players (Johnson, Johnson, & Krotee, 1986). The results indicated that (1) working cooperatively with peers and valuing cooperation result in greater psychological health than does competing with peers or working independently, and (2) cooperative attitudes are highly correlated with a wide variety of indices of psychological health. Competitiveness was in some cases positively and in some cases negatively related to psychological health, and individualistic attitudes were negatively related to a wide variety of indices of psychological health. Cooperativeness is positively related to a number of indices of psychological health, such as emotional maturity, well-adjusted social relations, strong personal identity, ability to cope with adversity, social competencies, and basic trust in and optimism about people. Personal ego strength, self-confidence, independence, and autonomy are all promoted by being involved in cooperative efforts. Individualistic attitudes tend to be related to a number of indices of psychological pathology, such as emotional immaturity, social maladjustment, delinquency, self-alienation, and self-rejection. Competitiveness is related to a mixture of healthy and unhealthy characteristics. Whereas inappropriate competitive and individualistic attitudes and efforts have resulted in alienating individuals from others, healthy and therapeutic growth depends on increasing individuals' understanding of how to cooperate more effectively with others. Cooperative experiences are not a luxury. They are absolutely necessary for healthy development.

Social interdependence theory has been extended to self-esteem. A *process of self-acceptance* is posited to be based on (1) internalizing perceptions that one is known, accepted, and liked as one is; (2) internalizing mutual success; and (3) evaluating oneself favorably in comparison with peers. A process of self-rejection may occur from (1) not wanting to be known, (2) low performance, (3) overgeneralization of self-evaluations, and (4) the disapproval of others. Since the 1950s, there have been over 80 studies comparing the relative impact of cooperative, competitive, and individualistic experiences on self-esteem (Johnson & Johnson, 1989). Cooperative experiences promote higher self-esteem than do competitive (effect size = 0.58) or individualistic (effect size = 0.44) experiences. Our research demonstrated that cooperative experiences tend to be related to beliefs that one is intrinsically worthwhile, others see one in positive ways, one's attributes compare favorably with those of one's peers, and one is a capable, competent, and successful person. In cooperative efforts, students (1) realize that they are accurately known, accepted, and liked by their peers; (2) know that they have contributed to their own, others, and group success; and (3) perceive themselves and others in a differentiated and realistic way that allows for multidimensional comparison based on complementarity of their own and others' abilities. Competitive experiences tend to be related to conditional self-esteem based on whether one wins or loses. Individualistic experiences tend to be related to basic self-rejection.

A number of studies have related cooperative, competitive, and individualistic experiences to perspective-taking ability (the ability to understand how a situation appears to other people; Johnson & Johnson, 1989). Cooperative experiences tend to increase perspective-taking ability, whereas competitive and individualistic experiences tend to promote egocentrism (being unaware of other perspectives other than . your own; effect sizes of 0.61 and 0.44, respectively). Individuals, furthermore, who are part of a cooperative effort learn more social skills and become more socially competent than do persons competing or working individualistically. Finally, it is through cooperative efforts that many of the attitudes and values essential to psychological health (such as self-efficacy) are learned and adopted.

An important aspect of psychological health is social competence. *Social skills and competencies tend to increase more within cooperative than in competitive or individualistic situations* (Johnson & Johnson, 1989). Working together to get the job done increases students' abilities to provide leadership, build and maintain trust, communicate effectively, and manage conflict constructively. Employability and career success depend largely on such social skills. Most modern work occurs within teams. Intelligence and technical expertise are of no use if individuals are not skillful group members. The social skills learned within cooperative learning groups, furthermore, provide the basis for building and maintaining lifelong friendships, loving and caring families, and cohesive neighborhoods.

When children, adolescents, and young adults are graduated from school, they need enough psychological stability to build and maintain career, family, and community relationships, to establish a basic and meaningful interdependence with other people, and to participate effectively within their society and world. States of depression, anxiety, and anger, furthermore, interfere with classroom functioning.

Reciprocal Relationships among the Three Outcomes

> *The reasons we were so good, and continued to be so good, was because he [Joe Paterno] forces you to develop an inner love among the players. It is much harder to give up on your buddy, than it is to give up on your coach. I really believe that over the years the teams I played on were almost unbeatable in tight situations. When we needed to get that six inches we got it because of our love for each other. Our camaraderie existed because of the kind of coach and kind of person Joe was.*
>
> —DAVID JOYNER, in a television interview

Each of the outcomes of cooperative efforts (effort to achieve, quality of relationships, and psychological health) influences the others and, therefore, they are likely to be found together (Johnson & Johnson, 1989). First, caring and committed friendships come from a sense of mutual accomplishment, mutual pride in joint work, and the bonding that results from joint efforts. The more individuals care about each other, the harder they will work to achieve mutual goals. Second, joint efforts to achieve mutual goals promote higher self-esteem, self-efficacy, personal control, and confidence in one's competencies. The healthier individuals are psychologically, the better able they are to work with others to achieve mutual goals. Third, psychological health is built on the internalization of the caring and respect received from loved ones. Friendships are developmental advantages that promote self-esteem, self-efficacy, and general psychological adjustment. The healthier people are psychologically (i.e., free of psychological pathology such as depression, paranoia, anxiety, fear of failure, repressed anger, hopelessness, and meaninglessness), the more caring and committed their relationships. Because each outcome can induce the others, one is likely to find them together. They are a package, with each outcome a door into all three. Together, they induce positive interdependence and promotive interaction.

Competitive and Individualistic Efforts

The basic social psychological query is, "Under what conditions are cooperative, competitive, and individualistic efforts effective?" The hundreds of studies that have been conducted to try to answer this question indicated that under most conditions, cooperation has more powerful effects on the variables studied than do competitive or individualistic efforts. Under most conditions, cooperative efforts are more effective than are competitive and individualistic efforts. There is some evidence that on very simple, overlearned, repetitive motor tasks, competition may produce higher achievement than does cooperation (Johnson & Johnson, 1989). It is unclear whether individualistic efforts have any advantage over cooperative efforts. There is considerably more research needed to clarify the conditions under which competitive or individualistic efforts may have more powerful effects than cooperation.

Mediating Variables: The Basic Elements of Cooperation

The truly committed cooperative learning group is probably the most productive tool humans have. Creating and maintaining truly committed cooperative groups, however, are far from easy. In most situations, truly committed cooperative groups are rare, perhaps because many individuals (1) are confused about what is (and is not) a cooperative group and (2) lack the discipline required to implement the basics of cooperative efforts in a rigorous way in every lesson.

Potential Group Performance

Not all groups are cooperative groups (Johnson & Johnson, 1994). Placing people in the same room, seating them together, telling them they are a cooperative group, and advising them to "cooperate," does not make them a cooperative group. Study groups, project groups, lab groups, committees, task forces, departments, and councils are groups, but they are not necessarily cooperative. Groups may be classified into at least four categories (Johnson & Johnson, 1994):

1. *Pseudogroups* are groups whose members have been assigned to work together, but they have no interest in doing so. There is competition at close quarters: Members may block each other's achievement, communicate and coordinate poorly, mislead and confuse each other, loaf, and seek a free ride.

The result is that the sum of the whole is less than the potential of the individual members.

2. *Traditional groups* are groups whose members agree to work together but see little benefit from doing so. There is individualistic work with talking. Members interact primarily to share information and clarify how to complete the tasks. Then, they each do the work on their own. Their achievements are individually recognized and rewarded. The result is that some members benefit, but others may be more productive working alone.

3. *Cooperative groups* are groups whose members commit themselves to the common purpose of maximizing their own and each other's success. Their defining characteristics are a compelling purpose to maximize all members' productivity and achievement, holding themselves and each other accountable for contributing their share of the work to achieve the group's goals, promoting each other's success by sharing resources and providing each other support and encouragement, using social skills to coordinate their efforts and achieve their goals, and analyzing how effectively they are achieving their goals and working together. The result is that the sum of the whole is greater than the potential of the individual members.

4. *High-performance cooperative groups* are groups that meet all the criteria for a cooperative group and outperform all reasonable expectations, given their membership.

Not every group is effective. Almost everyone has been part of a group that wasted time, was inefficient, and generally produced poor work. Pseudogroups and traditional groups are characterized by a number of dynamics that impair their effectiveness (Johnson & Johnson, 1994), such as group immaturity, uncritically and quickly accepting members' dominant response, social loafing, free-riding, and groupthink. Such hindering factors are eliminated by carefully structuring into the group five basic elements of cooperation.

The Basic Elements of Cooperation

Individuals fool themselves if they think well-meaning directives to "work together," "cooperate," and "be a team," will be enough to create cooperative efforts among members. *There is a discipline to creating cooperation.* Making teams work is like being on a diet. It does no good to diet one or two days a week. If you wish to lose weight, you have to control what you eat every day. Similarly, it does no good to structure a team carefully every fourth or fifth meeting. The basic elements are a regimen that, if followed rigorously, will produce the conditions for effective cooperation. The basic components of effective cooperative efforts are positive interdependence, face-to-face promotive interaction, individual and group accountability, appropriate use of social skills, and group processing.

Positive Interdependence: We Instead of Me

All for one and one for all.
—ALEXANDRE DUMAS

Within a football game, the quarterback who throws the pass and the receiver who catches the pass are positively interdependent. The success of one depends on the success of the other. It takes two to complete a pass. One player cannot succeed without the other. Both have to perform competently to assure their mutual success. If one fails, they both fail.

Positive interdependence exists when one perceives that one is linked with others in a way that one cannot succeed unless they do (and vice versa) and/or that one must coordinate one's efforts within the efforts of others to complete a task (Johnson & Johnson, 1989). The discipline of using cooperative groups begins with structuring positive interdependence. Group members have to know that they "sink or swim together"; that is, they have two responsibilities: to maximize their own productivity, and to maximize the productivity of all other group members. There are two major categories of interdependence: outcome interdependence and means interdependence (Johnson & Johnson, 1989). When persons are in a cooperative or competitive situation, they are oriented toward a desired outcome, end state, goal, or reward. If there is no outcome interdependence (goal and reward interdependence), there is no cooperation or competition. In addition, the means through which the mutual goals or rewards are to be accomplished specify the actions required on the part of group members. Means interdependence includes resource, role, and task interdependence (which are overlapping and not independent of each other).

Positive interdependence has numerous effects on individuals' motivation and productivity, not the least of which is to highlight the fact that the efforts of all group members are needed for group success. When members of a group see their efforts as dispensable for the group's success, they may reduce their efforts (Kerr, 1983; Kerr & Bruun, 1983; Sweeney, 1973). When group members perceive their potential contribution to the group as being unique, they increase their efforts (Harkins & Petty, 1982). When goal, task, resource, and role interdependence are clearly understood, individuals realize that their efforts are required in order for the group to succeed (i.e., there can be no "free-riders") and that their contributions are often unique. In addition, reward interdependence needs to be structured to ensure that one member's efforts do not make the efforts of other members unnecessary. If the highest score in the group determined the group grade, for example, low-ability members might see their efforts to produce as unnecessary, and they might contribute minimally, and high-ability members might feel exploited and become demoralized and, therefore, decrease their efforts so as not to provide undeserved rewards for irresponsible and ungrateful "free-riders" (Kerr, 1983).

A series of research studies was conducted to clarify the impact of positive interdependence on achievement. The results indicated the following:

1. Group membership in and of itself does not seem sufficient to produce higher achievement and productivity—positive interdependence is also required (Hwong, Casswell, Johnson, & Johnson, 1993). Knowing that one's performance affects the success of groupmates seems to create "responsibility forces" that increase one's efforts to achieve.

2. Interpersonal interaction is insufficient to increase productivity—positive interdependence is also required (Lew, Mesch, Johnson, & Johnson, 1985a,b; Mesch, Johnson, & Johnson, 1988; Mesch, Lew, Johnson, & Johnson, 1986a,b). Individuals attained higher achievement under positive goal interdependence than when they worked individualistically but had the opportunity to interact with classmates.

3. Goal and reward interdependence seem to be additive (Lew et al., 1986a,b; Mesch et al., 1988; Mesch et al., 1986). Although positive goal interdependence is sufficient to produce higher achievement and productivity than do individualistic efforts, the combination of goal and reward interdependence is even more effective.

4. Both working to achieve a reward and working to avoid the loss of a reward produced higher achievement than did individualistic efforts (Frank, 1984). There is no significant difference between working to achieve a reward and working to avoid a loss.

5. Goal interdependence promotes higher achievement and greater productivity than does resource interdependence (Johnson, Johnson, Ortiz, & Stanne, 1991).

6. Resource interdependence by itself may decrease achievement and productivity compared with individualistic efforts (Johnson, Johnson, Stanne, & Garibaldi, 1990; Ortiz, Johnson, & Johnson, 1996).

7. The combination of goal and resource interdependence increased achievement more than goal interdependence alone or individualistic efforts (Johnson et al., 1990; Ortiz et al., 1996).

8. Positive interdependence does more than simply motivate individuals to try harder; it facilitates the development of new insights and discoveries through promotive interaction (Gabbert, Johnson, & Johnson, 1986; Johnson & Johnson, 1981; Johnson, Skon, & Johnson, 1980; Skon, Johnson, & Johnson, 1981). Members of cooperative groups use higher-level reasoning strategies more frequently than do individuals working individualistically or competitively.

9. The more complex the procedures involved in interdependence, the longer it will take group members to reach their full levels of productivity (Ortiz et al., 1996). The more complex the teamwork procedures, the more members have to attend to teamwork and the less time they have to attend to taskwork. Once the teamwork procedures are mastered, however, members concentrate on taskwork and outperform individuals working alone.

The constructive effects that positive interdependence contribute to cooperative efforts do not mean that it is always advantageous. There are conditions under which positive interdependence may have negative effects on cooperation. Further research is needed to clarify the conditions under which positive interdependence does and does not contribute to cooperation's effectiveness.

Individual Accountability/Personal Responsibility

After positive interdependence, a key variable mediating the effectiveness of cooperation is a sense of personal responsibility for contributing one's efforts to accomplish the group's goals. This involves being responsible for (1) completing one's share of the work and (2) facilitating the work of other group members and minimally hindering their efforts. Personal responsibility is promoted by individual accountability. Certainly, lack of individual accountability reduces feelings of personal responsibility. Members will reduce their contributions to goal achievement when the group works on tasks where it is difficult to identify members' contributions, when there is an increased likelihood of redundant efforts, when there is a lack of group cohesiveness, and when there is lessened responsibility for the final outcome (Harkins & Petty, 1982; Ingham, Levinger, Graves, & Peckham, 1974; Kerr & Bruun, 1981; Latane, Williams, & Harkins, 1979; Moede, 1927; Petty, Harkins, Williams, & Lantane, 1977; Williams, 1981; Williams, Harkins, & Latane, 1981). If, however, there is high individual accountability and it is clear how much effort each member is contributing, if redundant efforts are avoided, if every member is responsible for the final outcome, and if the group is cohesive, then the social-loafing effect vanishes. The smaller the size of the group, in addition, the greater the individual accountability may be (Messick & Brewer, 1983).

Archer-Kath et al. (1994) investigated whether positive interdependence and individual accountability are two separate and independent dimensions. They compared the impact of feedback to the learning group as a whole with the individual feedback to each member on achievement, attitudes, and behavior in cooperative learning groups. Students received either individual or group feedback in written graph/chart form only on how frequently members engaged in the targeted behaviors. If individual accountability and positive interdependence are unrelated, no differences should be found in perceived positive interdependence between conditions. If they are related, students in the individual feedback condition should perceive more positive interdependence than students in the group feedback condition. Individual feedback resulted in greater perceptions of cooperation, goal interdependence, and resource interdependence than did group feedback, indicating that positive interdependence and individual accountability are related and that by increasing individual accountability, perceived interdependence among group members may also be increased.

The results of these studies indicated that individual accountability does increase the effectiveness of a group in ensuring that all members achieve and contribute to the achievement of their groupmates.

Promotive (Face-to-Face) Interaction

Promotive interaction may be defined as individuals encouraging and facilitating each other's efforts to complete tasks and achieve in order to reach the group's goals. Promotive interaction is characterized by students (1) providing each other with efficient and effective help and assistance; (2) exchanging needed resources such as information, materials, and processing information more efficiently and effectively; (3) providing each other with feedback in order to improve subsequent performance on assigned tasks and responsibilities; (4) challenging each other's conclusions and reasoning in order to promote higher quality decision making and greater insight into the problems being considered; (5) advocating exerting efforts to achieve mutual goals; (6) influencing each other's efforts to achieve mutual goals; (7) acting in trusting and trustworthy ways; (8) being motivated to strive for mutual benefit; and (9) feeling less anxiety and stress (Johnson & Johnson, 1989). The amount of research documenting the impact of promotive interaction on achievement is too voluminous to review here. Interested readers are referred to Johnson and Johnson (1989).

Social Skills

Placing socially unskilled students in a learning group and telling them to cooperate will obviously not be successful. Students must be taught the interpersonal and small-group skills needed for high quality cooperation and be motivated to use them. To coordinate efforts to achieve mutual goals students must (1) get to know and trust each other, (2) communicate accurately and unambiguously, (3) accept and support each other, and (4) resolve conflicts constructively (Johnson, 1993; Johnson & Johnson, 1997). Interpersonal and small-group skills form the basic nexus among individuals, and if individuals are to work together productively and cope with the stresses and strains of doing so, they must have a modicum of these skills. Students need to master and use interpersonal and small-group skills to capitalize on the opportunities presented by a cooperative learning situation. Especially when learning groups function on a long-term basis and engage in complex, free, exploratory activities over a prolonged period, the interpersonal and small-group skills of the members may determine the level of members' achievement and productivity.

In their studies on the long-term implementation of cooperation learning, Marvin Lew and Debra Mesch (Lew et al., 1986a,b; Mesch, Johnson, & Johnson, 1988, 1993; Mesch et al., 1986) investigated the impact of a reward contingency for using social skills as well as positive interdependence and a contingency for academic achievement on performance within cooperative learning groups. In the cooperative skills conditions, students were trained weekly in four social skills, and each member of a cooperative group was given two bonus points toward the quiz grade if all group members were observed by the teacher to demonstrate three out of four cooperative skills. The results indicated that the combination of positive goal interdependence, an academic contingency for high performance by all group members, and a social skills contingency promoted the highest achievement. Archer-Kath et al. (1994) trained students in the social skills of praising, supporting, asking for information, giving information, asking for help, and giving help. Students received either individual or group feedback in written graph/chart form on how frequently members engaged in the targeted behaviors. The researchers found that giving students individual feedback on how frequently they engaged in targeted social skills was more effective in increasing students' achievement than was group feedback. The more socially skillful students are, the more attention teachers pay to teaching and rewarding the use of social skills, and the more individual feedback students receive on their use of the skills, the higher the achievement that can be expected with cooperative learning groups.

Not only do social skills promote higher achievement, but also they contribute to building more positive relationships among group members. Putnam, Rynders, Johnson, and Johnson (1989) demonstrated that when students were taught social skills, observed by the teacher, and given individual feedback as to how frequently they engaged in the skills, their relationships became more positive.

Group Processing

In order to achieve, students in cooperative learning groups have to work together effectively. Effective group work is influenced by whether groups periodically reflect on how well they are functioning and plan how to improve their work processes. A *process* is an identifiable sequence of events taking place over time, and *process goals* refer to the sequence of events instrumental in achieving outcome goals. *Group processing* may be defined as reflecting on a group session to (1) describe what member actions were helpful and unhelpful and (2) make decisions about what actions to continue or change. The purpose of group processing is to clarify and improve the effectiveness of the members in contributing to the joint efforts to achieve the group's goals.

Yager, Johnson, and Johnson (1985) examined the impact on achievement of (1) cooperative learning in which members discussed how well their group was functioning and how they could improve its effectiveness, (2) cooperative learning without any group processing, and (3) individualistic learning. The results indicate that the high-, medium-, and low-achieving students in the cooperation with group processing condition achieved higher on daily achievement, postinstructional achievement, and retention measures than did the students in the other two conditions. Students in the cooperation groups without group processing condition, furthermore, achieved higher scores on all three measures than did the students in the individualistic condition.

Putnam et al. (1989) conducted a study in which there were two conditions: (1) cooperative learning with social skills training and (2) group processing and cooperative learning without social skills training and group processing. Forty-eight fifth-grade students (32 nonhandicapped students and 16 students with IQ's ranging from 35 to 52) participated in the study. In the cooperative learning with social skills training condition, the teacher gave students examples of specific cooperative behaviors to engage in, observed how frequently students engaged in the skills, gave students feedback as to how well they worked together, and had students discuss for

5 minutes how to use the skills more effectively in the future. In the uninstructed cooperative groups condition, students were placed in cooperative groups that worked together for the same period of time with the same amount of teacher intervention (aimed at the academic lesson and unrelated to working together skillfully). Both nonhandicapped and handicapped students were randomly assigned to each condition. The researchers found that more positive relationships developed between handicapped and nonhandicapped students in the cooperative skills condition and that these positive relationships carried over to postinstructional free-time situations.

Johnson et al. (1990) conducted a study comparing cooperative learning with no processing, cooperative learning with teacher processing (the teacher specified cooperative skills to use, observed, and gave whole-class feedback as to how well students were using the skills), cooperative learning with teacher and student processing (the teacher specified cooperative skills to use, observed, gave whole-class feedback as to how well students were using the skills, and had learning groups discuss how well they interacted as a group), and individualistic learning. Forty-nine high-ability African-American school seniors and entering college freshmen at Xavier University participated in the study. A complex, computer-assisted problem-solving assignment was given to all students. All three cooperative conditions performed higher than did the individualistic condition. The combination of teacher and student processing resulted in greater problem-solving success than did the other cooperative conditions.

Archer-Kath et al. (1994) provided learning groups with either individual or group feedback on how frequently members had engaged in targeted social skills. Each group had 5 minutes at the beginning of each session to discuss how well the group was functioning and what could be done to improve the group's effectiveness. Group processing with individual feedback was more effective than group processing with whole-group feedback in increasing students' (1) achievement motivation, actual achievement, uniformity of achievement among group members, and influence toward higher achievement within cooperative learning groups; (2) positive relationships among group members and between students and the teacher; and (3) self-esteem and positive attitudes toward the subject area.

The results of these studies indicated that engaging in group processing clarifies and improves the effectiveness of the members in contributing to the joint efforts to achieve the group's goals, especially when specific social skills are targeted and students receive individual feedback as to how frequently and how well they engaged in the skills.

Summary

There is nothing magical about telling individuals to work together as a team. The basic elements that both create cooperative efforts and mediate the relationship between cooperation and outcomes must be vigilantly structured into every group session. The basic elements are positive interdependence, individual accountability, promotive interaction, appropriate use of social skills, and group processing. These elements are a regimen that, if followed rigorously, will produce the conditions for effective cooperation.

Enhancing Variables: Trust and Conflict

During the 1950s and 1960s, Deutsch (1962, 1973) researched two aspects of the internal dynamics of cooperative groups that potentially enhanced outcomes: trust and conflict. His research was continued by the authors in the 1970s, 1980s, and 1990s. The greater the trust among group members, the more effective their cooperative efforts tend to be (Deutsch, 1962; Johnson, 1993; Johnson & Noonan, 1972).

Conflict within cooperative groups, when managed constructively, enhances the effectiveness of cooperative efforts. There are two types of conflict that occur frequently and regularly within cooperative groups: controversy and conflicts of interests (Johnson & Johnson, 1995a,b). Both controversies and conflicts of interests are inevitable results of the committed participation of members of cooperative learning groups. *Controversy* exists when group members have different information, perceptions, opinions, reasoning processes, theories, and conclusions, and they must reach agreement (Johnson & Johnson, 1995b). Compared with concurrence seeking, debate, and individualistic efforts, controversy results in greater mastery and retention of the subject matter, higher quality problem solving, greater creativity in thinking, greater motivation to learn more about the topic, more productive exchange of expertise among groups members, greater task involvement, more positive relationships among group members, more accurate perspective taking, and higher self-esteem. In addition, students enjoy it more. Controversies tend to be constructive when the situational context is cooperative, group members are heterogeneous, information and expertise are distributed within the group, members have the necessary conflict skills, and the canons of rational argumentation are followed.

A *conflict of interests* occurs when the actions of one person striving to achieve his or her goal interfere with and obstruct the actions of another person striving to achieve his or her goal (Johnson & Johnson, 1995a,c). Cooperative efforts tend to be more effective when group members (1) negotiate integrative agreements to resolve their conflicts of interests and (2) mediate the conflicts among their groupmates. What results is more constructive resolution of conflicts, fewer discipline problems, less teacher and administrator time spent in arbitrating student conflicts, and higher academic achievement. By teaching students integrative negotiation and peer mediation procedures, schools may not only enhance the quality and effectiveness of cooperative efforts, but also they create a schoolwide discipline program based on empowering students to regulate their own behavior.

Summary and Conclusions

> *It's easy to get the players. Getting them to play together, that's the hard part.*
> —Casey Stengel

Educators are faced with a number of issues that concern ensuring that schools are "world-class" in terms of achievement and higher-level reasoning, creating positive relationships among diverse students, and promoting students' psychological well-being and development. Because of its effectiveness in dealing with these issues, cooperative learning has surfaced as one of the most important educational practices. The popularity and widespread use of cooperative learning may be largely due to its being based on a theory validated by a great deal of research.

The application of social interdependence theory and research to education is one of the most successful and widespread applications of social psychology to practice. The theory provides a conceptual framework from which practical procedures that teachers may use to promote learning (cooperative learning) and improve instruction (teaching teams) may be developed. From the conceptual framework, educators may do such things as (1) define cooperative, competitive, and individualistic efforts; (2) define the teacher's role in conducting cooperative lessons; (3) use the five basic elements that guide the teacher's development and planning of lessons; and (4) use the five basic elements as a tool set to intervene in cooperative groups to solve problems students have in working together (Johnson et al., 1992, 1993).

On the basis of social interdependence theory and the validating research, a number of conclusions about cooperative learning can be made. *Cooperation is a generic human endeavor that affects many different instructional outcomes simultaneously.* Over the past 100 years, researchers have focused on such diverse outcomes as achievement, higher-level reasoning, retention, achievement motivation, intrinsic motivation, transfer of learning, interpersonal attraction, social support, friendships, prejudice, valuing differences, self-esteem, social competencies, psychological health, moral reasoning, and many others. These numerous outcomes may be subsumed within three broad categories: (1) effort to achieve, (2) positive interpersonal relationships, and (3) psychological health. Cooperative efforts, compared with competitive and individualistic ones, tend to result in higher levels of these outcomes, especially when five mediating variables (positive interdependence, individual accountability, promotive interaction, social skills, and group processing) and two enhancing variables (trust and conflict) are present.

The research on social interdependence has an external validity and a generalizability rarely found in the social sciences. Cooperative learning can be used with some confidence at every grade level, in every subject area, and with any task. The more variations in places, people, and procedures the research can withstand and still yield the same findings, the more externally valid the conclusions. The research has been conducted in 10 different historical decades. Research subjects have varied as to age, sex, economic class, nationality, and cultural background. A wide variety of research tasks, ways of structuring the types of social interdependence, and measures of the dependent variables have been used. The research has been conducted by many different researchers with markedly different theoretical and practical orientations, working in different settings and even in different countries. The diversity of subjects, settings, age levels, and operationalizations of social interdependence and the dependent variables give this work wide generalizability and considerable external validity.

Clear and specific operationalizations of cooperative learning have been made based on understanding social interdependence theory and the variables that mediate and enhance cooperation's effectiveness. The more educators understand the five basic elements and the two enhancing variables, the greater their ability to (1) structure formal and informal cooperative learning and cooperative base groups, (2) diagnosis problems students have in working together, (3) adapt cooperative learning to different student populations and subject areas, and (4) use cooperative learning for years with high fidelity and appropriate flexibility.

Cooperative learning should ideally be used the majority of the school day. In order to do so, teachers must know how to structure cooperative learning to include the five basic elements that mediate its effectiveness.

Cooperative learning is here to stay. Because it is based on a profound and strategic theory and there is substantial research validating its effectiveness, there probably will never be a time in the future when cooperative learning is not used extensively within educational programs.

References

Archer-Kath, J., Johnson, D. W., & Johnson, R. (1994). Individual versus group feedback in cooperative groups. *Journal of Social Psychology, 134,* 681–694.

Aronson, E. (1978). *The jigsaw classroom.* Beverly Hills, CA: Sage.

Deutsch, M. (1949). A theory of cooperation and competition. *Human Relations, 2,* 129–152.

Deutsch, M. (1962). Cooperation and trust: Some theoretical notes. In M. R. Jones (Ed.), *Nebraska symposium on motivation* (pp. 275–319). Lincoln: University of Nebraska Press.

Deutsch, M. (1973). *The resolution of conflict.* New Haven, CT: Yale University Press.

DeVries, D., & Edwards, K. (1974). Student teams and learning games: Their effects on cross-race and cross-sex interaction. *Journal of Educational Psychology, 66,* 741– 749.

Frank, M. (1984). A comparison between an individual and group goal structure contingency that differed in the behavioral contingency and performance–outcome components (Doctoral dissertation, University of Minnesota). *Dissertation Abstracts International, 45*/05, 1341-A.

Gabbert, B., Johnson, D., & Johnson, R. (1986). Cooperative learning, group-to-individual transfer, process gain and the acquisition of cognitive reasoning strategies. *Journal of Psychology, 120*(3), 265–278.

Harkins, S. G., & Petty, R. E. (1982). The effects of task difficulty and task uniqueness on social loafing. *Journal of Personality and Social Psychology, 43,* 1214–1229.

Hwong, N., Caswell, A., Johnson, D. W., & Johnson, R. (1993). Effects of cooperative and individualistic learning on prospective elementary teachers' music achievement and attitudes. *Journal of Social Psychology, 133,* 53–64.

Ingham, A., Levinger, G., Graves, J., & Peckham, V. (1974). The Ringelmann effect: Studies of group size and group performance. *Journal of Personality and Social Psychology, 10,* 371–384.

James, N., & Johnson, D. W. (1983). The relationship between attitudes toward social interdependence and psychological health within three criminal populations. *Journal of Abnormal and Social Psychology, 121,* 131–143.

James, S., & Johnson, D. W. (1988). Social interdependence, psychological adjustment, orientation toward negative life stress, and quality of second marriage. *Journal of Social Psychology, 128*(3), 287–304.

Johnson, D. W. (1970). *Social psychology of education.* New York: Holt, Rinehart and Winston.

Johnson, D. W. (1993). *Reaching out: Interpersonal effectiveness and self-actualization* (5th ed.). Englewood Cliffs, NJ: Prentice-Hall.

Johnson, D. W., & Johnson, F. (1994). *Joining together: Group theory and group skills* (5th ed.). Englewood Cliffs, NJ: Prentice-Hall.

Johnson, D. W., & Johnson, R. (1974). Instructional goal structure: Cooperative, competitive, or individualistic. *Review of Educational Research, 44,* 213–240.

Johnson, D. W., & Johnson, R. (1979). Conflict in the classroom: Controversy and learning. *Review of Educational Research, 49,* 51–70.

Johnson, D. W., & Johnson, R. (1981). Effects of cooperative and individualistic learning experiences on interethnic interaction. *Journal of Educational Psychology*, *73*(3), 454–459.

Johnson, D. W., & Johnson R. (1989). *Cooperation and competition: Theory and research*. Edina, MN: Interaction Book Company.

Johnson, D. W., & Johnson, R. (1995a). *Teaching students to be peacemakers*. Edina, MN: Interaction Book Company.

Johnson, D. W., & Johnson, R. (1995b). *Creative controversy: Intellectual challenge in the classroom*. Edina, MN: Interaction Book Company.

Johnson, D. W., & Johnson, R. (1995c). Teaching students to be peacemakers: Results of five years of research. *Peace and Conflict: Journal of Peace Psychology*, *1*(4), 417–438.

Johnson, D. W., Johnson, R., & Holubec, E. (1992). *Advanced cooperative learning* (2nd ed.). Edina, MN: Interaction Book Company.

Johnson, D. W., Johnson, R., & Holubec, E. (1993). *Cooperation in the classroom* (6th ed.). Edina, MN: Interaction Book Company.

Johnson, D. W., Johnson, R., & Krotee, M. (1986). The relationship between social interdependence and psychological health within the 1980 United States Olympic ice hockey team. *Journal of Psychology*, *120*, 279–292.

Johnson, D. W., Johnson, R., Ortiz, A., & Stanne, M. (1991). Impact of positive goal and resource interdependence on achievement, interaction, and attitudes. *Journal of General Psychology*, *118*(4), 341–347.

Johnson, D. W., Johnson, R., Stanne, M., & Garibaldi, A. (1990). Impact of group processing on achievement in cooperative groups. *Journal of Social Psychology*, *130*, 507–516.

Johnson, D. W., & Noonan, P. (1972). Effects of acceptance and reciprocation of self-disclosures on the development of trust. *Journal of Counseling Psychology*, *19*(5), 411–416.

Johnson, D. W., & Norem-Hebeisen, A. (1977). Attitudes toward interdependence among persons and psychological health. *Psychological Reports*, *40*, 843–850.

Johnson, D. W., Skon, L., & Johnson, R. (1980). Effects of cooperative, competitive, and individualistic conditions on children's problem-solving performance. *American Educational Research Journal*, *17*(1), 83–94.

Kerr, N., & Bruun, S. (1981). Ringelmann revisited: Alternative explanations for the social loafing effect. *Journal of Personality and Social Psychology*, *7*, 224–231.

Kerr, N., & Bruun, S. (1983). The dispensability of member effort and group motivation losses: Free-rider effects. *Journal of Personality and Social Psychology*, *44*, 78–94.

Latane, B., Williams, K., & Harkins, S. (1979). Many hands make light the work: The causes and consequences of social loafing. *Journal of Personality and Social Psychology*, *37*, 822–832.

Lew, M., Mesch, D., Johnson, D. W., & Johnson, R. (1986a). Positive interdependence, academic and collaborative-skills group contingencies and isolated students. *American Educational Research Journal*, *23*, 476–488.

Lew, M., Mesch, D., Johnson, D. W., & Johnson, R. (1986b). Components of cooperative learning: Effects of collaborative skills and academic group contingencies on achievement and mainstreaming. *Contemporary Educational Psychology*, *11*, 229–239.

Mesch, D., Johnson, D. W., & Johnson, R. (1988). Impact of positive interdependence and academic group contingencies on achievement. *Journal of Social Psychology*, *128*, 345–352.

Mesch, D., Lew, M., Johnson, D. W., & Johnson, R. (1986). Isolated teenagers, cooperative learning and the training of social skills. *Journal of Psychology*, *120*, 323–334.

Messick, D., & Brewer, M. (1983). Solving social dilemmas: A review. In L. Wheeler & P. Shaver (Eds.), *Review of personality and social psychology*, (Vol. 4, pp. 11–44). Newbury Park, CA: Sage.

Moede, W. (1927). Die richtlinien der leistungs-psycholgie. *Industrielle Psychotechnik*, *4*, 193–207.

Ortiz, A., Johnson, D. W., & Johnson, R. (1995). Effect of positive goal and resource interdependence on individual performance. *Journal of Social Psychology*, in press.

Petty, R., Harkins, S., Williams, K., & Latane, B. (1977). The effects of group size on cognitive effort and evaluation. *Personality and Social Psychology Bulletin*, *3*, 575–578.

Putnam, J., Rynders, J., Johnson, R., & Johnson, D. W. (1989). Collaborative skill instruction for promoting positive interactions between mentally handicapped and nonhandicapped children. *Exceptional Children, 55*(6), 550–557.

Sheingold, K., Hawkins, J., & Char, C. (1984). "I'm the thinkist, you're the typist": The interaction of technology and the social life of classrooms. *Journal of Social Issues, 40*(3), 49–61.

Skon, L., Johnson, D., & Johnson, R. (1981). Cooperative peer interaction versus individual competition and individualistic efforts: Effects on the acquisition of cognitive reasoning strategies. *Journal of Educational Psychology, 73*(1), 83–92.

Slavin, R. (1986). *Using student team learning* (3rd ed.). Baltimore: Johns Hopkins University.

Smith, K., Johnson, D. W., & Johnson, R. (1981). Can conflict be constructive? Controversy versus concurrence seeking in learning groups. *Journal of Educational Psychology, 73*, 651–663.

Sweeney, J. (1973). An experimental investigation of the free-rider problem. *Social Science Research, 2*, 277–292.

Tjosvold, D. (1986). *Working together to get things done.* Lexington, MA: D. C. Heath.

Williams, K. (1981). *The effects of group cohesiveness of social loafing.* Paper presented at the annual meeting of the Midwestern Psychological Association, Detroit, MI.

Williams, K., Harkins, S., & Latane, B. (1981). Identifiability as a deterrent to social loafing: Two cheering experiments. *Journal of Personality and Social Psychology, 40*, 303–311.

Yager, S., Johnson, D., & Johnson, R. (1985). Oral discussion, group-to-individual transfer, and achievement in cooperative learning groups. *Journal of Educational Psychology, 77*(1), 60–66.

3

Training People to Work in Groups

Richard L. Moreland, Linda Argote, and Ranjani Krishnan

As the end of the century approaches, dramatic changes are occurring in how work is performed in this country. One change that has received much attention is the growing emphasis on collaborative work. Workers have always helped one another, of course, but often in informal ways that received little recognition or support from organizations (see Brown & Duguid, 1991; Kram, 1988; Organ, 1988; Roethlisberger & Dickson, 1939). In contrast, activities in many organizations are now designed entirely around groups, so that collaboration among workers is formally mandated, structured, and evaluated.

A variety of groups, including management teams, special task forces, quality circles, and self-managed work teams, can be found in today's organizations (see Dumaine, 1994; Payne & Cooper, 1981). The latter groups have become especially popular. For example, in a 1990 study of Fortune 1000 companies by the General Accounting Office (see Lawler, Mohrman, & Ledford, 1992), nearly half of the companies surveyed were already using self-managed work teams, and more than half expected to expand their use of such teams in the future. A recent survey of human resource and development executives from hundreds of organizations (see "Trends," 1994) also indicated that the use of self-managed work teams will soon increase. The popularity of these teams is largely due to the benefits that they can produce (see Carr, 1992; Hoerr, 1989; Katzenbach & Smith, 1993; Montebello & Buzzotta, 1993; Wellins, Byham, & Dixon, 1994). Workers in self-managed teams often enjoy their jobs more, perhaps because they have greater autonomy and their work is more interesting. As a result, levels of absenteeism and turnover often decline in organiza-

Richard L. Moreland • Department of Psychology, University of Pittsburgh, Pittsburgh, Pennsylvania 15260.   **Linda Argote** • Graduate School of Industrial Administration, Carnegie Mellon University, Pittsburgh, Pennsylvania 15213.   **Ranjani Krishnan** • Katz Graduate School of Business, University of Pittsburgh, Pittsburgh, Pennsylvania 15260.

Theory and Research on Small Groups, edited by R. Scott Tindale et al. Plenum Press, New York, 1998.

tions that use such teams. And productivity levels often improve in those same organizations as workers help one another to produce more and better goods or services.

Despite these and other benefits, self-managed work teams can be problematic and have been criticized by several analysts. Some of these criticisms focus on the human costs that can arise when workers are forced to collaborate. For example, although many people enjoy working in groups, there are some loners who would rather work by themselves (Orsburn, Moran, Musselwhite, Zenger, & Perrin, 1990; Wetlaufer, 1994). And some groups demand so much from their members that workers' independence and psychological well-being are threatened (Barker, 1993; Herman, 1994). Finally, formal work groups can interfere with informal groups, in which some workers would rather participate (Sinclair, 1992).

Other criticisms of self-managed work teams focus on the special management problems that they often create. Although collaboration among workers can be beneficial, success is never guaranteed. Indeed, several examples can be found of self-managed work teams that failed (see Adler & Cole, 1993; Dubnicki & Limburg, 1991; Dumaine, 1994; Nahavandi & Aranda, 1994; Vogt & Hunt, 1988). These failures are usually attributed to some form of mismanagement, such as organizing groups in dysfunctional ways (e.g., unclear roles and norms), asking groups to do work that could be performed better by individuals, relying on evaluation and compensation policies that ignore group performance, and using groups as a tool for organizational downsizing. Another important factor, however, is the general lack of training provided for most members of self-managed work teams. Several analysts (e.g., Cannon-Bowers, Tannenbaum, Salas, & Volpe, 1995; Orsburn et al., 1990; Stevens & Campion, 1994; Wellins & George, 1991) have suggested that working in groups requires special knowledge, skills, and attitudes—qualities that may be rare in many organizations. Yet few organizations offer any special training for group work, and what little training is available may be misguided.

Much time, energy, and money are spent on training workers, but that effort is limited to a surprisingly small number of organizations. Most workers receive no formal training at all (Henkoff, 1993; U.S. Department of Labor, 1992), despite the fact that training seems to be a good investment (Grant, 1995; Guzzo, Jette, & Katzell, 1985). When training is provided, it is almost always designed for the individual worker. Training in many organizations is like going back to school, in the sense that each worker learns his or her job independently and often in an abstract and decontextualized manner (Huszczo, 1990; see also Resnick, 1987). The organizational settings in which work actually occurs are seldom considered.

Two Approaches to Group Training

How *should* people be trained to work in groups? The most common approach is to identify the qualities required for effective group work and then develop training programs to help workers acquire those qualities. The first of these steps is more difficult than it seems. Many kinds of knowledge, skills, and attitudes are relevant to working in groups (see Cannon-Bowers et al., 1995; Osburn et al., 1990; Stevens & Campion, 1994; Wellins & George, 1991). Cannon-Bowers and her colleagues, for example, argued that workers need such teamwork skills as leadership, situational awareness, and adaptability; team-relevant knowledge about such matters as group structure, dynamics, and performance (cf. Levine & Moreland, 1991); and positive team attitudes, such as confidence in the ability of groups to achieve their goals and the willingness to trust others. Orsburn and his colleagues argued that training should provide workers with technical, administrative, and interpersonal skills. Among the latter skills, those related to communication, conflict resolution, and goal setting are especially helpful. Finally, Stevens and Campion argued that changes in both selection and training practices can help work groups to succeed. Organizations should hire workers with prior group experience, for instance, or those whose personalities enable them to work well in groups. And workers should be trained in a variety of skills involving interpersonal relations (conflict resolution, collaborative problem solving, and communication) and self-management (goal setting/performance management, and planning/task coordination).

Even when there is agreement about what qualities are required to work effectively in groups, developing training programs that help workers to acquire those qualities can be difficult. These programs must be flexible, because participants may include prospective members of groups that have not yet formed, new members entering existing groups, and members of groups that are already failing. In the latter case, team-building interventions can often be used as well (see Buller, 1986; De-Meuse & Liebowitz, 1981; Nicholas, 1982; Tannenbaum, Beard, & Salas, 1992; Woodman & Sherwood, 1980). These interventions are aimed at strengthening the group as a whole, rather than improving individual members. Training programs, which can require considerable resources, must also be practical. How training is delivered to workers is an important factor in this regard. Many organizations deliver *group* training to *individual* workers, who learn to become effective group members either independently or in artificial groups created just for that purpose. This tactic allows more workers to be trained, with less disruption to other organizational activities.

Of course, training programs must also be effective: Workers should acquire whatever qualities they need for group work, and groups that contain those workers should become more productive as a result. Is this approach to group training effective? Although many claims for its benefits have been made, the evidence for those claims is limited and often unconvincing (see Nicholas, 1982; Stevens & Campion, 1994; Tannenbaum et al., 1992). And there are reasons to be skeptical about such training, because it reflects two related assumptions about work groups, both of which are probably wrong.

The first assumption is that someone with the "right stuff" will succeed in every work group. Put another way, all work groups are assumed to be similar, so that someone with a particular quality will influence group performance in similar ways across settings and over time. Research on a variety of group phenomena, including leadership (Chemers, 1987; Howell, Dorfman, & Kerr, 1986), group composition (Moreland & Levine, 1992a; Moreland, Levine, & Wingert, 1996), and group development (Worchel, 1996), clearly challenges this assumption. Many studies have shown, for example, that the effects of a given leadership style on group performance can vary considerably from one group to another. Such findings suggest that all work groups are *not* the same. Insofar as such groups differ in important ways, "generic" training programs that ignore those differences cannot be very effective.

In an insightful analysis of this issue, Cannon-Bowers and her colleagues (1995) argued that the qualities required for effective group work range along a dimension of specificity. At one end of that dimension are qualities relevant to all groups, whereas at the other end are qualities relevant to a single group. This suggests that in every organizational setting, there may be an optimal "mix" of generic and specific training methods for helping people work together in groups (Druckman & Bjork, 1991). The exact mix probably depends on many factors, including the level of task interdependence among a group's members and the probability of turnover in the group. In contrast, other analysts have argued that every work group is unique (see Brown & Duguid, 1991; Darrah, 1994; Huszczo, 1990; Levine & Moreland, 1991; Rentsch, 1990). This suggests that all group training should be specific rather than generic, focusing on whatever qualities are required for working effectively in particular groups.

A second assumption underlying this approach to group training is that learning to work with others and learning to do a job are largely independent matters. As a result, learning of the latter sort need not occur in the organizational settings where work actually occurs, but can be decontextualized instead, perhaps by creating a standard set of operating procedures that everyone must follow. This assumption, which reflects an idealistic view of work, can also be challenged (Feldman, 1989). As Darrah (1992) noted, real work is often ambiguous, unstable, and irrational, in part because it is a social construction. Many work groups seem to develop their own special operating procedures, which can differ considerably from the standard procedures taught to workers during formal training sessions (see Brown & Duguid, 1991; Darrah, 1992, 1994). These special operating procedures are often superior, because they reflect adaptations to local working conditions, but their merit is somewhat beside the point. The point is that people cannot become effective members of a work group until they learn to do their jobs in ways that are compatible with that group's *style* of working. Training programs that ignore this point cannot be effective, because they teach workers to do their jobs in unrealistic (and sometimes unproductive) ways.

As all of this suggests, another approach is needed for training people to work in groups. Many of the problems just discussed could be avoided if group training were carried out in the organizational settings where work actually occurs. So, when a work group forms, its members should be trained together, rather than apart. And when new members enter an existing work group, they should be trained by that group's members, preferably on the job (see Funk, 1992; Lave & Wenger, 1991; Scribner & Sachs, 1990). Finally, when a work group is already failing, retraining programs or team-building interventions should focus on that group's specific problems and be carried out within the group itself.

We have been especially interested in the advantages and disadvantages of training the members of a newly formed work group together rather than apart. Training of this sort has many advocates (e.g., Darrah, 1995; Hackman, 1993; Huszczo, 1990; Lawler & Mohrman, 1987), and has been used in a variety of organizations (see Andrews, Waag, & Bell, 1992; Druckman & Bjork, 1991; Henkoff, 1993; Hoerr, 1989; Kelly, 1994; Prince, Chidester, Bowers, & Cannon-Bowers, 1992; see also "Trends," 1994). Is this alternative approach to group training effective? Once again, the evidence is rather limited (Dyer, 1985). Training coworkers together has some clear disadvantages. For example, it may be difficult for an organization to keep a work group's members together, especially after their training has ended. Some workers may have to be transferred to other groups, and every work group experiences some turnover. But such training has several advantages as well. For example, it can help an organization to avoid several of the problems discussed earlier, by helping people learn to get along with the members of their own work group, and by teaching them to do their jobs in ways that are compatible with that group's special operating procedures. Training coworkers together might also strengthen a group's cohesion, raise the levels of commitment among its members, and increase its potency, all of which could improve the group's performance (see Griffith, 1989; Guzzo, Yost, Campbell, & Shea, 1993; Moreland, 1987; Mullen & Copper, 1994).

Our own research has focused on another advantage of training coworkers together, namely, the development of a *transactive memory system* within their work group. Wegner (1987, 1995) was the first to analyze transactive memory, especially as it occurs in couples (see Wegner, Erber, & Raymond, 1991; Wegner, Giuliano, & Hertel, 1985). He noted that many people supplement their own memories, which are limited and unreliable, with various external aids. These include objects (e.g., address or appointment books) and other people (e.g., friends or coworkers). Wegner was intrigued by the use of people as memory aids and speculated that a transactive memory system develops in many groups to ensure that important information is not forgotten. This system combines the knowledge possessed by individual group members with a shared awareness of who knows what. So when group members need information, but cannot remember it themselves or are uncertain about the accuracy of their memories, they can turn to one another for help. A transactive memory system thus provides access to more and better information that any single group member could remember alone (see Darrah, 1994).

Every work group probably develops some transactive memory system as people spend time together and learn how knowledge is distributed within the group. But such a system could develop more quickly and easily if the group's members were trained together rather than apart. Training coworkers together not only provides each person with the information needed to perform tasks well, but it also helps him or her to discover what everyone else in the group knows about those tasks. The potential benefits of such knowledge are clear. When group members know more about each other, they can plan their work more sensibly, assigning tasks to the people who will perform them best. As a result, the group can make optimal use of its human resources. Coordination is also likely to improve when workers know more about each other—people can *anticipate* behavior, rather than merely *react* to it (Wittenbaum, Vaughan, & Stasser, Chapter 9, this volume). Workers can thus interact more efficiently, even when task assignments are unclear. Finally, unexpected problems can be solved more readily when workers know more about each other (Moreland & Levine, 1992b). Problems can be matched with the people who are most likely to solve them. Those persons can then be asked for help, or the problems can simply be handed over to them.

Are these benefits real? Few researchers have studied transactive memory systems, but some indirect evidence for their benefits to work groups can be found. One area of relevant research involves the effects of familiarity among members on work-group performance (see Argote, 1993; Foushee, Lauber, Baetge, & Acomb, 1986; Goodman & Shah, 1992; Larson, Foster-Fishman, & Keys, 1994; Watson, Kumar, & Michaelsen, 1993; Watson, Michaelsen, & Sharp, 1991). As workers become more familiar to one another (usually through shared experience), the perfor-mance of their group often improves. Several factors may contribute to that improve-ment (see Katzenbach & Smith, 1993), but the development of a transactive memory system is probably a key factor, because it can improve so many of the processes related to group performance (e.g., planning, coordination, problem solving). Another area of relevant research involves the effects on work-group performance of the recognition of expertise by group members (see Henry, 1995; Libby, Trotman, & Zimmer, 1987; Littlepage & Silbiger, 1992; Stasser, Stewart, & Wittenbaum, 1995; Yetton & Bottger, 1982). Groups often perform a task better when their members can identify the person who is best at that task. A transactive memory system would obviously make that identification easier.

Our Research Program

Although research in these and other areas is suggestive, more direct evidence for the benefits of transactive memory systems in work groups is needed, along with research on how different types of group training can affect the development of those systems. We have begun a program of research designed to explore these issues (see Moreland, Argote, & Krishnan, 1996). This research involves laboratory experiments in which small groups of subjects are trained to perform a complex task. Various types of training, involving either groups or individuals, are used, and their effects on group performance are compared. Our two general predictions are that groups will perform better when their members are trained together rather than apart, and that the benefits of such training will depend largely on the operation of transactive memory systems.

Experiment One

We have completed three experiments so far, and others are underway. The subjects for our first experiment (Liang, Moreland, & Argote, 1995) were 90 students enrolled in undergraduate business courses. They were randomly assigned to small work groups, each containing three persons of the same sex. Their task was chosen to simulate the type of work found in many manufacturing organizations. Each group was asked to assemble the AM portion of an AM/FM radio, using materials from a radio kit. That kit included a circuit board with prepunched holes and dozens of mechanical and electronic components. The latter components included transistors, resistors, and capacitors. Subjects were asked to insert each component into the appropriate place on the circuit board, and then to wire all of the components together.

Two types of training were provided. Half of the groups were randomly assigned to a group training condition, and the other half were assigned to an individual training condition. In the group training condition, members of the same group were trained together, whereas in the individual training condition, they were trained separately. The content of training was exactly the same in both conditions.

The experiment was carried out in two hour-long sessions, separated by 1 week. The first session focused on training, and the second session focused on testing. In the group training condition, the members of each work group participated in both sessions together. In the individual training condition, each subject participated in his or her own individual training session, and then worked together with other subjects in a group for the testing session.

At the start of the experiment, subjects were told that the purpose of the research was to examine how training affects work-group performance. All participants knew that they would return a week later to perform the task as a group. Subjects in the group training condition expected to remain in the same group, whereas subjects in the individual training condition did not know who the members of their group would be.

The training session began with the experimenter demonstrating how to assemble the radio. Subjects were allowed to ask questions during this demonstration, which lasted for about 15 minutes. They were then allowed up to 30 minutes to practice assembling a radio themselves. In the group training condition, subjects worked together on one radio. After subjects completed their practice radios, the experimenter identified any assembly errors and explained how to correct them.

The testing session began with a memory test. Each group was given 7 minutes to recall how to assemble the radio. Group members collaborated on this task, recording what they remembered on a single sheet of paper. Each group was then given up to 30 minutes to assemble a radio, without consulting its recall sheet or the experimenter. Subjects were told to work as quickly as possible, but also to make as few errors as possible. Cash prizes were offered for members of the best performing groups. Finally, each subject completed a brief questionnaire that provided background information and assessed some beliefs about the group and its task.

We analyzed three measures of group performance. These were (1) how well each group recalled the procedure for assembling a radio; (2) how quickly each group assembled its radio; and (3) how many assembly errors each group made. Groups in the two training conditions did not differ in how quickly they assembled the radios. There were significant differences between training conditions, however, in both procedural recall and assembly errors. As we expected, groups whose members were trained together recalled more about how to assemble a radio and made fewer assembly errors than groups whose members were trained apart.

Why did groups whose members were trained together perform so well? Videotapes of group members working together on their radios allowed us to explore several factors. We were especially interested in three factors associated with the operation of transactive memory systems. The first of these factors was *memory differentiation*, or the tendency for group members to specialize in remembering different aspects of the assembly process. For example, one person might remember where particular components should be inserted into the circuit board, while another one remembered how those components should be wired together. The second factor was *task coordination*, or the ability of group members to work together efficiently while assembling the radio. In groups with stronger transactive memory there should be less confusion, fewer misunderstandings, and greater cooperation. Finally, the third factor was *task credibility*, or how much group members trusted each other's radio knowledge. In groups with stronger transactive memory systems, there should be less need to claim expertise, more acceptance of suggestions by other members, and less criticism of their work.

Three other factors, which seemed relevant to group performance and might have varied across training conditions, were also coded from the videotapes. The first of these factors was *task motivation*, or how eager group members were to win the award that we offered by assembling their radio quickly and correctly. The second factor was *group cohesion*, or the level of interpersonal attraction among group members. The final factor was *social identity*, or the tendency for subjects to think about themselves as group members rather than individuals.

Two judges, one of whom was blind to the research hypotheses and training conditions, were given a list of specific behaviors exemplifying each of these six factors. These judges watched each videotape, keeping those behaviors in mind, and made an overall rating of the group on each factor. The only exception was social identity, which the judges evaluated by counting how often personal pronouns (e.g., "I") and collective pronouns (e.g., "We") were used by the members of each group as they assembled their radio. We computed the ratio of collective pronouns to all pronouns and used that as a measure of social identity (cf. Cialdini et al., 1976; Veroff, Sutherland, Chadiha, & Ortego, 1993). Intraclass correlations, computed for each of the six factors, showed that the judges' evaluations were made reliably. Scores on the three factors associated with the operation of transactive memory systems were strongly correlated, so they were made into a composite index by averaging together each group's scores on those factors. The other three factors were not assumed to be related, nor were they strongly correlated with each other, so they were examined separately in our analyses.

Did these behavioral factors vary as a function of training? As we expected, scores on all three of the transactive memory factors (memory differentiation, task coordination, task credibility), and on the transactive memory index, were significantly higher in the group than in the individual training condition. Only one of the other factors, social identity, differed significantly across training conditions. Groups whose members were trained together had higher social identity scores than groups whose members were trained apart.

We believed that the effects of group training on group performance were due to the operation of transactive memory systems. To explore that issue, several multiple regression analyses were performed (see Baron & Kenny, 1986). Their purpose was to separate the direct and indirect effects (mediated by transactive memory) of training methods on group performance. Assembly errors served as our measure of group performance, transactive memory was measured using the composite index, and training methods were represented by a dummy variable. We began by using training methods to predict assembly errors, and then transactive memory index scores, in two separate regression analyses. As the results just described would suggest, training methods had significant effects in both analyses. We then regressed assembly errors on training methods and transactive memory simultaneously. The effects of transactive memory were significant, but the effects of training methods became nonsignificant. Just as we expected, the effects of training on group performance were thus mediated by the operation of transactive memory systems. When differences among groups in the strength of those memory systems were taken into account, training methods no longer mattered. Analogous regression analyses involving the social identity factor were also performed. The results provided no evidence of mediation— when any differences among groups in social identity were taken into account, the effects of training methods on group performance remained significant.

Our first experiment provided direct evidence that a work group's performance can be improved by training its members together rather than apart. As we expected, groups whose members were trained together recalled more about how to assemble a radio and made fewer assembly errors than groups whose members were trained apart. We also expected and found that stronger transactive memory systems developed in groups whose members were trained together. Members of those groups were more likely to specialize in remembering different aspects of the assembly process, coordinated their activities better while working on the radios, and displayed greater trust in one another's radio expertise. These findings are the first evidence that transactive memory systems can develop in work groups, as Wegner (1987) suggested. Finally, our results showed that the beneficial effects of group training on group performance were mediated by the operation of these transactive memory systems.

Experiment Two

These encouraging results led us to perform a second experiment, which was designed with three goals in mind. First, it seemed important to replicate the results from our initial experiment. We thus recreated the same individual and group training conditions and then reexamined their effects on group performance.

The second goal was to evaluate some alternative explanations for our results. Newly formed groups often suffer from special problems, for example, that limit their performance. These problems include anxiety about acceptance, interpersonal conflicts, and uncertainty about group norms (see LaCoursiere, 1980; Tuckman, 1965). Training the members of a work group together provides more time for them to resolve these problems. This suggests that enhanced development may have contributed to the performance advantages of group training. Several findings from the first experiment challenged this alternative explanation: Neither group cohesion nor social identity (potential indices of group development) mediated the effects of group training on group performance, and although a few groups contained subjects who were already acquainted, those groups (which were arguably more developed) did not perform any better than groups whose members were unacquainted. Nevertheless, the role of group development in group training and performance seemed to deserve a closer examination. Another alternative explanation involves strategic learning. Working in groups often creates coordination problems (see Wittenbaum, Vaughan, & Stasser, Chapter 9, this volume). It may be possible to solve at least some of those problems through simple strategies that are relevant to almost any group. These generic strategies, which include building commitment to the group and its task and organizing group activities, require little information about any specific group. Training a work group's members together provides more opportunities for them to employ such strategies. This suggests that strategic learning may have contributed as well to the performance advantages of group training. None of the results from the first experiment challenged this explanation, so the role of strategic learning in group training and performance seemed to deserve a closer examination as well.

To evaluate these alternative explanations, we added two new training conditions to the second experiment. One of these was identical to the individual training condition, except that a brief team-building exercise was conducted after the training session. This exercise, adapted from McGrath (1993), was meant to foster group development. Group members were asked to produce a brief quiz that the university could use to evaluate students who wanted to serve as mentors for freshmen during fall orientation. The other new condition was identical to the group training condition, except that all of the groups were scrambled between their training and testing sessions. Subjects were thus reassigned to new groups in ways that separated the people who were trained together. They were not told that this reassignment would occur until the end of the training session.

The team-building condition was designed to encourage group development, but without providing the kinds of information that group members needed about one another to develop transactive memory systems. The reassignment condition was designed to disable whatever transactive memory systems developed by making them irrelevant, leaving strategic learning as the major benefit of group training. Insofar as group development and strategic learning contribute to the performance advantages of group training, the performance of groups in these two new conditions should have been good. But if the performance advantages of group training depend on the operation of transactive memory systems, as we believe, then the performance of those groups should have been poor. Groups lacked transactive memory systems in the team-building condition, whereas in the reassignment condition, those systems were no longer relevant.

The third goal for this experiment was to explore the impact of turnover on transactive memory systems. One benefit of such systems is that each member of a work group can rely on the others for information about various aspects of the task. But what if someone leaves the group, taking with him or her valuable knowledge that nobody else possesses? This problem could have occurred in the reassignment condition of our experiment, where groups experienced sudden and dramatic turnover after their training sessions. By analyzing how those groups responded to that challenge, we hoped to learn something about how turnover affects group training and performance.

The subjects for this experiment were 186 students enrolled in introductory psychology courses. Many of the procedures were identical to those used in our first experiment. Once again, the subjects were randomly assigned to small, same-sex work groups. The task and materials were the same, and each group participated in both training and testing sessions. The training sessions in this experiment were modified slightly for groups in the individual training conditions. Rather than participating in separate sessions, the members of these groups were trained in the same room at the same time, but were not allowed to talk with or even observe one another while they practiced assembling their radios. This helped to make the experiences of subjects in the individual and group training conditions somewhat more comparable. Another minor procedural modification involved the testing sessions. At the beginning of those sessions, before working on their recall sheets, every subject was asked to complete a brief questionnaire. The general format (including time limits) for both the training and testing sessions was otherwise unchanged from the first experiment.

Our initial analyses focused on evaluating the two new training conditions. On their questionnaires, the subjects made ratings indicating their answers to a variety of questions. Some of those questions involved feelings about group development (e.g., "Does this work group seem more like one group or three separate individuals?"), whereas others involved thoughts about transactive memory (e.g., "How much do you think the other members of this work group know about your skills at assembling the radio?"). Ratings of questions in each category were strongly correlated, so we averaged them together (first within subjects and then within groups) to create indices of group development and transactive memory for each group. Scores on the group development index were significantly higher in the group training and team-building conditions than in the individual training or the reassignment conditions. Scores on the transactive memory index were significantly higher in the group training condition than in the individual training, team-building, or reassignment conditions. The two new conditions thus seemed to affect groups in the ways that we hoped. The team-building condition encouraged group development, but without producing transactive memory systems, whereas the reassignment condition disabled such systems by making them irrelevant.

Our next set of analyses focused on group performance. As in the first experiment, no differences were found in how quickly groups from different training conditions assembled their radios. There were, however, significant differences in procedural recall and assembly errors. As we expected, group training led to better performance on both of these measures than did any of the other training methods, which did not differ from one another.

Videotapes of the groups were again rated by two judges, using the same procedures as in the first experiment. Once again, intraclass correlations indicated that these evaluations were made reliably. Because scores on the transactive memory factors were again strongly correlated, they were averaged together to create a composite index for each group. As we expected, scores on that index were significantly higher in the group training condition than in the other three conditions, which did not differ from one another. Among the remaining factors, only social identity differed significantly across training conditions. Scores on that factor were higher in the group training and team-building conditions than in the individual training or reassignment conditions.

Were the effects of training methods on group performance mediated by transactive memory? Once again, we explored that issue using multiple regression analyses. Assembly errors served as our measure of group performance, and transactive memory was measured using the composite index, just as before. But training methods were represented by three dummy variables, using a coding scheme (Cohen & Cohen, 1983) that contrasted the group training condition with the other three training conditions. Once again, we began by using training methods to predict assembly errors, and then transactive memory index scores, in two separate analyses. Training methods had significant effects in both analyses. We then regressed assembly errors on training methods and transactive memory simultaneously. The effects of transactive memory were significant, but the effects of training methods became nonsignificant. Analogous regression analyses involving the social identity factor were also performed, but produced no evidence of mediation by that factor. The overall pattern of results was thus quite similar to what we observed in the first experiment. Differences in group performance across the training conditions were again mediated by the operation of transactive memory systems, as we expected.

The first goal for this experiment, to replicate the results from our initial experiment, was achieved. Once again, groups whose members were trained (and then remained) together outperformed groups whose members were trained in other ways, and this advantage clearly depended on the operation of transactive memory systems. Another goal for this experiment was to evaluate the contributions of group development and generic learning to the performance advantages of group training. Those contributions appeared to be minimal. Groups in both the new training conditions (where transactive memory systems were either missing or disabled) performed much worse than those in the group training condition, and no better than those in the individual training condition. The weak performance of groups in the reassignment condition can be taken as evidence that generic training programs, which assume that experiential learning about work groups will transfer from one group to another, are unlikely to succeed. Finally, the experiment also gave us a glimpse of how turnover can affect the operation of transactive memory systems. Groups in the reassignment condition experienced sudden and dramatic turnover, disabling their transactive memory systems and thereby harming their performance. But the damage was less severe than it might have been. Although these groups performed worse than those in the group training condition, they performed about as well as groups in the individual and team-building conditions. Put another way, turnover prevented groups from reaching the heights of performance, but did not plunge them into its depths.

Experiment Three

Our first two experiments suggested that group training really can help workers to learn who knows what about a task. But no direct measures of such knowledge were collected in either experiment. Instead, we measured several behaviors (memory differentiation, task coordination, task credibility) associated with the operation of transactive memory systems, and then *inferred* that such systems were stronger in groups where these behaviors were more common. The primary goal for our third experiment was thus to measure more clearly just what the members of a work group know about one another. We expected to find, as our earlier results suggested, that group members would know more about one another if they were trained together rather than apart. We also expected such knowledge to be *shared* more often when group members were trained together. Shared knowledge, after all, is a key feature of transactive memory systems (Wegner, 1987, 1995). The experiment had a secondary goal as well, namely, to see how social loafing and free-riding (see Karau & Williams, 1993; Shepperd, 1993) can affect group training and performance. Training the members of a work group together may encourage some of them to take advantage of the others by learning only those aspects of the task that seem most interesting. Because such workers never expect to perform the whole task on their own, they may hope that other group members will compensate for their ignorance by performing whatever aspects of the task they failed to learn. A transactive memory system would be helpful in this regard. Although such a system would reveal a lazy worker's ignorance to others, causing some embarrassment as a result, it would also help that person to identify which group members to ask for any help that was needed.

The subjects for this experiment were 78 students enrolled in introductory psychology courses. Many of the procedures were identical to those used in our first two experiments. The subjects were again assigned randomly to small, same-sex work groups. The task and materials were the same, and every group participated in both training and testing sessions. During the first session, each group was given either individual or group training, and those training sessions were conducted in exactly the same ways described earlier (for the second experiment). But a week later, when the testing sessions were held, important procedural changes were made. We began these sessions (again) by asking every subject to complete a brief question-naire. Up to 10 minutes were allotted for this task. Then, as usual, subjects were asked to complete a recall sheet and to assemble a radio as quickly and accurately as possible. The standard time limits were imposed on both of these tasks. In this experiment, however, the subjects were asked to perform those tasks *individually*, rather than together. In fact, they were not allowed to talk with or observe one another while working. This was an unpleasant surprise for the subjects, who were told during the training sessions that they would be working on the radios in groups.

The questionnaire was designed to measure in various ways what the members of each group believed about one another's radio expertise. The first question simply asked subjects to describe, in their own words, each person's strengths and weaknesses at building radios. Responses to this question were later rated by two judges (one of whom was blind to group training conditions) for their overall level of detail. Intraclass correlations showed that these ratings were made reliably. On the next portion of the questionnaire, subjects were asked to rate how skillful every member of their group was at various aspects of building a radio. These ratings included how much each person could remember about the procedure for assembling radios, how quickly that person could assemble a radio, and how many errors such a radio would contain. The third portion of the questionnaire was similar, except that the subjects were asked to rank every member of their group (from best to worst) for those same skills. The questionnaire ended with two unusual questions about the distribution of expertise among group members. One question asked subjects to guess what percentage of the knowledge needed to build radios well was possessed by everyone in their group (shared knowledge), rather than by just some members (unshared knowledge). The other question asked subjects to rate how similar the errors would be in radios built by different members of the group.

Responses from the questionnaires were used to produce three special indices for each group. These measured (1) the *complexity* of group members' beliefs about one another's radio expertise; (2) the *accuracy* of those beliefs; and (3) the level of *agreement* within a group about the distribution of expertise. The complexity index was produced using the first and the last two questions on the questionnaire. Subjects' responses on each question were first averaged within groups, then standardized (because the questions used different response formats), and finally (because they were strongly correlated) averaged together to produce a complexity index for each group. As we expected, complexity was significantly greater in groups whose members were trained together rather than apart. Subjects in the former groups wrote more detailed analyses of one another's strengths and weaknesses at building radios, guessed that less of the information needed to build radios well was known by everyone in their group, and expected more dissimilar errors to be made if the members of their group built radios alone.

The accuracy index was produced using the various rating and ranking questions on the questionnaire. The rating questions involved such radio-building skills as procedural recall, speed of assembly, and assembly errors. The subjects' answers to those questions revealed their *beliefs* about how strong those skills were in each group member. Because each of the subjects later completed a recall sheet and built a radio alone, we had objective information about how strong those skills *really* were. This made it possible to measure the accuracy of subjects' beliefs about one another. For a given skill, we first correlated a subject's ratings of the group's three members with the actual performance of those members. This yielded three correlations for each subject, reflecting his or her accuracy at perceiving the skills of each group member. [These correlations may seem odd, because they were based on few data, but their purpose was clearly descriptive rather than inferential.] Next, the subject's correlations were transformed (using Fisher's r-to-Z procedure) and averaged together. The resulting figures were then averaged within groups to produce a single score for each group. Subjects' responses to the ranking questions on the questionnaire were processed in much the same way. The result of all this computation was a set of six accuracy scores for each group, derived from its members' ratings or rankings of three radio-building skills. Because those scores were strongly correlated, they were averaged together to produce an accuracy index for each group. As we expected, significantly greater accuracy was found in groups whose members were trained together rather than apart.

The agreement index was produced in a similar way. Once again, the rating and ranking questions were used, but this time each subject's responses were correlated with responses from the other group members, rather than with any actual performance information. This yielded three more correlations for each subject, reflecting his or her agreement with each of the other group members about the distribution of skills within their group. These scores were then processed in the same way as before, creating a set of six agreement scores for each group. Those scores were also strongly correlated, so we averaged them together to produce an agreement index for each group. Significantly greater agreement was found in groups whose members were trained together rather than apart, as we expected.

These results provide clear evidence that training the members of a work group together rather than apart can help to produce a transactive memory system. When group members were trained together, they developed more complex beliefs about the distribution of radio-building skills within their group. In particular, they were more likely to see one another as unique individuals, each one with special skills that other group members might not possess. Beliefs about the distribution of radio-building skills were also more accurate, and more likely to be shared, in groups whose members were trained together. The advantages of creating a work group whose members share complex and yet accurate beliefs about who is good at what are easy to imagine. As we argued earlier, such a group should perform its task very well.

As assumption underlying our earlier experiments was that indirect and direct measures of transactive memory systems would be strongly correlated; that is, behavioral evidence of memory differentiation, task coordination, and task credibility should be found more often in groups whose members have complex, accurate, and shared beliefs about one another's expertise. Was this assumption correct? All of the subjects in our third experiment worked alone during their testing sessions, so no videotapes of group performance could be made. However, we *did* make videotapes of the training sessions in that experiment. Videotapes of subjects in the group training condition were thus evaluated by two judges, one of whom was blind to the research hypotheses. These judges rated the same three behavioral factors (noted earlier) as in our earlier experiments, using the same basic procedures. Once again, intraclass correlations indicated that these evaluations were made reliably. Because scores on the three factors were strongly correlated, each group's scores were averaged to create a composite index. That index was then correlated with the three questionnaire indices of complexity, accuracy, and agreement for each group. All these correlations were positive and significant, suggesting that indirect, behavioral measures (like those used in our earlier experiments) of transactive memory systems can detect their operation in work groups.

Finally, this experiment also provided some information about how social loafing or free-riding could affect group training and performance. As noted earlier, the usual performance measures (procedural recall, speed of assembly, assembly errors) were collected from every subject during the testing sessions. Although performance on all three measures was a bit worse in groups whose members were trained together rather than apart, none of these performance differences was significant, whether individuals or groups were used as the units of analysis. It would clearly be premature to dismiss the problem of social loafing or free-riding in group training, but these results suggest that it is not severe. Apparently, group members learn their task about as thoroughly whether they are trained together or apart.

Looking Ahead

Self-managed work teams, along with several other kinds of groups, have become an important part of many organizations. This trend seems likely to continue. Organizations that use such groups can enjoy a variety of benefits, but their success is not guaranteed. Some groups perform poorly, perhaps due to inadequate training of their members. Two broad approaches can be identified for training people to work in groups. One approach offers a kind of generic training, in which people learn (in abstract and decontextualized ways) whatever knowledge, skills, and attitudes are regarded as necessary for effective group work. Such training assumes that every work group is about the same, and that learning to do a job and learning to work well with others are independent matters. Both of these assumptions are probably wrong, however, suggesting that a second approach to group training is needed. That approach involves training people in the groups where they will actually be working. When a new work group is formed, for example, its members should be trained together rather than apart. Training of this sort has been done in a variety of organizations, but evidence for its effectiveness is limited. We attempted to collect such evidence, focusing on the role of transactive memory systems in producing any performance advantages of group training.

Our research program (so far) consists of three laboratory experiments, in which artificial work groups were created and observed under controlled conditions. The subjects in these groups were asked to learn and perform the complex task of assembling a transistor radio. Two types of training, individual and group, were provided for that task. The results from our first and second experiments provided clear evidence that the latter training was better. When a group's members were trained together rather than apart, they remembered more about the procedure for assembling radios and actually assembled radios with fewer errors. In fact, training group members together rather than apart reduced assembly errors by about 60% in the first experiment, and by about 50% in the second experiment. These effects were mediated by the operation of transactive memory systems. In all three experiments, those systems were stronger in groups whose members were trained together. And in our first two experiments, the performance advantages of such training disappeared when any differences across training conditions in the operation of transactive memory systems were taken into account. Finally, our second experiment showed that transactive memory systems, rather than group development or strategic learning, produced the performance advantages of group training.

Additional research, especially on natural work groups, will be needed to confirm these findings. Although both the experimental and mundane realism (see Aronson & Carlsmith, 1968) of our research paradigm are relatively high, the laboratory is a much simpler place than most organizations, where many factors can combine to influence a group's success. Research on natural work groups might involve archival or field studies and could be either correlational or experimental in form. For example, information about transactive memory systems could be obtained through self-report or observational data on work groups, and those data could then be correlated with various measures of group performance. In some organizations, it might even be possible to do field experiments on how different types of group training can affect transactive memory systems and group performance. These and other options will be explored as our program of research progresses.

We also hope to explore different ways to produce transactive memory systems in work groups. As noted earlier, training the members of a group together, and then keeping them together, can be difficult. If the performance advantages of group training really depend on the operation of transactive memory systems, then there may be easier means to the same end. When a work group's members must be trained apart, other kinds of activities might still help them to learn who knows what about their task. For example, Elias, Johnson, and Fortman (1989) found that simply encouraging group members to disclose their thoughts and feelings about a task led to improvements in group cohesion and performance. And Henry (1995) found that group performance could be improved if group members discussed how a task should be performed, or who might perform that task best. Workers could also be given direct information about one another's knowledge, by a manager (see Cannon-Bowers, Salas, & Converse, 1993) or some other authority. We are now planning a new experiment, for example, in which group members who were trained together or apart will receive some information (obtained during the training sessions) from the experimenter about everyone's radio-building skills. Such information should help create transactive memory systems in the groups whose members were trained apart, and thus improve their performance, perhaps to the level of groups whose members were trained together. Finally, much of the information embodied in transactive memory systems can be made available to workers in other ways. For example, some corporations are now building large computer databases in which the skills of their employees are catalogued (Stewart, 1995; see also Wegner, 1995). By searching through those databases, more workers may be able to learn more about one another than could ever be learned through direct experience or by word of mouth.

Another issue worth exploring is whether the effects of transactive memory systems on group performance are stable or depend on certain moderating factors. Moderation seems likely to us. Several factors could be important in this regard, including the composition of a work group, the coordination requirements of its task, and the level of stress under which it operates. A homogeneous work group, where knowledge is more likely to be shared, may have less need for a transactive memory system. But such a system could be quite valuable to a heterogeneous group (Griggs & Louw, 1995; Watson et al., 1993). Diversity among group members makes it more difficult to identify unshared knowledge, so workers may rely instead on stereotypical (and often inaccurate) beliefs about one another. The coordination requirements of a group's task may be important as well. If the group has a simple, routine task that requires little coordination among its members, then a transactive memory system may not be very useful. In such a group, each person knows just what to do and can work almost independently of the others. But a transactive memory system could be quite valuable to a group with a complex, nonroutine task that requires lots of coordination among its members (Cannon-Bowers et al., 1995; see also Argote, 1982; Murnighan & Conlon, 1991). In such a group, where the task itself can change from one moment to the next, a transactive memory system would enable workers to respond to such changes more readily. Finally, the level of stress under which a group operates may also be important. Stress can arise from many sources, including dangerous working conditions, time pressure, and conflict with other groups. As stress levels rise, groups can become more "rigid," suffering from restricted information processing and constricted social control (Staw, Sandelands, & Dutton, 1981). These changes can harm group performance, but the damage might be less severe in groups with stronger transactive memory systems. In those groups, workers are more likely to seek information from the right people, and control is more likely to be found in capable hands.

Although we have emphasized the benefits of transactive memory systems, their risks should not be ignored. We have explored two such risks in our research. First, turnover is a disruptive factor in most work groups, but especially in groups that rely on a transactive memory system. The departure of old members and arrival of new ones can create serious problems for such groups (see Cannon-Bowers et al., 1995; Levine & Moreland, 1991). Oldtimers who remain behind must replace whatever knowledge their group has lost, either by acquiring it themselves or by recruiting knowledgeable newcomers. And newcomers must learn what knowledge each old-timer possesses, so that they can participate in the group's transactive memory system. The results of our second experiment provided some evidence about how turnover can threaten the operation of transactive memory systems and thereby harm group performance. In the reassignment condition of that experiment, groups experienced sudden and dramatic turnover, which did impair both their transactive memory systems and performance. But damage of both sorts was less severe than it might have been. Perhaps a transactive memory system is *helpful* but not *essential* for a work group's success. The results from our third experiment revealed few differences in the *individual* performance of group members who were trained together or apart. In many groups, there may thus be enough redundancy in workers' knowledge to make turnover harmful, but not deadly.

It is also worth noting that real work groups seldom experience the kind of turnover that occurred in our reassignment condition. For example, in an archival study (using data from the U.S. Bureau of Labor Statistics) of American manufacturing organizations from 1948 to 1981, Ackerlof, Rose, and Yellen (1988) found that the average monthly turnover rate was less than 2%, regardless of why workers left their jobs. Schmittlein and Morrison (1983) found that the turnover rate for newly hired employees in a large corporation was just over 3% per month. These figures are far lower than the 66.6% *weekly* turnover rate for groups in the reassignment condition of our experiment. It is probably easier for work groups to preserve their transactive memory systems, and thereby reduce performance losses, when turnover rates are lower or more predictable. If turnover were expected, for example, then a group could prepare for it, perhaps by embedding the knowledge of department members in the group's structure or routines (see Devadas & Argote, 1995). These and other reactions to turnover are intriguing and deserve further study.

Another risk that we have explored in our research is social loafing or free-riding. When group members are trained together rather than apart, some of them may not learn the task thoroughly. Their ignorance need not be dangerous so long as other members of the group can and will compensate for it. But if everyone acts in this way, then there is a danger that some (difficult or unpleasant) aspects of the task will be learned by no one at all. And even when every aspect of a task has been learned by at least one group member, some people may refuse to compensate for the ignorance of others, preferring to let the group fail rather than allow coworkers to take advantage of them (Kerr, 1983). The results from our third experiment suggested that these kinds of problems are not severe—subjects learned their tasks about as well whether they received individual or group training. But social loafing and free-riding, like turnover, are complex phenomena that are probably shaped by many factors, including characteristics of the group's task (e.g., difficulty, meaningfulness, divisibility), the group's members (e.g., work values, self-esteem, beliefs about the group and one another), and the group itself (e.g., size, roles/norms, cohesion). The potential role of social loafing or free-riding in group training and performance thus deserve further study as well.

Clearly, much research will be needed to develop optimal programs for training people to work in groups. We have already devoted considerable effort to this goal, and our research has produced some important findings. But many issues remain to be explored, we hope, in an expanded research program that involves a wider variety of methods and settings. Is all this effort worthwhile? We believe that it is. Both organizations and workers would benefit enormously from more flexible, practical, and effective group training programs. Yet so far, the development of such programs has been somewhat haphazard. Few organizations seem to use small-group theory or research as a guide for training program development, and the effects of group training programs are seldom evaluated in rigorous ways. Social scientists, in our opinion, have much to offer in this regard. And, of course, organizations have much to offer social scientists, whose understanding of small groups would surely be enriched by efforts to identify and resolve the many complex issues related to work-group training and performance.

References

Ackerlof, G. A., Rose, A. K., & Yellen, J. K. (1988). Job switching and job satisfaction in the U.S. labor market. In W. C. Brainard & G. L. Perry (Eds.), *Brookings papers on economic activity* (Vol. 2, pp. 495–582). Washington, DC: Brookings Institution.

Adler, P. S., & Cole, R. E. (1993, Spring). Designed for learning: A tale of two auto plants. *Sloan Management Review*, pp. 85–94.

Andrews, D. H., Waag, W. L., & Bell, H. H. (1992). Training technologies applied to team training: Military examples. In R. W. Swezey & E. Salas (Eds.), *Teams: Their training and performance* (pp. 283–327). Norwood, NJ: Ablex.

Argote, L. (1982). Input uncertainty and organizational coordination in hospital emergency service units. *Administrative Science Quarterly, 27*, 420–434.

Argote, L. (1993). Group and organizational learning curves: Individual, system, and environmental components. *British Journal of Social Psychology, 32*, 31–51.

Aronson, E., & Carlsmith, J. M. (1968). Experimentation in social psychology. In G. Lindzey & E. Aronson (Eds.), *The handbook of social psychology* (Vol. 2, pp. 1–79). Reading, MA: Addison-Wesley.

Barker, J. R. (1993). Tightening the iron cage: Concertive control in self-managing teams. *Administrative Science Quarterly, 38*, 406–437.

Baron, R. M., & Kenny, D. A. (1986). The moderator–mediator variable distinction in social psychological research: Conceptual, strategic, and statistical considerations. *Journal of Personality and Social Psychology, 51*, 1173–1182.

Brown, J. S., & Duguid, P. (1991). Organizational learning and communities of practice: Toward a unified view of working, learning, and innovation. *Organization Science, 2*, 40–57.

Buller, P. F. (1986). The team-building-task performance relation: Some conceptual and methodological refinements. *Group and Organization Studies, 11*, 147–168.

Cannon-Bowers, J. A., Salas, E., & Converse, S. (1993). Shared mental models in expert team decision making. In N. J. Castellan (Ed.), *Individual and group decision making* (pp. 221–246). Hillsdale, NJ: Erlbaum.

Cannon-Bowers, J. A., Tannenbaum, S. I., Salas, E., & Volpe, C. E. (1995). Defining competencies and establishing team training requirements. In R. Guzzo & E. Salas (Eds.), *Team effectiveness and decision making in organizations* (pp. 333–380). San Francisco: Jossey-Bass.

Carr, C. (1992). *Teampower: Lessons from America's top companies in putting teampower to work.* Englewood Cliffs, NJ: Prentice-Hall.

Chemers, M. M. (1987). Leadership processes: Intrapersonal, interpersonal, and societal influences. In C. Hendrick (Ed.), *Review of personality and social psychology: Volume 8. Group processes* (pp. 252–277). Newbury Park, CA: Sage.

Cialdini, R. B., Borden, R. J., Thorne, A., Walker, M. R., Freeman, S., & Sloan, L. R. (1976). Basking in reflected glory: Three (football) field studies. *Journal of Personality and Social Psychology, 34*, 366–375.

Cohen, J., & Cohen, P. (1983). *Applied multiple regression/correlation analyses for the behavioral sciences.* Hillsdale, NJ: Erlbaum.

Darrah, C. (1992). Workplace skills in context. *Human Organization, 51*, 264–273.

Darrah, C. (1994). Skill requirements at work: Rhetoric vs. reality. *Work and Occupations, 21*, 64–84.

Darrah, C. (1995). Workplace training, workplace learning: A case study. *Human Organization, 54*, 31–41.

DeMeuse, K. P., & Liebowitz, S. J. (1981). An empirical analysis of team-building research. *Group and Organization Studies, 6*, 357–378.

Devadas, R., & Argote, L. (1995, May). *Organizational learning curves: The effects of turnover and work group structure.* Invited paper presented at the annual meeting of the Midwestern Psychological Association, Chicago.

Druckman, D., & Bjork, R. A. (1991). *In the mind's eye: Enhancing human performance.* Washington, DC: National Academy of Sciences.

Dubnicki, C., & Limburg, W. J. (1991, September/October). How do healthcare teams measure up? *Healthcare Forum, 34*, pp. 10–11.

Dumaine, B. (1994, September 5). The trouble with teams. *Fortune, 130*, 86–92.

Dyer, J. L. (1985). *Annotated bibliography and state-of-the-art review of the field of team training as it relates to military teams.* Fort Benning, GA: Army Research Institute for the Behavioral and Social Sciences.

Elias, F. G., Johnson, M. E., & Fortman, J. B. (1989). Task-focused self-disclosure: Effects on group cohesiveness, commitment to task, and productivity. *Organizational Designs in Communication, 20*, 87–96.

Feldman, D. C. (1989). Socialization, resocialization, and training: Reframing the research agenda. In L. Goldstein (Ed.), *Training and development in organizations* (pp. 376–416). San Francisco: Jossey-Bass.

Foushee, H. C., Lauber, J. K., Baetge, M. M., & Acomb, D. B. (1986). *Crew factors in flight operations: The operational significance of exposure to short-haul transport operations.* Moffett Field, CA: NASA Ames Research Center (Technical Report No. 88342).

Funk, J. L. (1992). *The teamwork advantage: An inside look at Japanese product and technology development.* Cambridge, MA: Productivity Press.

Goodman, P. S., & Shah, S. (1992). Familiarity and work group outcomes. In S. Worchel, W. Wood, & J. A. Simpson (Eds.), *Group process and productivity* (pp. 276–298). Newbury Park, CA: Sage.

Grant, L. (1995, May 22). A school for success. *U.S. News and World Report*, pp. 53–55.

Griffith, J. (1989). The Army's new unit personnel replacement system and its relationship to unit cohesion and social support. *Military Psychology, 1*, 17–34.

Griggs, L. B., & Louw, L.-L. (1995, October). Diverse teams: Breakdown or breakthrough? *Training and Development*, pp. 22–29.

Guzzo, R. A., Jette, R. D., & Katzell, R. A. (1985). The effects of psychologically based intervention programs on worker productivity: A meta-analysis. *Personnel Psychology, 38*, 275–291.

Guzzo, R. A., Yost, P. R., Campbell, R. J., & Shea, G. P. (1993). Potency in groups: Articulating a construct. *British Journal of Social Psychology, 32*, 87–106.

Hackman, J. R. (1993). Teams, leaders, and organizations: New directions for crew-oriented flight training. In E. L. Weiner, B. G. Kanki, & R. L. Helmreich (Eds.), *Cockpit resource management* (pp. 47–69). New York: Academic Press.

Henkoff, R. (1993, March 22). Companies that train best. *Fortune*, pp. 62–64, 68, 73–75.

Henry, R. A. (1995). Improving group judgment accuracy: Information sharing and determining the best members. *Organizational Behavior and Human Decision Processes, 62*, 190–197.

Herman, S. M. (1994). *A force of ones: Reclaiming individual power in a time of teams, work groups, and other crowds.* San Francisco: Jossey-Bass.

Hoerr, J. (1989, July 10). The payoff from teamwork. *Newsweek*, pp. 56–62.

Howell, J. P., Dorfman, P. W., & Kerr, S. (1986). Moderator variables in leadership research. *Academy of Management Review, 11*, 88–102.

Huszczo, G. E. (1990, February). Training for team-building. *Training and Development Journal*, pp. 37–43.

Karau, S. J., & Williams, K. D. (1993). Social loafing: A meta-analytic review and theoretical integration. *Journal of Personality and Social Psychology, 65*, 681–706.

Katzenbach, J. R., & Smith, D. K. (1993). *The wisdom of teams: Creating the high-performance organization.* Boston: Harvard Business School Press.

Kelly, K. (1994, March 28). Motorola: Training for the millennium. *Business Week*, pp. 158–162.

Kerr, N. L. (1983). Motivation losses in small groups: A social dilemma analysis. *Journal of Personality and Social Psychology*, *45*, 819–828.

Kram, K. E. (1988). *Mentoring at work: Developmental relationships in organizational life*. Lanham, MD: University Press of America.

LaCoursiere, R. (1980). *The life cycle of groups: Group developmental stage theory*. New York: Human Sciences Press.

Larsen, J. R., Foster-Fishman, P. G., & Keys, C. B. (1994). Discussion of shared and unshared information in decision-making groups. *Journal of Personality and Social Psychology*, *67*, 446–461.

Lave, J., & Wenger, E. (1991). *Situated learning: Legitimate peripheral participation*. New York: Cambridge University Press.

Lawler, E. E., & Mohrman, S. A. (1987). Quality circles: After the honeymoon. *Organizational Dynamics*, *15*(4), 42–54.

Lawler, E. E., Mohrman, S. A., & Ledford, G. E. (1992). *Employee involvement and total quality management*. San Francisco: Jossey-Bass.

Levine, J. M., & Moreland, R. L. (1991). Culture and socialization in work groups. In L. B. Resnick, J. M. Levine, & S. D. Teasley (Eds.), *Perspectives on socially shared cognition* (pp. 257–279). Washington, DC: American Psychological Association.

Liang, D. W., Moreland, R. L., & Argote, L. (1995). Group versus individual training and group performance: The mediating role of transactive memory. *Personality and Social Psychology Bulletin*, *21*, 384–393.

Libby, R., Trotman, K. T., & Zimmer, I. (1987). Member variation, recognition of expertise, and group performance. *Journal of Applied Psychology*, *72*, 81–87.

Littlepage, G. E., & Silbiger, H. (1992). Recognition of expertise in decision-making groups: Effects of group size and participation patterns. *Small Group Research*, *23*, 344–355.

McGrath, J. E. (1993). The JEMCO Workshop: Description of a longitudinal study. *Small Group Research*, *24*, 285–306.

Montebello, A. R., & Buzzotta, V. R. (1993, March). Work teams that work. *Training and Development*, pp. 59–64.

Moreland, R. L. (1987). The formation of small groups. In C. Hendrick (Ed.), *Review of personality and social psychology: Volume 8. Group processes* (pp. 80–110). Newbury Park, CA: Sage.

Moreland, R. L., Argote, L., & Krishnan, R. (1996). Socially shared cognition at work: Transactive memory and group performance. In J. L. Nye & A. M. Brower (Eds.), *What's social about social cognition? Research on socially shared cognition in small groups* (pp. 57–84). Thousand Oaks, CA: Sage.

Moreland, R. L., & Levine, J. M. (1992a). The composition of small groups. In E. J. Lawler, B. Markovsky, C. Ridgeway, & H. A. Walker (Eds.), *Advances in group processes* (Vol. 9, pp. 237–280). Greenwich, CT: JAI Press.

Moreland, R. L., & Levine, J. M. (1992b). Problem identification by groups. In S. Worchel, W. Wood, & J. A. Simpson (Eds.), *Group process and productivity* (pp. 17–47). Newbury Park, CA: Sage.

Moreland, R. L., Levine, J. M., & Wingert, M. L. (1996). Creating the ideal group: Composition effects at work. In E. H. Witte & J. H. Davis (Eds.), *Understanding group behavior: Volume 2. Small group processes and interpersonal relations* (pp. 11–35). Mahwah, NJ: Erlbaum.

Mullen, B., & Copper, C. (1994). The relation between group cohesiveness and performance: An integration. *Psychological Bulletin*, *115*, 210–227.

Murnighan, J. K., & Conlon, D. E. (1991). The dynamics of intense work groups: A study of British string quartets. *Administrative Science Quarterly*, *36*, 165–186.

Nahavandi, A., & Aranda, E. (1994). Restructuring teams for the re-engineered organization. *Academy of Management Executive*, *8*, 58–68.

Nicholas, J. M. (1982). The comparative impact of organization development interventions on hard criteria measures. *Academy of Management Review*, *7*, 531–542.

Organ, D. W. (1988). *Organizational citizenship behavior: The good soldier syndrome*. Lexington, MA: Lexington Books.

Orsburn, J. D., Moran, L., Musselwhite, E., Zenger, J. H., & Perrin, C. (1990). *Self-directed work teams: The new American challenge*. Homewood, IL: Business One.

Payne, R., & Cooper, C. L. (Eds.). (1981). *Groups at work.* Chichester, UK: Wiley.

Prince, C., Chidester, T. R., Bowers, C., & Cannon-Bowers, J. (1992). Aircrew coordination: Achieving teamwork in the cockpit. In R. W. Swezey & E. Salas (Eds.), *Teams: Their training and performance* (pp. 329–353). Norwood, NJ: Ablex.

Rentsch, J. R. (1990). Climate and culture: Interaction and qualitative differences in organizational meanings. *Journal of Applied Psychology, 75,* 668–681.

Resnick, L. B. (1987). Learning in school and out. *Educational Researcher, 16,* 13–20.

Roethlisberger, F. J., & Dickson, W. J. (1939). *Management and the worker.* Cambridge, MA: Harvard University Press.

Schmittlein, D. C., & Morrison, D. G. (1983). Modeling and estimation using job duration data. *Organizational Behavior and Human Performance, 32,* 1–22.

Scribner, S., & Sachs, P. (1990, February). *A study of on-the-job training.* New York: National Center on Education and Employment (Technical Paper No. 13).

Shepperd, J. A. (1993). Productivity loss in performance groups: A motivation analysis. *Psychological Bulletin, 113,* 67–81.

Sinclair, A. (1992). The tyranny of a team ideology. *Organization Studies, 13,* 611–626.

Stasser, G., Stewart, D. D., & Wittenbaum, G. M. (1995). Expert roles and information exchange during discussion: The importance of knowing who knows what. *Journal of Experimental Social Psychology, 31,* 244–265.

Staw, B. M., Sandelands, L. E., & Dutton, J. E. (1981). Threat-rigidity effects in organizational behavior: A multi-level analysis. *Administrative Science Quarterly, 26,* 501–524.

Stevens, M. J., & Campion, M. A. (1994). The knowledge, skill, and ability requirements for teamwork: Implications for human resource management. *Journal of Management, 20,* 503–530.

Stewart, T. A. (1995, October 30). Mapping corporate brainpower. *Fortune,* pp. 209–212.

Tannenbaum, S. I., Beard, R. L., & Salas, E. (1992). Team-building and its influence on team effectiveness: An examination of conceptual and empirical developments. In K. Kelley (Ed.), *Issues, theory, and research in industrial and organizational psychology* (pp. 117–153). Amsterdam: Elsevier Press.

Trends that will influence workplace learning and performance in the next five years. (1994, May). *Training and Development,* pp. 29–32.

Tuckman, B. W. (1965). Developmental sequence in small groups. *Psychological Bulletin, 63,* 384–399.

U.S. Department of Labor. (1992, August). *How workers get their training: A 1991 update.* Washington, DC: Bureau of Labor Statistics (Bulletin #2407).

Veroff, J., Sutherland, L., Chadiha, L., & Ortega, R. M. (1993). Newlyweds tell their stories: A narrative method for assessing marital experiences. *Journal of Social and Personal Relationships, 10,* 437–457.

Vogt, J. F., & Hunt, B. D. (1988, May). What *really* goes wrong with participative work groups? *Training and Development Journal,* pp. 96–100.

Watson, W. E., Kumar, K., & Michaelsen, L. K. (1993). Cultural diversity's impact on interaction process and performance: Comparing homogeneous and diverse task groups. *Academy of Management Journal, 36,* 590–602.

Watson, W. E., Michaelsen, L. K., & Sharp, W. (1991). Member competence, group interaction, and group decision making: A longitudinal study. *Journal of Applied Psychology, 76,* 803–809.

Wegner, D. M. (1987). Transactive memory: A contemporary analysis of the group mind. In B. Mullen & G. R. Goethals (Eds.), *Theories of group behavior* (pp. 185–205). New York: Springer-Verlag.

Wegner, D. M. (1995). A computer network model of human transactive memory. *Social Cognition, 13,* 319–339.

Wegner, D. M., Erber, R., & Raymond, P. (1991). Transactive memory in close relationships. *Journal of Personality and Social Psychology, 61,* 923–929.

Wegner, D. M., Giuliano, T., & Hertel, P. T. (1985). Cognitive interdependence in close relationships. In W. J. Ickes (Ed.), *Compatible and incompatible relationships* (pp. 253–276). New York: Springer-Verlag.

Wellins, R. S., Byham, W. C., & Dixon, G. R. (1994). *Inside teams: How 20 world-class organizations are winning through teamwork.* San Francisco: Jossey-Bass.

Wellins, R. S., & George, J. (1991, April). The key to self-directed teams. *Training and Development Journal,* pp. 26–31.

Wetlaufer, S. (1994, November/December). The team that wasn't. *Harvard Business Review*, pp. 22–25 (see also pp. 26–38).

Woodman, R. W., & Sherwood, J. J. (1980). The role of team development in organizational effectiveness: A critical review. *Psychological Bulletin, 88,* 166–186.

Worchel, S. (1996). Emphasizing the social nature of groups in a developmental framework. In J. L. Nye & A. M. Brower (Eds.), *What's social about social cognition? Research on socially shared cognition in small groups* (pp. 261–282). Thousand Oaks, CA: Sage.

Yetton, P. W., & Bottger, P. C. (1982). Individual versus group problem solving: An empirical test of a best-member strategy. *Organizational Behavior and Human Performance, 29,* 307–321.

4

Natural Development of Community Leadership

John C. Glidewell, James G. Kelly, Margaret Bagby, and Anna Dickerson

Our goal in this chapter is to provide some insights about the development of community leadership as it evolves in natural settings. The chapter presents comparisons between the ideas of established community leaders and those of research investigators. The leaders we quote spoke from firsthand experience; the investigators we cite wrote from their knowledge of the current data relevant to community leadership. First, we set out the conceptual framework that guided this community-based inquiry.

Conceptual Framework[1]

In our view, leadership is a relationship of interdependence between a person and a collection of people. Conceived as a part of a social structure, leadership is a position bearing certain kinds of social power over a collection of positions subject to that power. Thought of as a social process, leadership is the performance of some of a broad set of functions by one or more persons, functions that provide arousal, enablement, coordination, and direction to a collectivity. Although some persons are

---

[1]This framework was drawn from what we know of current, data-based knowledge about leadership. In this summary, we temporarily forego citing the sources of the framework, but we will cite them in the relevant subdivisions of the chapter, where we will make more detailed expositions of accumulated findings and their interpretations.

John C. Glidewell • Peabody College of Vanderbilt University, Nashville, Tennessee 37212.   **James G. Kelly** • Department of Psychology, University of Illinois at Chicago, Chicago, Illinois 60607-7137. **Margaret Bagby and Anna Dickerson** • Developing Communities Project, University of Illinois at Chicago, Chicago, Illinois 60607-7137.

Theory and Research on Small Groups, edited by R. Scott Tindale et al. Plenum Press, New York, 1998.

found in leadership positions more often than others, leadership, we maintain, is not *primarily* a trait of an individual.

Community leadership begins when citizens grow concerned about some threats to the well-being of the community, or some promises for the enhancement of that well-being, or usually both. For these threats and promises, we will use the term *focal concern* because, at a particular time, citizens focus on one or a few such concerns. Salient community events often shift the focus of the citizens. As small, face-to-face groups focus on particular concerns, possible actions are identified and agreed upon within the small groups. The roots of community leadership grow from the engaging actions of persons in small groups. Those groups provide the contexts through which persons influence and are influenced by the community.

The groups seek to mobilize sufficient numbers of people and groups to make concerted community actions effective. The most active members lead their small groups to form working alliances or coalitions and develop community organizations, often with different focal concerns. As intergroup conflicts over focal concerns and priorities for action are managed or settled for a time, members' identification with a focal concern and with the coalitions addressing it is intensified. In the course of managing intergroup conflict, ruling coalitions emerge and guide concerted actions directed toward one or a few focal concerns. Then, organizational dynamics apply.

Some of the most visibly active (and talkative) members of the groups, coalitions, and organizations become widely known as effective. They thereby become candidates for the leadership of the dominant coalitions. Dominant coalitions search for persons who could lead their joint actions on one or more current focal concerns. They often find a person who acts frequently and visibly; seems to know what she or he is doing; decides promptly; shows the courage to take important risks; articulates clear, attainable, short-term community goals, as well as the beginning of a long-term vision of the community; commits time and energy to mitigating the current focal concern; has visible access to people with great economic or political power and openly stated personal goals that complement or reflect the community goals.

Such a person becomes temporarily authorized to lead the coalitions on some immediate joint actions of one or a few focal concerns and becomes dependent on other active citizens to follow and implement his or her leadership. The authorization is manifested by acts such as these:

1. Leaders of the several influential coalitions attend meetings called by the person.
2. Those leaders accept assignments given by the person.
3. Citizens refer to the leadership of the person in their communication networks.
4. The news media identify the person as a leader.
5. Powerful people in the community's surrounding environment recognize her or him as a community leader.

As focal concerns change, the cycle begins again. Small groups reform, coalitions change, new ruling coalitions emerge, the most engaging citizens change, and the socially authorized community leadership changes.

With this conceptual background in mind, we will set out the context in which the community leaders emerged and acted, as well as the research approach of the investigators.

The Context and Approach

The Developing Communities Project

The Developing Communities Project (DCP) was formed to enhance the well-being of the citizens of the Greater Roseland Area on the South Side of Chicago. Currently, the specific goals of DCP are to facilitate housing and economic development, increase health-care options, increase affordable child care, and improve the quality of local public schools. Originally, DCP was part of the Calumet Community Religious Conference (CCRC), a joint effort of various churches on the South Side of Chicago to prevent the job closings and cope with the layoffs that Chicago's South Side faced in the late 1970s and early 1980s (the first focal concern).

In 1986, the DCP was incorporated as an independent organization serving the Greater Roseland Area (GRA). DCP is comprised of 20 component organizations from the GRA. Nineteen of these organizations are Christian churches of various denominations.

There are four structural groups that comprise the DCP: (1) Staff, (2) Board, (3) Core Teams, and (4) Task Forces. People from the GRA serve on a voluntary basis as members of the Board, a Core Team, or a Task Force, or all three.

The Board sets policies and priorities for the DCP. It consists of 20 pairs of community leaders. One member of the pair is the pastor from each of the 20 churches; the second is a layperson from each of those churches. Both serve as representatives for each participating church. The pastor chooses the lay board member based on such factors as personal values, position within the church, willingness to work on community issues, and an ability to motivate people. Once chosen, the lay board member also becomes the chairperson of the Core Team of his or her church.

The Core Team works on the strengths and cohesiveness of the church itself. Its members serve as the major communication channel between the DCP board and the congregation. The Core Teams are created at the church level by the pastor encouraging the involvement of interested people. Currently, there are 10 to 12 church Core Teams of 5 to 20 people. Tasks Forces are formed to address particular kinds of focal concerns in the community. Through these groups, the Board keeps abreast of the focal concerns of the community and the progress on and barriers to coping with those focal concerns. There are now four Task Forces, each working to enhance one of these aspects of community well-being: Youth and Education, Economic and Housing Development, Public Safety, and Health Care. Membership is open, but there must be at least one member from each church, because the Task Forces are also lines of Board–Church communication. Usually, a board member chairs a Task Force.

The Documentation Project

In 1989, the DCP Staff envisioned a community organizing approach to the prevention of alcoholism and substance abuse in their area. DCP made a proposal for such a prevention project and sought financial aid from the Illinois Department of Alcoholism and Substance Abuse (DASA). One criterion for the award of funds by DASA was that the community organizing effort be evaluated. The Illinois Department asked James G. Kelly to consider designing and conducting this evaluation. Following an initial meeting with DCP and DASA staff, Kelly proposed two foci for the proposed work: (1) documentation of the development of citizens who were being trained by DCP to be leaders (in contrast to generating outcome data such as prevalence and incidence rates for the area), and (2) collaboration between the UIC research team and the members of DCP on the design and implementation of the documentation. The DASA and DCP staffs agreed. Margaret Bagby, a member of the DCP Board, was appointed to serve as liaison to the UIC staff. In addition, a panel of citizens from the community, including Anna Dickerson, was selected by DCP to advise the UIC staff on the topics and methods to be used in the documentation.

Kelly, the principal investigator for the evaluation, was committed to a collaborative process. John C. Glidewell was quite interested in such research and has been a consultant to the project from the early days. He studied transcripts of the panel meetings as they were produced. He first suggested that the transcripts were rich in the participants' ideas of development of community leadership and should be analyzed. Kelly asked him to take on the task.

Glidewell accepted; this chapter is the outcome. It reports only one of the many outcomes of researcher–community collaboration in this research. In the spirit of collaboration, the last sections of the chapter are comments by some panel members after each had read a draft of the chapter. There, you will find both agreement and disagreement with the positions taken in the chapter.

The chapter reports an interpretation of the meetings of the advisory panel charged with developing recommendations for the documentation. In addition, the panel's responses provide an enlightening documentation of the development of community leadership. This chapter is based on verbatim transcripts of 18 panel meetings held between January 17, 1991 and November 19, 1992 (see Kelly, 1992).[2]

The discussions of the topics addressed in this chapter were only by-products of the panel's main task. That main task was to advise the research team about what to document and how to interview community leaders. As they discussed possible

---

[2]The panel members were (in alphabetical order): Hameedoh Akbar, Linda Bond, Anna Dickerson, Alma C. Jones, Doris Jones, Eugene Rogers, Booker Vance, and Verna Worsham. The panel members were leaders in educational, religious, labor, and other community organizations in the Greater Roseland Area. The following staff members from the Developing Communities Project (DCP) participated in panel discussions: Margaret Bagby, Liaison Person for DCP; Cassandra Lowe, then Associate Director of DCP; and John Owens, then Executive Director of DCP. The following were guests of the panel: Kimrob Hoskins, Rob Jagers, Kevin Jones. The research staff members from the University of Illinois at Chicago were Seán Azelton, James G. Kelly, Cecile Lardon, Lynne Mock, and Sandra J. P. Scheinfeld.

interview questions and approaches to community leaders, the panel members also articulated their own ideas about how community leadership develops. The data analyzed for this chapter consisted of the verbatim record of the subset of their statements that described their views of typical community leadership development.

The Data Analysis

The data analyses to be reported were made by Glidewell. The analysis was simple. From the verbatim record (Scheinfeld, 1992) of the first 18 meetings of the Advisory Panel, he created a database of the comments about leadership development made during the advisory sessions. He classified the comments with respect to the emergence of focal concerns, coalition formation, and the social authorization of community leadership. He then compared the ideas of the panel to those he drew from research investigators, including his own work. As you read the quotations from the meetings of the Community Research Panel, please keep in mind that they are necessarily fragments of a larger whole, taken out of context. The sequence of the quotations is often not the sequence in the meetings. (Note the nonserial meeting numbers and page numbers that are cited in brackets after the quotations.) Each of the statements has meanings in addition to those that can be inferred from the quotation alone. Nevertheless, we maintain that the meaning of the quotation alone is on the point of the issue addressed in that part of the chapter. Furthermore, many other quotations could have been selected. We present these quotations as typical of many such comments on the topic.

We begin with the comments made that reflect how emerging focal concerns sparked the beginning of interpersonal communication, consensus building, and the development of cohesion of the groups discussing a focal concern and possible actions to cope with it.

Emerging Focal Concerns

The Beginning

The roots of leadership were reflected in comments such as the following. The comments began when the panel was in its second meeting and continued in the ninth. The panel was discussing the origins of community leadership and how those origins were stimulated by some event that was seen as a threat to the well-being of the community. Here are some typical comments about events that caused concerns and the reactions to them.

MARGARET: I think most leaders at one time were reacting.... That's how they got started. [*General agreement on this point.*] Nobody says, "Well, I'm going to be an activist, I'm going to have a cause." Right? As we say, [they start off] mad as hell about something. [*General agreement.*]

LINDA: You have to—
ANNA: To get started—
LINDA: That's right.
MARGARET: And then you go from there. [9,13]*

*   *   *   *   *

JOHN: [People say], "We've got these problems and we really have to do something
   about ... [them]. [2,10]
ANNA: Some people are legitimately concerned.... I want a better center [in my
   neighborhood]. If it can work here, it can work there.... There are people out there
   who want to make a difference.
JOHN: You're right; and you're unique. In order to build something that is huge, you
   need access to a mass of people. I met you—how did I meet you?
ANNA: You forgot? The LSC [Local School Council]. Cassandra and you were doing
   the training. I called you up.
JOHN: We gave a shot at organizing parents. Anna was unique. [2,8]
ANNA: You're going to find out that they [active citizens] are talking to a neighbor....
   It's important how well we utilize friends, relatives and each other. [9,7]

The Nature of Focal Concerns

Focal concerns entail both a threat to the well-being of the community and a
promise of enhancing that well-being. Such concerns appear at both the lowest levels
of social power and at the highest.

Sometimes the focal concern is a vague worry, such as "That street crossing is
too dangerous so near a school"; sometimes it is a specific affront, such as "That gang
takes my child's money every day." Some threats and promises are economic: threats
of layoff and promises of hiring, property deterioration and renovation, loss and gain
of funds for community projects. Some threats and promises are political: irresponsible public officials and nomination of conscientious new officials, unjust discrimination in fire and police protection, and fair community services to all. Some threats and
promises are communal: the threat of community degradation and promise of community development; the threat of fights among gangs for exclusive access to
territory, and the promise of open, easy, and friendly access to all neighborhoods.
Some threats and promises are moral and ethical: crime and safety, graft and earned
equity, mutual aggression and mutual support, deception and honesty, abuse and
constructive use of social power.

As people recognize a threat and imagine a promise, the concerns grow and take
on salience in the minds of the citizens. Those citizens seek out concerned others, and
they talk more often and more intensely about their concerns and possible actions to
cope with them. The ways that growing salience increases communication and the

---

*In the bracketed numbers following a quotation of the panel, the first is the number of the meeting,
the second, the page number in the typescript of that meeting.

ways increasing communication intensifies salience were clearly expressed by the panel of community leaders. As John said earlier, "We've got these problems and we really have to do something about ... [them]." Again, in the second and ninth meetings, the salience of focal concerns, of communication about them, and of developing group cohesion was emphasized.

ANNA: A leader is going to talk. They'll tell you everything that is going on. [2,5]
MARGARET: You might say, "I've got a big pothole out here in the middle of the street," and I say, "Anna, this pothole has been here for the longest, and I've called and called," and you say, "Well, I know the ward chairman," or whatever he is. Well, you say, "Call such and such a thing and ask for such and such." Well, you have supported me because you have given me an avenue of a quicker response to what I did. And that's support.... You have a problem and you share it with somebody else and you find out they're having the same problem. [9,7]
LINDA: Many of us [black students] had varying feelings. Not all were active. Within my own home I was motivated to change, but my friend next door wasn't. My best friend ... was white and we became close because we had some common feeling about changing things. Not all black people feel one way. Look at where they're coming from ... [3,9]

The term *focal concern* is rarely used by researchers in the interpretation of the data marshaled until now. Even so, the concept can be readily inferred from the many case studies of concerted community action. Some examples are Freeman (1968), Jennings (1964), Kresh (1969), Thompson (1963), and Trounstine and Christensen (1982). Thompson portrayed the deep concern and mobilization of citizens against a threat and for a promise: against the threat of militant segregationists to force a halt to registering African-American voters and for the promise of a new, powerful citizen franchise.

Proximity, Similarity, Harmony, and Argument

Action groups are not random collections of strangers. Communication does increase cohesion, but also, cohesion increases communication. The closer in time and space that citizens live together, work together, play together, and worship together, the more frequent is communication. Some of the earliest studies of proximity and familiarity found that familiarity, proximity, and prior harmony increase the likelihood of people talking over their concerns (e.g., Festinger, Schachter, & Back, 1950; Whyte, 1956). As with Margaret and Anna's example of the pothole, the communication is sparked by a need to explore whether their concerns are shared with others, whether the estimates of respected others of the threats and promises are similar to the estimates that the individual is making. As a number of scientists have shown (e.g., Hill, Rueben, & Peplau, 1976; Kandel, 1978; Rosenbaum, 1986), when people want to talk about their concerns with others, they often select similar others who are likely to agree with them.

But people also seek out different others (as in the case of Linda and her white friend), especially when they expect the different others to accept them but to disagree with some of their views. People seek different others also because they need to put their ideas to test. If they can hold their own against others who disagree, they have more confidence in their ideas, as found by Novak and Lerner (1968), and Walster and Walster (1963).

Networks and Linkages

Participants become active along already-established and pervasive networks of human interaction. The most active sectors of the networks contain citizens who have positive linkages with people who hold influential positions in community organizations. Examples include churches, schools, political parties, workplaces, unions, neighborhood organizations, and the like. Some linkages entail compatible commitments that stimulate further activity. Some entail conflicting commitments that inhibit further activity. This initiation and inhibition of action has been found by a number of students of community action. Especially relevant are Jenkins and Eckert (1986), Glidewell (1993), McCarthy and Zald (1973), Tilly, Tilly, and Tilly (1975), and others reporting in the books edited by Hargrove and Glidewell (1990) and by Zald and McCarthy (1986).

Impact, Confidence, and Reinforcement

Kinder and Sears (1985) reviewed research on political participation. They concluded that active citizens tend to be those who have had enough success in trying to induce change that they perceive change as possible. In contrast, these Greater Roseland community leaders sought to *build* confidence, even in the face of little experience and success. They were trying to find or to develop leaders with internally based self-confidence, self-efficacy, and self-esteem, even when their experiences in community action were just beginning. Nevertheless, as the quotations in the series that follows illustrate, these leaders believed that to persist, one must feel that one has some influence on one's environment, whether due to internal confidence or to the external reinforcement of past successes. The dialogue began in the early meetings and continued through all the meetings.

LINDA: We can relate to this. The way to get it across is important. Even if you don't know everything, you come across so people follow you to the ends of the earth.
Verna: That's Mrs. Carr—she always comes across strong and she gets the results. [3,6]
JOHN: Self-efficacy. Define that again.
LYNNE: Your perception of how much impact you can have on your environment. What areas do you feel you have an impact (e.g., the church setting versus the job; is it just a job?). Which settings are important for people?

JOHN: That sounds like a good one to deal with. Do you have the power to change your environment? How do you get the power to do that?

ANNA: Yes.... One's ability to change the surroundings.... You have to feel you're making some kind of impact. [2,6 and 7]

Advocacy

This functioning self-efficacy is very often employed in the service of justice. One seeks impact as a concerned agent acting for a relatively deprived group[3] that cannot or does not act for itself. The "client" group is one deprived of resources, roles, and rewards that it deserves as much as more privileged groups who hold and control such resources, roles, and rewards. Among others, Jenkins and Eckert (1986) also found this phenomenon, and they called the deprived group "conscience constituents."

Consensus and Crisis

As citizens discuss and argue about what concerns are most important or urgent, a consensus sometimes emerges. Such a consensus clarifies the issue and specifies the action needed. It is usually an informal, implicit consensus, but sometimes it is a formal, articulated consensus about which threats are most important, which promises are most practical. Consensus builds more quickly when the issue is simple and the information about it is clear. Whether the consensus is formal or informal appears (given the lack of focus in current data) to be relatively independent of the complexity of the issue or the objective clarity of the information available. Explicit formality seems to be *associated with* the need for building a clear identity for the coalition seeking concerted action on the issue. Formality seems to answer the question, "Just what is the issue on which these citizens are seeking action, and just who are these citizens?"

Furthermore, publicized crises intensify the pressure for consensus and concerted action. Urgent action demands a clear focus, often oversimplified. Those demands also set the top priority on the crisis issue. For example, Motloch (1970) found such a quickly formalized consensus in the Santa Barbara oil spill. Useem (1980) observed it in the Boston antibusing uprising. Walsh (1981) found it in the community actions following the Three Mile Island nuclear leak, and Thompson (1963) observed it in the New Orleans voter registration in the face of segregationist threats. Likewise, the panel members believed that such crises facilitate consensus on a focal concern, as reflected in such statements as these:

[3]The concept of relative deprivation was developed by Samuel Stouffer and his colleagues in their studies of the morale of American soldiers in World War II (Stouffer, Suchman, DeVinney, Star, & Williams, 1949).

JOHN: They try to organize ... and they get only three people. Right? And then a crisis comes up and you can get 30 people. [8,3]

EUGENE: It may be sad to say but normally it takes some type of crisis to get people charged up.... In our area, we're complaining about ... the park, but it may take some kid down there getting hurt to get people to say, "Why can't we have this down there?" You have people come out to the meeting then. [8,5]

ANNA: You use a crisis to create resources [such as agreement to act quickly and eagerness to do so]. [8,8]

Activity and Leadership

All the conditions and motivations that lead a person to an activist's role are also conditions and motivations that initiate the emergence of leadership. High concern, much activity, especially speaking quickly and often, linkage to many social networks, acquaintance with and access to persons in influential positions—all bring the community's attention to an individual. The citizens notice closely a person's interpersonal and problem-related competencies, ability to influence others, attractiveness, and trustworthiness. Both highly active and less active citizens respond to and reinforce the influence attempts of those persons whom they would like to follow. Thereby, potential leaders come into awareness of all concerned.

Many scholars have found that emergent leadership was associated with high activity, quick and frequent talking in social settings, linkage to social networks, and acquaintance with and access to influential people in social organizations. Hare (1962) reported the association with quantity of talking, as did Bales (1954), Riecken (1958), Regula and Julian (1973), and Ginter and Linskold (1975). The amount of talking was perceived as a first sign of high motivation and involvement. Others who found such results also found that the "quality" of the talk was also a basis for following, but that quality was, at first, second to quantity (e.g., Bass, McGehee, Hawkins, Young, & Gebel, 1953; Morris & Hackman, 1969; Schneier, 1978). The last found that 25% of the variance in group leadership behaviors was accounted for by participation rates, suggesting a self-reinforcing cycle. Tilly et al. (1975), Kitschelt (1986), and Nelkin and Pollack (1981) found social linkages to community organizations to be a leading indicator of emerging leadership.

Summary: Focal Concerns and Leader Identification

Some events threaten the well-being of the community. The same events create promises of the enhancement of that well-being. The threat and the promise stimulate already active and *relatively* informed citizens to form small groups to discuss, clarify, and focus the threat and the promise. Crises accelerate the clarification and the focus, and stimulate quick action. The readiness to act, the concern for relatively deprived others, and the linkage to other powerful people lead to recognition of the talents of these active people, and they become potential community leaders. Their selection into a leadership group, however, is partly determined by their roles in forming the working alliances needed for concerted community action. The dynamics of small groups shifts to the dynamics of organizations. Accordingly, we turn to the next phase of community leadership development.

Development of Coalitions: The Bowl of Soup

Concerted Action

Active citizens see the weakness of individual and small-group action, and the need for widely concerted action; thus, working coalitions begin to form. During the panel discussions, Linda's "bowl of soup" metaphor for collective action carried special meaning. It symbolized the interdependency of the leaders for the many and varied talents available and the need for coalitions.

LINDA: I think the greatest success is the collective success.... I often get visual pictures—like a bowl of soup. It depends on the ingredients that go into the soup— that gives it taste.... You see what everyone has to offer—that makes the best soup. It makes it taste good. [3,5]

BOOKER: One person identifies the issue and clarifies what the issue is. Then one [person] does research around that issue. Then one develops a strategy on the basis of the research in order to address the issues that have been identified.... Once you help people develop an organizational framework, then crises don't seem to attack us, but we're ready to take on crises. [8,4–5]

JOHN: We try to lift up the purpose of organizing as "It makes just plain good sense to be organized ... to make things better." I guess what I'm trying to say, is there some way we could get at to what extent do people feel that an organization should be created just because it—for example, the steel industry, just like other organizations, they organized the trade associations, etc., etc., when they realized there was more than one of them in the business. They see it as being a way of organizing resources for their common good. [8,4]

EUGENE: If I come [to a conference that I had no part in planning] and say, "Well, look this isn't really what I want. I'd like to put so and so on the table," and you [and a lot of others] say, "Well, no. That may come up at a later date, but NOW this is the issue here." Well, at least I know that. If I want to stay on board, I know my issue is not going to be discussed this particular time. It may come up. I'm asking for the same consideration and cooperation, maybe at a later date, to put mine on the table. [I have to trust that my time will come.] [10,20]

As Eugene pointed out, joining a working alliance means that one must make some concessions. One may postpone action on the concern one believes is less agreed upon and support a concern one thinks is more consensual. Later, one collects on this implicit IOU by gaining support of an influential coalition for the postponed concern.

One tries to aggregate just the minimum number of influential people and organizations. The *minimum* means that power is generated at the least cost in concessions on one's own focal concerns. If one seeks maximum power and tries to bring all organizations on board, one may well be forced to pay a very high price in concessions, very much as Gamson (1961) would have predicted from his laboratory experiments on the theory of games.

Sometimes, however, one must gain the loyalty of large numbers of people in order to aggregate the great power necessary to influence the larger community. One is prepared to pay larger costs in concessions in order to form the larger coalition. A leading local coalition of organizations may invite, accept, and make concessions to *any* additional organization in order to aggregate the necessary power to influence a metropolitan agency. As far back as 1956, the conditions requiring a maximum aggregation of low-power groups to move a large community were observed and specified by a number of social scientists, for example, Caplow (1956) and Riker (1962) on political coalitions, and Kanter (1983) in business organizations. Coalition formation may be both formal and informal. Participant Alma C. Jones said, "... most of it is informal," [14,22], even in linking formal coalitions.

Conflict and Negotiation

As the coalitions of organizations develop effectiveness and linkages, the components must cope with the conflicting interests among them. As Deutsch (1973) and Pruitt (1981) found, such conflicts sometimes take the form of competition, as when each component tries to demonstrate the intensity its own pressing needs for support or funding and its superior ability to use resources effectively. Sometimes the conflict takes more destructive forms. An organization may try to derogate others' claims of pressing needs and may question their ability to use resources effectively.

EUGENE: There's a saying that they have in ... politics: "There are no permanent friends or enemies." You may not be able to work together on a particular issue, but you don't pull out to the extent that you can't come back and rebuild that "whatever it takes" to work on something that you might both agree on further down the road. [10,12]

Most organizations [have] certain boundaries, so to speak.... [In] my organization we may be dealing with certain things and you may be dealing with certain other things.... As long as you don't cross over into my turf.... There may be a rarity when we come together to pool our strength for something that's good for both organizations, that we both can share in. Other than that, we tend to deal independently. [8,16]

ALMA: You're talking about power. Anytime there is a power struggle, that conflict sometimes cannot be resolved. When you're talking about who's trying to get the money, that can destroy any relationship, in any family. [People laugh with Alma, acknowledging the truth of this statement.] [10,12]

JOHN: The reason why people jealously guard their ideas and their turf [is] because there is limited money to run these things.... Foundations ... in their idealistic vision sit up there and say, "Well, you all should be working with these other organizations. Right! But, in reality, we are looking at survival. [8,17]

Even given the risk of destructive conflict, vigorously advocating a competing position on a focal concern intensifies the identity of the coalition and intensifies the loyalty of the members of the coalition. As that identity and loyalty become strong, an "ingroup" versus "outgroup" suspicion develops among community organizations. Each is reluctant to give up any rights to champion the action on "our" focal concern (Eugene: "We tend to deal independently [8,16]). The panel confirmed some of the ideas of Simmel (1955) and Coser (1956), and the research of Sherif and his colleagues (1961) and of Blake and Mouton (1961a, 1961b, 1962a, 1962b). The latter found, consistent with the ideas of the former, that intergroup conflict induces an increase in group solidarity, more intense personal identification of members with their own group, and an exaggerated possessiveness of each group's assets. In Alma's words, "[If you cooperate], it's like you're giving them our ideas, or you're taking our ideas over there" [8,17].

The intercoalition conflicts have real dangers of mutual suspicion and mutual derogation, but they also stimulate interest, curiosity, creativity, and innovation. In that respect, community coalitions are like the public organization coalitions studied by Heffron (1989) and business organizations by Bolman and Deal (1991).

Conflict among coalitions is often mitigated by their interdependence. They need each other. Coalition formation is thus a conflict management technique. (Note the issue of the *Journal of Social Issues* edited by Boardman and Horowitz, 1994, on conflict management.) Not only do fund-granting agencies look for communitywide cooperation, but also citizen constituents look for that same cooperation. Coalition formation is a well-established means of aggregating power for organizations whose bases of power are individually small but, as a coalition member, collectively great.

The conflicts are real and continuing, but the interdependence and the prevention of mutual destruction is equally real and continuing. The organizations need each other if they are to mobilize the aggregate power they must have. Notice this comment:

ANNA: What are some of the strategies for dealing with rivalries and conflicts among organizations with whom you are developing relationships?... Yes, a lot of times you're doing the same things ... [8,16–17] ... "We didn't quite make it on this issue, but that one will come." Then those heads of organizations need to filter down to their own people that, you know, "It's okay. We still have a chance, but we've got to work on this [right now]".... I believe Eugene said something to that effect, that you jump on the bandwagon and work with whatever's going on, because yours is in there somewhere. [10,21]

Emergence of Dominant Coalitions

Some organizations recruit other organizations, and are recruited by them, to work on the now agreed upon focal concerns, temporarily expanding the influence of the recruiting organizations. One outcome of active competition for funds and for citizens' time and loyalty is that coalitions discover just what funds and citizen support they can command. Thus, the relative power of the coalitions becomes more nearly clear. In the minds of citizens, a temporary power ranking of coalitions develops for the purpose of acting on the current focal concern. The study by Laumann and Pappi (1976) of Altneustadt (a pseudonym for a German town of 20,000) provided a detailed, quantitative account of coalitions in the town and the power relationships of the coalitions on various community issues. Jennings's (1964) study of Atlanta is another example of such specifications of the power relationships of community coalitions.

The panel members never used the words "Ruling coalition." They did discuss communitywide action and the vital need for DCP's "connections" with other organizations. "Connections" and "coalitions" are not synonyms, but we maintain the DCP was an influential member of the dominant coalitions of organizations in the community. Here are samples of what they had to say.

JOHN: It's already complicated enough working with all these institutions, the different people that come out of them, right?... We are already trying to keep people focused on one agenda, one direction [11,23]

BOOKER: Generally [community organizations] deal with a competitive nature, but, then, there has to be times when one has to end up with a broader vision to bring them all together.... I'm just saying ... you need more nuances of the personal relationship. [8,16]

EUGENE: In our area, we encourage that each block organize a block organization—

CECILE: But not to stop there— [8,19]

EUGENE: But then there is also a communitywide organization. But we encourage blocks to organize and to do things just for your particular needs and your particular block, [things] that we don't have any interest in. So you target your needs and you fight for those, but then there are some overall things in the community that we need to organize as a group to do.... You set up your boundaries and then you can deal with this and you can deal with that, and every now and then ... you cross paths and then you have [to work together] to straighten things out. [8,20]

JOHN: I'm really working hard to generate a strong level of ownership.... We need to think about DCP not that we are "working" with these institutions [referring to a list headed "Organizations Working with DCP"] as though they are clients.... They ARE the organization.... Actually this title should be: "DCP is MADE UP of these Organizations," because there was no DCP prior to an organization of several organizations. [8,20]

The Context of Community Leadership

When the most powerful coalitions look for a joint leader, the personalities of potential community leaders get much attention. Yet, nearly all students of leadership have questioned whether personality accounts for much of the variations in leadership behavior anywhere. A review through 1985 is in Hollander (1985). Current considerations of whether some persons tend to take leadership in many different situations is contained in Albright and Forziati (1995). Taking account of these research reviews, we would suggest that between 10% and 20% of the variance in leadership *behavior* can be reliably accounted for by personality. The other 80% to 90% is accounted for by the *fit* between the focal concern of the community and the perceived abilities of the leader and of those influential people affiliated with the leader. Leadership *behavior* and leadership *effectiveness* are clearly not the same things. Accounting for effectiveness is considerably more difficult.

In community leadership, the altruism of the leaders has been much more an issue than the general personality of the leaders. On the one hand, the panel members said that leaders were motivated by their own self-interests. On the other hand, they said leaders were motivated by the focal concerns of the community. Clearly, the interests of the leader sometimes conflicted with those of the community. Sometimes the leader and the community had the same interests. The challenging issue arose when the leader had different interests from the community. Could a way be found to serve personal interests while also serving the interests of the community? The issue is a knotty one, and in this panel it persisted, unresolved.

The Fear That Power Corrupts

The concepts of social power and empowerment surged through the discussions like blood through arteries. The community needed not just action, but concerted action. The leader needed much power to inspire citizens to set aside personal concerns and act in concert. Concerted action was almost always both a risky pursuit of a short-term goal, and, in time, a vision of greater community well-being. The Reverend Doctor Martin Luther King and Chicago Mayor Harold Washington were mentioned repeatedly. They were the kind of heroic, public-spirited, charismatic, competent, courageous leaders who inspired other community leaders to join them in the leadership of community action. They also gained access to powerful political leaders. In time, they, themselves, became powerful political leaders.

The intensity of the interest of citizens in the personalities and egoism of community leaders have been widely noted. From our reviews so far (along with the authors of the special issue of the *Personality and Social Psychology Bulletin*, edited by Miller & Prentice, 1994), we believe that it is fair to say that the styles and effectiveness of community leaders are constructed in the minds of the active followers. The active citizens follow a leader whose style develops in their minds as they discuss their views of the leader. Commitment to followership is embedded, we maintain, in the resolve that lives in the minds of people. Yet each citizen conceived both a somewhat different knight and a somewhat different knave. One might say that effective leadership is based in compatible fantasies of citizens about the exercise of social power by a particular person.

As suspicious as these working leaders were of the exercise of power, they recognized that leadership necessarily entailed the exercise of great power over the community. Even so, they deeply believed that the leadership that they sought and practiced satisfied both the individual leader's need for power and the community's need for realizing the promises and mitigating the threats of the focal concerns of the community. Here are typical comments:

DORIS: How they get power is important. My aim is not to take power away from people ...

ALMA: There is also the positive side of taking power, having power. Politics, for instance, taking power politically [and using it in the interests of the community] ... [1,5]

ALMA: I'm still wondering what I'm getting out of [being a community leader].

JOHN: There's got to be more to it ... like job opportunities or ego. Dr. Jones [Alma], part of your self-interest in remaining active in the community is that it allows you to do your job better.

ALMA: [*Smiles.*]

ANNA: There's no underlying motive that says I want [to do] a better job.

ROB: It's probably a combination of things: Community changes make you feel good both in a general way and in a selfish way. [4,7]

MARGARET: I think it's more self-interest. [78,1] I feel the self-interest has to go along with the community self-interest. [7,4]

An abiding principle that would guide such an integration of personal and community interests was simply not forthcoming. Each time and place, each leader, each group of loyal workers, each focal community concern was too special; if not unique, it was too particular for generalization. But you knew when it happened; you felt the sense of enablement and empowerment of the followers by the leaders' perceived ability to assign roles and tasks astutely, to make resources available, to inspire committed, persistent, self-sacrificing action—and to attract funds.

Long-Term Vision and the Next Step

The durable leaders dramatize their long-term vision of enhanced community well-being. For example, many can dramatize a vision of a self-sustaining community that can and will protect itself against, and finds ways to prevent, threats of such infectious diseases as AIDS, such exploitation as drug peddling, and such betrayal as corrupt acts of police. They also dramatized their short-term competence to gain concessions to postpone the relatively less important community interests (e.g., potholes or trash removal) in favor of more vital focal concerns. A leader's inspiring, long-term vision was engaging, but her or his short-term competence to take the next step on vital concerns was reassuring. Hear some comments:

MARGARET: "Your vision develops as you go along."

CECILE: Different people do it differently. Some start with vision and no skills to accomplish it, or vice versa. You can start out at different points ... [*People disagree and start arguing about this, everyone talking at once.*]

ANNA: When I ran [for office] ... I knew I had the power to change it, but I didn't know how—I knew something had to be changed.

MARGARET: But you may not know what!

ANNA: Right ... step by step. We were folding flyers the week before the election. See what I'm saying?... It changed along the way. They got a vision as they talked.

MARGARET: Leaders may not see the vision.

LYNNE: They feel it, the vision.

MARGARET: They feel something.

ANNA: That's it. It's inside you. Something's got to change and we make it happen.

Margaret: ... Leave the word *vision* out of it. 'Cause people can see things and not feel it and then they are BSing you. [6,10]

The tilt of opinion in this group was that the actions on the next step were the experiences from which the dream was created. Furthermore, woven by visions of power, threaded through this fabric of the inspiring leader was the practical truism that leadership requires loyal followership. Implicit but compelling was the sense that the leadership of a person was, in some way, authorized by the actions of followers. Now we consider that process of social authorization.

The Social Authorization of Community Leaders

Most people do not follow abstractions. They follow a person, such as a Martin Luther King and the group of community leaders who choose to work with him. They follow the persons who inspire respect, act frequently and visibly, seem to know what they are doing, decide promptly, show the courage to take important risks, articulate a clear, attainable, short-term community goal, commit time and energy to addressing the current focal concern, have access to people with great economic and political power, and openly state personal goals that stimulate action on the current focal concern.

The leading coalitions come to recognize such a person, often, as with the Reverend Dr. King, a leader of influential organizations in powerful coalitions. Sometimes, however, the leader is an unaffiliated individual, such as Gandhi, who most represents the community ideals and seems most likely to act truly for the community, even as he or she acts for his or her own interests. The recognition becomes an authorization to act for the community on one or more of the current focal concerns. The authorization is manifested by leaders of powerful coalitions attending the meetings called by the person, by accepting assignments given by the person, and by referring to the leadership of the person in informal conversations within one's communication network or to the press. At the grass roots of the community, a central leader is known by the local leaders who follow her or him.

Sometimes a public meeting is called to make a public, formal recognition and authorization of the leadership of the person. The person is given a title that publicly establishes her or his authority and limits the domain of that authority to the current focal concern. The panel members both referred to and resisted the idea of a single person in a unitary position of community leadership, such as we have set out here. The discerning comments at the end of this chapter express their belief that leadership ought to be and is *plural*. They focused on the less recognized but no less socially authorized local leaders who regularly and frequently designed programs that implemented the suggestions and directions of the person who became known as the central leader. They believed, and the data available substantiate that the less visible local leaders of affiliated groups often exercised the most telling and essential leadership functions of the community. Yet the society around the community had a hand in this, too. Consider this proposition.

Implied but not explicitly stated in the panel discussions was the facilitating and, by inference, authorizing effect of the broader social and cultural systems. The local community was linked to, and greatly enabled by, the nation. It was enabled by laws governing the rights of local citizens and groups to talk among themselves, to meet in public settings to voice their focal concerns and authorize their leaders, to petition the government to set wrongs aright, and by laws governing allocation of financial aid for their endeavors.

Furthermore, some very basic, taken-for-granted norms of the society facilitated and socialized some leadership behaviors. For example, in spite of attempts to outshout each other, and in spite of mutual interruptions, people remarkably often conform to specific turn-taking cues while talking to others—cues of which they were usually unaware—as Duncan and Fiske (1979) have so painstakingly shown. And talking with others is the soil in which community leadership grows.

Prior research findings showing this enablement by the larger social system have been positively evaluated by Kitschelt (1986) and Nelkin and Pollack (1981). All enduring community leaders, then, depend upon other community leaders and coalitions, and upon the broader social system, all of which define their rights and their duties to the community and the society.

Summary

We have focused on the variations over time. Leadership development also varies widely over communities. The focal concerns vary from Syracuse to La Jolla, from middletown to metropolis. Likewise, the competition for influence, agreement on importance, and the formation of coalitions varies as communities vary from Des Moines to Lakeland, Fort Peck to El Paso. A leader in one community may find another community less inclined to follow her or his lead. We maintain, however, that the forms and processes summarized below appear in one guise or another wherever community leadership develops and changes.

The deepest roots of community leadership begin their growth when citizens see threats and feel concerns about the well-being of their community—and also see promises of enhancement of that well-being. They talk to each other about the threats and promises of the pressing focal concerns. They hear ideas and feelings about how to contain the threats and realize the promises. In time, coalitions form to gain supporters of a consensus on the most urgent concerns, on the actions needed to handle the concerns. The organized coalitions attract individuals and groups seeking mutual support for each of their several views of the most urgent community concerns. As the coalitions become experienced, they compete with other coalitions for the time, energy, and loyalty of already active citizens, and for resources from their environment.

Their negotiations, both smooth and rough, help to manage their conflicts with other working alliances, coalitions, groups, and organizations. The negotiations also intensify the coalitions' identity and the loyalty of their members. The manifest outcome of engaging other groups in the conflict makes the differing levels of the coalitions' power more clear to the coalitions and to the community. The more influential coalitions develop a consensus on the most urgent concerns, the most important threats and promises.

From the most influential coalitions, dominant coalitions often emerge. The dominant coalitions search for a person who could lead their joint action on one or more of the current focal concerns. They find a person who performs enough of these functions to capture their loyalty: acts quickly, frequently, and quite visibly, inspires the loyalty of local leaders, seems to know what she or he is doing, decides promptly, shows the courage to take important risks, articulates a clear, attainable, short-term community goal as well as the beginning of a long-term vision, commits time and energy to mitigating the current focal concerns, has visible access to people with great economic and political power, and quite openly states personal goals that complement the community goals.

If the person also has a magnetic charisma, that fact both encourages and discourages. The coalitions are attracted, but they seek protection from both emotional excesses and passive dependence. Such a person becomes temporarily authorized by the most influential coalitions to lead the community in some immediate joint actions on some of the current focal concerns. The authorization is manifested by members of the leading coalitions attending the meetings called by the person, by accepting assignments given by the person, by referring to the leadership of the person in informal conversations within one's communication network, acceptance by the news media, and recognition by the powerful people in the community's environment. The authorization need not be exclusive. The multiple focal concerns imply multiple leaders, each authorized to act on some but not all focal concerns.

Not discussed by this group of community leaders was the fact that the mantle of leadership was bestowed by the community and can be withdrawn by the community. As the focal concerns of the community change, as the composition of the community changes, as the political values and norms of the community change, the needed leadership qualities change. The process begins again. People discuss the threats to and promises of community well-being, form coalitions, compete for the time and energy of the citizens, compete with each other for influence, eventually agree on the most important current concerns, the focal concerns, and recognize leading coalitions. The leading coalitions authorize new community leaders to lead their joint actions on the then-current focal concerns. The mantle of central leadership is then on the shoulders of a new community leader.

Implications for Public Policy and Future Research

The main public policy implication of this research is that indigenous community leadership has important effects on the adaptive development of communities as safe, healthful, and challenging places for their citizens to live and develop. Community development and self-control can be enhanced by actions by all societal institutions and governments, actions that (1) provide accessible, legitimate settings in which citizens can discuss and evaluate the importance of focal concerns; (2) provide for the improvement and especially the enforcement of laws establishing the legal rights and duties of any concerted community action; (3) provide for the funding of urgent community action projects; and (4) encourage the legitimation and approval of community action by many community institutions.

The data available from this and other projects can be partly explained by existing group and organization theory. Three aspects, however, point to promising and possible inquiries. Enlightenment is much needed about how focal concerns of community groups change as the times change. Put in the context of social cognition, much can be discovered about how people change their minds about what is important and urgent. The second promise is in intellectually decomposing and synthesizing the system linkages by which many small-group agreements get organized into much larger coalitions of such groups, so that we understand better just what happens in the such group–community developments. The third issue demanding sound research is the explication of the mutual influences between the myth and the reality of consensual focal concerns and social authorization of community leaders.

The previous comments focused on the review of panel meetings and the observations of the panel meetings by Glidewell. These observations were connected to the research literature in social and organizational psychology. There are two concluding comments, one by the liaison person between the DCP Board and the University research group, the second by a member of the community research panel.

Comments by Some of the Community Leaders Involved: A View by a Liaison Person (Margaret Bagby)

I'm a board member of DCP. I got involved with the organization because I was sitting at home looking out my door and window, seeing things that were wrong and watching my community deteriorate. I didn't know what to do to correct what I saw was wrong, but I felt like I could effect a change. I certainly felt frustration and anger.

Then I joined DCP. I learned how to organize people, keep them focused on the issue, conduct research, and how to change some wrongs in our community.

I'm very protective of my organization. When I was asked to be a liaison person between DCP and the UIC staff, I didn't know what to expect. Traditionally, we African Americans have been studied, probed, and either told what to do or given what the system thinks we need. I believe we need to be able to work and get what we want, and not what others think we should have.

That's what was so great about the process in this evaluation project. Jim Kelly and the UIC staff were *just great* with the research we discussed at panel meetings and the articles they wrote and challenges they gave us. We were able to speak from the experience of living exactly what they talked about.

Our people are skeptical of anyone who comes to our community asking questions, asking why things are like they are, or why we do what we do. Everyone on the research advisory panel was a leader: a principal, union organizer, local school council person, school teacher, and community workers. Automatically they say, "What's going on? What are they [UIC] going to use the material for? What do we get out of this collaboration. Why are students interested in us?"

Most of their concerns were answered to the best of my ability. To "What's going on," I replied, "It was all about an evaluation that DASA had asked for because of the grant they had given the DCP."

The UIC research team would gather material such as quotes from the leaders being interviewed about issues those leaders had worked on, issues such as asbestos removed from apartments, school safety zones, refurbishing Gately stadium, and so on. That material would be analyzed and categorized to identify skills that leaders possess.

To "What would we achieve from the collaboration?" I replied that we hoped to get a document that could be used as a training tool and maybe a means of assessing the skills of leaders. That was, in fact, done with the help of Professor Kelly's research and that of the students working with him. I must say they did a magnificent job.

The students' interest in us was to complete their research and, in the end, gain their degree. They worked hard and long hours. They seemed to be totally committed, like the DCP leaders were.

I eliminated most of the doubts of the community leaders. After all, as I told them, that was my job. It was an evaluation called for by the Illinois DASA. We wanted a new, innovative way, since there are few available ways to document the development of community leaders.

We hope that the material gathered will one day become a tool for other organizations to use to train their leaders and a tool for Executive Directors to evaluate their leaders. The students are getting firsthand knowledge and hands-on experience from reality. In my book, that puts them head and shoulders above students that only do surveys with undergraduates. This makes their papers authentic and real. I feel that all the UIC staff members were genuinely interested.

Jim Kelly is the kind of person who believes in getting things done *now*. He plans his work, schedules meetings, and gives notices far in advance. That doesn't work with most of us African Americans. You have to notify us maybe a week, two at the most, in advance and then remind everyone the day before. That was my job. Jim soon realized this. I think that if anyone is going into a community, it is absolutely essential that you have a liaison person. She or he knows the habits of the community, can defuse negative reactions, can explain what really happened in a meeting, or just let the citizens bounce their feelings off someone they trust.

Everyone who participated in this collaboration discovered skills they didn't know they had, skills such as being able to research who you should talk to to get a pothole fixed. They learned how to get a meeting with the Mayor or Governor. They learned what agency to contact to have a stop sign or a safety sign erected. They also learned how to distinguish between an issue and a problem, how to make flyers that catch attention, how to get people out to meetings, how to raise money for a project. We didn't recognize a lot of the skills we had until we joined in this project.

In this chapter, I think Glidewell and Kelly captured exactly what was projected in the material from the 18 meetings. Glidewell never attended any of them, but it was as if he were there. I disagree with him about one thing. My sense is that Glidewell feels that we African Americans have one designated leader at any one given time or one issue (focal concern). I disagree. I feel that a leader emerges on certain issues. I think he confuses our *paid staff* with leaders. Paid staff are hired because of their skills in organizing and strategizing. I am not saying they are not leaders, but the real leaders select the issue. Paid staff figure the plan, and the leaders execute it. Otherwise, he is right on target.

This was such a great experience for me because this process was real, taken from experiences we all had lived. This interview was created from our soul, not from what someone says it should be according to statistics. It was real. We hope the interview will become an effective tool to be used in training seminars and in practice in organizations just starting out.

Comment on Community Leadership: Theory and Practice (Anna M. Dickerson)

Most of the ills of our community, and our society as a whole, are fostered by a sense of hopelessness and helplessness. Therefore, a good leader is challenged to try to make others feel that change is possible. To make change, you must feel and believe that reformation is possible.

The leader must have an inner vision. It seems that one does not always know what must be done but actually senses a feeling of how to do it. To be protective is preferable. However, it has not proven to be realistic. In reality, an issue usually gets more attention when it has escalated to the level of a crisis. Glidewell and Kelly seem to allude to this when they speak of the panel's discussion of activity, leadership, and crisis.

When they speak of the development of coalitions, I must agree with the conclusion. A twig can be easily broken when it stands alone. However, if that same twig is placed with a bunch of twigs, it cannot be broken so easily. There is indeed strength in numbers. This is part of the concept of this type of community action. The art of cooperatively working together encourages people to make concessions.

There has to be a certain degree of trust in the coalition entities if one is to set personal agendas aside and determine that the focal concern is the primary concern. The discussion of self and community interests was unresolved, because in many instances, self-interest and the focal concern of the community are one and the same. Glidewell and Kelly accurately capture the essence of the panel's thoughts here as well, when they speak of this need for organizational trust.

Some level of security has to be attained by an organization before the members can share certain ideas with people outside. The organization must be assured that its uniqueness will not be lost in the joint services and programs carried out by coalitions of organizations. Such assurance decreases the conflict generated by vying for the limited funds that are available.

Generally, choosing to be a follower requires submission. In this process, however, the follower experiences an empowerment from the strength of the joint effort. The individual does not feel slighted in any way, but readily celebrates the victories realized. An immediate, sure victory increases the leaders' self-confidence, motivates the followers, and reaffirms belief in the leader's competency and its use in the interests of all.

Slightly differing from the authors' assumption, I feel that the one authorized to assume leadership is not always the individual who is the most dramatically articulate. It seems to me that activity, commitment, courage in risk taking, tenacity, and willingness to vocalize the concerns outweigh how well one is able to articulate. A clear, attainable short-term community goal was usually identified, and it kept the followers motivated.

It is well understood that the community members choose who will lead them, and at one point this was discussed in the panel meetings. Individuals are drafted to lead, as I was when my peers selected me to run for the Local School Council and Union representative. My level of involvement in the school and in the union prompted others to propel me to the forefront.

As a member of the Research Panel, the experience was new and different. I recall that the decision to make the research planning a collaborative effort was mutually agreed upon by the DCP and the UIC. After panel meetings, each panel member was to review the documented materials, and each returned to the next panel meeting with input to that meeting. This was one of the less alluring portions of the process. There were occasions when individuals would fail to review the materials provided, come to the meeting, and rehash areas that had previously been solidified. This caused great frustration for me. I am quite sure that the UIC staff and other panel members were also stymied by these delays. Sometimes, however, very important issues were raised on time and proved to be beneficial to the end product.

Then, there was the testing of the interview. It was subjected to the initial trial interview prior to its revision. The procedure was long, time-consuming, and a feat of drudgery. I wanted to quit several times during the interview. As a member of the panel, I was committed to see the project through. My fatigue, nevertheless, was indicative of what other interviewee-leaders might encounter when they were interviewed. This contributed to the redrafting and condensing of the interview.

Overall, the process was rewarding. I also gained a strong sense of self-satisfaction, because I know I had a hand in something that may well be utilized in other settings. As a community worker and an individual, I have had a part in a collaborative work with a community organization, which operates on a grassroots level, and with the University, which is a structured, traditional institution. What a contrast; what a combination.

Acknowledgments

In addition to our appreciation of the time and effort of the persons writing the comments that are a part of this chapter, we also express our appreciation for the astute comments and very helpful suggestions of the following people: L. Seán Azelton, Lynne Mock, Darius Tandon, and André Martin, an anonymous reviewer, and our perceptive editor, Yolanda Suarez-Balcazar.

References

Albright, L., & Forziati, C. (1995). Cross-situation consistency and perceptual accuracy in leadership. *Journal of Personality and Social Psychology, 21,* 1269–1276.

Bales, R. F. (1953). The equilibrium problem in small groups. In T. Parsons, R. F. Bales, & E. A. Shills (Eds.), *Working papers in the theory of action* (pp. 111–161). New York: Free Press.

Bass, B. M., McGehee, C. R., Hawkins, W. C., Young, P. C., & Gebel, A. S. (1953). Personality variables related to leaderless group discussion behavior. *Journal of Abnormal and Social Psychology, 48,* 120–128.

Blake, R. R., & Mouton, J. S. (1961a). Comprehension of own and outgroup positions under intergroup competition. *Journal of Conflict Resolution, 5,* 304–310.

Blake, R. R., & Mouton, J. S. (1961b). Loyalty of representatives to ingroup positions during intergroup competition. *Sociometry, 24,* 177–183.

Blake, R. R., & Mouton, J. S. (1962a). Overvaluation of own group's product in intergroup competition. *Journal of Abnormal and Social Psychology, 64,* 237–238.

Blake, R. R., & Mouton, J. S. (1962b). Comprehension of points of commonality in competing solutions. *Sociometry, 25,* 56–63.

Boardman, S. K., & Horowitz, S. V. (1994). Constructive conflict management: An answer to critical social problems? [Special Issue]. *Journal of Social Issues, 50,* 1–211.

Bolman, L. G., & Deal, T. E. (1991). *Reframing organizations: Artistry, choice and leadership.* San Francisco: Jossey-Bass.

Caplow, T. A. (1956). A theory of coalitions in a triad. *American Sociological Review, 21,* 489–493.

Coser, L. (1956). *The functions of social conflict.* New York: Free Press.

Deutsch, M. (1973). *The resolution of conflict.* New Haven, CT: Yale University Press.

Duncan, S., Jr., & Fiske, D. W. (1979). Dynamic patterning in conversations. *American Scientist, 67,* 90–98.

Festinger, L., Schachter, S., & Back, K. (1950). *Social pressures in informal groups: A study of human factors in housing.* New York: Harper.

Freeman, L. C. (1968). *Patterns of local community leadership.* Indianapolis: Bobbs-Merrill.

Gamson, W. A. (1961). A theory of coalition formation. *American Sociological Review, 26,* 363–382.

Ginter, G., & Lindskold, S. (1975). Rate of participation and expertise as factors influencing leader choice. *Journal of Personality and Social Psychology, 32*, 1085–1089.

Glidewell, J. C. (1970). *Choice points.* Cambridge, MA: MIT Press.

Glidewell, J. C. (1987). Induced change in psychological and social systems. *American Journal of Community Psychology, 15*, 741–772.

Glidewell, J. C. (1993). How CEOs change their minds. In P. Hallinger, K. Leithwood, & J. Murphy (Eds.), *Cognitive perspectives on school leadership* (pp. 34–53). New York: Teachers College Press.

Glidewell, J. C., & Hargrove, E. C. (1990). Coping with impossible jobs. In E. C. Hargrove & J. C. Glidewell (Eds.), *Impossible jobs in public management.* Lawrence: University Press of Kansas.

Hare, A. P. (1962). *Handbook of small group research.* New York: Free Press.

Hargrove, E. C., & Glidewell, J. C. (Eds.). (1990). *Impossible jobs in public management.* Lawrence: University Press of Kansas.

Heffron, F. (1989). *Organization theory and public organizations: The political connection.* Englewood Cliffs, NJ: Prentice-Hall.

Hill, C. T., Rueben, Z., & Peplau, L. A. (1976). Breakups before marriage: The end of 103 affairs. *Journal of Social Issues, 32*(1), 147–168.

Hollander, E. P. (1985). Leadership and power. In G. Lindsey & E. Aronson (Eds.), *The handbook of social psychology* (3rd ed., Vol. 2, pp. 485–437). New York: Random House.

Jenkins, J. C., & Eckert, C. M. (1986). Channeling black insurgency: Elite patronage and professional social movement organizations in the development of the black movement. *American Sociological Review, 51*, 812–829.

Jennings, M. K. (1964). *Community influentials: The elites of Atlanta.* Glencoe, IL: Free Press of Glencoe.

Kandel, D. (1978). Similarity in real-life adolescent friendship pairs. *Journal of Personality and Social Psychology, 36*, 306–312.

Kanter, R. M. (1983). *The change masters: Innovations for productivity in the American corporation.* New York: Simon & Schuster.

Kelly, J. G. (1992, August 16). *Ecological inquiry and a collaborative enterprise: A commentary on the Chicago experience.* A paper presented at the 100th annual meeting of the American Psychological Association, Washington, DC.

Kinder, D. R., & Sears, D. O. (1985). Public opinion and political action. In G. Lindzey & E. Aronson (Eds.), *Handbook of social psychology* (3rd ed., pp. 659–741). Reading, MA: Addison-Wesley.

Kitschelt, H. P. (1986). Political opportunity structures and political protest. *British Journal of Political Science, 16*, 57–85.

Kresh, P. (1969). *The power of the unknown citizen.* Philadelphia: Lippincott.

Laumann, E. O., & Pappi, F. U. (1976). *Networks of collective action: A perspective on community influence systems.* New York: Academic Press.

McCarthy, J. D., & Zald, M. N. (1973). *The trend of social movements in America: Professionalization and resource mobilization.* Morristown, NJ: General Learning Press.

Miller, D. T., & Prentice D. A. (1994). The self and the collective. *Personality and Social Psychology Bulletin* (Special Issue), *20*, 451–610.

Morris, C. G., & Hackman, J. R. (1969). Behavioral correlates of perceived leadership. *Journal of Personality and Social Psychology, 13*, 350–361.

Motloch, H. (1970). Oil in Santa Barbara and power in America. *Sociological Inquiry, 40*, 131–141.

Nelkin, D., & Pollack, M. (1981). *The atom besieged.* Cambridge, MA: MIT Press.

Novak, D. W., & Lerner, M. J. (1968). Rejection as a consequence of perceived similarity. *Journal of Personality and Social Psychology, 9*, 147–152.

Pruitt, D. G. (1981). *Negotiation behavior.* New York: Academic Press.

Regula, C. R., & Julian, J. W. (1973). The impact of quality and frequency of task contributions on perceived ability. *Journal of Social Psychology, 89*, 115–122.

Riecken, H. W. (1958). The effect of talkativeness on ability to influence groups solutions to problems. *Sociometry, 21*, 309–321.

Riker, W. H. (1962). *The theory of political coalitions.* New Haven, CT: Yale University Press.

Rosenbaum, M. E. (1986). The repulsion hypothesis: On the nondevelopment of relationships. *Journal of Personality and Social Psychology, 51*, 1156–1166.

Scheinfeld, S. J. P. (1992, August 16). *Documenting the community research panel.* A paper presented at the 100th annual meeting of the American Psychological Association. Washington, DC.

Schneier, C. E. (1978). The contingency model of leadership: An extension to emergent leadership and leader's sex. *Organization Behavior and Human Performance, 21*, 220–239.

Schneier, C. E., & Barton, K. M. (1980). Sex effects in emergent leadership. *Journal of Applied Psychology, 65*, 341–345.

Sherif, M., Harvey, O. J., White, B. J., Hood, W. R., & Sherif, C. W. (1961). *Intergroup conflict and cooperation: The Robber's cave experiment.* Norman: University of Oklahoma Press.

Simmel, G. (1955). *Conflict.* New York: Free Press.

Stouffer, S. A., Suchman, E. A., DeVinney, L. C., Star, S. A., & Williams, R. M., Jr. (1949). *The American soldier: Adjustment during army life.* New York: Wiley.

Thompson, D. C. (1963). *The Negro leadership class.* Englewood Cliffs, NJ: Prentice-Hall.

Tilly, C., Tilly, L., & Tilly, R. (1975). *The rebellious century, 1830–1930.* Cambridge, MA: Harvard University Press.

Trounstine, P. J., & Christensen, T. (1982). *Movers and shakers: The study of community power.* New York: St. Martins Press.

Useem, B. (1980). Solidarity model, breakdown model, and the Boston antibusing movement. *American Sociological Review, 45*, 357–369.

Walsh, E. J. (1981). Resource mobilization and citizen protest in communities around Three Mile Island. *Social Problems, 29*, 1–21.

Walster, E., & Walster, G. W. (1963). Effects of expecting to be liked on choice of associates. *Journal of Abnormal and Social Psychology, 67*, 402–404.

Whyte, W. H., Jr. (1956). *The organization man.* New York: Simon & Schuster.

Zald, M. N., & McCarthy, J. D. (1986). *Social movements in an organized society.* New Brunswick, NJ: Transaction Books.

Zald, M. N., & McCarthy, J. D. (1987). Organizational intellectuals and the criticism of society. *Social Science Review, 49*, 344–362.

5

Group Interventions in Cancer

The Benefits of Social Support and Education on Patient Adjustment

Donna M. Posluszny, Kelly B. Hyman, and Andrew Baum

Research and theory on groups have been applied to treatment of mental health for years, and group therapy techniques have emerged as major components of psychological intervention. They are cost-effective, often bring together several useful perspectives or experiences, and provide environments that are fundamentally different from individual therapy. In group therapy, patients receive feedback and validation from peers rather than a single, "more powerful" therapist and can more effectively engage in rehearsal of new behaviors (Naar, 1982). Recently, group interventions have been applied to treatment of physical health problems, adapted for use with patients or families of people with AIDS, coronary heart disease, and genital herpes, among other diseases (e.g., Kelly, Murphy, Washington, & Wilson, 1994; Longo, Clum, & Yeager, 1988; van Elderen, Maes, Seegers, & Kragten, 1994). In particular, recent use of group interventions among cancer patients has met with success in affecting aspects of disease course and well-being, suggesting that the instructive, supportive, validating, and calming influences of group settings are particularly useful in treating this disease. In this chapter, we review the bases and outcomes of group-based psychosocial interventions among cancer patients, with an eye toward isolating the sources of group influence that are beneficial to cancer patients.

There is little doubt that cancer patients often need supportive and coping-focused assistance while fighting their disease. As a major cause of death, cancer is a

Donna M. Posluszny, Kelly B. Hyman, and Andrew Baum • University of Pittsburgh Cancer Institute, University of Pittsburgh, Pittsburgh, Pennsylvania 15213-3412.

Theory and Research on Small Groups, edited by R. Scott Tindale et al. Plenum Press, New York, 1998.

fearsome and highly threatening disease, and the experience of cancer is stressful at every stage, demanding substantial psychological and physical adjustment (Glanz & Lerman, 1992). Treatment for the disease is not always effective, and many still believe cancer inevitably leads to certain, painful death. Cancer patients report experiencing depression, anxiety, physical symptoms, disruption in marital and/or sexual relationships, lethargy and diminished levels of activity, and considerable fear regarding disease progression and death (Welch-McCaffrey, Hoffman, Leigh, Loescher, & Meyskens, 1989). Surgery, chemotherapy, and other cancer treatments also cause distress due to aversive side effects, threats to one's self-image, and negative effects on quality of life. Even after remission or successful treatment, survivors may exhibit chronic feelings of vulnerability (Burish, Meyerowitz, Carey, & Morrow, 1987; Schmale et al., 1983). Fear of recurrence and social stigmatization may also be substantial (Muzzin, Anderson, Figueredo, & Gudelis, 1994). To some extent, this heightened vigilance and worry is adaptive, but it must be managed and maintained at levels that maximize problem- or danger-focused coping rather than fear control (e.g., Leventhal, 1980). Because the rigorous demands and side effects of treatment are often unpleasant and stressful, and the disease is highly threatening, the diagnosis of cancer may require long-term coping efforts on the part of most patients (Maher, 1982). Behavioral interventions can often help with this process and when delivered in group settings can offer substantial assistance and stress relief to patients and their families.

Why Should Groups Help Cancer Patients?

Recent studies of group interventions have reported promising evidence of their benefit to cancer patients. Several properties of small groups may contribute to these benefits. Providing support, education, and coping skills is part of individual therapy as well, but groups may prove to be an unusually effective setting for providing them. Similarly, groups provide more extensive social support, the opportunity for social comparison, and may contribute to enhanced learning of coping skills.

Social Support

Defined as the belief that one is a valued member of a group and that one is loved and cared for (Cobb, 1976), *social support* appears to be one of the most useful and important tools for increasing quality of life and reducing distress associated with life-threatening disease. Groups can provide support to their members by giving a sense of belonging and universality that helps to offset the isolation often associated with cancer (Spiegel & Yalom, 1978). Discussion of cancer-related struggles and empathic listening to members' concerns can contribute to each member's belief of being an esteemed part of the group. In addition, being part of a group can provide a sense of security to members by letting everyone know that the group members' resources and services are available, should they be needed (Cobb, 1976).

There is abundant evidence that social support is linked to psychological and physical health outcomes (cf. Cohen & Wills, 1985). Prospective epidemiological studies have shown that social support is associated with decreased mortality (Berkman & Syme, 1979; House, Robbins, & Metzner, 1982). Mortality from all causes, as well as morbidity for several diseases, is greater among people with relatively low levels of social support than among those with more substantial support. Social support is also associated with lower levels of stress and appears to have a stress-buffering function as well, reducing psychological distress during times of threat or demand (e.g., Billings & Moos, 1982; Fleming, Baum, Gisriel, & Gatchel, 1982).

The mechanisms underlying the effects of social support and its relationship to health outcomes remain to be clarified. At a general level, it may be that a lack of positive social relationships is stressful or leads to negative psychological states such as anxiety and depression. These psychological states may ultimately influence physical health either by exerting a direct effect on physiological processes that influence susceptibility to disease or an indirect effect through behavioral patterns that alter physiological responses, thereby increasing risk for disease and mortality (Cohen & Wills, 1985). Alternatively, support may mediate the relationship between a stressful event and a potential stress reaction by altering stress appraisal and coping processes. Lazarus (1966) and Lazarus and Folkman (1984) have argued that the nature of one's appraisal of stressors determines both coping and the valence of outcomes. Social support may affect these appraisals and the likelihood that people see situations as threatening or harmful. This suggests that the perception that others can and will provide necessary help or support reduces threatening or harmful aspects of a situation and/or increases one's perceived ability to cope (Cohen & Wills, 1985). Support may also dampen stress reactivity, though a basis for this has not been specified (Kamarck, Jennings, & Manuck, 1990).

This intervening role of social support has been summarized in descriptions of the stress-buffering hypothesis; social support acts as a reserve and a resource to blunt the effects of stress, or to enable an individual to cope with stress more effectively when it is at high levels (Cohen & McKay, 1984). Along these lines, House, Landis, and Umberson (1988) suggest that support may also reduce the perceived importance of the problem, provide an actual solution to the problem, or facilitate healthy behaviors.

For cancer patients, having social support should be beneficial, but maintaining it may be difficult. Several studies suggest a positive association between social support and adaptive coping in cancer patients (Funch & Marshall, 1983; Smith, Redman, Burns, & Sagert, 1985), but others suggest that cancer patients often experience problems in obtaining or maintaining adequate support (Wortman, 1984). Cancer treatments and side effects, as well as the stigma associated with having cancer, significantly affect patients' social experiences, support processes, and emotional outcomes (Peters-Golden, 1982; Taylor, Lichtman, & Wood, 1984). For example, others may react to someone with cancer by providing support noncontingently or avoiding the person altogether, as if to avoid the possibility of contagion or threatening reminders of mortality (e.g., Coates & Wortman, 1980). This withdrawal of support, together with the demands of treatment, may make it difficult to remain active in one's primary reference groups (Wortman, 1984). Cella and Tross (1986) noted that although the cancer experience often strengthened the family unit, friends or acquaintances with less personal investment often avoided or abandoned people with cancer.

Consistent with this, cancer patients report that they are treated differently after people know they have cancer and feel misunderstood and avoided or feared (Peters-Golden, 1982). There is evidence that these perceptions are accurate, as healthy people tend to avoid contact with cancer patients (Peters-Golden, 1982). Many cancer patients report receiving adequate social support, but some clearly do not receive the extent and kind of support they want (for a review, see Taylor, Falke, Shoptaw, & Lichtman, 1986). For example, Peters-Golden (1982) found that only half of the patients surveyed regarded the support they received as adequate to fill their needs, and social support, when given, was often inappropriate and unhelpful. This group of unsatisfied cancer patients may be the most likely to seek out or benefit from group interventions because groups meet their needs for support (Taylor et al., 1986).

Although not extensive, research suggests that cancer patients' uncertainties and fears increase their need for support, while the intense fear and the stigma associated with the disease often create communication problems that can decrease their access to social support (Bloom, 1982; Wortman, 1984). The support needs of cancer patients may vary with the particular stage of their disease and the challenges they face at a given time in their cancer experience. The nature of support needed at diagnosis may be very different from that needed when faced with surgery at the end stage of terminal illness. At such, taxonomies have been proposed that consider stages of cancer and support strategies, starting with providing information and protection against isolation, and ending with existential support during the terminal phase (Broadhead & Kaplan, 1990). At this end stage, direct confrontation with fears of dying and venting of strong emotion in a supportive setting may be effective in helping the patient and family cope with the illness (Spiegel, 1993). The effectiveness of groups in providing support in these contexts is not surprising.

In addition, the need for reassurance from others is stimulated by external danger (e.g., Janis, 1968), in this case, the diagnosis of cancer. Groups can provide support by promising to stick by one another or by giving a sense of stability to a chaotic period of one's life. Schachter's (1959) work on emotional arousal and affiliative tendencies also suggests that the value of groups during periods of crisis is related to stability or validation of one's reactions to threat. His familiar finding that some anxious subjects sought to affiliate with others experiencing similar threats to reassure themselves during an uncertain experience has clear relevance for intervening with cancer patients.

Social Comparison

Although more than 1.2 million people are newly diagnosed with cancer each year (American Cancer Society, 1996), it remains a disease that affects a minority of people. As such, those who develop cancer often have no prior experience with it and have relatively few people in their immediate social network who share or have shared this experience. In addition, the potentially devastating nature of the disease may further contribute to feelings of uncertainty and unrealistic fears. Groups designed exclusively for cancer patients can provide an opportunity for social comparison, where patients can discuss and compare their thoughts and feelings with one another in hopes of making sense out of and normalizing their experiences.

Social comparison theory stems from Festinger's (1954) idea that people seek to evaluate their opinions and abilities. The method of choice is a physical test involving comparison with objective standards, but in the absence of standards, comparison with other people may be used. An opinion or belief is interpreted as "correct" or valid, or interpreted as "incorrect" or invalid, based on the consensus of the opinions that relevant others hold. The ideal place to get this evaluation is from members of a cohesive group of similar others. Thus, a group of cancer patients can allow people to discuss and validate their beliefs and fears, and provide an effective comparison for members to evaluate their experience. These groups can also have a corrective effect on each member's appraisal of external dangers (Janis, 1968).

Inherent in the nature of cancer, its course of treatment, potential recurrence, and disability are ambiguous situations leading to a range of fears, worries, and unknowns. These ambiguous situations or feelings lead to a desire to be with others as a means of socially evaluating and determining the appropriate reactions to the situation (Schachter, 1959). Consistent with this, Molleman, Pruyn, and van Kippenberg (1986) found that cancer patients preferred to affiliate with other cancer patients as uncertainty about aspects of their illness and treatment increased.

Recent work on social comparison and cancer patients indicates that patients seek better or poorer functioning individuals for different purposes (for a review, see Taylor & Lobel, 1989). Comparison may not always produce positive outcomes or improve mood, but in general, patients may compare themselves against less fortunate others when they need to enhance their well-being, but they often prefer to associate with better functioning patients in order to gain information and increase hope. This is consistent with research demonstrating that under conditions of threat, people prefer to compare themselves to those who are in worse shape in order to feel better about their own circumstances (Wills, 1981).

Coping and Modeling

Having several people with similar types of problems available for comparison also expands the number of ideas and strategies that can be adopted for solution of a given problem. Groups serve as reservoirs of special information and coping techniques proven successful in dealing with the common problems of group members (Adams, 1979). Members can share their personal methods of coping and others can learn effective strategies from their experiences. In this way, it is expected that members of disease-specific support groups serve as peer models for one another (Telch & Telch, 1985). When one group member is helped in this kind of setting, he or she is expected, after resolving this personal crisis, to offer help to others. Thus, in addition to observing a positive model of coping behavior, the individual has the opportunity and the obligation to master the crisis and to model successful coping behavior for another (Adams, 1979). In addition, through social learning, peer models can enhance members' self-efficacy, which may translate into more effective coping behavior (see Telch & Telch, 1985). The possibility remains that group members may model inappropriate or ineffective coping behaviors, though group processes may mitigate against this through comparison and invalidation of extreme opinions or options.

Group Interventions for Cancer Distress

Among cancer patients, the use of professionally led, group-based interventions has increased dramatically in the past dozen years. For the most part, these interventions have had measurable benefits, though research evaluating them has been uneven and often flawed. We briefly review this literature before discussing the bases for these effects and implications for future work in this area. First, we describe two early studies that investigated the basic efficacy of group intervention. Second, we discuss more detailed, support-focused interventions, including the work of Spiegel and colleagues. This is followed by a series of studies that used a somewhat standardized, educationally based format, modeled after the American Cancer Society intervention. Finally, we review a group of studies that have more specifically combined and/or compared education and support components in group intervention. For more critical reviews of this literature, the reader is referred to Andersen (1992).

One of the first attempts to determine the effectiveness of group interventions for cancer patients was a pilot study of an 8-week group counseling program focusing on issues of living and coping with cancer for patients and their families (Wood, Milligan, Christ, & Liff, 1978). Eleven of the 15 patients who participated reported that the group was generally helpful. Twelve indicated that they would recommend the group experience to other cancer patients. However, no data were reported that reflected changes in symptoms or other psychological measures, making it impossible to assess the efficacy of the group in any other comparable domain.

Another study addressing the basic efficacy of groups for cancer patients considered a more ambitious 12-session group intervention addressing specific themes such as perception of self, reallocation of roles, mourning, and adaptation (Baider, Amikam, & De-Nour, 1984). Following the intervention, comparisons were made between women who felt that participation had helped them and those who did not. Of the 24 patients who completed the intervention, 11 patients reported that they were "helped a lot," and 9 reported receiving "some help" from the group, whereas only 4 reported that they were "not helped." The women who reported being helped a lot showed statistically significant decreases in distress and improved adjustment from pre- to postintervention. Women in the other two categories exhibited no change or fared more poorly after the group experience. This intervention lacked a control group, and the study was characterized by a large refusal rate (55 out of 86 available patients declined to participate), thus raising serious questions about sampling bias and generalizability of the findings and making evaluation difficult.

Though useful in suggesting that small-group treatments for cancer patients may be beneficial, these early studies left a number of important questions unanswered. Without control groups, randomization, or clearly valid sampling procedures, the efficacy of these interventions could not be confirmed with any confidence. Fortunately, interest in applying group interventions to cancer treatment continues to grow, and several more definitive studies have been reported.

One of the more influential evaluations of cancer group interventions was reported in a series of articles by Spiegel and his colleagues (e.g., Spiegel & Bloom, 1983; Spiegel, Bloom, Kramer, & Gottheil, 1989; Spiegel, Bloom, & Yalom, 1981). They conducted an investigation of short- and long-term effects of a 1-year social support intervention for women with late-stage metastatic breast cancer. Complete data were collected from 16 of an original 34 experimental subjects and 14 of 24 controls. Treatment subjects met once each week for a full year of group supportive therapy, dealing with such areas as death and dying, related family problems, and difficulties with treatment. In addition, some treatment subjects received hypnosis training, while control subjects continued their regular treatment. At the end of the year, support-group subjects reported significantly less tension, depression, fatigue, and confusion, and significantly fewer maladaptive coping responses (Spiegel et al., 1981). Subjects who completed the group treatment reported less pain and suffering than did controls, and patients who received group support and hypnosis training reported less pain sensation than did subjects receiving group support alone. Decreases in pain were highly correlated with decreases in negative affect (Spiegel & Bloom, 1983). Of perhaps the greatest significance, 10-year survival rates for these women showed that the group support intervention was associated with enhanced survival: Women from the group treatment condition lived an average of 18 months longer than did women in the control condition, nearly a 100% increase in survival (Spiegel et al., 1989).

Jacobs, Ross, Walker, and Stockdale (1983) reported two studies of education and peer support groups among Hodgkin's disease patients 6 months or more after diagnosis. The peer-support-group intervention consisted of eight weekly sessions, in which 16 patients discussed common problems associated with having cancer. These treatment subjects were compared with 18 control subjects who received standard care. Relatively equal numbers of men and women participated and were equally represented in both groups. The effectiveness of treatment was evaluated on the Cancer Patient Behavior Scale (CPBS; Jacobs, Ross, & Stockdale, 1977), which has 10 subscales representing problem areas (depression, anxiety, treatment difficulties, interpersonal problems, life disruption, and personal habits) and support areas (activity, life satisfaction, self-competency, social competency). At the completion of the study, both the peer support and control groups showed improvement on most of these subscales and no significant differences between groups or across gender were reported.

The education intervention involved a 3-month distribution of pamphlets and mailings about Hodgkin's disease. The CPBS measures and answers to questions reflecting knowledge of disease were collected at baseline and 3 months later. Twenty-one Hodgkin's patients (15 males, 6 females) received this information, and 26 controls (16 males, 10 females) received standard care. Experimental subjects performed significantly better on the test of knowledge, exhibited significant reductions in anxiety and treatment problems, and had marginally significant decreases in depression and life disruption postintervention than controls. No gender differences were reported. These findings suggest that education may be more important than group context in determining efficacy of treatment; this possibility will be discussed in the next section of this chapter.

The importance of education and instruction *as a part* of group interventions has been evaluated by studies of the "I Can Cope" program adopted by the American Cancer Society in 1979. However, despite the common title and the use of education as a primary component, specifics of the interventions that have used the "I Can Cope" course have varied considerably from study to study.

The first of these "I Can Cope" studies was incorporated as part of a rehabilitation program for people living with cancer (Johnson, 1982). The sample consisted of 42 cancer patients who were diagnosed or rediagnosed with cancer within the year of the start of the intervention. The "I Can Cope" intervention was presented to 21 of the patients. The program included sessions focused on learning about the disease, coping with daily health problems, communicating with others, liking oneself, living with limits, and finding resources that can help. Subjects were matched for both pretest scores on the three dependent variables and for age and sex when possible. The treatment intervention was associated with significantly less anxiety and greater knowledge and sense of meaning compared to the control condition. The relative utility of individual versus group formats was evaluated among recently diagnosed gynecological cancer patients with an expected survival of at least 1 year (Cain, Kohorn, Quinlan, Latimer, & Schwartz, 1986). The treatment was again based on the "I Can Cope" educational program, presented to 21 patients on an individual basis and to 28 patients in groups of four to six. Both treatment conditions were compared with a standard care condition ($N = 31$). Topics included information about cancer, the impact of treatment of body image, relaxation, diet, exercise, and communicating with others. Some findings indicated that the group and individual formats were equivalent, as all participants exhibited decreased negative affect over time. However, there were significant treatment effects immediately after treatment and at a 6-month follow-up. Those participants who received individual treatment reported less anxiety and depression than did the subjects in the group treatment, who in turn reported less than did control subjects. Both individual and group subjects were more knowledgeable about their illness than were controls.

A third study based on the "I Can Cope" program added an individualized/ family counseling and stress management component in an effort to make the treatment more comprehensive (Reele, 1994). The educational topics included cancer diagnosis and treatment, self-esteem, diet and exercise, and the use of relaxation techniques. Twelve subjects in the treatment program were compared to eight graduates of the modified "I Can Cope" program (who met one additional time per month), and 12 subjects in a standard care control condition. Subjects had mixed cancer diagnoses and the length of time since diagnosis varied up to 5 years. Results indicated that quality of life remained unchanged among patients in the intervention group, whereas scores from subjects' in the other two conditions decreased slightly, resulting in a significant main effect of treatment postintervention. However, pre- to postchange scores were not significantly different between conditions.

In general, results of these studies are mixed, suggesting an effect of information that may or may not be enhanced by group treatments. With the exception of the results reported by Spiegel and his associates, most of these studies do not provide clear support for group interventions. There are several possible explanations for this, including likely gender differences in response to various formats, differences associated with a variety of cancers, and differences associated with various stages of disease and prognosis. Studies have not generally controlled for these factors, and most have not independently varied support and education components.

Some have tried to combine supportive and educational functions, with some success. The first of these examined group counseling with 30 men and 30 women with new diagnoses of advanced cancer (Ferlic, Goldman, & Kennedy, 1979). Subjects were randomly assigned to either treatment or control groups that met six times over a 2-week period. The educational component was comparable to the "I Can Cope" program and addressed the establishment of doctor–patient communication, basic disease and treatment information, self-esteem, and information on nutrition and physical activity. Additionally, an emphasis was added on examining feelings about death, pain and suffering, and discussion of other emotions that might be experienced as a result of having cancer. The primary outcome measures were self-esteem, adjustment, attitudes toward the disease, and perceptions of the illness. Participants in the treatment group exhibited significant increases in self-esteem immediately after the intervention, whereas the control group showed a slight decrease. In addition, treatment-group subjects knew more disease-related information and had greater positive changes on measures of hospital adjustment and death perception than did control subjects. A 6-month postintervention mailing did not provide sufficient numbers of returns to be reliable, so no information about the long-term maintenance of these changes was available.

Another comprehensive study assigned 51 (mostly male) patients and 25 spouses to either a stress and activity management treatment condition or a standard care control condition (Heinrich & Schag, 1985). Patients had a variety of cancers. Fifty percent of the sample had been diagnosed 2 years previously, and 50% were on chemotherapy, suggesting a more recent diagnosis. The treatment consisted of weekly meetings for 6 weeks, and sessions focused on relaxation training, cognitive therapy, problem-solving skills, and activity management. Both groups of patients exhibited better adjustment over time. Patients and spouses in the treatment condition reported feeling satisfied with care and with the help that they received in solving disease-related problems. Activity level did not differ between conditions, but the investigators speculated that the high baseline levels of time spent in physical activities each day may have caused a ceiling effect and restricted discovery of effects of the intervention. There was a significant main effect for knowledge about the illness for both the subjects and their spouses in the treatment condition.

More recently, Fawzy, Cousins, et al. (1990) examined the effect of a structured, short-term group intervention in 66 early-stage, recently diagnosed malignant melanoma patients, all of whom had a good prognosis for recovery. Thirty-eight treatment subjects completed the 6-week intervention in groups of 7 to 10 and were compared to 28 standard care controls. The intervention focused on health education, problem-solving skills training, relaxation training for stress management, and psychosocial support. Emotional benefits of the group and coping were evaluated before and after the group intervention, and at 6 months postintervention. Compared to control subjects, treatment subjects reported more vigor and active coping after the intervention, as well as 6 months later. They also reported less depression, anxiety, fatigue, and confusion at follow-up.

In addition, Fawzy, Kemeny, et al. (1990) reported 6-week and 6-month follow-up immune status data for these subjects, showing that immune system changes followed a similar pattern as the affective measures and were correlated with levels of anxiety and levels of anger. Immediately after the group intervention, treatment subjects' large granular lymphocytes (LGLs) were significantly increased above baseline, which may indicate enhanced immune system functioning. LGLs are found in both CD8+ T-cells and natural killer cells (NK cells), both of which are believed to be related to immune system defenses against cancer (Whiteside, Bryant, Day, & Herberman, 1990). Further analyses revealed that this change was associated with an increase in the percentage of CD8+ T-cells and not in the population of NK cells. Control subjects did not show this change, and treatment subjects continued to show this effect at 6 months. Numbers of natural killer cells and NK response were increased in the intervention group but not among control subjects at 6-months posttreatment. Of note, decreased anxiety and increased anger were positively correlated with positive immune changes, suggesting that affective change mediated immune changes in this study.

Compared with some of the other types of interventions that we have considered, more comprehensive small-group treatments appear to be beneficial for cancer patients. However, findings are not entirely consistent, and questions regarding efficacy of one form of treatment over another remain. Most interventions included several components; a more systematic approach would be to isolate the most effective aspects of these interventions so they can be more selectively applied. Two studies compared different types of programs in an attempt to better understand which treatment components are necessary to affect positive changes in cancer patients.

Telch and Telch (1986) investigated the benefits of a structured coping skills plus social support condition as compared with a social support only condition and a control condition. Forty-one male and female patients were assigned in groups of five to one of these conditions. Complete data were collected on 13 coping skills plus support subjects, 14 support-only subjects, and 14 control subjects. The treatment lasted 6 weeks for 90 minutes each week. The group coping skills instruction consisted of structured education and coping skills training similar to cognitive-behavioral therapy. The support group condition allowed patients to discuss feelings, concerns, and problems. Patients in the combined coping skills plus support condition did better than those in the support-only groups, and the patients in the support-only groups did better than did controls. Significant mood changes were observed for the total Profile of Moods States score and each of the six subscales, as were increases in self-efficacy and knowledge. These findings strongly suggest that support alone is useful but not as effective as support and coping skill training in managing distress associated with cancer. Education and coping skills training plus support was more beneficial than support alone, but support was better than nothing (Telch & Telch, 1986).

The second study assessed emotional status in patients receiving either an active treatment consisting of psychoeducation/coping skills plus supportive discussion or a control condition of supportive discussion alone (Cunningham & Tocco, 1989). The sample consisted of 53 patients (39 females, 14 males) with mixed cancer diagnoses. Approximately half of these patients were being treated, and half were experiencing a rediagnosis. Subjects were stratified according to age, sex, and apparent seriousness of disease, and randomly assigned to one of the two treatments. The programs ran for 6 weeks, meeting once each week for 2 hours. The psychoeducational component consisted of relaxation and positive mental imagery training, goal setting, and general life management. Coping techniques were also taught, and subjects were asked to continue practicing at home. In addition, the social support component consisted of discussion, expression of feelings, problem solving, and information sharing. Mood and distress were measured at the first and last sessions and again 2 to 3 weeks following completion of treatment. Both treatment groups produced significant improvements, but greater improvements were observed in the psychoeducation plus support group. By the end of the intervention and 2 to 3 weeks later, total mood disturbance was reduced significantly more in the psychoeducational group than in the support only group.

A related study examining the longer-term effects of the psychoeducational plus support intervention considered 39 patients who received this intervention and were assessed before, after, and at 3 months to measure improvement maintenance over time. The improvements gained by treatment intervention were comparable to those reported in the first study, and were maintained at 3 months. The lack of a no-intervention control group limits the conclusions one can draw from these studies, but their data suggest that providing both education and support is superior to support alone and that this kind of combined group intervention can successfully reduce distress (Cunningham & Tocco, 1989).

One final issue that has been examined in the literature is the extent to which benefits of small-group treatment generalize across patients; that is, can everyone benefit from treatment? Cunningham, Lockwood, and Edmonds (1993) used a number of mood, adjustment, and quality-of-life measures to identify patients who were most likely to benefit from a short-term, 7-week group intervention. They collected data on 400 cancer patients with varying diagnoses and stages of disease before, immediately following, and 3 months after the previously described treatment. Changes on all three measures were found at post and at follow-up, but patient characteristics predicted different outcomes. Mood and adjustment improved more for patients younger than 50 years old, whereas scores on the quality-of-life instrument showed that colorectal patients, recurrent disease patients, and those patients who did not expect the intervention to change the course of the disease improved less than did their counterparts. Marital status, religion, education, and gender were not related to outcomes. In general, there was no clear subset of this sample that consistently failed to benefit. Despite the lack of a control group (and the related questions of changes over time), this intervention appeared to provide benefits for a broad variety of cancer patients. Although other findings, largely from individual counseling interventions, suggest that characteristics of the cancer and the patient determine the usefulness of treatment programs (Andersen, 1992), evidence does not suggest a particular group most likely to be helped by group interventions.

How Well Do Group Interventions Work?

Overall, this literature has emphasized outcomes with little focus on mechanisms, and has favored determination of whether group interventions are effective rather than understanding why or how they work. There are a number of small-group processes that may mediate this treatment–outcome relationship, including social support, social comparison, and modeling. The increased social support experienced in these cancer treatment groups may decrease psychological distress and increase coping resources. Enhanced opportunities for social comparison with similar others allow patients validation of beliefs and fears and normalization of their cancer experience. Additionally, patients can benefit from both the intrinsic reward of being a model for someone else and from seeing others in similar situations as positive role models for successful coping. Despite the fact that research has not systematically evaluated these potential mechanisms, some tentative conclusions about the mechanisms can be drawn.

However, a number of important factors must be considered when attempting to consolidate the findings from these studies. Despite the results of the Cunningham et al. (1993) study demonstrating generalizability across a variety of cancers and characteristics, patients participating in these interventions have tended to be middle- to upper-middle-class women. In fact, cancer support attenders are more likely to be white, middle-class female patients than anyone else (Taylor et al., 1986). Related to this are high refusal rates, some greater than 70% (Baider et al., 1984). It is not clear what types of people seek out support groups but they may be those who report a greater number of problems or those who tend to use more social support resources (Taylor et al., 1986). These sources of bias have defied ready solutions of outreach and oversampling, and must be addressed as potential mechanisms mediating the effectiveness of these interventions.

In addition, there is great variability in the number and types of components that are used in these treatment programs. Unfortunately, descriptions of study procedures are sometimes vague, making it difficult to identify the components and timing of the interventions. Some interventions label themselves as educational, others as stress management or coping skills training, and still others as either social support or peer support. Given the group format of these interventions, it is likely that social support was, at least indirectly, a component of most of these interventions. Only one published study (Telch & Telch, 1986) allowed for direct comparison of specific treatment components of coping/education and social support; the coping/education intervention had positive effects above the effects from social support alone. Currently, a Carnegie Mellon University study is examining more directly the effectiveness of group support versus group education, as well as potential mechanisms of increased self-esteem and perceived control (Helgeson, personal communication, October 1994). This study and others like it will help clarify these issues. Together with greater standardization of measurement, these developments will expand our knowledge of the effects of group interventions in medical settings.

In general, conclusions from our literature review are consistent with the results of a meta-analysis of both individual and group psychosocial interventions with cancer patients (Meyer & Mark, 1995). These researchers found support for significant benefits of interventions on emotional and functional adjustment, treatment and disease-related symptoms, and for more global distress measures. The effect sizes from their meta-analysis for these variables ranged from .19 for functional adjustment to .28 for the global measures. Additionally, none of the effect sizes were significantly different among treatment categories. Where possible, effect sizes for studies presented in the current review were calculated based on pooled variance estimates. In these studies, medium to large effect sizes were found for the significant variables (Cohen, 1988). For example, in the studies conducted by Spiegel and colleagues, the effect size for the observed decrease in total mood disturbance between support group and control participants was .77. Even more impressive is the finding that the difference in survival (months from study entry to death) in these groups was .71. It also appears that combining education with support has a modest benefit (.31) over support alone (Cunningham & Tocco, 1989). Thus, professionally led small-group treatments are beneficial for cancer patients, and although most interventions are effective, some may be better than others.

Five general categories of outcome measures were used in these studies, including emotional adjustment, self-esteem, coping, general quality of life, and knowledge. Most used some measure of emotional adjustment, and most found benefits of treatment on measures of anxiety and depression. However, two studies found changes in treatment-group subjects that were comparable to changes in control groups (Heinrich & Schag, 1985; Jacobs et al., 1983). Patients in all conditions of these studies improved over time, thus masking any effects of the treatment intervention. Self-esteem-related measures were collected in two studies (Ferlic et al., 1979; Telch & Telch, 1986). The first of these studies found that subjects in the treatment condition increased slightly on measures from a self-concept test, whereas scores for control subjects decreased slightly. Telch and Telch (1986) measured patients' perceived self-efficacy with reference to their ability to cope in a variety of situations or to perform specific behaviors associated with having cancer. They found that subjects in both treatment conditions improved more than controls, but that subjects who received coping skills plus social support improved more than subjects who received social support alone. Group treatment interventions appear to be effective in improving emotional adjustment to cancer.

Measures of coping skills were collected in three studies (Fawzy, Cousins, et al. 1990; Reele, 1994; Spiegel et al., 1981). Due to small numbers, Reele (1994) only reported percentages for all subjects in the study, and little can be said about different uses of different strategies between groups. However, Fawzy and colleagues reported use of more active coping at the end of treatment and at 6-month follow-up for the treatment as compared to the control group. Spiegel et al. (1981) also found differences in coping between treatment and control groups. They found that treatment subjects used less of what they called "maladaptive coping," such as eating too much, drinking too much, and smoking. These findings suggest that interventions alter coping choices and provide patients with new coping options.

Three studies (Heinrich & Schag, 1985; Reele, 1994; Telch & Telch, 1986) assessed quality of life. Telch and Telch (1986) found that subjects in their coping plus social-support treatment reported fewer cancer-related problems following intervention. Subjects in the social-support condition also reported fewer problems than control subjects but more than the combination treatment subjects. Reele (1994) found that the treatment group reported better quality of life following treatment, but this effect was not the result of significant changes from baseline, as both treatment and control conditions improved over time. Finally, Heinrich and Schag (1985) did not report differences between groups in quality of life. These more global measures of quality of life may not capture the benefits of these treatment programs as well as more targeted measures of emotional adjustment, self-esteem, and coping. Additionally, other problems such as generalizing across stage and extent of disease further cloud some benefits of group interventions (Andersen, 1992).

Group Context and Psychological Well-Being

It is not possible to directly evaluate the specific psychological processes that are operating in small-group treatments on the basis of existing research. However, some speculations can be made. One can readily argue that social support is a central component of every intervention that involves more than one person, regardless of how it is labeled. Simply meeting with others may provide members with a basic level of incremental support, knowing that there are others who share their experience and are physically present. Of the interventions that were identified as social support and made special efforts to provide and mobilize support to its members, most were successful. The exception found no differences in distress or social functioning between the peer support group and control group after the intervention (Jacobs et al., 1983). Reasons for this finding are not clear, because peer support participants reported positive comments about the intervention.

Opportunities for social comparison are not necessarily assessable in most studies but can be measured indirectly by assuming that they are more likely to be increased by interventions that include discussion as opposed to the more structured, didactic interventions. Through discussion, patients can interact with one another and share their experiences and how they are handling their situations. This should help participants compare themselves to each other and facilitate the normalization of their experiences. Research has not directly addressed this possibility, and further investigation is warranted.

Theoretically, those interventions that were specifically targeted at a particular type of cancer or stage of disease should also make it easier for social comparison to occur and may be more beneficial to participants. In other words, patients at the same stage of disease or who all have just been diagnosed probably have more in common and face similar adjustment challenges than a group of patients who range from newly diagnosed to end-stage disease. This seemed to be the case, as interventions with homogenous groups were more likely to be successful (e.g., Fawzy, Cousins, et al., 1990; Ferlic et al., 1979; Spiegel et al., 1981). However, there are also studies that reported benefits of group interventions with more heterogenous groups (Cunningham & Tocco, 1989; Johnson, 1982). Interestingly, although Telch and Telch (1986) included mixed cancers and stages in their intervention, they made the sample more homogenous by screening for and recruiting participants who were experiencing psychological distress, obtaining positive results both for their psychoeducational and support interventions.

Modeling and coping skills were the focus of several interventions, most of which were successful. Perhaps the most striking evidence of the benefit of coping skills was reported by Telch and Telch (1986), who compared a coping skills intervention with a support-only intervention. Their results indicated that coping skills and support together are superior to support alone in improving mood and self-efficacy. Similar results were reported by Cunningham and Tocco (1989), who compared psychoeducation plus support against support alone and found that psycho-educational patients reported less distress. In addition, Fawzy, Cousins, and colleagues (1990) included substantial coping skills training components in their intervention and also obtained positive results. While Jacobs et al. (1983) found that informational mailings were more effective in reducing distress and improving behavioral functioning than was a peer support group, these mailings explained the target groups' cancer and gave helpful suggestions on how to cope with the cancer experience. It appears that providing patients with information and some coping skills training is effective in reducing distress, improving daily functioning and problem solving. In addition, providing this in a group environment appears to be enhanced by the benefits of the group, including social support, social comparison, and real-life modeling.

Conclusions

This review and discussion of applications of group research and theory to intervention with seriously ill populations are by no means definitive. This literature is still small, despite recent interest, and much of the research on group interventions with cancer patients is plagued by methodological problems, such as lack of appropriate control groups, small samples, and nonstandard measurement. Some studies are stronger, providing appropriate comparisons and larger, well-instrumented designs. Regardless, these studies generally indicate that group interventions among cancer patients enhance emotional adjustment to disease and treatment. Despite a number of important differences among studies and diversity in disease type, extent of disease, and prognosis, the findings from this growing literature are fairly consistent: group intervention among cancer patients is beneficial.

Of course, if this basic conclusion were not the case, then we would likely need to question our basic assumptions and orientations toward applied psychology and behavioral intervention. The extent of some of the findings, including extensions to immune function and patient survival reported by recent investigations (Fawzy, Kemeny, et al., 1990; Spiegel et al., 1989), demonstrate that these interventions work and can help patients cope with cancer. The conclusion that they reduce distress is a very basic one that is not informative beyond confirming our assumptions.

This is not to suggest that this literature indicates that groups are better than individual interventions. There is no systematic support for such a claim, though one can build a reasonably strong model to predict such differences. Increased social support, opportunities for social comparison, and coping skills modeling are all positive factors that should be increased in group settings and are likely to facilitate adjustment and coping. Reduction in distress, enhanced quality of life, and facilitation of coping are among the outcomes of these interventions, but systematic comparisons of the relative efficacy of individual and group approaches have not been reported. Because groups are more cost-effective than individual treatment (they require less time and staff to reach more people), their further use and investigation of mechanisms by which they work are indicated.

It may be the case that different patients are better served by different interventions. Interestingly, studies that included mostly men failed to find group intervention effects (Heinrich & Schag, 1985; Jacobs et al., 1983). It is not clear why this was the case, but it may reflect a mismatch of the type of intervention chosen and the gender-based coping preferences of the group. Two separate studies with comparable, predominately male samples, one with an education intervention, and one with a peer support intervention, yielded inconsistent findings, such that education was effective and peer support was not (Jacobs et al., 1983). Heinrich and Schag (1985) found similar results in their mostly male sample with a skills training/social support intervention. Three other interventions that included approximately equal numbers of men and women found positive results in a mixed component intervention (Fawzy, Cousins, et al., 1990; Ferlic et al., 1979; Reele, 1994). It may be that interventions composed solely or primarily of support are not as useful for men, and that men respond more readily to education-based or coping skills–focused intervention or to individual intervention (see Taylor et al., 1986). Many researchers have suggested that men are less comfortable sharing distress than are women, and the group format may not work for them as a result. Similarly, men report different patterns of social support than women, and the kind of support provided by groups may be more effective among women. This issue also needs systematic investigation as we refine our understanding of group interventions and target them to particular diseases, gender, age, and other important mediating factors.

In a matter of a few generations, knowledge of and approaches to treating disease have changed so much that in some instances it is difficult to imagine now what once was. Our understanding of health, disease, and the genetic and molecular bases of normal function have been revolutionized by technological advances and new knowledge. Our treatment of disease and our emphasis on prevention and maintenance of good health have changed dramatically; consequently, behavioral scientists and psychologists have found themselves increasingly involved in these endeavors. The advent of interventions to help patients adapt to the realities of serious disease, to ease emotional distress, to enhance quality of life, and, perhaps, to affect the course of the disease is as revolutionary as breakthroughs in molecular biology and opens vast new arenas for application of theory and research in psychology, particularly behavioral medicine. The systematic investigation and application of what we know about groups and interventions offer one promising and important avenue to pursue in the fight against the initiation, progression, and the effects of diseases such as cancer, AIDS, and heart disease.

References

Adams, J. (1979). Mutual-help groups: Enhancing the coping ability of oncology clients. *Cancer Nursing*, *2*, 95–98.

American Cancer Society. (1996). *Cancer facts and figures*. Washington, DC: Author.

Andersen, B. L. (1992). Psychological interventions for cancer patients to enhance the quality of life. *Journal of Consulting and Clinical Psychology*, *60*, 552–568.

Baider, L., Amikam, J. C., & De-Nour, A. K. (1984). Time-limited thematic group with post-mastectomy patients. *Journal of Psychosomatic Research*, *28*, 323–330.

Berkman, L., & Syme, S. L. (1979). Social networks, host resistance and mortality: A nine year follow-up study of Alemeda County resident. *American Journal of Epidemiology*, *109*, 186–204.

Billings, A. G., & Moos, R. H. (1982). Social support and functioning among community and clinical groups: A path model. *Journal of Behavioral Medicine*, *5*, 295–312.

Bloom, J. R. (1982). Social support, accommodation to stress, and adjustment to breast cancer. *Social Science and Medicine*, *16*, 1329–1338.

Broadhead, W. E., & Kaplan, B. H. (1990). Social support and the cancer patient. *Cancer*, *67* (Suppl. No. 3), 794–799.

Burish, T. G., Meyerowitz, B. E., Carey, M. P., & Morrow, G. R. (1987). The stressful effects of cancer in adults. In A. Baum & J. E. Singer (Eds.), *Handbook of psychology and health: Vol. 5, Stress* (pp. 137–173). Hillsdale, NJ: Erlbaum.

Cain, E. N., Kohorn, E. I., Quinlan, D. M., Latimer, K., & Schwartz, P. E. (1986). Psychosocial benefits of a cancer support group. *Cancer*, *57*, 183–189.

Cella, D. F., & Tross, S. (1986). Psychological adjustment to survival from Hodgkin's disease. *Journal of Consulting and Clinical Psychology, 54*, 616–622.

Coates, D., & Wortman, C. B. (1980). Depression maintenance and interpersonal control. In A. Baum & J. E. Singer (Eds.), *Advances in environmental psychology: Vol. 2. Applications of personal control* (pp. 149–182). Hillsdale, NJ: Erlbaum.

Cobb, S. (1976). Social support as a moderator of life stress. *Psychosomatic Medicine, 38*, 300–314.

Cohen, J. (1988). *Statistical power analysis for the behavioral sciences* (rev. ed.). Hillsdale, NJ: Erlbaum.

Cohen, S., & McKay, G. (1984). Social support, stress and the buffering hypothesis: A theoretical analysis. In A. Baum, S. E. Taylor, and J. E. Singer (Eds.), *Handbook of psychology and health: Vol. 4. Social psychological aspects of health* (pp. 253–267). Hillsdale, NJ: Erlbaum.

Cohen, S., & Wills, T. A. (1985). Stress, social support and the buffering hypothesis. *Psychological Bulletin, 98*, 310–357.

Cunningham, A. J., Lockwood, G. A, & Edmonds, C. V. I. (1993). Which cancer patients benefit most from a brief, group, coping skills program? *International Journal of Psychiatry in Medicine, 23*, 383–398.

Cunningham, A. J., & Tocco, E. K. (1989). A randomized trial of group psychoeducational therapy for cancer patients. *Patient Education and Counseling, 14*, 101–114.

Fawzy, F. I., Cousins, N., Fawzy, N. W., Kemeny, M. E., Elashoff, R., & Morton, D. (1990). A structured psychiatric intervention for cancer patients: I. Changes over time in methods of coping and affective disturbance. *Archives of General Psychiatry, 47*, 720–725.

Fawzy, F. I., Kemeny, M. E., Fawzy, N. W., Elashoff, R., Morton, D., Cousins, N., & Fahey, J. L. (1990). A structured psychiatric intervention for cancer patients: II. Changes over time in immunological measures. *Archives of General Psychiatry, 47*, 729–735.

Ferlic, M., Goldman, A., & Kennedy, B. J. (1979). Group counseling in adult patients with advanced cancer. *Cancer, 43*, 760–766.

Festinger, L. (1954). A theory of social comparison processes. *Human Relations, 7*, 117–140.

Fleming, R., Baum, A., Gisriel, M. M., & Gatchel, R. J. (1982). Mediating influences of social support on stress at Three Mile Island. *Journal of Human Stress, 8*, 14–22.

Funch, D. P., & Marshall, J. (1983). The role of stress, social support and age in survival from breast cancer. *Journal of Psychosomatic Research, 27*, 77–83.

Glanz, K., & Lerman, C. (1992). Psychosocial impact of breast cancer: A critical review. *Annals of Behavioral Medicine, 14*, 204–211.

Heinrich, R. L., & Schag, C. C. (1985). Stress and activity management: Group treatment for cancer patients and spouses. *Journal of Consulting and Clinical Psychology, 53*, 439–446.

House, J. S., Landis, K. R., & Umberson, D. (1988). Social relationships and health. *Science, 241*, 540–545.

House, J. S., Robbins, C., & Metzner, H. L. (1982). The association of social relationship and activities with mortality: Prospective evidence from the Tecumseh Community Health Study. *American Journal of Epidemiology, 116*, 123–140.

Jacobs, C., Ross, R., & Stockdale, F. E. (1977). Cancer patients behavior scale. *Proceedings of the American Society of Clinical Oncology, 18*, 334.

Jacobs, C., Ross, R. D., Walker, I. M., & Stockdale, F. E. (1983). Behavior of cancer patients: A randomized study on the effects of education and peer support groups. *American Journal of Clinical Oncology, 6*, 347–350.

Janis, I. L. (1968). Group identification under conditions of external danger. In D. Cartwright & A. Zander (Eds.), *Group dynamics: Research and theory* (3rd ed., pp. 80–90). New York: Harper & Row.

Johnson, J. (1982). The effects of a patient education course on persons with a chronic illness. *Cancer Nursing, 5*, 117–123.

Kamarck, T. W., Jennings, J. R., & Manuck, S. B. (1990). Social support reduces cardiovascular reactivity to psychological challenge: A laboratory model. *Psychosomatic Medicine, 52*, 42–58.

Kelly, J. A., Murphy, D. A., Washington, C. D., & Wilson, T. S. (1994). The effects of HIV/AIDS intervention groups for high-risk women in urban clinics. *American Journal of Public Health, 84*, 1918–1922.

Lazarus, R. S. (1966). *Psychological stress and the coping process.* New York: McGraw-Hill.

Lazarus, R. S., & Folkman, S. (1984). *Stress, appraisal, and coping.* New York: Springer.

Leventhal, H. (1980). Toward a comprehensive theory of emotion. In L. Berkowitz (Ed.), *Advances in experimental social psychology* (Vol. 13, pp. 139–207). New York: Academic Press.

Longo, D. J., Clum, G. A., & Yaeger, N. J. (1988). Psychosocial treatment for recurrent genital herpes. *Journal of Consulting and Clinical Psychology, 56,* 61–66.

Maher, E. L. (1982). Anomic aspects of recovery from cancer. *Social Science and Medicine, 16,* 907–912.

Meyer, T. J., & Mark, M. M. (1995). Effects of psychosocial interventions with adult cancer patients: A meta-analysis of randomized experiments. *Health Psychology, 14,* 101–108.

Molleman, E., Pruyn, J., & van Knippenberg, A. (1986). Social comparison processes among cancer patients. *British Journal of Social Psychology, 25,* 1–13.

Muzzin, L. J., Anderson, N. J., Figueredo, A. T., & Gudelis, S. O. (1994). The experience of cancer. *Social Science and Medicine, 38,* 1201–1208.

Naar, R. (1982). *A primer of group psychotherapy.* New York: Human Sciences.

Peters-Golden, H. (1982). Breast cancer: Varied perceptions of social support in the illness experience. *Social Science and Medicine, 16,* 483–491.

Reele, B. L. (1994). Effect of counseling on quality of life for individuals with cancer and their families. *Cancer Nursing, 17,* 101–112.

Schachter, S. (1959). *The psychology of affiliation.* Stanford, CA: Stanford University Press.

Schmale, A. H., Morrow, G. R., Schmitt, M. H., Adler, L. M., Enelow, A., Murawski, B. J., & Cates, C. G. (1983). Well-being of cancer survivors. *Psychosomatic Medicine, 45,* 163–169.

Smith, E., Redman, R., Burns, T. L., & Sagert, K. M. (1985). Perceptions of social support among patients with recently diagnosed breast, endometrial, and ovarian cancer: An exploratory study. *Journal of Psychosocial Oncology, 3,* 65–81.

Spiegel, D. (1993). Psychosocial intervention in cancer. *Journal of the National Cancer Institute, 85,* 1198–1205.

Spiegel, D., & Bloom, J. R. (1983). Group therapy and hypnosis reduce metastatic breast carcinoma pain. *Psychosomatic Medicine, 45,* 333–339.

Spiegel, D., Bloom, J. R., Kraemer, H. C., & Gottheil, E. (1989). Effect of psychosocial treatment on survival of patients with metastatic breast cancer. *Lancet, 2,* 888–891.

Spiegel, D., Bloom, J. R., & Yalom, I. (1981). Group support for patients with metastatic cancer: A randomized prospective outcome study. *Archives of General Psychiatry, 38,* 527–533.

Spiegel, D., & Yalom, I. (1978). A support group for dying patients. *International Journal of Group Psychotherapy, 28,* 233–245.

Taylor, S. E., Falke, R. L., Shoptaw, S. J., & Lichtman, R. R. (1986). Social support, support groups, and the cancer patient. *Journal of Consulting and Clinical Psychology, 54,* 608–615.

Taylor, S. E., Lichtman, R. R., & Wood, J. V. (1984). Compliance with chemotherapy among breast cancer patients. *Health Psychology, 3,* 553–562.

Taylor, S. E., & Lobel, M. (1989). Social comparison activity under threat: Downward evaluation and upward contacts. *Psychological Review, 96,* 569–575.

Telch, C. F., & Telch, M. J. (1985). Psychological approaches for enhancing coping among cancer patients: A review. *Clinical Psychology Review, 5,* 325–344.

Telch, C. F., & Telch, M. J. (1986). Group coping skills instruction and supportive group therapy for cancer patients: A comparison of strategies. *Journal of Consulting and Clinical Psychology, 54,* 802–808.

van Elderen, T. M. T., Maes, S., Seegers, G., & Kragten, H. (1994). Effects of a post-hospitalization group health education programme for patients with coronary heart disease. *Psychology and Health, 9,* 317–330.

Welch-McCaffrey, D., Hoffman, B., Leigh, S. A., Loescher, L. J., & Meyskens, F. L. (1989). Surviving adult cancer: Part 2. Psychosocial implication. *Annals of Internal Medicine, 111,* 517–524.

Whiteside, T. L., Bryant, J., Day, R., & Herberman, R. B. (1990). Natural killer cytotoxicity in the diagnosis of immune dysfunction: Criteria for a reproducible assay. *Journal of Clinical Laboratory Analysis, 4,* 102–114.

Wills, T. A. (1981). Downward comparison principles in social psychology. *Psychological Bulletin, 90,* 245–271.

Wood, P. E., Milligan, M., Christ, D., & Liff, D. (1978). Group counseling for cancer patients in a community hospital. *Psychosomatics, 19,* 555–561.

Wortman, C. B. (1984). Social support and the cancer patient. *Cancer, 53* (Suppl. 10), 2339–2360.

6

Applying Group Processes to International Conflict Analysis and Resolution

Ronald J. Fisher

For over 30 years, applied social psychologists and other scholar–practitioners have been developing small group methods for the analysis and resolution of violent and protracted international conflict. These applications, termed *interactive conflict resolution* by Fisher (1993, 1997), directly engage informal representatives of the conflicting parties in intensive discussions facilitated by an impartial team of third-party consultants. The objectives include individual attitude change, including realizations about the other party and the nature of the conflict, and the creation of ideas and policies for deescalation and peace building to be transferred back to the relationship between the antagonists. The third party's role is to improve communication, facilitate dialogue, induce analysis of the conflict, and guide the participants through a process of joint problem solving. One social-psychological premise is that face-to-face interaction is necessary to address relationship issues that hinder deescalation and to develop mutually acceptable and sustainable solutions. A typical workshop lasts 4 or 5 days and involves approximately 15 participants, five from each of the two conflicting parties and the third party. Thus, the approach is clearly a small group method both in size and in the nature of the interaction.

Although these innovative applications fall within the domain of small group theory and research, little has been written about them from that perspective. This may be because few of the developers were trained in group dynamics, or perhaps because the larger context of the work has been the interdisciplinary field of conflict resolution, rather than one of the social sciences that studies small groups. Nevertheless, descriptions have been provided on the nature of the interaction, the role of the third party, the developments within workshops over time, the processes of joint

Ronald J. Fisher • Department of Psychology, University of Saskatchewan, Saskatoon, Canada, S7N 5A5.

Theory and Research on Small Groups, edited by R. Scott Tindale et al. Plenum Press, New York, 1998.

problem solving, and the changes that are induced in the participants. Thus, the information exists for constructing an analysis using concepts and models drawn from theory and research on small groups, with the intention of improving the understanding of the method and its usefulness.

This chapter will first provide a brief overview of this field of application, identifying its various forms, common functions, and typical outcomes. Concepts from group development will then be used to understand the typical phases of workshops and the role transitions experienced by participants. The role of the third party will be analyzed as a form of facilitative leadership essential to the successful operationalization of the method. The changes that participants generally undergo will be described as part of a reeducative experience that has parallels in other forms of group work. The group problem-solving sequence will then be used as the basis for understanding the critical process of joint problem solving. Finally, the need for increased assessment of the effects, both on the participants and on the wider conflict between the parties, will be addressed.

Interactive Conflict Resolution: Forms, Functions and Outcomes

The application of small group discussion methods to international conflict started with the efforts of international relations scholar John Burton and his colleagues at University College London in the mid-1960s. Searching for an alternative to traditional analyses and interventions, the Burton group invited informal, high-level representatives from three East Asian countries (Malaysia, Indonesia, and Singapore), which were engaged in serious hostilities, to a series of discussions in London. The resulting analysis, facilitated by an interdisciplinary team of scholars, produced a framework of understanding that served as the basis for the Manila peace accord between Malaysia and Indonesia. Burton's group then turned its attention to the escalating intercommunal conflict on the Eastern Mediterranean island of Cyprus, holding a 5-day workshop with high-level representatives from the Greek and Turkish Cypriot communities. One result was a return to UN-brokered negotiations, which had previously broken off. Burton (1969) described these interventions as a new methodology of "controlled communication" in which the third-party panel facilitates changes in perception, more accurate understanding, and an analysis of the conflict using concepts from social science. According to Burton, these experiences can pave the way for successful negotiations and for the development of functional cooperation between previously conflicting parties.

Burton subsequently developed the "problem-solving" approach, articulating a set of rules for its implementation (1987) and a description of its role in conflict prevention and resolution in the context of political decision making (1990). He collaborated with political scientist Edward Azar in applications to the Sri Lankan, Falklands/Malvinas, and Lebanese conflicts. For his part, Azar (1990) developed a conceptual model for "problem-solving forums," describing the selection of participants, the interactive process, and the role of the facilitators.

Social psychologist Herbert Kelman was a member of the third party in Burton's Cyprus workshop and developed his model of the "problem-solving workshop" in collaboration with Stephen Cohen, initially focusing on the Arab–Israeli conflict (Kelman & Cohen, 1976, 1986). Kelman and other colleagues continued the development of "interactive problem solving" with a series of applications to the Israeli–Palestinian conflict, culminating in a continuing workshop and ongoing working group alongside formal negotiations (Kelman, 1986, 1992, 1995a; Rouhana & Kelman, 1994). It is very likely that Kelman's workshops over a 25-year period, with increasingly influential Israelis and Palestinians, have had a positive influence on the political dialogue and the peace negotiations between these longtime enemies.

Social psychologist Leonard Doob initiated the application of human relations training to destructive international conflicts. In the mid-1960s, Doob and his multidisciplinary team organized and facilitated a 2-week "workshop" focusing on the border conflicts in the Horn of Africa among Ethiopia, Somalia, and Kenya. This application of sensitivitiy training, supplemented by other techniques, resulted in increased understanding and improved attitudes, but the total group was not able to reach agreement on an overall solution (Doob, 1970). Doob later arranged a 10-day workshop on the conflict in Northern Ireland, using the Tavistock training method and other techniques, with a mixed group of grassroots leaders from the Catholic and Protestant communities of Belfast. Besides the training designed to increase understanding about group and intergroup processes, the participants worked on plans for back-home applications. Unfortunately, the experience had negative effects for some and resulted in highly mixed evaluations (Alevy et al., 1974; Boehringer, Zeruolis, Bayley, & Boehringer, 1974; Doob & Foltz, 1973, 1974). Doob also organized a series of discussions that brought together influential Turkish and Greek Cypriots, but these were terminated without any apparent positive outcomes (Doob, 1987).

Based on the work of Burton, Doob, and others, I developed a general model of "third-party consultation" to emphasize the essential role of the scholar–practitioners who organize and facilitate the problem-solving sessions (Fisher, 1972, 1976). The model specified the impartial and skilled identity of the third party, the nature of the consulting relationship, the neutral and informal small-group setting, the core functions and tactics of the method, and the desired outcomes in terms of improved attitudes, a more cooperative relationship, and, ultimately, resolution of the conflict. The model served as a useful guide for practice in applications to the India–Pakistan conflict (Fisher, 1980) and, more recently, the Cyprus conflict (Fisher, 1992, 1994).

During the early 1980s, a group affiliated with the American Psychiatric Association organized a series of six meetings in "unofficial diplomacy" that focused on the Middle East conflict (Julius, 1991; Volkan, Montville, & Julius, 1991). The participants were influential Egyptian, Israeli, (and later) Palestinian academics, former politicians, diplomats, and so on, who came together to increase their mutual understanding of psychological issues in the conflict. This psychodynamic approach emphasizes the role of victimization and dehumanization, and the necessity of mourning losses and seeking forgiveness. Volkan and his colleagues are now engaged in an ongoing project centered on the relationships between Russia and the Baltic Republics, which focuses in part on the intergroup relations among ethnic Russians in each of the states (Volkan & Harris, 1992, 1993).

Harold Saunders, a former U.S. government official, has developed the approach of a "public peace process," first within the context of the Dartmouth Conference (Chufrin & Saunders, 1993; Saunders, 1991), and more recently with the support of the Kettering Foundation (Saunders & Slim, 1994). During the 1980s, the regional conflict task force of the Dartmouth Conference met on more than 20 occasions to analyze U.S. and U.S.S.R. interactions, including the underlying perceptions and motivations that characterized their relationship. The resulting insights and policy options were constantly fed back to decision makers and may have had some influence in the ending of the Cold War. Saunders and colleague Randa Slim have articulated a five-stage process of unofficial dialogue and are applying it to the conflict in the former Soviet republic of Tajikistan (Saunders & Slim, 1994; Slim, 1995).

This overview demonstrates the vitality and variety of this form of small group practice, but does not capture the diversity and growing sophistication of the field. Reviews are provided by Fisher (1972, 1983, 1986, 1990) and detail on particular approaches is available in Azar (1990), Burton and Dukes (1990), Kelman and Cohen (1986), Mitchell (1981), Volkan et al. (1991), and Saunders and Slim (1994). I have introduced the term *interactive conflict resolution* (ICR) to cover all approaches that involve small group, problem-solving discussions between unofficial representatives of parties (identity groups or states) engaged in destructive conflict, which are organized and facilitated by an impartial third party of social scientist–practitioners (Fisher, 1993). A recent review of ICR provides a detailed account and assessment of over 75 applications and discusses the issues that need to be addressed for the field to advance (Fisher, 1997).

One important agenda is to further elucidate ICR as a form of small group practice, and this requires theoretical understanding of the structures and processes of this form of interaction. It also necessitates an appreciation of the third party's role as a group leader who requires both the conceptual knowledge and the behavioral compe-tence to facilitate productive confrontation between representatives from antagonistic parties. This role fuses group facilitation with conflict management in a uniquely challenging manner, and it is incumbent upon those who enact it to be equal to the task in both behavioral and ethical terms.

Group Development: One Out of Three

The systematic study of group processes in social psychology was initiated by Lewin and his colleagues in the late 1930s. One of the pioneers in this enterprise, Dorwin Cartwright (1951), defined the field as follows:

> "Group dynamics" refers to the forces operating in groups. The investigation of group dynamics, then, consists of a study of these forces: what gives rise to them,

what conditions modify them, what consequences they have, etc. The practical application of group dynamics (or the technology of group dynamics) consists of utilization of knowledge about these forces for the achievement of some purpose. (pp.382–383)

Anthony de Reuck, a member of the Burton group, was familiar with group dynamics and indicates that the decision to limit the size of the first workshops was based on previous experience with small problem-solving groups. In particular, he notes that "it was the intention to exploit previous experience of unstructured meetings and to employ the insights of small group theory in conducting the proceedings" (de Reuck, 1974, p.66).

de Reuck (1974, 1983) observes that the workshop really begins as three groups, that is, the two parties and the third-party panel. The first duty of the antagonistic groups is to present and argue for their side of the conflict. However, as a deeper analysis of the situation occurs through the interventions of the third party, each party comes to cooperate with and thereby form a temporary group with the panel members. Eventually, as the interaction moves toward problem solution, each party comes to consider the other as legitimate members of the same task group. As de Reuck points out: "In short, the parties begin by co-operating with the panel in analysis and end by co-operating together in resolving their conflict" (1983, p.58).

A similar point is advanced by Rouhana (1995), based on his collaboration with Kelman on a continuing Israeli–Palestinian workshop. He stresses that workshop dynamics are different from those of a natural group process, because the two teams of participants compose two distinct and cohesive groups who are in conflict. These differences are not erased, even though the two teams eventually come to cooperate in the workshop. Nonetheless, Rohana (1995) indicates that the third-party team must be sensitive to the natural development of group processes and take this into account in making its interventions.

Concurrent with the development of one group out of three is a role transition experienced by the participants from that of combatant to conflict analyst and finally to cooperative representative (de Reuck, 1974). Initially, the delegates feel bound by their role as representatives to defend their peoples' or countries' positions and to attack those of the adversary. However, as they join with the third party in the analysis of the conflict, they take on a role akin to that of a scholar or researcher, working to understand the situation in a detached fashion using relevant concepts and theories. On the basis of increased mutual understanding, the parties are then able to move into a cooperative role in which they engage in joint problem solving. A similar role transition is noted by Christopher Mitchell, another member of the Burton team. In discussing the Cyprus workshop, Mitchell (1981) describes how the participants begin by making the case for their respective sides, but as the discussion moves into the analytical phase, their role changes to that of "honorary academic" working alongside the third-party panel to apply general principles to their specific conflict.

The process of role transition as part of group socialization has been a focus of theoretical development by Moreland and Levine (1984). They posit that individuals go through a series of role transitions (entry, acceptance, divergence, exit) that correspond to different phases of group membership and levels of commitment. The socialization phase between entry and acceptance is the critical period in ICR workshops, during which time the participant is expected to accept the more detached role of academic analyst. At this point, the individual's commitment to the group is heightened, and a shared sense of purpose develops.

These comments point to the importance of group development in ICR workshops. In their review of small group research, Levine and Moreland (1990) indicate that the goal of most work on group development is to understand how and why groups change over time. Unfortunately, only a minority of studies offer quantitative data as opposed to qualitative analyses, and even these are limited, because most theories of group development are difficult to confirm or disconfirm. Moreland and Levine (1988) point out that although a great deal of research on group development took place in the 1950–1980 period, most of it was limited to observational field studies of therapy, training, or other self-analytic groups. Thus, most theories of group development are primarily descriptive, rather than explanatory, and are founded on limited empirical evidence.

One theory that stands out for being based on a wide range of studies, and for including natural and laboratory groups as well as training and therapy groups, is that of Tuckman (Moreland & Levine, 1988). In his initial study, Tuckman (1965) reviewed 55 studies of group development and induced a general model specifying typical changes over time in both task activities and interpersonal relations. Similarities in developmental trends in these two domains allowed Tuckman to posit an overall model consisting of four stages: forming, storming, norming, and performing. A later review by Tuckman and Jensen (1977) covered 22 additional studies, and while confirming the initial model also resulted in the addition of a fifth and final stage—adjourning. Tuckman's revised model will be used here to organize and describe the developmental sequence that appears to occur in ICR workshops. General observations that illustrate behaviors at each stage will be drawn from the author's experience in facilitating workshops on the Cyprus conflict (Fisher, 1991, 1992, 1994), although comments from other third-party consultants will also be included.

In the first stage of *forming*, participants are dependent upon the panel for information and direction, and are looking for orientation toward the task of the workshop. At this time it is common for the third party to provide statements on the objectives and activities of the workshop, and to provide guidelines that will alleviate some of the concerns and anxiety of the participants. For example, typical ground rules include respecting the confidentiality of the proceedings, particularly not attributing any statements to individuals following the workshop, and taking an analytical approach to the discussions rather than an adversarial or argumentative one (Fisher, 1992; Kelman & Cohen, 1986). Time is usually devoted to individual statements by the participants on their background and experience, often in relation to the conflict.

During or following the introductions, and regardless of the agenda or the ground rule calling for analysis, the workshop typically moves quickly into the second stage of *storming*. In Tuckman's model, this involves differences and arguments among group members, criticism of the leader, and emotional resistances to working together on the task. In an ICR workshop, this conflict stage can be considerably more intense, because the two parties bring a reservoir of grievances, blame, and hostility to the table. At the same time, part of the role of the third party is to constrain and channel this negative energy so that the group climate is not unduly damaged, and so that the participants can move on to the more important analytic and creative tasks. As de Reuck (1974) and others note, one of the first obligations of the representatives is to make the case for their peoples' concerns and positions, and in doing so to attack the other side. Although the panel needs to listen carefully and respectfully to these statements, in order to release the hostility behind them and to better understand the conflict, an attack–counterattack mode must not be allowed to dominate the workshop. In this stage, the panel can also expect to be questioned or criticized, for example, on an intervention, or even the workshop design or agenda, as participants hold the leadership responsible for some of the distress they are experiencing. Volkan (1991), for example, describes in psychoanalytic terms the phenomenon of a "mini-conflict" that brings forward a relatively trivial problem that the third party is challenged to resolve in order to have leadership bestowed upon it by the participants. Adversarial interchanges and challenges to the third party in the storming stage need to be handled effectively in order for the group to move forward in its development and on its agenda.

In the third stage of *norming*, a degree of cohesion develops, participants exchange their comments openly, and there is a shared sense of the expectations and standards of appropriate behavior. In the ICR workshop, this stage is signaled by an acceptance of the analytic norms, proffered by the third party, which changes the discussion into one akin to an academic seminar. Ideas and interpretations are tossed about freely, and the participants develop a more objective stance in which they are able to see the conflict more as a totality of related behavior. Kelman and Cohen (1986) speak of the tone of the workshop as involving an element of seriousness, due to the policy relevance of the discussions, combined with a playfulness to entertain novel ideas and scenarios in an off-the-record, low-risk environment.

The analytic and respectful atmosphere then encourages the group to move into the next stage of *performing*, which in Tuckman's model is signaled by the enactment of interrelated functional roles and the emergence of solutions. At this point in the ICR workshop, the participants take more responsibility for jointly creating alternative directions and activities that would engender deescalation and ultimately resolution. The third-party consultants can offer various social technologies, such as force field analysis or project planning formats, to assist the creative process, but at this stage, it is essential that the two parties act as one. Only the representatives from a people or a country know their situation intimately enough to predict resistances to peace building and how to overcome them successfully. Thus, a shared sensitivity and a pooling of resources is required for joint problem solving, and this will only occur if the performing stage is attained in a genuine fashion.

Finally, in the stage of *adjourning*, the issue of group termination, including concerns about separation, is addressed. In ICR workshops, the third party encourages closure through such activities as planning back-home activities and sharing evaluations of the experience. Participants often make arrangements for continuing communication or working together in some appropriate fashion. In cases where a series of workshops is held, these connections can develop into an interparty coalition working for peace across conflict lines (Kelman, 1992).

Facilitative Leadership: The Role of the Third Party

Leadership is generally acknowledged as an essential element of group functioning, and most definitions emphasize a process of social influence that is directed toward achievement of the group's goals (Shaw, 1981). In ICR workshops, the individuals who enact the third-party role engage in a variety of behaviors designed to move the sessions toward positive outcomes. The ICR leadership role is a unique hybrid of at least three subroles: (1) a discussion chair who moderates and coordinates the flow of the interaction, (2) an expert analyst who provides conceptual input relevant to the conflict under discussion, and (3) a human relations trainer who works to improve communication and manage conflict among participants, and to focus attention on group and intergroup process occurring in the workshop.

In the first major review of work in this area, Fisher (1972) highlighted the essential role of the third-party consultant as being primarily facilitative and diagnostic. The third party serves as the catalyst for the processes of mutual exploration and creative problem solving, and as the analyst who applies social science theory in the ongoing discussions. The role is further defined by the core strategies or functions of the third party: inducing positive motivation, improving communication, diagnosing the conflict, and regulating the interaction. In a similar vein, Burton (1987) notes that the role of the third-party panel is to facilitate analysis and then to help deduce outcomes based on that analysis.

In order to enact the role, the third party requires a large repository of knowledge and skills, both individually and collectively as a team. These include knowledge of generic conflict processes, moderate knowledge about the conflict in question, understanding of group processes, and the professional and personal expertise to intervene effectively in the ongoing discussion in a variety of ways (Fisher, 1972). Kelman and Cohen (1986) maintain that although the workshop discussion is relatively unstructured, it needs to be guided by social scientists who possess knowledge of both conflict theory and group processes. In addition, the leaders must be capable of carrying out three different kinds of intervention to promote the analytical norms and maintain productive discussions: (1) theoretical inputs to provide participants with conceptual tools to understand and distance themselves from their conflict, (2) content observations to interpret the discussion in ways that increase participant understanding and bring about new realizations, and (3) process observations that suggest how interaction in the workshop parallels the ongoing relations between the groups (Kelman & Cohen, 1986). Given the scope of the third-party role, it is not surprising that most ICR theorists propose that the panel be composed of an interdisciplinary team of consultants (e.g., Azar, 1990; Burton, 1987).

The third-party role can thus be seen as a form of facilitative leadership that has connections to theory and research on small group processes. The third party must provide both task and socioemotional leadership to the group, where in the first instance, participants will look to the panel to both implement the agenda and provide support to the members. The third party needs to enact a variety of both task (e.g., giving information, seeking opinions) and maintenance functions (e.g., encouraging others, opening up communication) in the group. At the same time, the third party must deal with any disruptive or aggressive behavior that would undermine the analytical, respectful norms of the interaction. The panel members must therefore collectively bring a wide repertoire of interpersonal and group skills to bear on the discourse.

The more demanding elements of the third-party role show resemblance to the role of trainer in human relations workshops, such as sensitivity training and encounter groups. In this context, the trainer is a facilitator who helps the group to learn about interpersonal and group processes by analyzing its ongoing interaction (Fisher, 1982). More specifically, the trainer helps set the group norms, models appropriate values and behavior, facilitates communication and conflict resolution among members, and diagnoses group functioning using relevant concepts and theories. In ICR workshops, the third party carries out similar functions in a manner uniquely tailored to a setting involving members of two conflicting collectivities. Thus, process interventions are not only directed toward the group level but to the intergroup level, wherein the third party uses interactions within the workshop as the primary data for analyzing the nature of the intergroup relationship and the conflict (Kelman & Cohen, 1986).

Furthermore, the third party may propose "structured exercises" (Kelman & Cohen, 1986) or "procedures" (Fisher, 1972) that engage the participants in novel forms of interaction that might illuminate some aspect of the conflict. For example, the two groups of representatives might meet separately to develop their image of the opposing group or a list of possible steps toward reconciliation, which are then shared and discussed. Exercises such as these were initially developed by Blake, Shepard, and Mouton (1964) in their work on intergroup conflict in industrial settings and are now part and parcel of the practice field of organization development (e.g., French & Bell, 1995). The use of such procedures again adds to the complex demands of the third party's role as a facilitative leader.

ICR as a Reeducative Experience

It is important to acknowledge and articulate the ways in which ICR workshops are designed to change participants' attitudes and behavior. The method is essentially a reeducative experience in which group processes play a central role. In considering applications of group dynamics, Cartwright (1951) described three ways that groups can enter into the process of change. As a *medium of change*, the group is a source of influence on members; as a *target of change*, the group is the focus of influence attempts (e.g., on its norms, leadership style, etc.) designed to ultimately affect members; and as an *agent of change*, organized efforts by the group bring about modifications in the wider social environment. ICR primarily involves the group as a medium of change, and there is considerable evidence that such group methods are capable of producing behavior change in individuals (e.g., Lieberman, 1976). However, from the third party's point of view, the ICR group is also a target of change, in that the proffered norms, strategies, and orientations of conflict resolution will be adopted by the group and thereby influence all members. In addition, there is typically an intention that the group will become an agent of change, engaging in some form of policy influence or peace building following the workshop.

Kelman (1995b) has recently summarized his thinking on the role of group processes in conflict resolution and the ways in which the workshop group is a vehicle for change. First, the group serves as a microcosm of the larger system, in that dynamics of the conflict are played out in workshop interactions. Elements of the relationship between the parties, such as mutual distrust, majority–minority status, and power differences, are often reflected in participants' behavior and are thus available for observation and analysis initiated by the third party. The resulting insights that participants gain into the dynamics of the conflict are comparable to the corrective emotional experiences of group psychotherapy, but the level of intervention and analysis is at the intergroup rather than the interpersonal. Second, the workshop group serves as a laboratory in which the interaction yields products (new ideas, differentiated images, mutual reassurances) that can be fed into the political discourse and policy making in the two societies. Third, the group provides a setting for direct interaction where representatives of the parties can engage in behaviors that are central to conflict resolution, such as taking the other's perspective or engaging in joint problem solving. The workshop is thereby a unique forum supporting a special kind of interaction in which opposing representatives need to address and listen to each other and work cooperatively in confronting their conflict. Fourth, the group becomes an uneasy coalition across the conflict line, which requires continuous, mutual testing and the maintenance of a working trust. Finally, the workshop group promotes and models a new relationship between the parties that is based on equality and reciprocity, and that embodies empathy, mutual responsiveness, and trust.

As a reeducative experience, ICR can be placed in the context of general strategies for producing change in human social systems articulated by Chin and Benne (1985). These forms of *planned change* involve the conscious and systematic applications of social scientific knowledge for the modification of social institutions and the solution of social problems (Bennis, Benne, & Chin, 1985). The *empirical–rational strategy* assumes that people will act in their own best interests when a change agent provides them with valid knowledge about social problems and reasonable proposals for change. The *power–coercive strategy* assumes that people change through the application of social influence, that is, economic, moral, or political rewards and punishments, administered by a powerful agent. The *normative–reeducative strategy* assumes that people are committed to social norms and will only change their behavior if changes occur in their normative orientations and related attitudes, values, skills, and important relationships. Although this strategy also requires a knowledge base and an intellectual rationale, the distinguishing feature is the conscious, planned intervention of a change agent that involves the client system in a participative analysis of problems and a collaborative search for solutions.

The basic process of reeducation was articulated by Kurt Lewin in the 1940s to describe how individuals can change their patterns of thinking, valuing, and behaving in directions that are more socially valid, appropriate, and satisfying. An initial set of principles developed by Lewin and Grabbe (1945) have been assessed by Benne (1976) in the light of 30 years of experience in applied social science and planned change. These principles affirm that reeducative experiences must affect cognitive structures, values (including attractions and aversions to other groups), and behavioral skills, that is, the whole person, in order to be effective. Lewin considered reeducation as essentially a change in culture that needs to affect both individuals and the social system. For this to happen, the norms of the reeducative experience must include an openness to communication, a willingness to share information and perceptions for analysis, and a commitment to face problems and contribute to their solution (Benne, 1976). These norms underlie the functioning of the ICR workshop as a reeducative experience. However, as Bargal (1992) points out, Lewin did not articulate in a detailed manner how the structure and processes of intergroup workshops should be operationalized to foster a reeducative experience. Based on a major, long-term project providing conflict management workshops to mixed groups of Palestinian and Jewish youth in Israel, Bargal (1992) outlines the tasks required in the planning, implementation, and assessment of this form of ICR interventions.

As a reeducative experience, ICR shares with other group methods a two-phase process of behavior change, first identified by Kelman (1952) as involving a practice phase and an action phase. In the first instance, the existing dysfunctional behavior and problem analysis are challenged and hopefully changed, while in the second, the new behavior is tested against social reality and integrated with other elements to help resolve the problem. This distinction leads to the question of how individual changes in the group setting are transferred to the social environment of the participants. In an early analysis of problem-solving workshops, Kelman (1972) noted that this problem of transfer actually involves two questions: (1) Will individual changes in attitudes and approach in the workshop be maintained when the participant returns to the home environment, and (2) how likely is it that these changes can be brought to bear on the policy-making process? The field of ICR is still asking these same questions today, and thus the issue of assessing the effects of these reeducative experiences remains paramount.

Group and Intergroup Problem Solving

Problem-solving groups designed to address a difficulty or make a decision are a common phenomenon, at least in Western society (Shaw, 1981). Problem solving is generally seen as involving a series of stages, from identifying and diagnosing the problem, through the creation of and selection from alternative solutions, to the implementation and evaluation of the chosen solution. Basically, problem solving is the scientific method applied to practical affairs (Morris & Sashkin, 1976). The systematic study of group problem solving has identified a variety of factors that facilitate the process and some that impede it (Maier, 1970; Shaw, 1981). Although it is generally acknowledged that groups possess advantages over individuals in problem solving, it is also important to note that groups are susceptible to some counterproductive processes, such as groupthink, wherein blind consensus seeking drives ineffective decision making (Janis, 1982). Thus, successful problem solving requires a combination of both task and social behaviors in order to use the group's human resources effectively toward the achievement of shared objectives (Morris & Sashkin, 1976).

ICR workshops clearly involve problem solving, although most sessions are not intended to result in the solution of the conflict outright. More typically, workshops are designed to yield products, such as principles for resolution or project plans for peace-building activities, which may contribute to deescalation and ultimate resolution. Thus, the third party works hard to form the group into a adequately cohesive problem-solving unit and to implement the problem-solving sequence in some fashion. Two elements that are critical to the process are the engendering of creativity and a norm to move forward by consensus as the modal form of decision making (Hare, 1982).

A pilot workshop on the India–Pakistan conflict organized by Fisher (1980) provides some indication of the problem-solving nature of ICR. Because the participants were graduate students and research associates living in Canada, the political sensitivity of the meeting was very low in comparison to most ICR work, and thus more intrusive research procedures were deemed appropriate. All workshop sessions, including single meetings with each of the groups and joint meetings with the third-party team, were tape recorded and subjected to Interaction Process Analysis, a scheme developed by Bales (1950) to code behaviors occurring in small groups. The analysis of the joint meetings yielded percentages on the behavioral categories that were very similar to the comparative percentages found in other types of problem-solving sessions. In 11 of 12 categories, the coded percentages were within the limits suggested by Bales as indicative of problem-solving activities. The one deviant category, "shows tension release," may have been attenuated by the relatively high degree of structure provided by the third-party procedures.

A unique aspect of ICR workshops is that they involve *intergroup problem solving* in which representatives of two conflicting parties form a problem-solving team to address their common difficulty. The genesis of intergroup problem solving lies in the fields of social and organizational psychology, led by the groundbreaking work of Blake and Mouton (1961) following on the intergroup conflict research of Sherif and his colleagues (Sherif & Sherif, 1953; Sherif, Harvey, White, Hood, & Sherif, 1961). Blake and Mouton first demonstrated the destructive consequences of intergroup competition and conflict, in contrast to the benefits of intergroup cooperation, during training workshops for organizational managers. As professional practitioners, they then developed a social technology of intergroup problem solving, which they applied in a variety of organizational settings and relationships, including labor and management, headquarters and field, and new and old organizations in a merger (Blake et al., 1964). Interventions that they pioneered to turn dysfunctional intergroup relationships into productive ones are now part of the practice field of organization development (Blake & Mouton, 1984; Burke, 1974; French & Bell, 1995).

The pioneers of ICR, such as Burton, Doob, and Kelman, were likely aware of these developments in organizational psychology, although it is unclear how much it directly affected their thinking. Nonetheless, intergroup problem solving has come to be at the core of most ICR interventions in one fashion or another. As noted earlier, the development of one cohesive group out of three and the role transition from adversary to cooperator are prerequisites to this. Beyond that, intergroup problem solving requires that the opposing representatives, with the facilitation of the third party, come to think and act together at every stage of the process. What this means is that there must be problem definition by consensus, problem diagnosis from two perspectives, the creation of alternatives with reciprocal sensitivity to each side's concerns and constraints, the evaluation and selection of alternatives with awareness of the pros and cons as seen by each side, and implementation and evaluation with mutual support and feedback. In other words, the two sides must come to work together with a great deal of empathy and willingness to incorporate each other's reality.

The mutuality of the joint problem-solving process is shown clearly in the recent work of Harold Saunders and his colleagues, initially identified as "public, intercommunal problem solving," and more recently as "dialogue to change conflictual relationships" (Saunders, 1992; Saunders & Slim, 1994). Saunders's model was first applied to U.S.–Soviet relations within the context of the Dartmouth Conference (Chufrin & Saunders, 1993) and is now being used to assist in addressing the Tajikistan conflict (Saunders & Slim, 1994; Slim, 1995). The model consists of five developmental stages, which, similar to the problem-solving sequence, are not fixed in stone; that is, different groups will move at different rates and may move back and forth if necessary, for example, to complete a deeper analysis of a core issue or to look again for an alternative solution that is acceptable to both sides. The first stage of *deciding to engage* essentially involves a commitment to explore joint problem solving, both by the representatives and the official leadership of the parties. The second stage of *mapping the relationship together* requires an analytical approach in which the participants identify the underlying interests and difficulties that exist. The third stage of *probing the dynamics of the relationship* involves listening with greater sensitivity to the other's hopes and fears so as to understand how relations evolve over time. The fourth stage, *experiencing the relationship by thinking together*, engages the participants in jointly building scenarios on how to deal with a specific difficulty. The fifth and final stage of *acting together* involves the participants in implementing the scenarios in ways that influence the conflictual relationship. In a concrete fashion, Saunders's model represents intergroup problem solving realistically translated into the domain of unofficial diplomacy.

In a complementary fashion to Saunders's model, Rouhana (1995) has articulated a series of four phases that capture the dynamics of joint thinking as represented in a continuing Israeli–Palestinian workshop (Rouhana & Kelman, 1994). Although the third party steers the participants through the phases, the workshop's readiness to move forward is determined by the natural development of the group. The first phase involves movement from the unilateral explication of collective concerns and needs by each side to the comprehension of the concerns of both sides. This development of mutual, realistic empathy is a prerequisite to the second phase, wherein each side now explores the other's willingness to respond to its concerns. Toward the end of this phase, the two teams, along with the third party, begin to develop a sense of common membership in the workshop group. This working relationship allows for the shift to phase three—joint thinking sensitive to both sets of needs that creates ideas, options, and directions acceptable to both parties. The final phase involves working together to disseminate and implement the new ideas—the ultimate product of intergroup problem solving.

Another example of using the problem-solving process in ICR workshops comes from the author's work on the protracted intercommunal conflict on the Eastern Mediterranean island of Cyprus (Fisher, 1992, 1994). A conflict-analysis workshop organized in 1991 brought together influential, informal representatives of the Greek Cypriot and Turkish Cypriot communities for 4 days of intense dialogue at a neutral location near London, England. The problem-solving sequence was initiated through an identification of the major issues in the conflict as perceived by the participants. Deeper analysis was encouraged by looking at the fundamental fears and basic needs of the two sides. Before creating alternatives, the workshop discussed the acknowledgments and assurances that each side needed from the other and also created a future vision in terms of the desired relationship that the two communities wanted. This laid the groundwork and provided a context for discussing potential peace-building activities at the intercommunal level. A number of possible projects in social research, business, culture, and education were discussed, with the third party advising on how intergroup collaboration could deal with the numerous constraints and resistances that would be encountered. Activities implemented in whole or in part as a result of the workshop included a series of cross-line meetings by business leaders, an intercommunal steering committee to plan bicommunal activities, and an annual joint exhibit by Turkish Cypriot and Greek Cypriot artists. In addition, the outcomes influenced the decision to focus the next workshop on the field of education.

Two further workshops were held in 1993 on the island, highlighting the manner in which the education systems of the two communities work to maintain the conflict rather than contributing to deescalation and resolution (Fisher, 1994). Participants were influential educationalists from a variety of settings and roles in the two communities who were generally committed to peace building. The problem-solving stages were again initiated by considering the major issues and underlying fears and needs of the two communities. The third party then used the technique of force-field analysis to produce a deeper understanding of the dynamics pushing toward a renewed relationship and the resistances working against it, with particular reference to education. A further discussion detailed how the education systems of the two communities contributed to maintaining the conflict versus the strengths and re-sources they possessed to assist in rapprochement. Moving to the creation of alternatives, participants first identified potential areas for peace building, such as student and teacher exchanges and the development of new curriculum materials. Based on interests, participants then formed bicommunal subgroups to develop proposals for peace-building activities, which were reviewed by the full workshop.

Following the two workshops, two further meetings of participants with the now-functioning intercommunal steering committee were facilitated by the third party to form larger project teams to carry forward some combined project proposals. Unfortunately, a distorted and vicious attack on intercommunal activities occurred shortly after these meetings in the nationalist media on the Greek Cypriot side. Although this campaign was directed primarily at an American-based training program in conflict resolution, it had the effect of derailing the intercommunal educational initiatives. This outcome illustrates some of the difficulties in transferring the changes and products of ICR workshops to the wider relationship between the parties.

Evaluating ICR Interventions

One challenge for ICR is that it involves a complex reeducative process that includes both individual changes in the workshops and the transfer of these to a social system. Neither of these phases is being evaluated in an adequate manner in ongoing work, given that most assessments are simply descriptive accounts by the organizers. In a recent assessment of the field, I noted that almost 90% of published interventions were evaluated using only the case study method (Fisher, 1997, Chapter 9). Moreover, most of these are brief accounts provided by the intervenors and not the level of detailed case study that would allow for meta-analysis. A small number of interventions employ postassessments in the form of questionnaires or interviews, and a similarly small number use pre- and postmeasures. However, few of these are quantitative measures with demonstrated psychometric properties. In terms of experimental design, before and after studies are the highest level of control, with no control-group designs in evidence. As for longitudinal research on transfer effects, it is virtually nonexistent, although some third parties, such as Kelman and Rouhana, and Saunders and Slim, do attempt to track developments in the wider conflict that have potential connections to workshop outcomes. In summary, the state of research in the field is rudimentary.

There are many reasons why research on ICR is not well developed, all of which is related to understandable limitations or constraints. To start with, the third party typically feels a strong ethical obligation to protect the welfare of the participants and the integrity of the discussions, and gathering more systematic data might put either or both at risk. Participants are assured of anonymity and confidentiality, and the keeping of research records or follow-up studies that might identify them could be problematic. There is also a concern about the research agenda intruding on the practice work in important ways. For example, tape or video recording of workshop sessions would likely cause considerable anxiety for participants who fear being identified or quoted at some point, and might also constrain their behavior in the workshop. Also, on a practical note, most ICR practitioners have a difficult enough time acquiring funding for the intervention itself, let alone a research component. However, as funders become more attuned to the importance of evaluation, such activities may become expected, and support will be made available. On the wider question of assessing transfer effects, complex, multimethod, longitudinal, and therefore costly research designs would be required. In addition, some of the necessary information about linkages between products of workshops and policy making may be politically sensitive or secret, thus precluding access to some of the outcome data. Finally, a multitude of variables affect public opinion and policy making, and to document the actual effects of ICR interventions would be difficult if not close to impossible.

In spite of all these difficulties, it is incumbent upon ICR scholar–practitioners as social scientists and as professionals to move the research agenda forward. Not to do so is tantamount to assuming that the method has utility and deserves support when there is limited evidence to support these contentions. A number of avenues for progress are available (Fisher, 1997, Chapter 11). First, ICR specialists could develop more demonstration projects that are more educational than political in nature, and as such are more amenable to a research agenda. These interventions would involve lower level influentials or ordinary citizens who would not be as sensitive to the need for anonymity and confidentiality, and would thus be more amenable to taking part in a research component. Second, the fuller range of research methods in social science could be brought to bear. Methods for the evaluation of social programs have seen much development over the past 20 years and are generally applicable to ICR. The methodology of evaluability assessment could be used to clarify intervention goals, activities, and the logical linkages between these. Process evaluation would be valuable to document whether workshop activities are actually being implemented as planned, whether desired interactions such as dialogue are occurring, and whether important conditions such as improved communication or a working trust are actually established. Outcome evaluation methods are applicable both to the attitudinal and behavioral changes experienced by participants and the transfer effects on policy making. Through a delayed control-group design, demonstration projects could achieve a high level of rigor in assessing whether the intervention resulted in the predicted changes. When workshops of a more political nature are held with influentials, follow-up research using a variety of methods could be undertaken to track the transfer process and outcomes in the societal context. Finally, ICR intervenors should also consider developing a form of participatory action research for their assessments, so that participants become partners in developing research designs and methods that are culturally and politically sensitive to their societies.

Conclusion

Interactive conflict resolution is a diverse, vital, and growing field in the interdisciplinary domain of conflict analysis and resolution. It has the potential to be a powerful and useful small-group method that contributes to the management of international conflict. For this to happen, it is essential to understand and develop ICR as a form of small-group practice that is linked to theory and research on group dynamics.

In understanding ICR as a group method, a number of areas of theorizing are useful. Models of group development, particularly Tuckman's, appear to illuminate the method in useful ways if appropriate adaptations are made. The hybrid and challenging role of the third party, which is primarily facilitative, places considerable responsibility on those who enact it. There is therefore a need for greater emphasis on the professional development of third-party consultants, partly through some form of apprenticeship training. One unique element of this role is the capacity to understand and facilitate the process of intergroup problem solving, which is at the heart of ICR.

Research methods from small-group work have an especially important role to play in improving the documentation and evaluation of ICR interventions. Observational and questionnaire methods for tracking process variables and assessing outcomes are particularly relevant. Coding schemes that capture behavioral interaction, group development variables, and third-party interventions would be highly useful in process evaluations. Experiences in assessing individual changes from other areas of group work, such as sensitivity training or group psychotherapy, could shed light on design and measurement approaches that would be useful in outcome evaluations of ICR. Studies on the transfer effects of various types of training workshops to organizational and community settings would also have some utility. There is therefore much potential to be developed through the active collaboration of ICR practitioners and small-group researchers.

Acknowledgments

The author would like to thank Eaaron Henderson-King and Pamela Pomerance Steiner for helpful comments on a previous version of this chapter.

References

Alevy, D. I., Bunker, B., Doob, L. W., Foltz, W. J., French, N., Klein, E. B., & Miller, J. C. (1974). Rationale, research, and role relations in the Stirling Workshop. *Journal of Conflict Resolution, 18*, 276–284.

Azar, E. E. (1990). *The management of protracted social conflict*. Hampshire, UK: Dartmouth Publishing.

Bales, R. F. (1950). A set of categories for the analysis of small group interaction. *American Sociological Review, 15*, 257–263.

Bargal, D. (1992). Conflict management workshops for Arab Palestinian and Jewish youth—A framework for planning, intervention and evaluation. *Social Work with Groups, 15(1)*, 51–68.

Benne, K. D. (1976). The process of re-education: An assessment of Kurt Lewin's views. In W. G. Bennis, K. D. Benne, R. Chin, & K. E. Corey (Eds.), *The planning of change* (3rd ed., pp. 315–327). New York: Holt, Rinehart and Winston.

Bennis, W. G., Benne, K. D., & Chin, R. (1985). *The planning of change* (4th ed.). New York: Holt, Rinehart & Winston.

Blake, R. R., & Mouton, J. S. (1961). *Group dynamics: Key to decision-making*. Houston, TX: Gulf.

Blake, R. R., & Mouton, J. S. (1984). *Solving costly organizational conflicts*. San Francisco, CA: Jossey-Bass.

Blake, R. R., Shepard, H. A., & Mouton, J. S. (1964). *Managing intergroup conflict in industry.* Houston, TX: Gulf.

Boehringer, G. H., Zeruolis, V., Bayley, J., & Boehringer, K. (1974). Stirling: The destructive application of group techniques to a conflict. *Journal of Conflict Resolution, 18,* 257–275.

Burke, W. W. (1974). Managing conflict between groups. In J. D. Adams (Ed.), *Theory and method in organization development: An evolutionary process* (pp. 255–268). Arlington, VA: NTL Institute.

Burton, J. W. (1969). *Conflict and communication: The use of controlled communication in international relations.* London: Macmillan.

Burton, J. W. (1987). *Resolving deep-rooted conflict: A handbook.* Lanham, MD: University Press of America.

Burton, J. W. (1990). *Conflict: Resolution and provention.* New York: St. Martin's Press.

Burton, J. W., & Dukes, F. (1990). *Conflict: Practices in management, settlement and resolution.* New York: St. Martin's Press.

Cartwright, D. (1951). Achieving change in people: Some applications of group dynamics theory. *Human Relations, 4,* 381–392.

Chin, R., & Benne, K. D. (1985). General strategies for affecting changes in human systems. In W. G. Bennis, K. D. Benne & R. Chin (Eds.), *The planning of change* (4th ed., pp. 22–45). New York: Holt, Rinehart & Winston.

Chufrin, G. I., & Saunders, H. H. (1993). A public peace process. *Negotiation Journal, 9,* 155–177.

de Reuck, A. V. S. (1974). Controlled communication: Rationale and dynamics. *The Human Context, 6(1),* 64–80.

de Reuck, A. V. S. (1983). A theory of conflict resolution by problem solving. *Man, Environment, Space and Time, 3(1),* 53–69.

Doob, L. W. (Ed.). (1970). *Resolving conflict in Africa: The Fermeda workshop.* New Haven, CT: Yale University Press.

Doob, L. W. (1987). Adieu to private intervention in political conflicts? *International Journal of Group Tensions, 17,* 15–27.

Doob, L. W., & Foltz, W. J. (1973). The Belfast Workshop: An application of group techniques to a destructive conflict. *Journal of Conflict Resolution, 17,* 489–512.

Doob, L. W., & Foltz, W. J. (1974). The impact of a workshop upon grassroots leaders in Belfast. *Journal of Conflict Resolution, 18,* 237–256.

Fisher, R. J. (1972). Third party consultation: A method for the study and resolution of conflict. *Journal of Conflict Resolution, 16,* 67–94.

Fisher, R. J. (1976). Third party consultation: A skill for professional psychologists in community practice. *Professional Psychology, 7,* 344–351.

Fisher, R. J. (1980). A third party consultation workshop on the India–Pakistan conflict. *Journal of Social Psychology, 112,* 191–206.

Fisher, R. J. (1982). *Social psychology: An applied approach.* New York: St. Martin's Press.

Fisher, R. J. (1983). Third party consultation as a method of conflict resolution: A review of studies. *Journal of Conflict Resolution, 27,* 301–334.

Fisher, R. J. (1986). Third party consultation: A problem-solving approach for de-escalating international conflict. In J. P. Maas & R. A. C. Stewart (Eds.), *Toward a world of peace: People create alternatives* (pp. 18–32). Suva, Fiji: University of the South Pacific Press.

Fisher, R. J. (1990). *The social psychology of intergroup and international conflict resolution.* New York: Springer-Verlag.

Fisher, R. J. (1992). *Peacebuilding for Cyprus: Report on a conflict analysis workshop, June 1991.* Ottawa: Canadian Institute for International Peace and Security.

Fisher, R. J. (1993). Developing the field of interactive conflict resolution: Issues in training, funding and institutionalization. *Political Psychology, 14,* 123–138.

Fisher, R. J. (1994). *Education and peacebuilding in Cyprus: A report on two conflict analysis workshops.* Saskatoon, Canada: University of Saskatchewan.

Fisher, R. J. (1997). *Interactive conflict resolution.* Syracuse, NY: Syracuse University Press.

French, W. L., & Bell, C. H. (1995). *Organization development* (5th ed.). Englewood Cliffs, NJ: Prentice-Hall.

Hare, A. P. (1982). *Creativity in small groups*. Beverly Hills, CA: Sage.

Janis, I. L. (1982). *Groupthink* (2nd ed.). Boston: Houghton Mifflin.

Julius, D. A. (1991). The practice of track two diplomacy in the Arab–Israeli conferences. In V. D. Volkan, J. V. Montville, & D. A. Julius (Eds.), *The psychodynamics of international relationships: Volume II: Unofficial diplomacy at work* (pp. 193–205). Lexington, MA: Lexington Books.

Kelman, H. C. (1952). Two phases of behavior change. *Journal of Social Issues, 8(2)*, 81–88.

Kelman, H. C. (1972). The problem-solving workshop in conflict resolution. In R. L. Merritt (Ed.), *Communication in international politics* (pp. 168–204). Urbana: University of Illinois Press.

Kelman, H. C. (1986). Interactive problem solving: A social-psychological approach to conflict resolution. In W. Klassen (Ed.), *Dialogue toward interfaith understanding* (pp. 293–314). Jerusalem: Ecumenical Institute for Theological Research.

Kelman, H. C. (1992). Informal mediation by the scholar–practitioner. In J. Bercovitch & J. Rubin (Eds.), *Mediation in international relations: Multiple approaches to conflict management* (pp. 64–96). New York: St. Martin's Press.

Kelman, H. C. (1995a). Contributions of an unofficial conflict resolution effort to the Israeli–Palestinian breakthrough. *Negotiation Journal, 11*, 19–27.

Kelman, H. C. (1995b, August). Group processes in the resolution of international conflicts: Experiences from the Israeli–Palestinian case. Paper presented at the Annual Conference of the American Psychological Association, New York.

Kelman, H. C., & Cohen, S. P. (1976). The problem-solving workshop: A social-psychological contribution to the resolution of international conflict. *Journal of Peace Research, 13*, 79–90.

Kelman, H. C., & Cohen, S. P. (1986). Resolution of international conflict: An interactional approach. In S. Worchel & W. G. Austin (Eds.), *Psychology of intergroup relations* (2nd ed., pp. 323–342). Chicago: Nelson-Hall.

Levine, J. M., & Moreland, R. L. (1990). Progress in small group research. *Annual Review of Psychology, 41*, 585–634.

Lewin, K., & Grabbe, P. (1945). Conduct, knowledge and acceptance of new values. *Journal of Social Issues, 1(3)*, 53–63.

Lieberman, M. A. (1976). Change induction in small groups. *Annual Review of Psychology, 27*, 217–250.

Maier, N. R. F. (1970). *Problem solving and creativity in individuals and groups*. Belmont, CA: Brooks/Cole.

Mitchell, C. R. (1981). *Peacemaking and the consultant's role*. Westmead, UK: Gower.

Moreland, R. L., & Levine, J. M. (1984). Role transitions in small groups. In V. L. Allen & E. van de Vliert (Eds.), *Role transitions: Explorations and explanations* (pp. 181–195). New York: Plenum Press.

Moreland, R. L., & Levine, J. M. (1988). Group dynamics over time: Development and socialization in small groups. In J. E. McGrath (Ed.), *The social psychology of time: New perspectives* (pp. 151–181). Newbury Park, CA: Sage.

Morris, W. C., & Sashkin, M. (1976). *Organization behavior in action: Skill building experiences*. St. Paul, MN: West.

Rouhana, N. N. (1995). The dynamics of joint thinking between adversaries in international conflict: Phases of the continuing problem-solving workshop. *Political Psychology, 16*, 321–345.

Rouhana, N. N., & Kelman, H. C. (1994). Promoting joint thinking in international conflict: An Israeli–Palestinian continuing workshop. *Journal of Social Issues, 50(1)*, 157–178.

Saunders, H. H. (1991). Officials and citizens in international relationships: The Dartmouth conference. In V. D. Volkan, J. V. Montville, & D. A. Julius: (Eds.), *The psychodynamics of international relationships: Volume II: Unofficial diplomacy at work* (pp. 41–69). Lexington, MA: Lexington Books.

Saunders, H. H. (1992, July). *Thinking in stages: A framework for public intercommunal problem-solving from experience in the Dartmouth Conference Regional Conflicts Task Force, 1982–92.* Paper presented in a Symposium on Nonofficial Interaction Processes in the Resolution of International Conflict at the Annual Scientific Meeting of the International Society of Political Psychology, San Francisco.

Saunders, H. H., & Slim, R. (1994, July). *Dialogue to change conflictual relationships: The Tajikistani dialogue.* Paper presented at the Annual Scientific Meeting of the International Society of Political Psychology, Santiago, Spain.

Shaw, M. E. (1981). *Group dynamics: The psychology of small group behavior* (3rd ed.). New York: McGraw-Hill.

Sherif, M., Harvey, O. J., White, B. J., Hood, W. R., & Sherif, C. W. (1961). *Intergroup conflict and cooperation: The Robbers Cave experiment*. Norman: University of Oklahoma Book Exchange.

Sherif, M., & Sherif, C. W. (1953). *Groups in harmony and tension*. New York: Harper.

Slim, R. M. (1995, July). *A framework for managing conflict in divided societies: The Tajikistan case study*. Paper presented at the Annual Scientific Meeting of the International Society of Political Psychology, Washington, DC.

Tuckman, B. W. (1965). Developmental sequence in small groups. *Psychological Bulletin, 63*, 384–399.

Tuckman, B. W., & Jensen, M. A. C. (1977). Stages of small group development revisited. *Group and Organizational Studies, 2*, 419–427.

Volkan, V. D. (1991). Psychological processes in unofficial diplomacy meetings. In V. D. Volkan, J. V. Montville, & D. A. Julius (Eds.), *The psychodynamics of international relationships: Volume II: Unofficial diplomacy at work* (pp. 207–222). Lexington, MA: Lexington Books.

Volkan, V. D., & Harris, M. (1992). Negotiating a peaceful separation: A psychopolitical analysis of current relationships between Russia and the Baltic republics. *Mind and Human Interaction, 4*, 20–39.

Volkan, V. D., & Harris, M. (1993). Vaccinating the political process: A second psychopolitical analysis of relationships between Russia and the Baltic states. *Mind and Human Interaction, 4*, 169–190.

Volkan, V. D., Montville, J. V., & Julius, D. A. (Eds.). (1991). *The psychodynamics of international relationships: Volume II: Unofficial diplomacy at work*. Lexington, MA: Lexington Books.

7

Improving Group Performance
The Case of the Jury

Steven Penrod and Larry Heuer

> *No Man shall be taken and imprisoned or dis-seized of any free tenement or of his liberties or free custom or outlawed or exiled, or in any other way destroyed— except by the lawful judgment of his peers.*
>
> Magna Carta

The jury is among the most visible decision-making groups in American society. The decisions rendered by juries are in the public eye in a variety of ways: The group members are citizens fulfilling their public duties, the cases they decide are presented in a public arena, and their decisions are matters of public record. Perhaps because it operates so publicly, the jury has often been a target for both praise and criticism. Supporters praise the jury for individualizing the administration of justice, enhancing the legitimacy of government authority, serving as a catalyst to legal reforms, and serving as a balance to the special interests of judges (see, e.g., Hans & Vidmar, 1986; Landsman, 1993; Lempert, 1981; Rembar, 1980; Sperlich, 1982; Van Dyke, 1977).

Despite such praise, it is tempting to conclude that critiques of the jury have not reached so fevered a pitch as in recent years. Outpourings of criticism have followed, for example, the acquittals of police officers in the first trial of Rodney King's assailants, the acquittal of Lorena Bobbitt, the large damage award given to an elderly woman who spilled hot McDonald's coffee on herself, the hung jury in the first trial of the Menendez brothers, and the more recent acquittal of O. J. Simpson. However, as Landsman (1993) documents, attacks on the jury have been popular since the turn of the century, and it is not difficult to find pungent characterizations of the jury by

Steven Penrod • Law/Psychology Program, University of Nebraska–Lincoln, Lincoln, Nebraska 68588.
Larry Heuer • Department of Psychology, Barnard College, New York, New York 10027.

Theory and Research on Small Groups, edited by R. Scott Tindale et al. Plenum Press, New York, 1998.

thoughtful and responsible critics. In *Roughing It*, Mark Twain caustically observed: "The jury system puts a ban on intelligence and honesty, and a premium upon ignorance, stupidity and perjury. It's a shame that we must continue to use a worthless system because it was good a thousand years ago." Judge Jerome Frank complained:

> While the jury can contribute nothing of value so far as the law is concerned, it has infinite capacity for mischief, for twelve men can easily misunderstand more law in a minute than the judge can explain in an hour. (*Skidmore v. Baltimore and Ohio Railroad*)

Dean Griswold of the Harvard Law School deplored:

> The jury trial is the apothesis of the amateur. Why should anyone think that 12 persons brought in from the street, selected for their lack of general ability, should have any special capacity for deciding controversies between persons? (cited in Kalven & Zeisel, 1966, p. 5)

English legal scholar Glanville Williams quipped sarcastically: "It is an understatement to describe a jury ... as a group of twelve men of average ignorance" (cited in Hans & Vidmar, 1986, p. 114).

The fires of jury criticism have further been fueled by the recent publication of two popular books (Abramson, 1994; Adler, 1994) that examine the jury and jury performance. Federal Court of Appeals Judge (and former University of Chicago Law professor) Richard A. Posner (1995) echoes the themes of jury criticism in his review of the Abramson and Adler books:

> In recent years, a series of highly publicized criminal trials in which obviously guilty defendants were acquitted by juries (or convicted only of much lesser offenses than they had actually committed) has made the American jury a controversial institution. Civil juries have rendered some astonishing verdicts as well, ladling out billions in other people's money with insouciance and attracting a drumbeat of criticism from the business community. (p. 14)

Posner directly questions the ability of laypersons to handle the cases they are presented:

> Even though federal jurors are a reasonably select group of people, and are given by most federal judges all the help they could reasonably ask, the jury system in civil cases remains time-consuming and, if the case is complex, unreliable. I think it is romanticizing, or pandering to the "every man a king" strain in American culture, to suppose that average people are deep wells of wisdom with a pumping station in every jury room. (p. 19)

The jury found its way into the 1996 Presidential election:

> The legal guardrails that protected our society—that ensured a certain fundamental level of security and safety for America's families ... have in many places been knocked down, even dismantled, often by the very judges and juries who have been entrusted with the sacred duty of upholding the law. (Robert Dole, quoted in Tackett, 1996, p. 1)

The question of jury performance is prominent in the case law as well. Most recently, in *Markman v. Westview Instruments* (April 23, 1996), the Supreme Court circumscribed the reach of the jury by allocating to trial judges a responsibility that had previously rested in the hands of the jury. In future patent cases involving disputes about limits of a patent, the judge will now have the responsibility for determining those limits rather than the jury. Justice Souter, writing for the majority in *Markham* had this to say about the jury:

> Judges, not juries, are the better suited to find the acquired meaning of patent terms. The construction of written instruments is one of those things that judges often do and are likely to do better than jurors unburdened by training in exegesis. Patent construction in particular is a special occupation, requiring, like all others, special training and practice. The judge, from his training and discipline, is more likely to give a proper interpretation to such instruments than a jury; and he is, therefore, more likely to be right, in performing such a duty, than a jury can be expected to be. (not paginated)

In some ways this predation on the turf of the jury is not surprising: What is surprising is that it has taken the Supreme Court so long to address fundamental questions of jury competence. The groundwork for such a decision was laid more than 15 years ago by two U.S. appellate court decisions in which courts in two different federal circuits disagreed on a proposed complexity exception to the Seventh Amendment right to a jury trial. In *In re U.S. Financial Securities Litigation* (1979), the Supreme Court denied certiorari on a Ninth Circuit holding that there is not a complexity exception to the Seventh Amendment. However, in *In re Japanese Electronic Products Antitrust Litigation*, (1980) the Third Circuit held that due process considerations may preclude the right to a jury trial in complex civil suits and observed:

> Any assessment of a jury's ability to decide complex cases should include consideration not only of a jury's particular strengths and the possible enhancement of its capabilities but also of the particular constraints that operate on a jury in complex cases. The long time periods required for most complex cases are especially disabling for a jury.... Furthermore, a jury is likely to be unfamiliar with both the technical subject matter of a complex case and the process of civil litigation. The probability is not remote that a jury will become overwhelmed and confused by a mass of evidence and issues and will reach erroneous decisions. The reality of these difficulties that juries encounter in complex cases is underscored by the experience of some federal district judges who have found particular suits to have exceeded the practical abilities of a jury. (cites omitted, p. 1086)

It cannot be denied that many juries are confronted with a challenging task. For example, in 1991, 217,871 civil cases were filed in the federal courts of the United States. Of the 20,433 trials held in the 12-month period ending June 30, 1990, 11,502 were civil trials, 4,765 of which were tried to juries. Many trials were quite lengthy: 2,393 required between 4 and 9 days, 347 lasted between 10 and 19 days, and 85 lasted more than 20 days (Administrative Office of the Courts, 1990). All told, nearly 60%

of these civil jury trials lasted 4 or more days. The jurors participating in such trials clearly can confront complex group decision-making tasks.

On the other hand, some commentators have defended the jury, noting that critics of the jury have made their criticisms without the benefit of solid empirical evidence that would support their claims, and without having examined the promise of various procedural modifications that might assist the jury. Judge William Schwarzer (1991) suggests that jurors' problems are not inherent, but rather result from a failure to present the trial material in an understandable fashion. Sociologist Richard Lempert (1981) has questioned whether judges can perform any better than juries in complex cases. Political scientist Peter Sperlich (1980, 1982) observed that however overwhelmed the jury may be by complex litigation, the same problems are likely to exist for judges.

Are juries performing poorly, and can their performance be improved? The evidence on these matters is mixed. Certainly jury critics raise important empirical questions about the jury, though rarely do they provide more than anecdotes in support of their positions, and even less frequently do they display proficiency at specifying what should be studied or how. Despite the poor guidance from critics, the psychological community has begun to explore various aspects of jury performance. For example, a growing body of research has examined jurors' understanding of the law and, unfortunately, the jury has not fared much better in the hands of the research community than it has in the hands of critical legal pundits. Reifman, Gusick, and Ellsworth (1992) observed that the research indicates that jurors understand less than half of the judge's instructions. There is considerable consensus regarding the jury's struggle with legal language, and one response from the social science community has been to rework instructions into simpler English. Although these reworkings prove fairly successful (see, e.g., Charrow & Charrow, 1979; Elwork, Sales, & Alfini, 1982), courts have not been quick to revamp instructions in light of these findings.

Some researchers have given the jury high marks for its performance with trial evidence (e.g., Cecil, Lind, & Bermant, 1987; Guinther, 1988; Hans & Vidmar, 1986; Hastie, Penrod, & Pennington, 1983; Kalven & Zeisel, 1966; Visher, 1987). However, as Cecil, Hans, and Wiggins (1991) point out, most of these studies have focused on ordinary trials, and there are reasons to believe that juries might struggle in longer, more complex trials.

Systematic study of jury performance in complex cases has been undertaken only recently (see, e.g., Bourgeois, Horowitz, & ForsterLee, 1993a, 1993b; Horowitz & Bordens, 1990). Horowitz and his colleagues have used laboratory techniques to look at aspects of complex civil litigation such as the impact of variations in the number of plaintiffs, the size of the plaintiff classes represented by a litigant, variations in the severity of injuries sustained by plaintiffs (Horowitz & Bordens, 1988), and structural variations in trials such as ordering of liability/damage decisions and the number of decisions (Horowitz & Bordens, 1990).

Intensive studies of jury decision making in actual complex cases are limited in number and tend to take the form of anecdotal accounts of jury decision making (e.g.,

Adler, 1986; Austin, 1984; Frankel, 1990; Pacelle, 1986; Weinstein & Kushen, 1991). A somewhat more systematic effort to study jury decision making in complex cases was undertaken by an American Bar Association (ABA) subcommittee that interviewed jurors in four cases (American Bar Association, 1989). Clearly these anecdotal studies provide some useful insights into possible problems that juries may encounter, but they suffer from the fact that they are retrospective, the trials are viewed from the perspective of the authors, there are no systematic or reliable measures of performance, and authors emphasize different aspects of the trials. Thus, the anecdotes can be used to develop hypotheses and measures, but they are largely uninformative about systematic strengths and weaknesses in jury decision making.

Among the few studies that have systematically examined complex cases, one of the most interesting was a field study conducted by Cecil, Lind, and Bermant (1987; see also Cecil, Hans, & Wiggins, 1991). These researchers interviewed 180 of 400 jurors who had served in 29 civil trials lasting more than 20 trial days each, and compared their responses to jurors in a matched set of shorter trials. The study examined jurors' reports about (1) their interest in the trials, (2) their understanding of the trial evidence and judge's instructions, and (3) the burdens imposed on them. Though the jurors reported that the lengthy and shorter trials were similarly interesting, nearly half (46%) of jurors in long trials rated the evidence as very difficult or difficult compared to 29% in the short trials. In addition, 8% of short-trial and 30% of long-trial jurors rated the instructions as very difficult or difficult to understand. These jurors' reports suggest that jurors find the evidence more difficult in lengthy trials, but most jurors asserted they could adequately understand the evidence. Cecil et al. (1991) observed that claims about evidence difficulty may be overstated by critics. The Cecil et al. field study provides some valuable insights into jury decision making in complex cases, yet it obviously leaves many questions about jury performance unanswered.

Although a compelling argument can be made that the case against the jury is unproven, the harshest jury critics nonetheless call for the end of the jury. Other critics advance proposals that would limit the ambit of the jury while preserving the institution in cases that are thought suitable for lay decision makers. Less strident critics such as Abramson and Adler are more inclined to offer reforms that they believe will assist the jury in its decision making without limiting the number and types of cases juries are permitted to decide (see also Royal Commission on Criminal Justice, 1993; Schwarzer, 1991).

Numerous possibilities for jury reform have been suggested. One suggestion is to restructure cases. Examples of restructuring include limiting the amount of evidence presented or the time allowed for presenting it, eliminating parties, severance of consolidated actions, special verdicts, or special masters. Another suggestion is to restructure juries. Possibilities have included selecting better educated jurors and greater reliance on 12-person juries. A third possibility includes more aggressive case management techniques.

Posner (1995) particularly cites, with approval, some reforms championed by Abramson and Adler:

For complex modern cases, both Abramson and Adler propose a series of reforms
to make the jury's task easier: allowing jurors to take notes and ask questions;
authorizing the judge to instruct the jury in the law at the beginning and during the
trial, as well as when it is over ... (p. 16)

A growing body of laboratory experimental research has demonstrated the
benefits of procedures intended to aid jurors, for example, providing jurors access to
trial transcripts (ForsterLee, Horowitz, & Bordens, 1993); preinstructing jurors (Kassin & Wrightsman, 1979; Bourgeois, Horowitz, & ForsterLee, 1993a; Smith, 1988,
1991); notetaking (Hastie, 1983); and rewriting instructions (e.g., Charrow & Charrow, 1979; Elwork et al., 1982).

This chapter summarizes the results of two courtroom field experiments that
complement laboratory experiments evaluating jury reforms. These field experiments
examine the consequences of permitting jurors to take notes and direct questions to
witnesses during trials. The data for the first experiment were obtained from 29
different judges (sitting in 63 trials), 95 lawyers, and 550 jurors—all of whom participated in the same 67 Wisconsin state court trials. The data for the second experiment
were obtained from a national sample. The final sample included 75 civil and 85
criminal trials in the courtrooms of 103 different judges from 33 states. Data were
supplied by 103 judges, 220 lawyers, and 1,229 jurors. Our previously published
reports of these experiments provide greater detail about such issues as sampling
procedures and design and analysis. Our courtroom experiments have also examined
the effects of preliminary instructions, written instructions, juror orientations, special
verdicts, and pattern instructions. Readers interested in our findings regarding these
procedures are referred to Heuer and Penrod (1988, 1989, 1994a, 1994b).

Prior Research on Notes and Questions as Jury Aids

Arguments for and against juror notetaking and question asking have been
advanced by social scientists and legal scholars alike, and the debate over these
procedures is not new. Appellate decisions about juror questioning of witnesses date
back to as early as 1825, and decisions about juror notetaking date to at least 1900.
Despite the fact that many appellate courts have addressed these issues over a period
of a century or more, there is no consensus on the advantages and disadvantages of
these procedures. The lack of consensus does not arise because courts are unable to
agree on the criteria by which the procedures should be evaluated—indeed, across
cases, the same criteria appear repeatedly. Likewise, the appellate opinions suggest
that the problem is not one of inadequate information about or experience with these
procedures. The appellate judges writing these decisions appear secure with the
information they use to evaluate the procedures. This information ranges from the
judges' own experience to anecdotes from others to small-scale "studies" of the
procedures. We believe that an important reason for the lack of a consensus about the
use of these procedures is the paucity of systematic evaluations of their effects.

Elsewhere (Heuer & Penrod, 1988), we have summarized and critiqued the published reports of studies examining juror notetaking and questioning. Among the limitations of these studies are reliance on laboratory methods, research designs with small sample sizes, and a tendency to focus on juror reactions to the procedures while ignoring the experiences of judges and attorneys. Field studies of these procedures typically do not employ random assignment of trials to experimental conditions.

We presume that readers of this chapter understand the value and importance of random assignment of trials to experimental conditions. Judges generally do not. Although judges in our studies occasionally offered to participate in the study under the condition that their participation be limited to those trials in which juror questions are now allowed, we insisted, as a condition of participation, that judges be willing to allow us to randomly assign cases to experimental conditions. The procedures in these experiments were similar. Both studies included approximately equal numbers of criminal and civil trials. Both are true experiments—each trial in both studies was randomly assigned to be one in which jury questioning and notetaking were or were not allowed. In other words, each trial was randomly assigned to one of the four possible combinations of these two procedures. In both studies, the judge received a packet of materials including (1) instructions about the particular combination of questioning and notetaking procedures they were to employ in their next jury trial; (2) suggestions about how the procedures should be administered; and (3) questionnaires to be completed by the judge, the lawyers, and the jurors after the trial.

At the end of each trial, questionnaires were distributed to the jurors, the lead attorneys, and the judge. All respondents were asked to provide demographic information and asked a series of questions assessing their general evaluations of the trial, the trial actors, and the experimental procedures. When possible, all questions were answered on nine-point bipolar adjective scales. In most trials, judges had the jurors complete the questionnaires before they left the courtroom. The judges and lawyers were asked to complete as much of the questionnaire as possible while the jury was deliberating.

Our evaluation of juror questions and notetaking began with a survey of legal and psychological literatures in order to determine the advantages and disadvantages that might be associated with the procedures. In the following sections we present our conclusions regarding those advantages and disadvantages.

Juror Questions

Several years ago, during the trial of a drug case, the jury in U.S. Chief Judge Scott O. Wright's courtroom was permitted to ask questions. One of the jury questions requested that a videotape introduced into evidence be played a second time. During deliberations, the jury asked to see the tape a third time. Judge Wright initially thought the jurors were trying to get a better look at the face of the dealer who was delivering crack to an undercover police officer—until they asked to see the defendant's pants, which the U.S. prosecutor had almost not introduced into evidence. One of Judge

Wright's jurors had noticed a tear in the dealer's pants in the videotape and discovered a matching tear in the defendant's pants. Within minutes the jury returned a verdict of guilty. According to Judge Wright, the police, the FBI, and the U.S. attorneys had probably seen the videotape 1,000 times but not noticed a critical piece of evidence that ultimately persuaded the jury. Experiences like this have convinced some judges that jurors should routinely be allowed to ask questions during trials. Other judges favor juror questions because they see more mundane benefits to an increased jury role—such as an increased likelihood jurors will stay awake and alert during long and occasionally boring trials.

Whatever their reasons, an increasing number of judges are assessing the effects of allowing jurors in their courtrooms to ask questions of witnesses. Critics, however, suggest that jurists should proceed cautiously down this path, if at all. Proponents and critics have advanced a number of testable hypotheses about the impact of such questions on trial outcomes and the trial process. These hypotheses informed the development of our dependent measures. The juror questioning procedure generally conformed to the following recommendations given to the trial judges.

For trials randomly assigned to permit juror questions, judges received the following instructions:

> In this trial, we request that you allow the jurors to direct written questions to any witness. After direct and cross examination of each witness is complete, please ask jurors to submit any additional questions they may have, in writing, to you. If you find any such question patently objectionable, decline to ask it and explain to the jury that no adverse inference should be drawn from your ruling. If the question is facially acceptable, confer with counsel and rule on any objection (outside the hearing of the jury) raised before posing the question to the witness. If an objection is sustained, explain to the jury that no adverse inference should be drawn from your ruling.

Judges also were asked to deliver the following recommended instructions to jurors:

> Ladies and gentlemen of the jury, you will be given the opportunity to ask written questions of any of the witnesses called to testify in this case. Because that is the primary responsibility of the counsel, you are not encouraged to ask large numbers of questions. After both lawyers have finished questioning a witness, if there are matters that have not been explained you may then seek permission to ask that witness a written question. No oral questions will be permitted. Questions must be directed to the witness and not to the lawyer or the judge. Should you desire to ask a question, simply raise your hand and the bailiff will furnish you with pencil and paper. After consulting with counsel, I will determine if your question may properly be asked under the law. I will then present it myself to the witness. If I cannot allow a particular question to be asked, you should not speculate about what the answer might have been.

In trials assigned not to include juror questions, judges were asked not to allow the jurors to direct questions to any witness.

In the Wisconsin study, juror questioning of witnesses was permitted in 33 trials.

Jurors in these trials asked a total of 88 questions (2.3 questions per trial), of which two-thirds were directed to prosecution/plaintiff's witnesses, and one-third were addressed to defense witnesses. Of the 88 questions, 15 were objected to by either the prosecution or defense attorney. The attorneys displayed considerable agreement about which were objectionable, and both lawyers typically objected to the same questions.

In the national study, juror questions were permitted in 71 trials, and at least one question was asked in 51 of those trials. Not counting those questions that were submitted but not asked (due to lawyer objections or the judge's screening), jurors asked an average of 5.1 questions per civil trial (median = 1.8) and an average of 4.4 questions per criminal trial (median = 1.3). In both civil and criminal trials, questions were asked at the mean rate of approximately one question for every 2 hours of trial time (the median was somewhat lower—about .2–.3 questions per hour of trial time, with a modal rate of 0.0).

The majority of jury questions in the national study were directed to plaintiff or prosecution witnesses (79% in civil trials, 77% in criminal trials). Though this suggests some disparity in the rate of questions directed to the opposing sides, when we take into consideration the amount of time that prosecution and defense witnesses spent on the stand, the rate of questioning is much more evenly distributed: Questions were submitted to prosecution witnesses at a rate of approximately .7 questions per hour of testimony, compared with a rate of approximately .5 per hour for defense witnesses. Twenty-four percent of the jurors' questions were objected to by one or both attorneys.

As in the Wisconsin study, the attorneys in trials in the national study were in considerable agreement about which questions were objectionable—44% of the questions that were objected to were challenged by both lawyers. Defense attorneys reported that 81% of their objections were sustained, compared to 81% for prosecutors. (Here and throughout this chapter, the word *prosecutor* is used to refer to both the prosecuting and plaintiff's attorneys, except when a distinction is drawn between criminal and civil trials).

Evaluation of Purported Advantages of Juror Questions

Do juror questions promote juror understanding of the facts and issues and alleviate juror doubts about trial evidence? In *Ratton v. Busby* (1959), jurors asked questions about such matters as downwind leg, base leg, final approach, left-hand rectangular flight pattern, altitudes, banking, visibility, and bell crank. The court upheld the propriety of juror questions that were clearly designed to gain an understanding of the vernacular of flying, familiar to pilots but not to jurors. In numerous similar instances, courts have found no prejudice, stating that the questions assisted the jurors in their attempts to clarify complicated evidence (e.g., *Krause v. State*, 1942; *Schaefer v. St. Louis & Suburban R. Co.*, 1895).

Our findings generally support the view that juror questions serve a clarifying function. In the national study, the jurors in question-asking trials were asked how helpful their questions were for clarifying the evidence, clarifying the law, and getting to the truth. Overall, their answers indicated modest but positive appraisals. The jurors also indicated that they felt somewhat better informed by the evidence and were more confident that they had sufficient information for reaching a responsible verdict in trials where questions were allowed. In the Wisconsin cases, jurors permitted to ask questions were more satisfied that the questioning of witnesses had been thorough, seldom believed that a witness needed to be further questioned, and were more satisfied that the jury had sufficient information to reach a responsible verdict.

   Do juror questions help jurors get to the truth? McLaughlin (1982) observed, "Rather than an indifferent battle of legal minds with jurors as mere spectators, a trial is above all a search for truth ... while justice is blind, jurors need not also be" (pp. 697–698). In *State v. Kendall* (1907), the court held there was nothing improper in a juror asking a question with the apparent purpose of discovering the truth. The court pointed out that jurors ask often pertinent questions that help in advancing the investigation. In at least two cases (*Louisville Bridge & Terminal Co. v. Brown*, 1925; *White v. Little*, 1928), courts have observed that juror questions might aid the jury in finding out and learning the real facts.

   Our findings do not offer much support for this purported advantage of juror questions. In both the national and Wisconsin studies, the judges and attorneys were asked whether they thought juror questions helped get to the truth. Their answers indicate that they did not expect juror questions to help get to the truth, and after participating in a trial in which questions were allowed, judges and attorneys reported that the questions were not very helpful. Lawyers in the Wisconsin study were also asked whether they thought juror questions had brought up information that they had deliberately omitted—this question was asked because preliminary questioning of trial attorneys about juror questions revealed some fear that juror questions would play havoc with attorney trial strategies. However, attorneys who participated in trials with questions reported this was not a problem.

   Do juror questions alert trial counsel to particular issues that require further development? In *United States v. Callahan* (1979), the court observed that trials exist to develop the truth, and jurors' questions might helpfully alert counsel that particular factual issues need additional development. In both of our studies, we asked the lawyers and judges whether juror questions had signaled juror confusion about the law or the evidence. In both studies, lawyers and judges expected juror questions to provide useful information about the jury's thinking, but after participating in a trial in which questions were allowed, judges and lawyers agreed that questions did not yield these benefits.

   Do juror questions increase juror, attorney, or judge satisfaction with the trial or the verdict? Jurors' overall satisfaction with the trial was assessed in both the Wisconsin and the national study. In both studies, the conclusion was the same: Jurors were quite satisfied with their experiences, and their assessment was not influenced by the presence or absence of juror questions. Other survey questions revealed that jurors' satisfaction with their verdict and their attitudes toward jury service were unaffected by their opportunity to ask questions. The lawyers and judges in the national trial were also asked how satisfied they were with the jury's verdict. Overall, both parties indicated that they were reasonably satisfied (with judges somewhat more satisfied than attorneys). These assessments were not influenced by the presence or absence of juror questions.

Evaluation of Purported Disadvantages of Juror Questions

Do jurors ask inappropriate questions? One concern of trial attorneys is that jurors, because they are untutored in the law, will ask impermissible questions and should therefore be discouraged from asking any question at all. Examples of jurors asking classically impermissible questions can be found in the case law. For example, in *Maggart v. Bell* (1931), one juror asked the defendant whether he was covered by accident insurance. Examples of impermissible questions such as this one contribute to views such as the one expressed by Chief Judge Donald Lay in the Eighth Circuit case of *United States v. Johnson* (1989): "Because lay jurors will not understand the rules of evidence, they may well ask impermissible questions, such as those directed at the defendant's character" (p. 713).

Despite these reservations, our observation from both studies is that although the jurors do not know the rules of evidence, they nonetheless ask appropriate questions. In the Wisconsin study, both lawyers and judges reported that they did not expect juror questions to be inappropriate or inept, and they did not find them to be so. Lawyers in the national study were more skeptical if they had not experienced the procedure in a trial. However, among attorneys who participated in a trial with juror questions, neither of these expectations was realized. The judges in the national trial did not expect such harm to result from juror questions, and were clearly convinced after experiencing the procedure that such harm does not occur.

Are trial counsel reluctant to object to inappropriate juror questions? Numerous courts have refused to reverse when counsel did not object, during trial, to permitting jurors to ask questions (e.g., *Chicago Hanson Cab Co. v. Havelick*, 1869), or to improper juror questions (e.g., *Louisville Bridge & Terminal Co. v. Brown*, 1925). In considering whether counsel should be *required* to object to improper juror questions in order to preserve the point for appeal, the court in *State v. Sickles* (1926) asked whether this standard was appropriate when objections raise the risk of offending the juror.

Both of our studies show that lawyers are not immobilized by such concerns. In the national and Wisconsin studies, respectively, lawyers objected to 20% and 17% of the questions submitted by jurors (in the national study the lawyers objected to at least one question in 40% of the trials in which one was asked). Of course, our instructions to judges in question-asking trials offered some protection to an objecting attorney in that judges were asked to rule on objections outside the hearing of the jury. Furthermore, if an objection was sustained, judges were asked to explain the basis of the ruling to the jury to minimize the possibility that jurors would draw an adverse inference.

Are jurors embarrassed or angry when attorneys object to juror questions? Whereas many courts have refused to reverse when the attorneys did not object to juror questions during the trial, other courts have expressed concern that objections would offend the questioning juror and thereby prejudice the juror against the objecting attorney's client. The court, in *DeBenedetto v. Goodyear* (1985) also raised this concern, indicating that even though the court could take remedial steps in response to an improper question, these steps may make the questioning juror feel uncomfortable and perhaps even angry.

Responses from jurors whose questions drew objections in our studies make it clear they were neither embarrassed nor angry when this happened. In the national study, 65 of the 145 jurors who asked questions indicated that their questions had been objected to. Of these 65 jurors, 52 and 54, respectively, circled an 8 or a 9 (*Not at all*) on questions asking whether they were embarrassed or angry. Responses from jurors in the Wisconsin study were similar. In addition, the Wisconsin jurors whose questions drew objections typically reported that they understood the basis for the lawyer's objection.

If counsel objects and the objection is sustained, does the jury does draw inappropriate inferences from the unanswered question? In *Johnson*, Chief Judge Lay noted:

> If the defendant had refused to answer, as was his right, or if counsel had objected, the prejudicial effect on the jury could have been more devastating than were the defendant's answers. A jury frustrated in its pursuit of "truth" might well speculate on the defendant's probable answer, perhaps inferring more from the failure to answer than it would have gleaned from the answer itself. (*United States v. Johnson*, 1989, p. 712)

Chief Judge Lay argued that such a risk is always present when a question goes unanswered, but it is exacerbated when the question comes from a juror, because jurors will overemphasize their own questions.

We asked the lawyers in the national study two questions about such problems (*"Juror questioning caused prejudice to my client." "The juror questioning procedure undermined the goals of the adversarial process."*). The lawyers' responses indicated they did not expect and did not observe such consequences. Judges responses were similar.

When jurors are allowed to ask questions, do they become advocates rather than neutrals? In *Johnson*, Chief Judge Lay observed:

> The fundamental problem with juror questions lies in the gross distortion of the adversary system and the misconception of the role of the jury as a neutral factfinder in the adversary process. Those who doubt the value of the adversary system or who question its continuance will not object to distortion of the jury's role. However, as long as we adhere to an adversary system of justice, the neutrality and objectivity of the juror must be sacrosanct. (p. 713)

McLaughlin (1982) described the potential for jurors to fall prey to the "12 angry men syndrome," in which jurors lose their objectivity and begin to deliver accusatorial questions in an inquisitorial style at the witness.

We examined several types of evidence that indirectly address this concern. The first was the pattern of jury decisions. The verdict data from the national study indicate that jury questions did not have a significant effect on the verdicts. We also asked the judges what their preferred verdict would have been in the trial. This allowed us to examine the rate of agreement between judge and jury verdicts. The agreement rate was not affected by the jury questioning procedure—judges and jurors agreed on the appropriate verdict in about 69% of all cases. Agreement was slightly higher in cases in which questions were permitted (74% vs. 65%), but this difference was not statistically significant. In addition, juror responses indicated that neither lawyer was perceived less favorably as a result of the question-asking procedure (a result that might be expected if the jurors lost sight of their neutrality). In fact, both attorneys were perceived somewhat more favorably in question asking trials.

Do jurors overemphasize answers to their own questions at the expense of other trial evidence? Chief Judge Lay in *Johnson*, suggested that "Over the course of a trial, the jury develops a sense of cohesiveness and camaraderie, placing more importance on the reactions and questions of each other than on questions and answers presented in the normal adversarial process" (p. 712). Two findings from the national study led us to conclude that this was not a problem. First, the jurors in questioning trials were quite modest in their appraisal of the helpfulness of juror questions. Second, the jurors in trials in which questions were asked estimated that approximately 10% of their deliberation time (an average of 15 minutes) was devoted to discussing the answers to juror questions. Neither of these are the responses we would expect if the jurors were exaggerating the importance of such information relative to other trial evidence; however, in at least one case, jurors reported that more than half their deliberation was devoted to matters that were the subject of juror questions. It is impossible to determine whether that was a problem or a strength of the juror questions in that case.

Do juror questions have a prejudicial effect? Purver (1970) observed that appellate courts generally require "an affirmative showing that the improper questioning did actually operate to the complaining party's detriment" (p. 882). Though such showings are uncommon, courts have reversed where a juror's question revealed a prejudicial intent, or had a prejudicial effect (e.g., *Rojas v. Vuocolo*, 1944). A somewhat more skeptical view has been expressed by Chief Judge Lay, writing in *Johnson*. Lay argued that "allowing juror questions during trial is inherently prejudicial and should not be condoned" (p. 711). According to Chief Judge Lay, juror questioning might have subtle psychological effects that are difficult to identify.

Of course, if a procedure is prejudicial on its face, then the propriety of the procedure is really a policy matter, not an empirical one. However, any prejudicial effects that can be postulated should be measurable. In our investigations of jury questioning, signs of prejudice were explored most thoroughly in the national study, using dependent measures such as jury verdicts, judge–jury agreement on verdicts, lawyer satisfaction with verdicts, and juror impressions of the lawyers. This evidence is clearly contrary to what would be expected if questions had prejudicial effects: Jury questions did not affect the pattern of jury verdicts; they did not affect judge–jury verdict agreement; the lawyers and judges in this study did not see such biasing effects (even though the lawyers expected them); and the jurors had more favorable views of both attorneys in trials where juror questions were allowed.

General Evaluations of Juror Questions by Judges and Attorneys

In the Wisconsin study, the judges and the lawyers were asked about their reactions to jury questions. Their responses make it clear that neither group has serious objections to this procedure, and both tended to be more favorably disposed after participating in trials in which juror questions were permitted. The attorneys in the national study also did not expect any remarkable benefits prior to being exposed to the procedure, and after exposure they reported there were none. The reasons for their more favorable attitude after exposure appears to parallel their realization that there was no harm. Prior to exposure, attorneys think juror questions might uncover deliberately omitted information, interfere with their trial strategy, disrupt their case presentation, prejudice their client, or cause them to lose command over their case, but after exposure, the attorneys report that these problems did not occur.

The judges and attorneys in the national study were specifically asked to indicate their agreement with the statement: "I am in favor of allowing jurors to ask questions of witnesses during the trial" ($1 = Strongly Agree$; $9 = Strongly Disagree$). Both the judges and the attorneys who had experience with juror questions were more enthusiastic about the procedure than were their counterparts who had not experienced the procedures. For the judges, this represented a change from essentially undecided about the procedure before exposure ($M = 4.5$) to a moderate endorsement after exposure ($M = 3.7$); for attorneys this represented a change from modest opposition before ($M = 6.3$) to a more neutral stance after ($M = 4.9$).

Juror Notetaking

In trials assigned to the notetaking condition, judges were asked to permit jurors to take notes during all phases of the trial and to instruct the jurors about this permission as soon as practicable after the jury was impaneled. Judges were instructed that if they were unwilling to allow notes during the closing arguments by the trial attorneys, jurors should be allowed to take notes up to the closing arguments and the trial should kept in the study. Judges were also provided with suggested instructions about notetaking. In trials assigned to non-notetaking, judges were asked to bar notes and to state on the record the reason for this decision (a practice required by Wisconsin statutes).

Across our two studies, juror notetaking was allowed in 135 trials. When the jurors in both of our studies were given the opportunity to take notes, most of them did so (66% in the Wisconsin study, 87% in the national study), but they did not take extensive notes. In the Wisconsin study, with an average trial length of 2.3 days, the jurors took an average of 5.4 pages of notes. In the national study, the averages were 14.4 pages of notes for civil trials (which lasted an average of nearly 10 days) and 7.1

pages of notes for criminal trials (which lasted an average of nearly 6 days). In the national study, we estimate that jurors in both civil and criminal trials took about .6 pages of notes per hour of trial time.

Evaluation of the Purported Advantages of Juror Notetaking

Does juror notetaking serve as a memory aid? Some earlier studies (e.g., Flango, 1980; Sand & Reiss, 1985) reported that jurors found the notetaking procedure helpful as a memory aid, and at least one appellate decision has expressed this seemingly reasonable expectation, arguing there is no reason why notes should not be made by jurors, given that judges and lawyers make notes, and given the possibility notes might aid their memories and enable them to consider the evidence more intelligently (*United States v. Carlisi*, 1940).

In both of our studies, jurors were asked a variety of questions about their ability to recall the evidence. In the Wisconsin study, jurors also completed a multiple-choice test of their understanding of the judge's instructions. Our conclusion from both studies was that there was no evidence to suggest better recall in trials where note-taking was permitted, nor for jurors who elected to take notes. Although we believe the evidence from our two field studies is more compelling than findings from prior field research (for reasons discussed earlier), we would not argue that there is no memory advantage to juror notetaking. As in prior studies, the measures available in our study may not be sufficiently sensitive to detect one. We were forced to rely on quite general measures of recall rather than measures tailored to each case. General inquiries such as ours rely on jurors' impressions of their recall ability, sometimes reported many days after the trial. In this instance, the benefits of experiments in controlled environments (e.g., mock trials) are much more powerful test settings for memory effects—such studies can readily control the content of the trial, can vary the complexity of the trial, and can directly measure juror performance as a function of the opportunity to take notes. We briefly summarize a recent experiment that exploits some of these advantages.

Does notetaking increase juror satisfaction with the trial or the verdict? Though we have not located appellate decisions suggesting such an advantage, the social science literature provides numerous reasons to expect notetaking jurors to be more satisfied. Among the clearest examples are prior nonexperimental studies in which the jurors who took notes report that they participated more in the jury's deliberations because of them (Flango, 1980) and that jurors, attorneys, and judges had a generally positive reaction to the procedure (Sand & Reiss, 1985). In the Wisconsin experiment, we detected a slight increase in juror satisfaction with trials, but this finding was not replicated in our national experiment, nor did the national study find an effect of notetaking on jurors' verdict confidence. However, jurors were already quite satisfied with the procedures and verdicts in their trial (on nine-point scales, with higher scores indicating greater satisfaction, jurors' mean satisfaction with the trial procedure was 7.2, and their mean satisfaction with the verdict was 7.0).

Evaluation of the Purported Disadvantages of Juror Notetaking

Do jurors' notes produce a distorted record of the case? This concern has taken various forms, several of which were examined in our studies. According to the majority in *Thornton v. Weaber* (1955), jurors are unable to distinguish important from unimportant evidence and will therefore miss the important evidentiary points while noting the unimportant ones. These biased notes will, according to this analysis, then distort the jurors' evaluation of the trial evidence. The majority in *Thornton v. Weaber* also suggested that notetakers will be unable to keep pace with the trial, and will therefore miss important points. Both these critiques suggest that juror notetaking will actually interfere with the transmission of information from the trial to the deliberations.

With respect to the most important trial outcome, we found no evidence that verdicts were affected by notetaking. Data collected in the national study revealed that notetakers were overwhelmingly convinced that the trial did not proceed too quickly for them to keep pace.

Does notetaking distract jurors? This criticism takes many forms. According to Flango (1980), notetakers may distract nonnotetakers, or distract themselves by doodling rather than attending to trial proceedings. McLaughlin (1982) suggests that jurors, while making notes on a trivial point, will miss important evidence. Hastie (1983) suggests that notetakers might be distracted from assessing witness credibility if they devote too much attention to their notes. In both of our studies, notetakers and nonnotetakers in notetaking trials agreed they were not distracted by other notetakers. Notetakers additionally reported that their own notetaking was not distracting. And in the Wisconsin study, the judges and attorneys said they neither expected nor found notetaking to be distracting.

Do notetakers have an undue influence over nonnotetakers? Several decisions (e.g., *Fischer v. Fischer*, 1966; *Thornton v. Weaber*, 1955; *United States v. Davis*, 1900) have sounded this concern. In *Watkins v. State* (1965), the court observed that traditionally jurors were not permitted to take with them to the deliberation room any paper introduced into evidence except with the consent of both parties. The reason for this was that, at the time the rule developed, most jurors were illiterate and the prohibition on juror notetaking was an outgrowth of this rule. The concern was that if a single juror could read the materials, that juror could exert inordinate influence on less literate jurors. The Tennessee court, writing in 1965, observed that concerns about literacy were no longer justified. However, in an opinion written about the same time, the court in *Fischer v. Fischer* (1966), concluded that jurors should not be allowed to take notes, because skilled notetakers will gain a marked influential advantage over other jurors. In *Thornton v. Weaber* (1955), the court cleverly speculated that note-takers might have more influence because they might seem more alert and informed than nonnotetakers. And in *United States v. Davis* (1900), the court speculated that a juror who can refer to notes could have undue influence in conflicts of memory.

The reports from jurors in both of our studies suggest that this type of concern is not a problem. In both studies, notetakers and nonnotetakers both agreed that note-takers should not and did not have an advantage over nonnotetakers during deliberations. In addition, in the Wisconsin experiment we found no evidence that better educated jurors participated more in the jury's deliberations when aided by trial notes.

Are juror notes an accurate and useful record of the trial? In *United States v. Davis* (1900), the court considered whether it was appropriate that a judge, upon noticing that two jurors had occasionally taken notes, directed them to discontinue the practice and turn their notes over to the marshal. In ruling that notetaking was improper, the appeals court stated, "Without corrupt purpose, his notes may be inaccurate, or meager or careless, and loosely deficient, partial, and altogether incomplete" (p. 839). Eighty years later, Flango (1980) suggested that because they are inexperienced at notetaking, or because they cannot keep pace with the trial, juror notes will be an inaccurate record of the trial. Others have suggested that jurors would spend too much time doodling to be keeping an accurate record.

In both of our studies, we concluded that notes tended to be a fair and accurate record of the trial proceedings. We asked jurors whether their notes tended to be valuable records of the trial or mostly doodles, and they reported that they were considerably more likely to be accurate records. More impressive, perhaps, are the comments from one of the participating judges in this experiment—who approached the experiment quite skeptical about jurors' notetaking abilities. Upon reviewing the notes from eight trials, his report included the following comments:

> Approximately one-third of all the jurors, with the exception of the disorderly conduct trial, took surprisingly detailed notes. The notes were so clearly written and organized that I had little trouble determining what went on in the case…. Out of all of the notes reviewed there was only one juror who doodled on the notes…. I was surprised at how much in agreement the jurors' notes were for a particular case and how well the jurors seemed to have grasped the issues of the case. Many of the notes were extremely articulate and well organized. I concluded that jurors have far better notetaking capacity than I had realized … (Barland, 1985)

Jurors in notetaking trials in both experiments overwhelmingly reported that the trial did not proceed too quickly for them to keep pace with the proceedings—85% of the jurors in the Wisconsin study, and 87% of the jurors in the national study, said this was not a problem.

Do juror notes favor one side or the other? The plausible basis for this concern is that jurors may take more notes early in the trial but become fatigued and bored with notetaking as the trial wears on. Such practices could favor the prosecution or plaintiff who presents its case first. However, neither of our studies found the jurors to be more diligent notetakers during the earlier phases of a trial. In the Wisconsin study, jurors in notetaking trials reported a slightly less favorable impression of the defense attorney, but this was a small effect, and the pattern was not replicated in the larger national study. The national study also found no effect of notetaking on verdicts, a difference one would expect if the procedure provided an advantage to either party. Overall, the clear conclusion is that notetaking does not favor either the prosecution or the defense.

Does juror notetaking consume too much trial time? Several appellate decisions have indicated that notetaking is acceptable only if it does not require substantial court time (e.g., *Cahill v. Baltimore*, 1916; *Tift v. Towns*, 1879). Hastie (1983) speculated that notetaking might lengthen jury deliberations as jurors try to resolve discrepancies in their notes. However, Hastie's study came to the same conclusion as ours: In neither study was deliberation time affected by juror notetaking. The jurors in our national study reported that very little deliberation time was devoted to discussions of notes (the median estimate was 1% of deliberation time; the modal estimate was 0%). In the Wisconsin study, the jurors in notetaking trials also did not report any increase in acrimonious debate, in the difficulty of agreeing on the meaning of the law, or on the application of the judge's instructions to trial facts. In the national study, we also did not find a difference in the time devoted to any portion of the trial as a function of notetaking.

General Evaluations by Judges and Attorneys

In both the Wisconsin and the national studies, we asked the judges and the lawyers in notetaking and in nonnotetaking trials for their general impressions of this procedure. In both studies, the indication from both parties was the same: Neither the judges nor the attorneys expected notetaking to be especially problematic and neither of them found it to be so. Furthermore, both parties were more enthusiastic about the notetaking procedure after they had participated in a notetaking trial.

Conclusions from Courtroom Experiments

Tables 3 and 4 summarize our findings regarding the notetaking and question-asking procedure. With the exception of the finding that juror questions promote juror understanding and alleviate their doubts about the trial evidence, our findings reveal relatively little support for the purported advantages of notetaking and questions. However, the findings also are overwhelmingly contrary to notions about harmful consequences. In short, our findings suggest that the effects of these procedures are quite innocuous. Nonetheless, several considerations prompt us to conclude that these procedures deserve serious consideration as a way to assist jurors with their often complicated task.

First, it is clear that jurors favor of the opportunity to ask questions and take notes. Second, judges and attorneys are more favorably disposed to both procedures after they have participated in a trial in which they were permitted. Third, the findings do not support critiques of the procedures that emphasize possible harmful consequences. Finally, our conclusions are based on the highly consistent findings from two studies, comprising 227 trials, and generally consistent reports from the judges in 213 of those trials, 315 attorneys, and 1,779 jurors.

Where Are the Advantages?

It is natural to ask why our findings do not produce more evidence to support the claimed benefits of these procedures. Two reasons are immediately apparent: Either these benefits simply do not exist or our study methods were insensitive to the benefits. Several considerations lead us to suspect that studies employing different methods might find more evidence to support some of these benefits. In the simplest view, there are essentially three benefits that might be expected to result from both procedures: (1) Jurors and trial observers will perceive trial procedures as fairer and more satisfying; (2) jurors will be more confident that they have made the correct decision, and more satisfied with their jury experience; (3) jurors will better understand and recall the trial evidence, leading to more competent and fairer jury verdicts.

Although we did not find juror satisfaction or fairness perceptions to be consistently affected by the presence or absence of these procedures, this is most likely due to the generally high levels of juror satisfaction that already exist with the judicial system in this country. However, such procedures might enhance fairness perceptions in circumstances where other factors cause justice perceptions to be most strained. Additional studies, focusing on highly visible, highly charged, or controversial cases, where the fairness of trial procedures is being closely monitored, might be especially likely to reveal benefits of increased juror participation.

As for juror confidence and satisfaction with their performance, we have already suggested that our findings support the claim that the juror questioning procedure promotes jurors' understanding of the trial evidence and alleviates their doubts about trial testimony. Furthermore, in the national study, we found evidence that such benefits were especially likely to result from the question-asking procedure in cases in which the evidence or the law were particularly complex—precisely the setting where the questioning procedure might be expected to be most helpful (Heuer & Penrod, 1994b). However, neither of our studies have been very supportive of this claim for the notetaking procedure, nor have we found this procedure to be especially helpful in longer, or more complex cases (Heuer & Penrod, 1994b). This counterintuitive finding deserves closer examination. At least one possibility to be investigated is that jurors are not typically very skilled at notetaking. Even though they report little difficulty keeping pace with the trial, jurors might not be adept at deciding which evidence needs to be recorded for later recall, or at recording information in a well-organized fashion. Additional research could explore whether a brief training period, as part of jury indoctrination, might add to the effectiveness of the notetaking procedure. Alternatively, attorneys might tailor their presentation so as to assist notetaking jurors—emphasizing key points, or explicitly stating the general outline of their argument.

Finally, what about findings of increased juror comprehension, better recalled evidence, and better reasoned decisions? Despite the strengths of the field experiments summarized here, this type of design is not very well suited to administering measures that would best capture these types of benefits. For example, because our juror questionnaires were given to the judges prior to the start of the trial, we were unable to include questions tailored to the particular case the jurors had observed. Similarly, our questions about the judge's instructions in the Wisconsin study could only address the most general instructions that were likely to be present in all trials. So our questionnaire was probably not very sensitive to variations in jurors' comprehension of the judge's instructions or of the trial evidence. Furthermore, jurors completed

Table 3. Summary of Findings Regarding the Advantages and Disadvantages of Juror Questions to Witnesses

National Courtroom Experiment (1994)	Wisconsin Courtroom Experiment (1988)
Advantages	
Juror questions promote juror understanding of the facts and issues and alleviate juror doubts about trial evidence: (1) Jurors modest but positive in appraisal of helpfulness of questions for clarifying evidence, law, and getting to truth; (2) Juror responses indicate jurors felt better informed when questions permitted.	Same conclusion: Jurors reported that the questioning of witnesses was sufficiently thorough and that the jury had sufficient information to reach verdict.
Juror questions *do not* help get to the truth: (1) Juror response to questions about being well informed suggests modest benefit; (2) Virtually no endorsement from attorneys and judges that juror questioning yields this benefit.	Same conclusion: Attorneys say they did not expect and did not find this benefit to result from juror questions.
Juror questions *do not* alert counsel that particular issues require further development: Both lawyers and judges expected juror questions to provide feedback about the law or the evidence, but report that their expectations were not realized.	Same conclusion: Attorneys found feedback from questions helpful, but not for identifying juror confusion about evidence or law: (1) Attorneys expected to get useful feedback about confusion over law and evidence, but report they did not; (2) attorneys expected and received some feedback about jurors' perceptions of the trial.
Juror questions *do not* increase juror, attorney, or judge satisfaction with the trial or the verdict: Overall, jurors, lawyers, and judges were reasonably well satisfied with the trial and the verdict—a reaction unaffected by question procedure.	Same conclusion regarding juror satisfaction: Attorney and judge satisfaction measures not collected.
Disadvantages	
Jurors *do not* ask inappropriate questions: (1) Lawyers expected inappropriate and unwelcome questions, but report that neither occurred; (2) judges did not expect nor find the jurors' questions inept; (3) judges' expectation that juror questions would interfere with lawyers' strategies was not confirmed	Same conclusion: (1) Lawyers expected juror questions to upset their strategy or to result in unwated surprises, but say this didn't happen; (2) judges did not expect or find the questioning procedure to be either impractical or a nuisance.

Counsel *are not* reluctant to object to inappropriate juror questions:
(1) Lawyers from either side objected to 20% of questions asked; (2) lawyers objected to at least one juror question in 40% of trials in which one was asked.

If the lawyers do object, the jurors *are not* embarrassed to angry:
Of the 145 jurors who asked a question, 65 had their question objected to. Of these, 52 and 54 circle and 8 or 9 (*Not at All*) to the questions: (1) "Were you embarrassed?" (2) "Were you angry?"

If counsel objects and the objection is sustained, the jury *does not* draw inappropriate inferences from the unanswered question: Lawyers and judges both reported that such problems did not occur.

Jurors allowed to ask questions *do not* become advocates rather than neutrals:
(1) Questioning procedure had no effect on verdicts or on judge–jury verdict agreement rate; (2) questioning procedure had no negative effect on juror impressions of attorneys—jurors were more satisfied with both prosecution/plaintiff and defense when questions permitted.

Jurors *do not* overemphasize answers to their own questions at the expense of other trial evidence:
(1) Overall, jurors were modest in their appraisal of the helpfulness of juror questions (see advantage 2); (2) juries in trials where questions were asked devote approximately 10% of deliberation time (15 min.) to discussing answers to juror questions.

Juror questions *do not* have a prejudicial effect:
(1) The questioning procedure had no effect on verdicts; (2) the questioning procedure had no effect on judge–jury verdict agreement rate; (3) lawyers report virtually no biasing effect of juror questions (even though they expected some); (4) judges neither expect nor find significant biasing effects.

Global evaluation: Both judges and attorneys who experienced the questioning procedure were more enthusiastic than those who did not experience it.

Same conclusion: Lawyers objected to 17% of questions asked and generally agreed about which were objectionable.

Same conclusion: Jurors whose questions were objected to said they were definitely not embarrassed or angry. They also said they understood the basis for the lawyer's objection.

Same conclusion: Lawyers expected that juror questions would cause prejudice to their client, but after participating in trials where questions are allowed, they report that this did not happen.

Global evaluation: Both lawyers and judges were mnore favorabley disposed after participating in a trial in which questions were allowed. Lawyers did not expect any remarkable benefits form procedure, and after exposure, they say there were none.

**Table 4.   Summary of Findings Regarding the Advantages
and Disadvantages of Juror Notetaking**

National Courtroom Experiment (1994)	Wisconsin Courtroom Experiment (1988)
Advantages	
Juror notes *do not* serve as memory aid. No direct measures of recall, but no difference in juror self-reports of evidence recall as a function of notetaking.	Same conclusion: With the additional measure of juror performance on multiple choice questions about judge's instructions.
Juror notetaking *does not* increase juror satisfaction with the trial or the verdict. Juror satisfaction is high regardless of notetaking condition.	Same conclusion: This study found a small ($M = 7.3$ vs. $M = 7.0$) but statistically significant increase in juror satisfaction when notetaking was permitted, but no increase in verdict confidence.
Disadvantages	
Jurors *do not* produce a distorted record of the case: (1) Majority of the jurors (85%) reported that they did not have difficulty keeping pace with trial; (2) neither jury verdicts nor rate of judge–jury verdict agreement were affected by juror notetaking.	
Notetaking *does not* distract jurors. Both notetakers and nonnotetakers said they were not distracted by notetakers. Notetakers also said their own notetaking did not distract from the trail.	Same conclusion: Based on different evidence: (1) No decrement in performance on multiple choice test of judge's instructions; (2) jurors did not expect or find notetaking distracting; (3) lawyers and judges did not expect or find notetaking distracting to themselves or to other jurors.
Notetakers *do not* gain an undue influence over nonnotetaker. Both notetakers and nonnotetakers in notetaking trials agreed notetakers should not and did not have more influence.	Same conclusion: Again, notetakers and nonnotetakers in agreement. No evidence that more literate jurors gained influence by virtue of notes.
Juror notes are an accurate record of the trial. Jurors reported their notes were valuable records, not doodles. Jurors also reported that trial did not proceed too quickly for accurate notetaking (see 2 above).	Same conclusion: Similar evidence to 1994 study; additional evidence from one judge's analysis of juror notes from trial in his courtroom.
Notetaking *does not* favor either the prosection/plaintiff or defense: (a) No advantage to either party in terms of pages/hour or notes recorded; (2) no effect on juror impressions of attorneys; (3) no effect on verdicts.	Same conclusion: (1) No advantage to either party in quantity of notes; (2) no effect on evaluation of prosecution/plaintiff's attorney; (3) slightly less favorable impression of defense when notetaking permitted.
Notetaking *does not* consume too much time: (1) No difference in trial time; (2) no difference in deliberation time; (3) little deliberation time spent discussing notes (median = 1% of deliberation time, mode = 0%).	Same conclusion: (1) No difference in reported difficulty reaching verdict; (2) no acrimonious debates; (3) no evidence for more frequent vot changes when notes allowed.

Overall impressions of judges and attorneys: Neither the judges nor the attorneys expected juror notetaking to be problematic. Still, their evaluations became more positive after seeing the procedure employed in a trial.

these questionnaires after the trial was completed, sometimes days afterward. Thus, our assessment of the benefits of jury notetaking was taking place without the jurors having the opportunity to look at their notes while answering our questions (they did, however, have access to their notes during their deliberations). Finally, we were not able to observe the juries' deliberations—something that would permit an assessment of the juries' competence at reconstructing the relevant evidence and law, weighing it, and integrating it into a final decision. Such sensitive methods have not been available in actual courtroom settings for some time. Thus, the best methods for assessing the efforts of notetaking and question asking should combine the advantages of field experiments with experiments conducted in more controlled settings. Fortunately, one recent study of juror notetaking exploits some of these advantages. In doing so, the study also suggests advantages for juror notetaking that the field experiment did not detect.

Rosenhan, Eisner, and Robinson (1994) conducted a laboratory experiment in which 144 jury-eligible college students viewed a 75-minute videotaped simulation of an actual civil trial. The authors report that the case was realistic and fairly complex, and therefore placed considerable demands on juror comprehension and memory. The researchers tested jurors' recall and comprehension of trial material immediately after the trial. Most of the jurors did not deliberate but immediately completed questionnaires—the authors report that their conclusions are not qualified by the presence or absence of jury deliberations. Jurors were asked questions tailored to the particular case they had observed—with their notes available for reference while answering the questions.

On the measure of recall, notetakers outperformed nonnotetakers by a modest but significant margin. The authors report, for example, that 7 of the 10 highest scores on the recall measure were attained by notetakers, whereas 8 of the 10 lowest scores were attained by nonnotetakers. Among notetakers, the authors found a positive relation between the quantity of notes taken and recall and between the degree of organization in notes and recall. The authors did not find an effect for notes on jurors' private verdicts.

Conclusions

Commentators, scholars, attorneys, and judges have long complained about jury performance. It is noteworthy that the criticisms and some jury reforms that have been advanced to meet the criticisms have both been advanced despite the lack of relevant systematic data. This situation is beginning to change as studies such as those discussed in this chapter provide new insights into the strengths and weaknesses of jury decision making and allow us to identify procedural reforms and decision aids that will optimize jury performance.

Overall, the evidence from our field experiments, in combination with the findings from earlier nonexperimental studies and findings from laboratory studies like that of Rosenhan et al. (1994) converge on the conclusion that notetaking and question asking offer promise as aids to jurors, and especially so in more complex cases.

Furthermore, these field studies, particularly in combination with sophisticated and realistic trial simulations, offer more authoritative evidence about these procedures than has been garnered in more than a century of debate about their merits. As critiques of the jury and erosion of jury powers such as those produced in the recent *Markman* decision accumulate, it is imperative that additional research be conducted on other trial procedures that might assist juries. Among the many proposed reforms that are susceptible to systematic investigation are providing the jury with a written copy of the judge's instructions, instructing the jury prior to the evidence, limiting the volume of evidence presented to juries, limiting the time for the presentation of evidence, more aggressive stipulation to facts before the trial, selection of specially qualified (blue ribbon) juries, appointment of special masters to assist juries, expanded use of special verdict forms, bifurcation of issues, and bifurcation of parties.

Of course, courts must cooperate in this evaluative effort; they must be persuaded that a few sound courtroom experiments will almost invariably provide a sounder basis for policy making than will a century's worth of appellate court speculations about the merits and disadvantages of procedures deployed in a haphazard manner. The judiciary must be enlisted in the effort to provide sound answers to the questions they are so adept at posing. Our experience with the courts suggest that some members of the judiciary already understand the merits of systematic study of the jury and other components of the justice system. We believe that successful field experiments such as the ones described here can serve as sound models for and demonstrations of the advantages of future courtroom experiments.

References

Abramson, J. (1994). *We, the jury: The jury system and the ideal democracy*. New York: Basic Books.

Adler, S. J. (1986, January/February). How to lose the bet-your-company case. *American Lawyer*, pp. 27–30, 107–110.

Adler, S. J. (1994). *The jury: Trial and error in the American courtroom*. New York: Times Books.

Administrative Office of the Courts. (1990). Annual Report of the Director of the Administrative Office of the U.S. Courts. Washington, DC.

Austin, A. (1984). *Complex litigation confronts the jury system: A case study*. Frederick, MD: University Publications of America.

Barland, T. (January 10, 1985). Letter addressed to the Executive Secretary of the Judicial Council of Wisconsin.

Bourgeois, M. J., Horowitz, I. A., & ForsterLee, L. (1993a). The effects of technicality and access to trial transcripts on verdicts and information processing in a civil trial. *Personality and Social Psychology Bulletin, 19*, 220–227.

Bourgeois, M. J., Horowitz, I. A., & ForsterLee, L. (1993b). Nominal and interactive groups: Effects of preinstructions and deliberations on decisions and evidence recall in complex trials. *Journal of Applied Psychology, 80*, 58–67.

Cahill v. Baltimore, 129 Md 17, 98 A 235 (1916).

Cecil, J., Hans, V. P., & Wiggins, E. C. (1991). Citizen comprehension of difficult issues: Lessons from civil jury trials. *American University Law Review, 40*, 727–774.

Cecil, J. S., Lind, E. A., & Bermant, G. (1987). Jury service in lengthy civil trials. *Federal Judicial Center*.

Charrow, R. P., & Charrow, V. R. (1979). Making legal language understandable: A psycholinguistic study of jury instructions. *Columbia Law Review, 79*, 1306–1374.

Chicago Hanson Cab Co. v. Havelick, 131 Ill 179, 22 NE 797 (1869).

DeBenedetto v. Goodyear, 754 F2d 512, 80 ALR Fed 879 (1985).

Elwork, A., Sales, B. D., & Alfini, J. J. (1982). *Making jury instructions understandable*. Charlottesville, VA: The Michie Company.

Fischer v. Fischer, 31 Wis 2d 293, 142 NW 2d 857 (1966).

Flango, V. E. (1980). Would jurors do a better job if they could take notes? *Judicature, 63*(9), 436–443.

ForsterLee, L., Horowitz, I. A., & Bourgeois, M. J. (1993). Juror competence in civil trials: The effects of preinstruction and evidence technicality. *Journal of Applied Psychology, 78*, 14–21.

Frankel, M. (1990). A trial judge's perspective on providing tools for rational jury decision making. *Northwestern University Law Review, 85*, 221.

Guinther, J. (1988). *The jury in America*. New York: Facts-on-File Publications.

Hans, V. P., & Vidmar, N. (1986). *Judging the jury*. New York: Plenum Press.

Hastie, R. (1983). *Final report to the National Institute for Law Enforcement and Criminal Justice*. Unpublished manuscript. Northwestern University, Evanston, IL.

Hastie, R., Penrod, S. D., & Pennington, N. (1983). *Inside the jury*. Cambridge, MA: Harvard University Press.

Heuer, L., & Penrod, S. (1988). Increasing jurors' participation in trials: A field experiment with jury notetaking and question asking. *Law and Human Behavior, 12*, 409–430.

Heuer, L., & Penrod, S. D. (1989). Instructing jurors: A field experiment with written and preliminary instructions. *Law and Human Behavior, 13*, 231–262.

Heuer, L., & Penrod, S. D. (1994a). Juror notetaking and question asking during trial: A national field experiment. *Law and Human Behavior, 18*(2), 121–150.

Heuer, L. B., & Penrod, S. (1994b). Trial complexity: A field investigation of its meaning and its effects. *Law and Human Behavior, 18*, 29–52.

Horowitz, I. A., & Bordens, K. S. (1988). The effects of outlier presence, plaintiff population size, and aggregation of plaintiffs on simulated civil jury decisions. *Law and Human Behavior, 12*, 209–229.

Horowitz, I. A., & Bordens, K. S. (1990). An experimental investigation of procedural issues in complex tort trials. *Law and Human Behavior, 14*, 269–285.

In re United States Financial Securities Litigation, 609 F.2d 411 (1979).

Jury comprehension in complex cases, ABA Subcommittee Report, 1989, Washington, DC.

Kalven, H. (1964). The dignity of the civil jury. *Virginia Law Review, 50*, 1055–1075.

Kalven, H., & Zeisel, H. (1966). *The American jury*. Boston: Little, Brown.

Kassin, S. W., & Wrightsman, L. S. (1979). On the requirements of proof: The timing of judicial instruction and mock juror verdicts. *Journal of Personality and Social Psychology, 37*, 1877–1887.

Krause v. State, 75 Okla Crim 381, 132 P2d 179 (1942).

Landsman, S. (1993). The civil jury in America: Scenes from an unappreciated history. *Hastings Law Journal, 44*, 579.

Lempert, R. (1981). Civil juries and complex cases: Let's not rush to judgment. *Michigan Law Review, 80*, 68–132.

Maggart v. Bell, 116 Cal App 306, 2 P2d 516 (1931).

Markman v. Westview Instruments, U.S. Supreme Court, 95-26 (April 23, 1996).

McLaughlin, M. A. (1982). Questions to witnesses and notetaking by the jury as aids in understanding complex litigation. *New England Law Review, 18*, 687–713.

Pacelle, M. (1986, December). Contaminated verdict. *American Lawyer*, pp. 75–80.

Posner, R. A. (March 1, 1995). Juries on trial. *Commentary, 99*, 49.

Purver, J. M. (1970). Propriety of jurors asking questions in open court during course of trial. *American Law Reports, 3rd Series, 31*, 872–892.

Ratton v. Busby, 230 Ark 667, 326 SW2d 889 (1959).

Reifman, A., Gusick, S. M., & Ellsworth, P. C. (1992). Real jurors understanding of the law in real cases. *Law and Human Behavior, 16*, 539–554.

Rembar, C. (1980). *The Law of the land*. New York: Simon & Schuster.

Rojas v. Vuocolo, 142 Tex 152, 177 SW2d 962 (1944).

Rosenhan, D. L., Eisner, S. L., & Robinson, R. J. (1994). Notetaking can aid juror recall. *Law and Human Behavior, 18,* 53–61.

Royal Commission on Criminal Justice. (1993). *Report* (Cm 2263), London: Her Majesty's Stationer's Office.

Sand, L. B., & Reiss, S. A. (1985). A report on seven experiments conducted by district court judges in the second circuit. *New York University Law Review, 60,* 423–497.

Schaefer v. St. Louis and Suburban R. Co., 128 Mo 64, 30 SW 331 (1895).

Schwarzer, W. W. (1991). Reforming jury trials. *132 Federal Rules Decisions 575,* Minneapolis, MN: West.

Skidmore v. Baltimore and Ohio Railroad, 167 F.2d 54 [2d Cir. 1948].

Smith, V. L. (1988). *The psychological and legal implications of pretrial instruction in the law.* Doctoral dissertation, Stanford University, Stanford, CA.

Smith, V. L. (1991). The feasibility and utility of pretrial instruction in the substantive law: A survey of judges. *Law and Human Behavior, 14,* 235–248.

Sperlich, P. W. (1980). ... And then there were six: The decline of the American jury. *Judicature, 63,* 262, 275–277.

Sperlich, P. W. (1982). The case for preserving the trial by jury in complex civil litigation. *Judicature, 65,* 395–419.

State v. Kendall, 142 NC 659, 57 SE 340 (1907).

State v. Sickles, 220 Mo App 290, 286 SW 432 (1926).

Tackett, M. (April 20, 1996). Dole fires a salvo at Clinton judges. *Chicago Tribune,* p. 1.

Thornton v. Weaber, 380 Pa 590, 112 A2d 344 (1955).

Tift v. Towns, 63 Ga 237 (1879).

United States v. Callahan, 588 F2d 1078 (1979).

United States v. Carlisi, DC NY, 32 F Supp 479 (1940).

United States v. Davis, CC Tenn, 103 F 457, affd CA6, 107 F 753 (1900).

United States v. Johnson, 892 F2d 707 (1989).

Van Dyke, J. M. (1977). *Jury selection procedures.* Cambridge, MA: Ballinger.

Visher, C. A. (1987). Juror decision making: The importance of evidence. *Law and Human Behavior, 11,* 1–18.

Watkins v. State, 216 Tenn 545, 393 SW2d 141 (1965).

Weinstein, J. B., & Kushen, R. (1991). Scientific evidence in complex litigation. ALI-ABA Course—C607 *ALI-ABA* 709.

White v. Little, 131 Okla 3123, 268 P 221 (1928).

8

An Evaluation of the Biasing Effects of Death Qualification

A Meta-Analytic/Computer Simulation Approach

Joseph W. Filkins, Christine M. Smith, and R. Scott Tindale

Social science research has had a long history of influencing court decisions (see *Muller v. Oregon*, 1908), but the last 20 years has seen a substantial increase in the focus of social psychological research on various aspects of the legal system (Monahan & Walker, 1985). Although a number of important topics have received attention (e.g., eyewitness testimony, Wells, 1993; repressed memories, Loftus, 1993), the functioning of criminal juries has remained a key point of inquiry (Davis, 1980; Hans & Vidmar, 1986; Hastie, Penrod, & Pennington, 1983; Tindale & Davis, 1983). The main issues of the 1970s involved the appropriate jury size and decision rule (Davis, Kerr, Atkin, Holt, & Meek, 1975), following from a number of Supreme Court rulings on both matters (e.g., *Ballew v. Georgia*, 1978; *Williams v. Florida*, 1970). Probably the central issue of the 1980s, however, was the use of "death qualification" procedures for capital trials (Bersoff & Ogden, 1987; Cowan, Thompson, & Ellsworth, 1984; Thompson, 1989).

Death Qualification and the Initial Debate

Death qualification involves voir dire procedures through which potential jurors in a capital case are excluded from jury service for cause because of their views

Joseph W. Filkins • Office of Institutional Planning and Research, DePaul University, Chicago, Illinois 60604.   **Christine M. Smith** • Department of Psychology, Grand Valley State University, Allendale, Michigan 49401.   **R. Scott Tindale** • Department of Psychology, Loyola University of Chicago, Illinois 60626.

Theory and Research on Small Groups, edited by R. Scott Tindale et al. Plenum Press, New York, 1998.

toward the death penalty. Gross (1984) reports that up until 1968, it was common practice to exclude from service any person professing opposition to the death penalty. Indeed, in one case, the trial judge challenged for cause 47 potential jurors on the basis of their attitude toward the death penalty after having been quoted as saying, "Let's get these conscientious objectors out of the way without wasting any time on them" (*Witherspoon v. Illinois*, 1968, p. 514; Gross, 1984). This procedure was challenged in *Witherspoon v. Illinois*.

In his petition to the Supreme Court, Witherspoon argued that a death qualified jury must "necessarily be biased in favor of conviction" (*Witherspoon v. Illinois*, 1968, p. 516) because a death qualified juror would be the kind of juror who would "too readily ignore the presumption of the defendant's innocence" (p. 516) and return a guilty verdict, because his attitudes toward the death penalty are such that this juror "would be unperturbed by the prospect of sending a man to his death" (p. 516). Witherspoon argued his Sixth Amendment right to a trial by an impartial jury and his Fourteenth Amendment right to due process were being violated because his jury entered the trial prejudiced against him.

To support his claim that death qualified jurors are conviction prone, Witherspoon presented the Court with evidence obtained from three empirical studies: Wilson (1964, cited in Thompson, 1989), and early drafts of Zeisel (1968) and Goldberg (1970). Each of these studies used attitudes and scruples against the death penalty to distinguish different classes of jurors, and each study found that individuals favoring the death penalty were more likely to convict. The Court dismissed this evidence, citing methodological flaws with each of the studies. For instance, the Court found the stimulus materials used in the Wilson and Goldberg studies not realistic enough to draw confident generalizations to the real world (Bersoff & Ogden, 1987). The Court also criticized the use of student jurors, the fact that these jurors did not deliberate, and the fact that these groups were distinguished using standards that had not been properly articulated (Bersoff & Ogden, 1987). As such, the Court ruled that the empirical evidence was "too tentative and fragmentary to establish that jurors not opposed to the death penalty tend to favor the prosecution in the determination of guilt" (*Witherspoon v. Illinois*, 1968, p. 527).

However, because the state of Illinois does not employ a bifurcated system in capital cases (i.e., using two different juries for the guilt and penalty phases of the trial, respectively), the same jury that convicted Witherspoon also sentenced him to death. The Court overturned this sentence, citing the obvious lack of impartiality on the part of the jurors. The Court also specified the appropriate criteria to use for death qualification in the future. The *Witherspoon* court suggested that potential jurors be excluded only if they make it "unmistakably clear (1) that they would *automatically* vote against the imposition of capital punishment without regard to any evidence that might be developed at the trial before them, or (2) that their attitude toward the death penalty would prevent them from making an impartial decisions as to the defendant's guilt" (*Witherspoon v. Illinois*, 1968, p. 522, n. 21, as cited in Thompson, 1989). The first criterion eliminates those jurors commonly called "penalty nullifiers," while the second criterion eliminates "guilt nullifiers" (Thompson, 1989).

Research after Witherspoon

The arguments specified by the *Witherspoon* court, particularly the "too tentative and fragmentary" comment, served as a catalyst for research on death qualification procedures and conviction proneness. This new wave of research attempted to classify participants according to the standards set forth by the Court and to simulate conditions more like those found in a courtroom setting (Bersoff & Ogden, 1987). Bronson (1970) surveyed over 700 prospective jurors in Colorado and had them respond to a number of statements that purportedly assessed their conviction proneness. Bronson found a general pattern of association between a favorable death penalty attitude and relative conviction proneness. However, this study did not have jurors making a verdict decision in any particular case. Jurow (1971) used employees of the Sperry Rand Corporation to represent actual jurors and classified them according their attitudes toward the death penalty. He had these participants listen to two audiotaped descriptions of simulated murder trials and make individual verdict decisions. For one case, he found a definite effect of death penalty attitudes on conviction rates where jurors "not opposed" to the death penalty were more likely to convict; the other case resulted in a trend in the same direction. A third study, coming close on the heels of the *Witherspoon* decision, was a 1971 survey conducted by the Harris group (as reported in White [1973] and the Bersoff & Ogden [1987] *amicus curiae* brief provided for the American Psychological Association to the Supreme Court for *Lockhart v. McCree*). In this study, a nationwide, random sample of adults were given four descriptions of criminal cases, and the consistent finding was that death qualified jurors voted to convict more often than excludable jurors.

As research in this field progressed, more elaborate experimental designs were used to assess the effects of death qualification, primarily by Ellsworth and her colleagues at Stanford University (Cowan et al., 1984; Ellsworth, Bukaty, Cowan, & Thompson, 1984; Thompson, Cowan, Ellsworth, & Harrington; 1984) and Haney at the University of California–Santa Cruz (Haney, 1980, 1984; Haney, Hurtado, & Vega, 1994). Cowan et al. (1984) contributed to the growing body of evidence indicating the conviction proneness of death qualified jurors. Adult participants were classified as death qualified or excludable and then watched a 2½-hour videotape of a simulated murder trial. They then gave an initial verdict, were divided into 12-person juries that then deliberated for one hour, and finally filled out a postdeliberation questionnaire designed to assess the different aspects of the deliberation process. Half of the constructed juries were comprised exclusively of death qualified jurors, and the other half were comprised of a majority of death qualified jurors, along with two to four excludable jurors. On both the predeliberation and postdeliberation ballots, death qualified jurors were more likely to vote for conviction than excludable jurors.

In a follow-up to the above study, Thompson et al. (1984) suggested that the greater conviction proneness of death qualified jurors is due, in part, to their tendency to interpret the evidence presented at trial in a way more favorable to the prosecution and less favorable to the defense. Ellsworth et al. (1984) assessed the impact of death qualification on interpretations of an insanity defense. Excludables were found to be more likely than death qualified jurors to vote for a "not guilty by reason of insanity" verdict for cases involving a schizophrenia defense. The groups did not differ in cases where the insanity defense was based on a physical disorder (e.g., retardation and epilepsy). They also found that death qualified jurors tended to be more skeptical of an insanity defense than excludable jurors.

Haney (1980, 1984) examined the effects of death qualification procedures during voir dire. Do the questions posed to prospective jurors at the outset of a capital trial affect their subsequent impressions and interpretation of the evidence? Haney (1984) had participants classified as death qualified watch one of two videotapes of a simulated voir dire in which one of the tapes included a 30-minute death qualification segment. Those participants who watched the death qualification voir dire were more likely to believe that the defendant was guilty and would be convicted by the jury. The differences in the voir dire also affected their impressions of the prosecuting and defense attorneys, the judge, and the legal process in general. These findings suggest that the death qualification *process* affects not only who can serve, but also the perceptions of the trial held by people who are selected to serve.

Despite the evidence to the contrary, some researchers remain skeptical about the conviction proneness of death qualified jurors. Elliot (1991) presents, in a footnote, the results of three small studies, all of which failed to find any appreciable difference in the conviction rates of death qualified jurors and excludable jurors. Elliot and Robinson (1991) investigated whether attitudes toward the death penalty were related to conviction proneness and a proprosecution bias. They found that attitudes toward the death penalty were unrelated to verdicts in a capital case. Furthermore, they found that strong opponents of the death penalty were no different than others in attitudes toward attorneys, witnesses, or other impressions of the trial.

Another constitutional issue at the heart of the death qualification debate centers around the consistent findings of researchers that certain groups within the community are disproportionately underrepresented in capital juries. The Sixth Amendment guarantees the right of the accused to a "speedy and public trial by an impartial jury of the State ... wherein the crime shall have been committed." Way (1980, p. 337) suggests that the presumed first step in impaneling an impartial jury is to be certain that the jury panel is a representative cross-section of the community:

> The American tradition of trial by jury ... necessarily contemplates an impartial jury drawn from a cross section of the community.... Prospective jurors shall be selected by court officials without systematic and intentional exclusion of any groups. (*Thiel v. Southern Pacific Company*, 1946, p. 220)

In *Duren v. Missouri* (1979), the Court lists three elements that must be present before a violation of the fair cross-section doctrine will be found:

> In order to establish a prima facie violation of the fair cross section requirement the defendant must show (1) that the group alleged to be excluded is a "distinctive" group in the community; (2) that the representation of this group in venires from which juries are selected is not fair and reasonable in relation to the number of such persons in the community; and (3) that this underrepresentation is due to

systematic exclusion of this group in the jury-selection process. (Finch & Ferraro, 1986, p. 30)

Finch and Ferraro (1986) note that in the typical fair cross-section challenge applying these elements usually centers on the sufficiency of the statistical proof. They report that several courts have refused to recognize excludable jurors as such a group.

Although "excludables" do not form such a "distinctive" group in society, recent research has demonstrated that death penalty attitudes correlate with demographic characteristics that have been perceived by the courts as defining distinctive groups, namely, race and gender (Bersoff & Ogden, 1987). After undergoing the death qualification screening, 21% of female respondents were classified as excludables in the Fitzgerald and Ellsworth (1984) study, as compared to 13% of males. In addition, Cowan et al. (1984) and Neises and Dillehay (1987) found significant associations between gender and death qualification status. Death qualification has also been questioned because of an apparent disparity in the proportions of white and minority jurors who are excluded. Fitzgerald and Ellsworth (1984) found in their study that 26% of African-American respondents would be classified as excludables in a capital case, as compared to 16% of white jurors. Similar results were found in the Cowan et al. (1984) study. Furthermore, a number of studies that simply looked at death penalty attitudes have found that both gender and race covary with such attitudes (e.g., Bronson, 1970; Zeisel, 1968). African-Americans and women tend to hold more negative attitudes toward the death penalty than do whites and men. Fitzgerald and Ellsworth (1984) report that the proportion of people responding that they are "strongly opposed" to the death penalty comes very close to the number of *Witherspoon* excludables. Again, African-Americans and women tend to be heavily represented in the "strongly opposed" category.

The findings regarding race and gender, on face value, suggest a possible violation of the *Duren* fair cross-section doctrine. Minorities and women obviously constitute a distinct group within the community, representing a sizable proportion of the jury pool, and are disproportionately excluded from service due to death qualification. Furthermore, the underrepresentation of minorities and women in the pool of death qualified jurors results from the systematic exclusion of these people because of their attitudes toward the death penalty, regardless of their evaluations of their abilities to perform the functions of jurors. At the least, these data suggest a second look by the Supreme Court is advisable.

Court Cases since **Witherspoon**

Armed with this new evidence not available to the Court in *Witherspoon*, attorneys and psychologist argued that the evidence was not "too tentative and fragmentary" to suggest problems with death qualification. The issue of death qualification once again returned to the courts, where the constitutionality of death qualification was questioned on the grounds that the process violated a defendant's

Sixth and Fourteenth Amendment rights. The California Supreme Court took up this issue in 1980, with *Hovey v. Superior Court*, where the petitioner, who was accused of kidnapping and murder, challenged California's death qualification practice. The *Witherspoon* ruling allowed for the exclusion of both guilt and penalty nullifiers, and Hovey challenged the exclusion of the penalty nullifiers for the guilt phase of the trial.

The court, in this case, had before it the preliminary reports of the Ellsworth and Haney studies. However, Chief Justice Byrd, writing for the court, ruled that the groups defined as "death qualified" in the Ellsworth studies were fundamentally different than "California death qualified" jurors because, in California, three groups of people are excluded from service: guilt nullifiers, penalty nullifiers, and those who would automatically impose the death penalty at the sentencing stage on a defendant found guilty during the guilt phase (these the court referred to as the "automatic death penalty group" or ADPs). Because none of Ellsworth's studies expressly considered ADPs as part of the excludable group, the court was unable to make a decision favorable to the petitioner on the basis of this work alone. However, because of the aforementioned research findings of Haney (1984), the court decided that the death qualification procedure could potentially bias jurors and thus ordered that the death qualification portion of the voir dire be conducted individually for each prospective juror.

In light of this ruling, Kadane (1984) reanalyzed the Ellsworth (Cowan et al., 1984) data, taking into account the ADP group. He found that those people who could be fair and impartial during the guilt phase, and yet still would automatically impose the death penalty during sentencing, accounted for about 1% of the total juror population. Thus, the inclusion of these people would change the fundamental results of the Ellsworth studies very little. With this finding, the Arkansas Supreme Court in *Grigsby v. Mabry* (1983) concluded that the social science evidence established a link between death qualification and conviction proneness. The Arkansas court dismissed the *Hovey* ruling on the grounds that the number of people falling into the ADP group was negligible.

Returning to the U.S. Supreme Court, two rulings since *Witherspoon* have had significant ramifications on the process of death qualification. In *Wainwright v. Witt* (1985), the Court essentially changed the rules by which jurors are excluded in capital cases. As Thompson (1989) discusses the case, *Witherspoon* called for the exclusion of jurors (1) who would automatically vote against the death penalty and (2) whose attitude toward the death penalty was such that they would be unable to render an impartial verdict. In *Witt*, the Court relaxed this standard by stating that a juror whose views would "prevent or substantially impair the performance of his duty as a juror in accordance with his instructions and oath" could be excluded (*Witt*, p. 850, as cited in Thompson, 1989). According to Thompson, this new standard substantially increased the proportion of people who would be classified as nullifiers, because jurors now do not have to qualify their bias against the death penalty as an "automatic" vote against the death penalty. Neises and Dillehay (1987) found that the *Witt* standard would exclude approximately 21% of their sample, whereas the combined *Witherspoon* criteria would exclude 14%. When combined with ADPs, the total percentage of excludables for a case using the *Witt* standard would be 40.6%, while using the *Witherspoon* standard, it would be 38.6%. Indeed, *Witt* potentially increases the size of the excludable group.

In *Lockhart v. McCree* (1986), the Supreme Court overturned the ruling in *Grigsby*, with the majority criticizing the empirical studies by finding flaws in each. *McCree* is an important case for social scientists because, for this case, the American Psychological Association provided the Court with an *amicus curiae* brief (Bersoff & Ogden, 1987) that outlined most of the evidence presented earlier. In making the ruling of the Court, Justice Rehnquist examined each study piecemeal and dismissed anyone he determined to be flawed (Thompson, 1989). According to Thompson, eight of the studies presented by *McCree* were dismissed with the single sentence "[these] studies dealt solely with generalized attitudes and beliefs about the death penalty ... and were thus ... only marginally relevant" to the issue of conviction proneness (*McCree* at 1773, as quoted by Thompson, 1989). The remaining studies were essentially ignored by the Court, which claimed that the research added little to what was known to the Court at *Witherspoon*. This claim was based, in part, on the argument that none of the new studies demonstrated that *juries*, as opposed to *jurors*, would be biased against the defendant after death qualification procedures. Thus, with a single stroke, the Court shot down the claim that death qualification led to a conviction-prone jury and thus violated a defendant's Sixth and Fourteenth Amendment rights.

Similarly, the Court in *McCree* rejected the claim that death qualification results in an biased jury, declaring the social science evidence legally irrelevant, because the data only speak to the aggregate tendencies of the jury (Thompson, 1989). Thompson further reports that the Court adopted an individual view to impartiality in this case, claiming that "an impartial jury consists of nothing more than jurors who will conscientiously apply the law and find the facts," (*McCree* at 1767, quoting *Witt* at 844, 852, as quoted by Thompson, 1989). The Court essentially claimed that the jury is nothing more than the sum of the individual jurors, without necessitating consideration of any aggregate qualities. If as Fitzgerald and Ellsworth (1984) claim, death qualified jurors tend to favor the prosecution, then it would seem important to consider what happens when a group of like-minded individuals interact. Studies of group polarization (Myers & Lamm, 1976) and mock jury decision making (Davis, 1980) suggest that the group can become more extreme in its position as compared to the average of the individual tendencies. Results such as these suggest a need to consider the group-level effects of death qualification.

Purpose of Present Research

In their consideration of the social scientific evidence presented, the Court has been criticized for considering each study individually and, subsequently, for failing to see the overall pattern of results that suggest the biasing effects of death qualification (e.g., Thompson, 1989). Furthermore, the Court defined *impartial* at the *juror* as opposed to the *jury* level, in addition to claiming that no evidence of *jury* bias had been demonstrated. The present research attempts to address these concerns using two different but complementary methodological approaches. First, a series of meta-analyses was performed on the effects of death qualification and death penalty attitudes on conviction proneness and the exclusion of certain groups. Meta-analysis has an advantage over the written summary approach used in the American Psychological Association (APA) brief in that it moves the focus from the individual study to the overall pattern of evidence. In addition, it provides a quantitative measure of the consistency with which a body of research provides evidence for a particular position.

Based on the results of the meta-analyses, we attempted to address the issue of the effects of death qualification on jury verdicts using computer simulations derived from empirically supported formal models of jury behavior. The computer simulation approach has worked well in addressing the implications of other issues surrounding the jury, such as changes in jury size and decision rule (Davis, 1980), and the potential impact of using social scientists to help choose jurors favorable to a particular side (Tindale & Nagao, 1986). Given the inherent difficulties of studying real capital juries and the equally problematic nature of empirical simulations (i.e., mock jury studies) for capital offenses (where the mock jurors are well aware that their decisions do not affect real life-and-death issues), meta-analytic and computer simulation approaches may be the only ways to scientifically address the concerns surrounding death qualification procedures.

Meta-Analyses

Literature Search

We conducted literature searches using the keywords *death qualification* and *death penalty attitudes* of the PsycLIT database covering the period January 1974–January 1994. We then used the reference lists provided by these empirical studies and thought pieces written by legal philosophers to locate other studies of potential relevance. After a list was compiled, we sent the list to several of the researchers who conducted this work, along with a description of the intended project and a request for any other relevant studies of which they might have knowledge. In total, 14 articles provided nonredundant information useful for our analyses.

Coding of Variables

For each study, the following information was coded: (1) the type of participants used, either college students or actual jurors; (2) the procedure used to determine death qualification, either *Witherspoon* or *Witt* criteria; and (3) the type of stimulus materials used, whether they were written, audio, or video reenactments of trials. Where applicable, depending upon the study, the following information was also recorded: (1) race and gender differences in death qualification; (2) pre- and post-deliberation verdict decisions reached; (3) sentence decisions; (4) differences in death penalty attitudes between qualified and excludable groups; and (5) ratings of willingness to convict in capital cases. Differences for the variables (except for 4) listed above were also recorded using differences in death penalty attitudes as the grouping factor.

Six meta-analyses were performed, focusing primarily on the following empirical issues: (1) differences for conviction proneness between death qualified and excludable jurors; (2) racial differences in the proportions of death qualified jurors; (3) gender differences in the proportions of death qualified jurors; (4) racial differences in death penalty attitudes; (5) gender differences in death penalty attitudes; and (6) differences in reported need for additional evidence in capital cases between death qualified and excludable jurors.

Results

Hedges and Olkin (1985) have advocated the use of g, the differences between the means of the experimental and control groups divided by the pooled within-groups standard deviation, as a measure of effect size. These values of g are converted into unbiased estimates of the population parameters, d. Effect sizes for the individual studies were calculated and combined using the DSTAT statistical package for meta-analysis (Johnson, 1989).

Death Qualification and Conviction Proneness

For this analysis, 12 separate effect sizes were combined to yield an index of the effect of death qualification on conviction proneness. The effect sizes for each of the individual studies used in this meta-analysis, as well as the sample sizes for the death qualified and excludable groups, are displayed in Table 5. Most of the studies included employed student participants. The exceptions were the studies by Cowan et al. (1984), Ellsworth et al. (1984), Jurow (1971), and Harris (1977), who selected participants from at-large adult populations. Most of the studies distinguished death qualified from excludable jurors using the *Witherspoon* criteria. However, Jurow (1971) used attitudes toward the death penalty to define death qualified from non-death qualified jurors. Harris (1970) distinguished between scrupled and nonscrupled jurors, based on attitudes toward the death penalty. Bernard and Dwyer (1984) distinguished juror types based upon their willingness to impose the death penalty under certain circumstances. Those participants who expressed any willingness to impose the death penalty, even if only in extreme cases, were classified as death qualified.

In each of these studies, jurors were asked to make (at least) one verdict decision. The cases on which these decisions were based differed across studies. Several of the studies (Cowan et al., 1984; Elliot, 1991, all studies; Elliot & Robinson, 1991, Study 1)

**Table 5. Effect Sizes for Conviction Proneness
of Death-Qualified Jurors Meta-Analysis**

Study	Death-qualified group size	Excludable group size	Effect size
Bernard and Dwyer (1984)	135	45	.104
Cowan et al. (1984)	258	30	.534
Elliot (1991)			
Study 1	83	24	−.182
Study 2	89	21	.054
Study 3	43	13	.144
Elliot and Robinson (1991)			
Study 1	87	23	−.127
Study 2	45	37	.000
Study 3a	61	22	.049
Study 3b	83	10	−.311
Ellsworth et al. (1984)	19	16	.243
Jurow (1971)	190	21	.288
Louis Harris & Associates (1971)	1593	475	.145

used some variation of the Hastie et al. (1983) videotaped murder trial simulation. Elliot and Robinson (1991), Study 2, used a slide presentation of the case depicted in the Hastie et al. (1983) videotape. Jurow (1971) used two audiotaped murder cases: a robbery–murder and a rape–murder. Elliot and Robinson (1991), Studies 3a and 3b, used a written transcript of the Jurow rape–murder scenario. Bernard and Dwyer (1984) used a written murder scenario. In this study, although jurors were combined into three different jury types and asked to reach jury decisons, the authors also provided the individual first-ballot verdict decisions. These decisions were used in the analyses here. Harris (1970) had respondents make verdict decisions for four cases: the theft of a typewriter; the manslaughter of a police officer; the assault of a police officer; and the larceny of an automobile. Ellsworth et al. (1984) had participants reach four verdict decisions for cases in which defendants were utilizing an insanity defense where the root cause of the insanity was "organic" (retardation or epilepsy) or "non-organic" (schizoaffective-type schizophrenia or paranoid schizophrenia) in nature. For the studies in which the same jurors made multiple verdict decisions (Ellsworth et al., 1984; Harris, 1970; Jurow, 1971), the results were combined within each study into a single effect size, which was entered into the computations for the overall effect size.

Each of the individual effect sizes presented in Table 5 were combined to yield an overall index of the effects of death qualification on conviction proneness. The meta-analysis indicated that death qualified jurors tend to be more conviction prone ($d = .125$, with a 95% confidence interval of .04 to .21) than jurors who would be excluded. Although the effect is not large, the 95% confidence interval does not contain 0, indicating that the effect across studies is reliable.

Race and Gender Differences and Death Qualification

The effects of death qualification on the eligibility of different strata within the population were also investigated. Studies that explicitly determined the effects of death qualification on the racial and gender diversity within the population of eligible jurors were utilized in the following meta-analyses. To study racial differences, three studies were utilized, the individual effect sizes for which can be found in Table 6. All of the studies utilized prospective jurors as participants. Cowan et al. (1984) and Fitzgerald and Ellsworth (1984) established death qualification status through the use of the *Witherspoon* criteria. Bronson (1970) established death qualification status through the use of an attitude questionnaire. Those respondents who expressed strong opposition to the death penalty were classified as excludable. Two of the three studies reported large differences in the proportions of different ethnic groups being excluded. Our comparisons distinguished between whites and nonwhites. The third study (Cowan et al., 1984) reported that there were no significant differences in the qualification status of the different races, and an effect size of 0 was entered into the analyses. However, it should be noted that 93% of their sample was white.

To study gender differences, five separate effect sizes were combined into the overall effect size. The individual effect sizes can be found in Table 7. In addition to information provided by the Bronson, Cowan et al., and Fitzgerald and Ellsworth studies mentioned earlier, information was also taken from Cox and Tanford (1989) and Neises and Dillehay (1987). Cox and Tanford utilized student participants in their study and classified them as death qualified or excludable using the *Witherspoon* standards. Neises and Dillehay compared the effects of the *Witherspoon* criteria with the criteria set forth in *Witt* on a sample of jury-eligible adults. The reported gender differences in death qualification were found using the *Witt* criteria.

The results of these meta-analyses indicate that minority jurors are more likely to be excluded than white jurors ($d = .304$, with a 95% confidence interval of .13 to .47). Also, women are more likely to be excluded from jury service than are men ($d = .195$, with a 95% confidence interval of .11 to .28). Both of these analyses indicate that death qualification systematically excludes minorities and women from service on capital juries, seemingly because of their attitudes toward the death penalty.

Table 6. Effect Sizes for the Meta-Analysis on the Impact of Death Qualification on the Racial Composition of Jury Panels

Study	Proportion non-whites excluded	Proportion whites excluded	Effect size
Bronson (1970)	.294	.095	.655
Cowan et al. (1984)	n/a	n/a	.000
Fitzgerald and Ellsworth (1984)	.255	.165	.236

Note: The proportions for Bronson (1970) are for whites and all others, whereas the proportions for Fitzgerald and Ellsworth (1984) compare blacks to all others. The effect size for Cowan et al. (1984) results from their assertion that, in their sample, death qualifieds and excludables did not differ on this variable.

Table 7.   Effect Sizes for the Meta-Analysis on the Impact
of Death Qualification on the Gender Composition of Jury Panels

Study	Proportion males excluded	Proportion females excluded	Effect size
Bronson (1970)	.084	.132	.159
Cowan et al. (1984)	n/a	n/a	.296
Cox and Tanford (1989)	.112	.098	−.047
Fitzgerald and Ellsworth (1984)	.131	.210	.214
Neises and Dillehay (1987)	.117	.284	.417

Racial and Gender Differences in Death Penalty Attitudes

Because death qualification is closely related to death penalty attitudes (Fitz-gerald & Ellsworth, 1984), we compared minorities to whites and males to females in their opposition to the death penalty. The effect sizes for the individual studies can be found in Tables 8 (for race) and 9 (for gender). To investigate racial and gender differences in death penalty attitudes, information was taken from four sources. The specifics of Cowan et al. (1984) have already been mentioned. Goldberg (1970) used a student population and asked her participants whether they held any conscientious scruples toward the death penalty. Luginbuhl and Middendorf (1988) sampled from a population of eligible jurors in North Carolina and assessed death penalty attitudes using a four-point scale. Racial and gender differences were indicated in terms of differences in mean scores on this scale. All effect sizes from this source were calculated from the inferential statistics provided. Thus, no proportions are provided in Tables 8 or 9 for this study. One effect size for race and two effect sizes for gender were taken from this study. Finally, information on racial and gender differences in death penalty attitudes was taken from Zeisel (1968), which provided a combination of several Gallup polls measuring gender and race differences in death penalty attitudes.

The results of these meta-analyses revealed that women are more likely to hold negative death penalty attitudes than men ($d = .280$, with a 95% confidence interval

Table 8.   Effect Sizes for the Meta-Analysis
on Racial Differences in Death Penalty Attitudes

Study	Proportion nonwhites opposed to DP	Proportion whites opposed to DP	Effect size
Bronson (1970)	.676	.397	.573
Goldberg (1970)	.760	.470	.622
Luginbuhl and Middendorf (1988)	.680	.420	.519
Zeisel (1968)	.671	.518	.310

Table 9.   Effect Sizes for the Meta-Analysis
on Gender Differences in Death Penalty Attitudes

Study	Proportion males opposed to DP	Proportion females opposed to DP	Effect size
Bronson (1970)	.309	.533	.467
Goldberg (1970)	.590	.640	.102
Luginbuhl and Middendorf (1988)			
Study 1	n/a	n/a	.521
Study 2	n/a	n/a	.258
Zeisel (1968)	.467	.590	.248

of .23 to .33). Also, members of minority groups are more likely to hold negative death penalty attitudes than white jurors ($d = .370$, with a 95% confidence interval of .28 to .46).

Need for More Evidence by Nondeath Qualified Jurors

One point raised by critics of the research on death qualified juries (e.g., Elliot, 1991; Robinson & Elliot, 1991) was that excludables, as compared to death qualified jurors, would be less likely to follow the law in capital cases. In an attempt to demonstrate this, Robinson and Elliot asked study participants to choose one of five statements concerning the need for more evidence in order to convict in a capital case. The categories were No More Evidence, A Little More Evidence, Somewhat More Evidence, Much More Evidence, and Could Never Vote Guilty in a Capital Case. A group of Loyola University students were also asked the same question. Excluding the Could Never Vote category, we collapsed the categories of A Little, Somewhat, and Much into one (because all three technically would be a violation of jury instructions) and compared the number of death qualified verses excludable jurors that claimed they would need more evidence for a capital case. The effects sizes and proportions needing no more evidence for the Elliot and Robinson study, and our Loyola study are presented in Table 10. The results showed that excludable jurors were more likely than death qualified jurors to need more evidence in a capital trial ($d = .470$, with a 95% confidence interval of .21–.73).

Computer Simulations

The first set of simulations attempted to ascertain the impact of death qualification procedures on jury verdict distributions. The simulations were generated using a computer program based on social decision scheme theory (Davis, 1973). The theory attempts to model the processes by which individual group members combine their preferences into a single group response. For example, the members of a 12-person

**Table 10.   Effect Sizes for the Meta-Analysis
on Need for More Evidence and Death Qualification
Proportion Needing No More Evidence**

Study	Excludables	Nonexcludables	Effect size
Loyola Study (1995)	.35	.45	.468
Robinson et al. (1992)	.16	.38	.471

jury can array themselves over two response alternatives (e.g., guilty vs. not guilty) in 13 different ways (i.e. 12 for guilty and none for not guilty, 11 for guilty and 1 for not guilty,... none for guilty and 12 for not guilty). Given the probability that a juror randomly selected from some population would vote guilty, a probability distribution across the different group preference structures can be estimated. This probability distribution is then multiplied by a social decision scheme (SDS) matrix. An SDS matrix contains the conditional probabilities associated with a particular group preference distribution choosing a particular decision alternative (for a more complete description of the theory, see Davis, 1973; Stasser, Kerr, & Davis, 1989).

Table 11 presents the SDS matrix that we used for the first set of simulations. As indicated in the table, any time at least two-thirds of the jury members favor the same alternative, that alternative is chosen by the jury. When no two-thirds majority exists, the model assumes that the jury will choose not guilty with a probability of .75, and

**Table 11.   Two-Thirds
Majority, Defendant
Protection Otherwise
Social Decision Scheme**

Juror verdict distribution		Predicted jury verdict probabilities		
G	NG	G	NG	Hung
12	0	1.0	0.0	0.0
11	1	1.0	0.0	0.0
10	2	1.0	0.0	0.0
9	3	1.0	0.0	0.0
8	4	1.0	0.0	0.0
7	5	0.0	0.75	0.25
6	6	0.0	0.75	0.25
5	7	0.0	0.75	0.25
4	8	0.0	1.0	0.0
3	9	0.0	1.0	0.0
2	10	0.0	1.0	0.0
1	11	0.0	1.0	0.0
0	12	0.0	1.0	0.0

will reach no decision (hang) with a probability of .25. This model, referred to as a two-thirds majority–defendant protection otherwise model, has received substantial empirical support in mock jury studies (e.g., Davis, Kerr, Stasser, Meek, & Holt, 1977).

Our first two simulations were based on the following assumptions. First, we assumed an average jury-pool size of 50 members, from which the final 12 jurors would be chosen. Second, we used the two-thirds majority model described in Table 10 to model the outcome of the jury deliberation process. Third, we assumed that ADP jurors and guilt nullifiers (using the *Witherspoon* criteria) would be struck for cause and would never end up on a jury. Thus, these categories of jurors are not included in any of the simulations. The death qualified jury condition simply assumed that all of the jury members were drawn from a pool of potential jurors (all death qualified) with a particular probability for voting for conviction. The nondeath qualified jury condition assumed that jurors were being sampled from two distinct populations: one comparable to the death qualified condition, and the other (impartial jurors but penalty nullifiers) .125 standard deviations less likely to vote for conviction. This value (.125) was taken from the meta-analysis for conviction proneness discussed earlier. Based on some recent data collected in our lab, we sampled twice as often from the death qualified group as compared to the penalty nullifier group. For example, in a jury pool of size 50, with an initial probability of conviction of .35, the standard deviation around .35 would be .067. This value, when multiplied by .125, would lead to an estimate of the probability of a vote to convict from the penalty nullifier group of .342. Sampling from the two groups with the aforementioned weights would give an overall nondeath qualified jury pool estimate of .347, as compared to .35 when only death qualified jurors are included. Such a calculation was done for the range of possible individual probability of conviction values starting at 0 and continuing to 1.0 in increments of .05. A second, similar set of calculations was performed using a value of .21 for the difference between death qualified and nondeath qualified jury pools. This value represents the upper end of the 95% confidence interval, which could be perceived as the most biased case possible, given the meta-analytic results we obtained.

The results of the first two simulations are presented in Figure 2. The points along the abscissa represent the probability of an individual, death qualified juror voting for conviction. The points along the ordinate represent the probability of a jury voting for conviction, given a particular individual conviction probability. The black bars represent death qualified juries. The other two bars represent nondeath qualified juries, one using the mean effect-size estimate and the other using the upper end of the 95% confidence interval or maximum effect-size estimate. The figure shows that death qualified juries would have higher conviction rates than nondeath qualified juries. However, these differences, even using the maximum effect-size estimate, are very small. The largest differences in the figure are only 1.4%, which occurred using the maximum effect-size estimate at the individual conviction levels of .60, .65, and .70. Using the mean effect-size estimate, the largest differences are .8% at these same points. Such differences would translate into two or three fewer convictions per 200

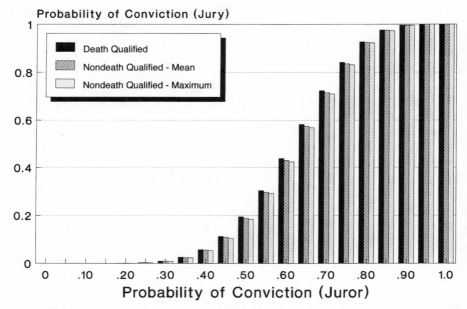

Figure 2. Probability of conviction estimates for death qualified and non-death qualified juries (mean effect size = .125, Maximum effect size = .210).

capital trials by using nondeath qualified juries (see Davis & Kerr, 1986, for a discussion of a similar finding based on a very different simulation strategy).

The relatively small differences found in the first two simulations led us to run a similar simulation using the largest effect size obtained in any of the studies we included. This effect size (.53) came from the Cowan et al. (1984) paper, which probably represents the best study included from a methodological standpoint. Table 12 shows a portion of the results from this third simulation. As indicated in the table,

Table 12. **Estimated Jury Conviction Probabilities for Death Qualified and Nondeath Qualified Juries Assuming an Effect Size of .53**

Individual	Death qualified	Nondeath qualified	Difference
.50	.194	.171	.023
.55	.304	.275	.029
.60	.438	.404	.034
.65	.583	.549	.034
.70	.724	.693	.031

over the range of individual conviction probabilities that produce the largest jury-level differences, the differences still are not large, ranging from 2.3% to 3.4%.

One limitation of the simulations presented thus far is that they were based on models encompassing only two verdict categories—guilty and not guilty. However, in many murder trials (and the mock trial used by Cowan et al., 1984), there are four possible verdicts: (1) guilty of first-degree murder, (2) guilty of second-degree murder, (3) guilty of manslaughter, and (4) not guilty. Thus, we ran one final simulation comparing verdict propensities for death qualified and nondeath qualified juries. Using data presented by Hastie et al. (1983), we developed a social decision scheme model that mimicked the predictions of the JUS model developed by Hastie et al. The SDS model that best fits their data was a two-thirds majority, weighted averaging model, with considerably more weight given to the second-degree murder verdict. We then used this model to simulate the jury verdicts that might have occurred in the Cowan et al. Study had their juries been allowed to deliberate until a consensus was reached. The death qualified and nondeath qualified jury panels were defined based on the initial, individual verdict preference data from Cowan et al. The results are presented in Figure 3. Again, as indicated in the figure, the differences in conviction rates are small, with the increase in the number of not guilty verdicts as a function of using nondeath qualified juries only reaching 3%. For this mock trial, the probabilities associated with first-degree murder verdicts (the only verdict that actually could

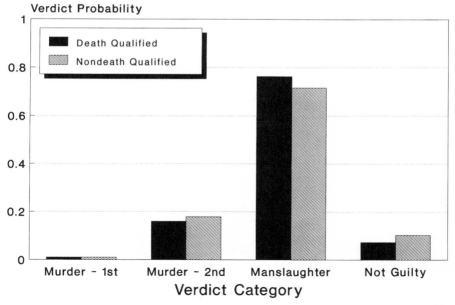

Figure 3. Verdict probabilities for death qualified and nondeath qualified juries using data from Cowan et al. (1984).

lead to a death sentence) were trivially small, regardless of whether the juries were death qualified.

Given the meta-analytic results obtained concerning racial differences and death qualification, we decided to estimate the probability of minority (specifically African-American) representation on juries trying capital cases. Using the data from Fitzgerald and Ellsworth (1984), we calculated the probability of a jury having no African-American jurors impaneled. Fitzgerald and Ellsworth reported that approximately 25% of African-Americans would be struck for cause due to death qualification (i.e., would be categorized as penalty nullifiers—again, guilty nullifiers were not considered in our simulations). Using binomial probabilities, we estimated the probability that a jury would contain no African-American members for three different populations. The three populations were 5% African-Americans, 12.7% African-Americans (the current percentage in the U.S., based on the U.S. Census Report, 1995), and 40% African-American. The results of the simulation are presented in Figure 4. As indicated in the figure, when African-Americans represent about 40% of the local population (i.e., jury pool), the effects of death qualification on the likelihood of having no African-American representation on the jury is relatively small. However, for populations typical of the United States as a whole, or for populations where African-Americans are underrepresented, death qualification increases the probability of having no African-American representation on the jury by between 9% and

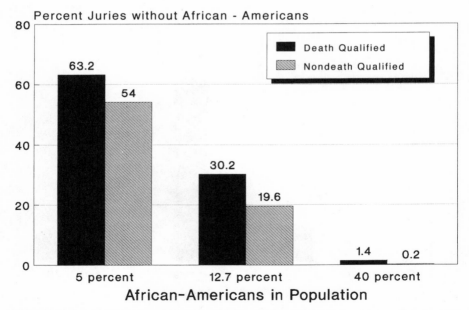

Figure 4. Estimated percentages of juries impaneled containing no African-American members for death qualified and nondeath qualified juries.

11%. A similar analysis could have been performed for gender. However, given that women make up about 50% of the population on average, the odds of selecting an all-male jury would be extremely small, regardless of whether death qualification procedures were used.

Implications and Conclusions

The meta-analyses and computer simulations reported here attempted to address a number of aspects related to the controversy surrounding death qualified juries. In *Lockhart v. McCree* (1986), the Supreme Court ruled that death qualified juries do not violate a defendant's constitutional rights. Their arguments were based, in part, on a piecemeal interpretation of the social science evidence and on the lack of direct evidence concerning the biasing effects of death qualification on *jury* verdicts. The meta-analytic results concerning the argument that death qualified jurors are more likely to vote for conviction than nondeath qualified jurors are at odds with the Court's decision. Summing across multiple studies using different trials, methods, and participants, the evidence remains firm: Death qualified jurors are more conviction prone than nondeath qualified jurors. Even though the effect size is small by general social science standards, it is statistically reliable. In addition, our results support a number of other claims made in the APA *amicus curiae* brief (Bersoff & Ogden, 1987). Males and females differ in terms of their death penalty attitudes and in their propensities to be excluded from juries due to death qualification procedures. Minorities also are more negative toward the death penalty and will be excluded more often from juries than will majority group (i.e., white) members. However, our results also confirm a point made by critics of the APA brief (Elliot, 1991). Although based on only two studies, a significant effect size was found between death qualified persons and penalty nullifiers in terms of the reported need for more evidence in order to vote for conviction in a capital trial. More penalty nullifiers report that they would need more evidence to convict in a capital trial as compared to the death qualified group. Given that jurors are not supposed to consider the potential penalties in the guilt phase of a trial, these results indicate that penalty nullifiers are less likely to follow the judge's instructions to the letter than are death qualified jurors. However, in the data we collected, only 45% of the death qualified participants reported that they would need no more evidence in a capital case, whereas 35% of the penalty nullifiers responded this way. Thus, not all of our penalty nullifiers would refuse to follow the judge's instructions, and over half of our death qualified participants would refuse to do so.

The results of the simulations focused on conviction rates for death qualified and nondeath qualified juries were somewhat surprising and only weakly supportive of the arguments made in the APA brief. The brief argued that the evidence at the individual-juror level demonstrated that death qualified juries, if allowed to deliberate to a final verdict, would be more likely than nondeath qualified juries to convict. Our results support this claim, but using the average effect size from the meta-analysis, the differences between death qualified and nondeath qualified juries would be minute (approximately .8%). The simulation results predict that only one more conviction per 100 capital trials would occur due to using death qualification procedures. Even using inappropriately large estimates of the effect size does not produce substantial differences at the jury level (largest difference = 3.4%). Obviously, from the defendant's perspective, any increase in the probability of conviction would be unfair. However, other decisions made by the Supreme Court (e.g., *Ballew v. Georgia*, 1978) have tolerated much larger biases against the defendant on practical grounds (e.g., the maximum difference found between simulation of 6- and 12-person juries is 15% and can favor the prosecution over the defense; Nagao & Davis, 1980).

Based on our simulations, potentially the most negative aspect of death qualification concerns the representation of minority group members (particularly African Americans) on capital juries. One of the key issues in the *Furman v. Georgia* (1972) case, where the death penalty, as then used, was declared unconstitutional, was the overwhelming evidence that African-Americans were given the death penalty far more often than whites (Hans & Vidmar, 1986). However, even with newly written death penalty statutes, early research showed that racial bias was still substantial (Bowers & Pierce, 1980). Currently, about 40% of the prisoners on death row are African-Americans. In addition, although over 50% of murder victims are African-Americans, the victims of over 82% of the inmates on death row were white.[1] Thus, African-American representation on capital juries, particularly for cases with white victims, would seem to be an important Sixth Amendment concern. However, our simulation showed that, in some cases, death qualification would reduce the odds of having even one African American on the jury by over 10%.

Although the findings presented here are potentially relevant to judicial policy, there are a number of limitations that should be mentioned. First, the meta-analyses present summaries of the findings as they are now. However, as previously mentioned, most of the cases used to generate the data we summarized were not capital cases. Whether, and to what degree, death qualification affects juror's judgments on capital cases has not been addressed empirically to a sufficient extent. However, such empirical investigations are not likely in the near future, due to the inherent difficulties of studying highly emotional behaviors in obviously nonreal settings. In addition, the ambiguity of the *Wainwright v. Witt* (1985) decision makes it even more difficult to define clearly how juries are death qualified. Judges in different jurisdictions may use very different criteria to decide whether a juror's views on capital punishment would "prevent or substantially impair the performance of his (her) duties as a juror in accordance with his (her) instructions" (*Wainwright v. Witt*, 1987, p. 852, as cited in Thompson, 1989, sections in parentheses inserted by current authors). Thus, future empirical work on this issue will be more difficult than was the case with the *Witherspoon* criteria.

---

[1]The statistics reported here were obtained from two cites on the World Wide Web. The percentage of murder victims by race was obtained from the U.S. Department of Justice FBI statistics—http://www.fbi.gov/ucrpress.htm. The death row statistics were obtained from NAACP Legal Defense Fund as reported from http://sun.soc.niu.edu/~critcrim/dp/dp.breakdown.96.

Although the models used for the jury simulations have received a fair amount of empirical support, various other assumptions were necessary for the simulations presented here. Changes in these assumptions would not necessarily change the shapes of the predicted curves or the direction of the effects, but the sizes of the relative differences would almost certainly change to some degree. In addition, the simulations did not take into account effects due to the voir dire proceedings (Haney, 1984), or the inclinations of penalty nullifiers to want additional evidence in capital cases (Elliot, 1991). It is also possible that death penalty attitudes have changed since many of the studies reviewed here were run. However, the data we collected for the simulations (obtained within the last 4 years) were not substantially different from those reported elsewhere. Overall, we hope these results will help inform future debates about death qualification procedures and provide policy makers with some benchmarks for evaluating present and future policy decisions.

References

Ballew v. Georgia. (1978). *United States Law Week, 46,* 4217–4224.

Bernard, J. L., & Dwyer, O. W. (1984). *Witherspoon v. Illinois*: The court was right. *Law and Psychology Review, 8,* 105-114.

Bersoff, D. N., & Ogden, D. W. (1987). In the Supreme Court of the United States: *Lockhart v. McCree. American Psychologist, 42,* 59–68.

Bowers, W., & Pierce, G. (1980). Arbitrariness and discrimination under post-*Furman* capital statutes. *Crime and Delinquency, 26,* 563–635.

Bronson, E. J. (1970). On the conviction proneness and representativeness of the death qualified jury: An empirical study of Colorado veniremen. *University of Colorado Law Reveiw, 42,* 1–32.

Cowan, C. L., Thompson, W. C., & Ellsworth, P. C. (1984). The effects of death qualification on jurors' predisposition to convict and on the quality of deliberations. *Law and Human Behavior, 8,* 53–80.

Cox, M., & Tanford, S. (1989). An alternative method of capital jury selection. *Law and Human Behavior, 13,* 167–183.

Davis, J. H. (1973). Group decision and social interaction: A theory of social decision schemes. *Psychological Review, 80,* 97–125.

Davis, J. H. (1980). Group decision and procedural justice. In M. Fishbein (Ed.), *Progress in social psychology* (pp. 157–229). Hillsdale, NJ: Erlbaum.

Davis, J. H., & Kerr, N. L. (1986). Thought experiments and the problem of sparse data in small-group performance research. In P. S. Goodman (Ed.), *Designing effective work groups* (pp. 305–349). San Francisco: Jossey-Bass.

Davis, J. H., Kerr, N. L., Atkin, R. S., Holt, R., & Meek, D. (1975). The decision processes of 6- and 12-person juries assigned unanimous and 2/3 majority rules. *Journal of Personality and Social Psychology, 32,* 1–14.

Davis, J. H., Kerr, N. L., Stasser, G., Meek, D., & Holt, R. (1977). Victim consequences, sentence severity, and decision processes in mock juries. *Organizational Behavior and Human Decision Processes, 18,* 346–365.

Duren v. Missouri. 439 U.S. 357 (1979).

Elliot, R. (1991). Social science data and the APA: The *Lockhart* brief as a case in point. *Law and Human Behavior, 15,* 59–76.

Elliot, R., & Robinson, R. J. (1991). Death penalty attitudes and the tendency to convict or acquit: Some data. *Law and Human Behavior, 15,* 389–404.

Ellsworth, P. C., Bukaty, R. M., Cowan, C. L., & Thompson, W. C. (1984). The death qualified jury and the defense of insanity. *Law and Human Behavior, 8,* 81–93.

Finch, F., & Ferraro, M. (1986). The empirical challenge to death qualified juries: On further examination. *Nebraska Law Review, 65,* 21–74.

Fitzgerald, R., & Ellsworth, P. C. (1984). Due process vs. crime control. *Law and Human Behavior, 8,* 31–51.

Furman v. Georgia. 408 U.S. 238 (1972).

Goldberg, F. (1970). Toward expansion of *Witherspoon*: Capital scruples, jury bias, and the use of psychological presumptions in the law. *Harvard Civil Rights Law Journal, 5,* 53–69.

Grigsby v. Mabry. 569 F. Supp. 1273 (E. D. Ark.) (1983).

Gross, S. R. (1984). Determining the neutrality of death qualified juries: Judicial appraisal of empirical data. *Law and Human Behavior, 8,* 7–30.

Haney, C. (1980). Juries and the death penalty: Readdressing the *Witherspoon* question. *Crime and Delinquency, 26,* 512–527.

Haney, C. (1984). On the selection of capital juries: The biasing effects of the death qualification process. *Law and Human Behavior, 8,* 121–132.

Haney, C., Hurtado, A., & Vega, L. (1994) "Modern" death qualification: New data on its biasing effects. *Law and Human Behavior, 18,* 619–633.

Hans, V. P., & Vidmar, N. (1986). *Judging the jury.* New York: Plenum Press.

Louis Harris & Associates. Study No. 2016, 1971. (On file at the NAACP Legal Defense Fund, 10 Columbus Circle, New York, NY 10019.

Hastie, R., Penrod, S., & Pennington, N. (1983). *Inside the jury.* Cambridge, MA: Harvard University Press.

Hedges, L. V., & Olkin, I. (1985). *Statistical methods for meta-analysis.* San Diego, CA: Academic Press.

Hovey v. Superior Court. 28 Cal 3d 1 (1980).

Johnson, B. T. (1989, updated 1993). *DSTAT: Software for the meta-analytic review of research literatures.* Hillsdale, NJ: Erlbaum.

Jurow, G. L. (1971). New data on the effect of a "death qualified" jury on the guilt determination process. *Harvard Law Review, 83,* 567–611.

Kadane, J. B. (1984). After *Hovey*: Taking account of the automatic death penalty jurors. *Law and Human Behavior, 8,* 115–120.

Lockhart v. McCree. 106 S. Ct. 1758 (1986).

Loftus, E. F. (1993). The reality of repressed memories. *American Psychologist, 48,* 518–537.

Luginbuhl, J., & Middendorf, K. (1988). Death penalty beliefs and jurors' responses to aggravating and mitigating circumstances in capital trials. *Law and Human Behavior, 12,* 263–282.

Monahan, J., & Walker, L. (1985). *Social science in law: Cases and materials.* New York: Foundation Press.

Muller v. Oregon. 208 U.S. 412 (1908).

Myers, D. G., & Lamm, H. (1976). The group polarization phenomenon. *Psychological Bulletin, 83,* 602–627.

Nagao, D. H., & Davis, J. H. (1980). Some implications of temporal drift in social parameters. *Journal of Experimental Social Psychology, 16,* 479–496.

Neises, M. L., & Dillehay, R. C. (1987). Death qualification and conviction proneness: *Witt* and *Witherspoon* compared. *Behavioral Sciences and the Law, 5,* 479–495.

Stasser, G., Kerr, N. L., & Davis, J. H. (1989). Influence processes and consensus models in decision-making groups. In P. Paulus (Ed.), *Psychology of group influence* (2nd ed., pp. 279–326). Hillsdale, NJ: Erlbaum.

Thiel v. Southern Pacific Co. 328 U.S. 217 (1946).

Thompson, W. C. (1989). Death qualification after *Wainwright v. Witt* and *Lockhart v. McCree.* *Law and Human Behavior, 13,* 185–216.

Thompson, W. C., Cowan, C. L., Ellsworth, P. C., & Harrington, J. C. (1984). Death penalty attitudes and conviction proneness: The translation of attitudes into verdicts. *Law and Human Behavior, 8,* 95–113.

Tindale, R. S., & Davis, J. H. (1983). Group decision making and jury verdicts. In H. H. Blumberg, A. P. Hare, V. Kent, & M. F. Davies (Eds.), *Small groups and social interaction* (Vol. 2, pp. 9–38). Chichester, UK: Wiley.

Tindale, R. S., & Nagao, D. H. (1986). An assessment of the potential utility of "Scientific Jury Selection": A "Thought Experiment" approach. *Organizational Behavior and Human Decision Processes, 37,* 409–425.

Wainwright v. Witt 105 S. Ct. 844 (1985).

Way, H. F. (1980). *Criminal justice and the American Constitution.* North Scituate, MA: Duxbury Press.

Wells, G. L. (1993). What do we know about eyewitness identification. *American Psychologist, 48,* 553–571.

White, W. (1973). The constitutional invalidity of convictions imposed by death qualified juries. *Cornell Law Reveiw, 58,* 1176–1220.

Williams v. Florida, 90 S. Ct. 1893 (1972).

Wilson, W. (1964). *Belief in capital punishment and jury performance.* Unpublished manuscript, University of Texas, Austin.

Witherspoon v. Illinois, 391 U.S. 550 (1968).

Zeisel, H. (1968). *Some data on juror attitudes toward capital punishment.* Monograph, Center for Studies in Criminal Justice, University of Chicago Law School, Chicago, IL.

9

Coordination in Task-Performing Groups

Gwen M. Wittenbaum, Sandra I. Vaughan, and Garold Stasser

Groups are often called upon to perform tasks in organizations. Hiring decisions are made by selection committees, product ideas are generated by teams, products are assembled by a collective of individuals, and problems regarding how to cut labor and time costs are solved by task forces. Often, these groups are composed of members with different expertise, skills, and roles, who work on a task that requires them to combine their efforts in a way that facilitates successful task completion. For example, the selection committee may try to pool all members' unique information about the job candidates in order to reach a well-informed decision, team members who generate product ideas may wish to avoid duplication of ideas in order to maximize the quantity of ideas produced, and members assembling a product may build the part that is assigned to them by occupational roles or standard operating procedures. The way in which group members synchronize their actions in order to complete successfully the group task is referred to as *group coordination*. In other words, group coordination involves who among the members does what, as well as when, where, and how they complete their designated tasks. This chapter explores different ways that members can coordinate their actions, the factors that moderate such coordination attempts, and implications for group performance effectiveness.

Coordination is an essential component of successful group performance. As Steiner (1972) suggested, groups whose actual productivity does not equal their potential productivity may have incurred such "process losses" because of either reduced motivation or poor coordination. We will focus on the latter cause of process losses, namely, performance deficits due to group actions that are poorly orchestrated. Coordination losses can stem from inappropriate allocation of resources (e.g., unnec-

Gwen M. Wittenbaum • Department of Communication, Michigan State University, East Lansing, Michigan 48824.   **Sandra I. Vaughan and Garold Strasser** • Department of Psychology, Miami University of Ohio, Oxford, Ohio 45056.

Theory and Research on Small Groups, edited by R. Scott Tindale et al. Plenum Press, New York, 1998.

essary duplication of efforts, leaving some subtasks undone) or failure to time efforts wisely. The lack of temporal coordination is demonstrated when work group members experience scheduling problems in their use of organizational resources or in finding a mutually satisfying meeting time (McGrath & Rotchford, 1983). Coordination losses can also occur when members do not weigh others' contributions in an optimal way or make incorrect assumptions about what subtasks others will perform. In recognition of the role that group coordination plays in impacting group performance, this chapter will review the existing literature related to group coordination and offer a theoretical integration.

Group coordination can vary on at least two dimensions: time and explicitness. Member attempts to coordinate may occur before group work begins or during the process of working together. Coordination may be *tacit*, based on unspoken expectations and intentions, or it may be *explicit*, based on verbal agreements or formally adopted plans that fully and clearly designate who is to do what and when they are to do it. Although the dimensions of time and explicitness theoretically represent continuums instead of dichotomies, for ease of presentation, we will discuss four modes of coordination located at the extreme of the continuums: (1) preplans, (2) in-process planning, (3) tacit precoordination, and (4) in-process tacit coordination. These coordination modes are depicted in Figure 5.

Before interaction begins, *preplans* explicitly indicate ways for members to coordinate their efforts. Preplans include job descriptions, organizational rules, poli-

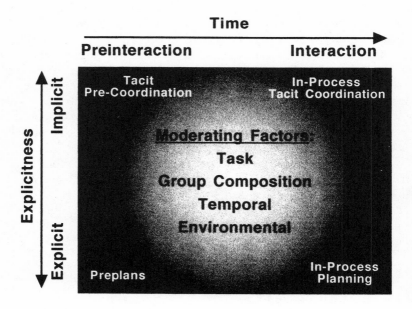

Figure 5. Model of Coordination mode in task-performing groups.

cies, schedules, and standard operating procedures. The explicitness of preplans is often established through written memoranda or verbal instructions from group leaders. For example, a task force set up to improve production efficiency may consist of members with different occupational roles: plant superintendent, engineer, accountant, assembler, and human resource manager. If the supervisor who composed the group circulated a memo defining what each member was expected to add to the group before the group's meeting (e.g., the accountant will be expected to analyze the plant's budget), such communication would constitute preplans. Along with operating rules and production schedules, these role descriptions and procedures explicitly identify what each member is expected to accomplish.

Like preplans, *in-process planning* explicitly defines each member's work role. However, in-process planning takes place through the communication of strategy plans during interaction or while members are working on their task. Thus, in-process planning is evidenced by discussion that mentions members' skills, abilities, and expertise, assigns subtasks to specific members, questions what others are doing to complete the task, or asserts how and when the task should be completed.

Although coordination can be explicit, several observations from the small-group process literature suggest that it is often tacit. Gersick (1988) found that work groups established patterns of interacting early during each group's first interaction. She assumed that the sheer speed with which behavioral patterns emerged suggests that they stem from processes operating before groups convene, such as "members' expectations about the task, each other, and the context and repertoires of behavioral routines and performance strategies" (p. 33). In a similar vein, Bettenhausen and Murnighan (1985) purported that newly formed bargaining groups quickly developed a norm for how to approach the task by incorporating task scripts that were shared among members before interaction. These examples illustrate *tacit precoordination*—preinteraction hypotheses about other group members, the task, and the work environment that influence coordination intentions; that is, members make assumptions about the task demands and others' likely task contributions, and adjust their own actions accordingly. Studies that examine how members allocate their resources in anticipation of group task completion (e.g., Wittenbaum, Stasser, & Merry, 1996) assess tacit precoordination strategies.

In-process tacit coordination occurs when members make mutual strategy adjustments tacitly while working. In other words, members tacitly adjust their own behavior to fit with the observed behavior of others during interaction. Hackman and Morris (1975) suggested that in-process tacit coordination is a prevalent phenomenon given that the task-oriented groups that they observed rarely discussed strategies for how to go about performing the task unless explicitly instructed to do so. They noted that "while most tasks do not constrain a group from overtly discussing and reformulating its performance strategies, there appears to be a pervasive norm in groups *not* to address such matters explicitly" (p. 67). These researchers claimed that in-process planning is normatively rare, suggesting that tacit coordination may be a prevalent phenomenon in task-oriented groups.

Members of jazz quartets (Bastien & Hostager, 1988; Eisenberg, 1990; Rose, 1994) and string quartets (Murnighan & Conlon, 1991) may exemplify in-process tacit coordination while they perform for an audience. Such groups often improvise while performing: "Decisions concerning when and how songs end, the length of the solos, when to change to a different section of the song, or how many verses of the lyrics to sing are frequently made on stage" (Rose, 1994, p. 418). Group norms, which dictate that the time between songs should be kept to a minimum, the band should appear "polished," and the band should foster the sense of spontaneous "jamming," make explicit communication of coordination difficult. Thus, improvisations often are guided by knowledge about which member takes the lead at which times, musical cues that indicate that a member is wrapping up her or his solo, and other nonverbal gestures (e.g., head nod, gaze).

The following section presents the growing empirical evidence for tacit coordination in anticipation of and during group work. After reviewing the literature that focuses directly on tacit coordination, we will turn our attention to two questions. First, what are the risks and benefits of tacitly, rather than explicitly, coordinating group performance? Second, what task, compositional, temporal, and environmental factors encourage and discourage reliance on tacit coordination?

Tacit Coordination

Supporting Literature

Questions regarding the process of tacit coordination have surfaced recently. Thus far, the areas of research and theorizing that have emerged concern (1) how group members coordinate their actions in anticipation of small-group task completion, and (2) the development and utility of transactive memory systems in small groups.

Anticipated Interaction

Coordination implies that members are adjusting their behavior based on observed or expected actions of other members and on task demands. Thus, the lack of explicit communication in tacit coordination does not imply coincidental or accidental divisions of labor that may occur if members simply follow their own predilections. To qualify as tacit coordination, members must be responding to characteristics of their fellow members and of the task to be completed. Wittenbaum et al. (1996) noted that tacit coordination entails at least three components: member expectations, task assessment, and resource allocation. *Member expectations* are subjective predictions about other members' actions: What are others likely to do? Assumptions about others' actions can be based on distal and fallible social cues, such as social stereotypes. In groups that work together often, these expectations can be determined by past behaviors in similar circumstances. *Task assessment* is the perceived demand of the collective task: What needs to be done? *Resource allocation* is each member's deployment of resources, such as attention, time, and effort, to subtasks.

Wittenbaum et al. (1996) noted that members hold a rich array of preinteraction knowledge about themselves, other members, and the collective task. In a similar vein, Rouse, Cannon-Bowers, and Salas (1992) suggested that groups develop mental models consisting of shared knowledge about the team (e.g., relationships and roles between members, purpose of the team) and task (e.g., procedures and strategies needed to complete the task, performance criteria). Although mental models can be explicitly negotiated, members often use them to form expectations about how others likely will respond to the group task, consequently allowing members to coordinate their actions with the behaviors anticipated by others. To the extent that team members hold congruent member expectations and similar task assessments, they can allocate their resources in mutually complementary ways.

Wittenbaum et al. (1996) conducted an experiment to assess directly whether members are sensitive to cues about other members' likely actions and the demands of the task when coordinating their actions in anticipation of small-group task completion. In their study, members read information about three candidates for student-body president and anticipated discussing the candidates in small groups with others who were "experts" in some topics addressed by the candidates. Anticipated task demands were varied by telling subjects that their group would be asked to either remember collectively as many candidate statements as possible (*recall set*) or decide collectively on the best candidate (*decide set*). In lieu of group interaction, subjects were asked unexpectedly to recall individually the candidate information. Results showed that members coordinated their activities differently depending on the task demands. Those expecting a collective recall task remembered more information in topics that fell outside of the other members' anticipated expertise (items that the others probably would not remember), whereas those expecting a group decision remembered more information in topics associated with others' anticipated expertise (items that the others probably would remember). Presumably, recall-set subjects supplemented others' expected recall to enhance the group's recall output and decide-set subjects duplicated others' expected recall to facilitate reaching a group consensus.[1] These results held both when subjects were explicitly told about others' areas of expertise and when subjects needed to infer others' expertise from remote social cues. This research provides some evidence that members form expectations about the task and anticipated actions of coworkers and attempt to allocate their resources in a way that facilitates successful task completion.

Vaughan and Stasser (1996) investigated how members of problem-solving groups adjusted their allocation of attention among subtasks over repeated trials. Groups worked on sets of four word scrambles and four logic problems on each of three trials. The word scrambles and logic problems also varied in difficulty. All three trials were identical in structure, and before each group interaction, individuals could review the problems their group would be solving. Across all trials, members tended to work on the problem type (logic problems or word scrambles) for which they felt

---

[1] Although the results are consistent with this interpretation, the authors did not directly assess members' information-processing strategies or their assumptions about what others would remember.

they had superior ability relative to others. Thus, individuals apparently imported self-knowledge of their relative skill at the two task types that guided their distribution of effort. Moreover, there was evidence for an emergent self-knowledge of general problem-solving ability that guided members' allocation of effort especially on the third trial; that is, members who, on a postexperimental questionnaire, rated themselves as generally better than others, tended to work on difficult problems, whereas those who rated themselves as less able tended to work on easy problems. However, this relationship between ability and problem choice did not emerge until the second trial and was strongest on the third trial. The implication is that members not only gain a sense of what others will do over repeated interaction but also gain a sense of what they can do better than others and allocate their efforts accordingly.

In summary, several lines of research have found evidence for tacit coordination. Members form expectations about each other based on social cues (Wittenbaum et al., 1996), past experience (Vaughan & Stasser, 1996), or shared mental models (Rouse et al., 1992), and use these expectations to guide their own behavior. Moreover, Wittenbaum et al. showed that varying task demands affects how members adjust their own behavior in relation to others' expected actions. Finally, members may also use perceived relative ability as a guide for behavior by allocating effort to tasks for which they feel they have superior ability relative to other members (Vaughan & Stasser, 1996).

Transactive Memory

Although not specifically a model of tacit coordination, Wegner's (1987, 1995) theory of transactive memory articulates some processes that involve the tacit coordination of collective memory. According to his theory, other people are sources of external memory storage, similar to phone books, computer databases, and dictionaries. For example, if Matt needs to know his brother-in-law's new phone number, he could ask his wife, Sue, where she placed the number or whether she remembers it herself. Matt's request may be based on an array of prior knowledge and assumptions; he may know that (1) he frequently misremembers others' phone numbers, (2) Sue maintains an address book, (3) Sue was able to locate quickly the last number he requested, or (4) Sue is likely to know the number because it is her brother.

This example illustrates several components of transactive memory. Members possess knowledge about their own memory, abilities, and expertise, as well as beliefs about other members' interests, skills, and expertise. From these beliefs, assumptions are made about the likelihood that information is stored in a particular member's mind. These assumptions can not only be based on beliefs about others' interests, skills, and expertise, but also history (e.g., Sue stored that kind of information in the past), occupational roles, circumstances (e.g., Sue was the last person who saw the number), access to information, and social cues, such as age, race, dress, and gender (e.g., it is the wife's role to keep track of phone numbers). Because Sue is more interested in keeping track of phone numbers relative to Matt, is more expert in information regarding her own family, and has a successful history of locating phone numbers, she is considered responsible for remembering her brother's number. In other words, in a group, "known experts in a domain are usually held responsible for the encoding, storage, and retrieval of any new information encountered in that domain" (Wegner, 1987, p. 192). In order to obtain the information from the "experts," members need to inquire with a label that will help the others retrieve the information. In the case of Matt, asking Sue for her "brother's new phone number" would probably be an adequate label from which Sue could search her own memory for the information or use the tag placed in her memory for where to find it in an external source ("Oh yeah, I wrote it down on a napkin and placed it in my purse"). Moreover, Sue's success in locating the phone number likely will solidify her role as the group member who collects and organizes phone numbers.

Transactive memory systems can develop tacitly over time as members learn about each others' areas of expertise and make assumptions about what information others will remember. Conceptually, this is similar to the member expectations component in the Wittenbaum et al. (1996) model. Moreover, members are sensitive to the task demands, which, in the case of transactive memory, involve the collective encoding, storage, and retrieval of information. If members wish to save time and energy, it is efficient to distribute the memory load among group members such that different members are responsible for different types of information. In this way, the memory load of any single member is lessened. Also, members allocate their own memory resources to actions that help the group retain the most information by remembering information in their own area of expertise. Thus, the development and use of transactive memory systems often involves tacitly coordinated action.

In one of the few studies to explore empirically the development and utility of transactive memory, Wegner, Erber, and Raymond (1991) examined the memory performance of couples who were paired with their intimate partner (*natural pairs*) or a member of another couple (*impromptu pairs*). Couples were instructed to memorize a list of words together without discussion. In half of the couples, a memory structure was imposed that made one member responsible for remembering items within some domains and the other member responsible for remembering items from the remaining domains (*assignment of expertise*). The other half of the couples received no imposed memory structure (*no assignment of expertise*). In support of the transactive memory hypothesis, natural pairs with no expertise assignment performed the best on the recall task, whereas natural pairs operating under an imposed memory structure performed the worst. Wegner et al. suggested that the structure of the natural memory system was disrupted by artificial responsibility assignments, thereby inhibiting memorization of the words. Also, as expected, impromptu pairs with expertise assignments performed better than those without such assignments. Wegner et al. concluded that the impromptu pairs did not have an intact transactive memory system and needed the assigned responsibility (preplans) to aid performance. In contrast, the acquainted couples were able to coordinate tacitly their performance based on their knowledge of each other's interests and abilities.

In summary, transactive memory systems that tacitly develop in groups through the experience of working together seem effective. Consequently, artificially imposing strategies on efficient tacit systems hurts group performance. However, it is possible that imposed strategies may inhibit performance initially but may lead to better performance over time as the group adjusts to the new role assignments. The imposition of strategies may prove fruitful in new groups whose members do not have the experience working together to know who is best at remembering particular types of information. In such cases, the formal assignment of responsibility may create effective and long-lasting transactive memory systems.

Liang, Moreland, and Argote (1995) applied the work on transactive memory to training in work groups. They proposed that training members of a work group together, rather than separately, may facilitate production due to the formation of a transactive memory system among members during training. To test this hypothesis, group members were trained individually or as a group to assemble the AM section of a radio. All subjects anticipated assembling the radio section in three-person, same-gender groups. However, participants in the individual training condition did not know who would be in their groups, and participants trained in groups understood they would remain in their groups for the radio assembly. One week after training, groups met to assemble the AM radio section, and their interaction was videotaped. Groups who were trained together remembered more of the assembly procedure and produced better assembled sections than groups whose members were trained separately. Furthermore, evidence from coders' ratings of the group interaction suggested that group members who were trained together performed better due to the development of transactive memory systems during training. Specifically, Liang et al. cited increased diversity of assembly recall, coordination of task activities, and trust in one another's task expertise as evidence for transactive memory systems among members trained together.

Apparently, the experience of being trained together allowed members to assess their own and other members' skills, abilities, and expertise (e.g., which members were good at building certain parts of the radio, who remembered what information from training) and to get a sense of what the task demanded (Moreland, Argote, & Krishnan, 1996). Because the task permitted members to assemble individually different parts of the radio (a divisible task according to Steiner, 1972), members may have realized that dividing the assembly responsibilities likely would improve efficiency. Given members' beliefs about themselves, others, and the task, they could allocate their own effort to building parts that facilitated effective in-process tacit coordination.[2]

Consequences of Tacit Coordination

The existing evidence suggests that groups often tacitly coordinate their activities, both when preparing for group performance (tacit precoordination) and when

[2]Examination of the group discussions revealed little explicit discussion of coordination issues, thereby providing some support for an interpretation of the results as evidence of in-process tacit coordination. (R. L. Moreland, personal communication, March 4, 1996).

performing (in-process tacit coordination). This reliance on tacit coordination may be both functional and dysfunctional.

Functional

The primary potential advantage of tacit coordination is efficiency: Groups who successfully coordinate their activities without explicit strategy discussion free more time for task completion than groups who must use task time to explicitly plan (Gersick & Hackman, 1990). This advantage may be especially beneficial for groups who work under time pressure, such as tight deadlines. Also, this temporal benefit may be most clearly evidenced in groups whose members are familiar with the task and have a shared understanding of the best way to go about completing it (Rouse et al., 1992). In this case, task time would be wasted making explicit what members already know, and a more efficient use of time would be to simply start working on the task (Hackman & Morris, 1975).

If tacit coordination is based on valid cues of member expertise, it also increases the likelihood that members complete the tasks for which they are most capable. Using an example from the transactive memory paradigm, if an academic hiring committee consists of three people with respective expertise in research, teaching, and service, they can tacitly coordinate their processing of information about job candidates by assuming responsibility for information within their domain of expertise. Each can evaluate the candidates in the area for which he or she is most capable of making discriminating judgments. In this way, tacit precoordination allows for efficient processing of information, because members attend to and retain the types of information that they are best qualified to evaluate.

Finally, tacit coordination may allow groups to make decisions about who should be responsible for which tasks, without the evaluative implications of explicit assignment. Hackman and Morris (1975) suggested that individuals in groups alleviate the evaluation apprehension and uncertainty that the group situation invokes by implementing comfortable norms and familiar patterns of behavior. Members may use tacit role assignment to avoid the discomfort of making others' strengths and weaknesses explicit. For example, in a student work group assigned to complete a problem for a statistics course, members may hold the belief that Chris performs poorly in statistics. Without explicitly indicating that Chris lacks competence, other members can assume the more complicated parts of the task (e.g., determining what statistical test to employ), while tacitly leaving the simple parts (e.g., adding up the numbers) to the less competent member. In this way, members can avoid the social discomfort of explicit task assignment, maintain their cohesiveness, and remain satisfied with their task performance.

Dysfunctional

Despite the potential benefits of tacit coordination, groups face inevitable risks by coordinating implicitly. One apparent drawback is the potential for coordination failure. By relying on assumptions, group members increase the likelihood that their coordination attempts will fail. Suppositions about how others will approach the task are likely to be less accurate than overt statements from others about what they will do. Because member expectations are formed from a limited set of cues, they may often be faulty. Incorrect assumptions could lead members to unnecessarily duplicate their efforts and leave some subtasks undone. Or members' assumptions may incorrectly identify the most and least capable members, leading to an inappropriate weighting of members' contributions.

In other cases, duplication of members' interests and expertise may leave tasks undone that each member would have completed if alone. For example, family members may understand the need to coordinate household chores such as grocery shopping. However, if everyone in the household assumes that someone else will buy the groceries, they will soon have cupboards that are bare. Interestingly, this kind of oversight may occur not because no one wants to shop for groceries, but because many want to shop for groceries. If several members of the household like shopping for groceries, and everyone correctly recognizes this duplication of interest, they may individually assume that someone else will do the grocery shopping. In this way, their sensitivity to coordination issues and their tacit reaction to the expected actions of others may unwittingly lead them to forego the very activity that many of them would have chosen based on their own interests and abilities.

Wittenbaum et al. (1996) discussed this paradox in their study of anticipated group interaction. Recall that subjects anticipated discussing student-body president candidates in small groups with others who were "experts" in some of the five topic areas addressed by the candidates: academic life, campus crime and safety, dorm life, minority issues, and social life.[3] Suppose that a subject, with personal interests in college social life, anticipated interacting with two others who were socially active on campus, one other who was involved in dormitory life, and one other who was concerned with minority issues. If the anticipated group task is to collectively recall as much candidate information as possible, the subject should try to avoid duplication of member efforts so that members do not attend to and retrieve the same pieces of information. Using this strategy, the subject should not attend to candidate information about social issues, because the other two presumed members of the group are interested in that topic and likely will remember information in their area of expertise; that is, subjects under these conditions should reduce their efforts in remembering social life information to the extent that they see their efforts as dispensable for the group's success (i.e., it is not necessary that three members remember social life information; Kerr, 1983; Kerr & Bruun, 1983). Indeed, results showed that when subjects anticipated a collective recall task, they remembered more information outside of others' expertise (in this example, either campus crime or academic issues) than information associated with others' expertise. This resulted in subjects not remembering information in topic areas necessarily associated with their own interests. As Wittenbaum et al. pointed out, if *all* members adopted this tacit strategy, the

---

[3] Each of the five topic areas was represented an equal number of times as others' expertise across all conditions of the study.

result would be poorly coordinated group performance; that is, subjects in this example may have focused on social life issues if working on the task alone, but in the group setting, they may assume that attention to social life issues will duplicate others' efforts and avoid such information, leaving no members able to remember social life issues.

Member expectations may be especially prone to mistake and mistreatment when they are based on stereotypes about members of particular social groups. Diffuse status cues, such as race and gender, often are used to infer members' task competence (Berger, Fisek, Norman, & Zelditch, 1977). According to expectation states theory, these inferences can lead to behaviors that tend to validate the inferences. Members who are presumed to be less competent are given fewer behavioral opportunities to demonstrate competence (e.g., they are frequently interrupted during conversation, their contributions are less positively evaluated), leading them to appear less capable—a confirmation of the initial stereotype that created the confirming behavior. This process likely would have damaging effects on the tacit coordination process. For example, Ann may be presumed by other work-group members to be incompetent because she is female, leading members to tacitly assign her to simple subtasks or to ignore her contributions. Failure may come about in this case for several reasons. First, Ann may complete a more challenging subtask, knowing that she is particularly skillful in that domain. If others completed this subtask, assuming that she would not, the result would be duplication of member efforts. Second, Ann may have generated the best solution to the problem, but if other members discounted her ideas, the group would fail to perform as well as they could have (i.e., process loss; Steiner, 1972; Torrance, 1954). Last, Ann may come to internalize the expectations that others have for her, leading her to accept inappropriate task assignments and the low evaluation of her work. In a damaging way, using stereotypes to guide group coordination may not only inhibit the chances of utilizing all members' unique abilities, but it may also serve to perpetuate stereotypic beliefs about members of certain social groups. Established interaction patterns based on status cues may be especially stable and difficult to break out of once they are established (Berger et al., 1977).

Recomposition is inevitable as groups age; old members retire or quit, and new members replace them. Groups that tacitly coordinate are most vulnerable to changes in member composition. Because members' unique abilities and expertise were never made explicit, it may not be clear to the remaining members what role the ex-member played, what subtasks will be left undone due to the vacancy, or what area of expertise is needed to fill the gap. Thus, recruitment for a new member may be difficult. Also, the group may have developed an unspoken language for understanding other members' behavior. A new member may not be privy to the tacit cues that members use to signal their task intentions. Consequently, it may take a while for the newcomer to become socialized into the group's culture (Levine & Moreland, 1991), thus retarding the functioning of the tacit system. In summary, the more tacit group members' roles, the more difficult it will be to replace members, maintain a functioning group, and socialize new members. However, problems associated with turnover may be most pronounced in organizations low in structure (procedures and roles are unspecified), when highly skilled workers leave, or when groups work on complex tasks (Argote, 1993; Argote, Insko, Yovetich, & Romero, 1995).

Factors Moderating the Mode of Coordination

Although tacit coordination may be a prevalent phenomenon, coordination attempts may become explicit when particular task, compositional, temporal, and environmental factors operate. Figure 5 depicts a model of one interaction episode for a group. Before the group meets to work on the task, members may engage in tacit precoordination and use preplans established by the organization. The moderating factors determine whether tacit precoordination or preplans operate and whether subsequent coordination efforts during interaction involve tacit adjustments or whether members explicitly discuss strategy plans. After this interaction episode, members may anticipate meeting again to continue task completion. If so, any coordination patterns established during the first episode then influence the coordination mode for the second and subsequent interactions via the moderating factors. For example, a group that explicitly discusses coordination issues during its first meeting and then implicitly uses this initial experience as a guide for approaching a second task or meeting has exhibited tacit coordination in its second interaction.

Thus far, we have discussed the four coordination modes in their purest forms, implying that each is distinctly different from the others. These pure modes may exist. However, most instances of group performance probably represent a blend of explicit and tacit coordination and of preinteraction and in-process coordination. Our model of coordination, as shown in Figure 5, graphically depicts the gradual blending of the coordination modes. According to the model, the manner in which group members coordinate their actions likely involves some mixture of more than one mode. For example, standard operating procedures, once made explicit during the early part of a group's history, may be evoked tacitly at a later time. In this case, the mode of coordination seems most appropriately placed somewhere between preplans and tacit precoordination. Furthermore, as tasks or working environments change, old standard operating procedures may become outdated, forcing group members to modify or reject them tacitly or explicitly during interaction. Thus, preplans may not only be executed somewhat tacitly, but they may also be revised and implemented during interaction. The gradual blending of the coordination modes in the model indicates that these modes are not necessarily distinct, rarely operate in their pure forms, and may operate concurrently.

In addition, our discussion has equated implicit with tacit coordination and explicit with spoken coordination. Although the implicit–explicit and tacit-spoken dimensions covary for most instances of coordination, they are not always equivalent. The behavior of jazz quartets may exemplify a case in which tacitly coordinated behavior involves explicit communication. Jazz groups use nonverbal gestures (e.g., head nods, body posture, arm raising) to signal their task intentions (e.g., ending or beginning a solo) during a performance. These nonverbal gestures may characterize in-process planning when such signals have mutually agree-upon meaning among group members (e.g., Bastien & Hostager, 1988; Rose, 1994). Thus, nonverbal signals may, at times, represent a symbolic language that explicitly communicates actions without speech.

Although the moderating factors indicated in the model represent some of the most relevant factors influencing the mode of coordination, this list is by no means comprehensive. Certainly other factors not identified (e.g., group structure), and additional variables associated with the identified factors may affect how group members coordinate. The manner in which each identified moderating factor potentially impacts the mode of coordination is delineated further.

Task Factors

Task Interdependence

Collective tasks require varying degrees of dependence among members in order to complete the task. Some tasks demand that members work together to integrate their efforts, whereas others allow members to perform well while working independently. Tasks that create high dependence among members add to the complexity of synchronization and may render tacit coordination strategies ineffective. Therefore, the more coordination required of members, the more they should use explicit strategies, particularly during interaction. Van de Ven, Delbecq, and Koenig (1976) found that as the group's task required greater worker interdependence, members used preplans to the same extent but increased their use of group coordination in the form of scheduled and unscheduled meetings. We suspect that the need for group meetings to complete the task indicates that members needed to discuss and reformulate strategy plans. However, evidence from this study cannot preclude that tacit forms of coordination predominated during the group meetings.

Clearer evidence comes from a study conducted by Hackman, Brousseau, and Weiss (1976). In their experiment, four-person groups assembled various electrical components from "order lists" provided by the experimenter. The work arrangement was set up so that members could work individually in assembling components for the group. Half of the groups received "unequal information," in that some information was missing from each member's order lists, but collectively the group had access to all of the component information. In this condition, members needed substantial coordination and sharing of information among members in order to complete the task. In the other half of the groups, each member received all of the component information and could thus construct the components individually. In addition, groups were given one of three strategy instructions. Some were told to spend the first 5 minutes of their work time in explicit strategy planing activities (*strategy*), others were instructed not to waste time and to get to work immediately (*antistrategy*), and a *control* group was given no special instructions. Results showed that the strategy condition discussed strategy more than the antistrategy and control conditions. In fact strategy discussion did not emerge spontaneously during interaction when groups were not explicitly instructed to discuss strategies. Interestingly, strategy planning only improved group productivity when the task required coordination (unequal information condition). When group members all shared the same information, those in the antistrategy condition actually performed better than those in the strategy condition. These results suggest that in-process planning does not seem to emerge spontaneously, and when it does occur, it enhances performance only when the coordination requirement for the task is high. When members are not highly interdependent, planning may consume time that would be better used for working.

Task Uncertainty

Van de Ven et al. (1976) defined task uncertainty as "the difficulty and variability of the work undertaken by an organizational unit" (p.324), where variability refers to the degree to which a task changes over time and difficulty refers to the complexity and ease involved in completing the task. As task uncertainty increases, groups tend to engage in more in-process planning. The results observed by Van de Ven et al. are consistent with this position. They discovered that as task uncertainty in organizational work units increased, units decreased their use of preplans and increased their use of coordination by feedback, including personal meetings with other unit workers and scheduled and unscheduled group meetings. We presume that these group communications were used to provide workers with information about what others were doing so that they could explicitly coordinate how to complete the task.

Similar results were obtained by Argote (1982), who observed the means of coordination in hospital emergency units. Such units are composed of nurses and physicians who must engage in substantial information sharing and coordination to treat patients. Argote specifically examined *input uncertainty*, expressed as a high probability of various patient conditions occurring. For example, if an emergency unit generally sees patients who have conditions that fall into six different categories that occur equally often, that unit experiences less input uncertainty than one that sees patients who have conditions that generally fall into 20 different, but equally likely categories. In the latter unit, diagnoses are more difficult. Organizational effectiveness was used as the dependent measure, which assessed promptness of care, quality of nursing care, and quality of medical care. Argote found that when uncertainty was low, preplans made a significant contribution to organizational effectiveness, whereas when uncertainty was high, coordination during interaction contributed significantly to organizational effectiveness. Like Van de Ven et al. (1976), Argote did not specify whether teams that worked out their activities during interaction used tacit or explicit means of coordination. Nonetheless, Argote's results suggest that task uncertainty increases the use of in-process planning.

Weldon and Weingart (1993) urged that more research is needed examining the impact of particular task variables on the planning process. They suggested that task complexity and task variability may increase the use of in-process planning. These factors represent the components of task uncertainty, and thus may have the same impact as uncertainty on the mode of coordination used by groups. Weldon and Weingart noted that coordination for a highly variable task would require that members plan while working on the task so that discussions of who should do what, when, and where could keep up with the changing demands of the task. Also, groups that work on a complex task learn about the task as they work, increasing the need for in-process planning. Thus, the more variability and complexity involved in the task, the greater the coordination demand, and the more likely that in-process planning will be needed to achieve successful group performance.

Group Composition Factors

Group Size

Much of the group process research has shown that as group size increases, several negative consequences result (Moreland & Levine, 1992). Members of larger groups participate less, are less cooperative, and suffer from greater coordination problems compared to smaller groups (Bray, Kerr, & Atkin, 1978; Gooding & Wagner, 1985; Kerr 1989; Steiner, 1972). The greater communication difficulty in large groups would seem to discourage explicit discussion of strategy plans during interaction. Indeed, larger groups may be more likely to rely on tacit means of coordination as well as preplans, which do not require intragroup communication. Although there is no empirical evidence to date regarding whether group coordination in larger groups is mostly tacit, there is some evidence to suggest that use of preplans increases in larger groups. Van de Ven et al. (1976) observed organizational units that ranged in size from 2 to 21 members. They found that as the number of unit personnel increased, units increased their reliance on preplans, whereas discussion between workers and group meetings remained constant. This increase in use of plans, rules, and schedules was more pronounced in units with 10 or more workers. These results do not bode well for the coordination efficacy of larger groups. If large groups face a variable task or one that makes members highly interdependent—tasks for which in-process planning is most ideal—then their performance may suffer given the added difficulty of communicating. However, new technologies in communication (e.g., E-mail, on-line conversations) may make communication in large groups easier, thus facilitating effective in-process planning.

Recomposition

Work groups often need to recruit new members to cope with increased task demands or to replace old members who retire or are lost through attrition. The periodic replacement of old members with new members can benefit the productivity of small work groups due to older members passing down their knowledge to new members (Insko et al., 1982). "Old-timers" are likely to hold valuable information regarding the group (e.g., norms, history of success), its members (e.g., how members differ, who is good at what), and the group's work (e.g., what work is done, how performance is evaluated), particularly if existing norms are functional for group performance (Levine & Moreland, 1991; Moreland & Levine, 1989). However, coordination problems may arise when old-timers leave the group, particularly if the organization is low in structure and formalization (few embedded rules and standard operating procedures), if highly skilled workers leave, or if groups work on complex tasks (Argote, 1993; Argote et al., 1995). Valuable old-timers may take their knowledge about how the group works with them, leaving the others without such knowledge. Such group-level memory loss may leave the group unable to retrieve important information once stored and retrieved by former members (Larson & Christensen, 1993). And, as mentioned earlier, when groups use tacit means of coordination, it may be unclear what niche the ex-member filled, making recruitment for a replacement member difficult. Given the disruption in the group's functioning and knowledge base caused by attrition, it may become necessary to adopt more explicit means of coordination, even if the group had formerly relied on tacit means of coordination. The departure of one or more members may precipitate discussion among members regarding how to proceed with the task, what the ex-members' skills and abilities were, what subtasks will now go undone, and how to fill the gap left by their absence.

Although there is no empirical evidence to support this hypothesis, the theorizing of Gersick and Hackman (1990) is consistent with this position. They claimed that a group develops an *habitual routine* when it "repeatedly exhibits a functionally similar pattern of behavior in a given situation without explicitly selecting it over alternative ways of behaving" (p. 69).[4] It seems that groups develop a pattern of interacting quite early during the first interaction (Gersick, 1988) that becomes so entrenched in the group's functioning that members do not discuss whether their approach to their task is the most appropriate one. In this way, tacit coordination represents a kind of habitual routine, in that groups can develop a pattern of interacting based on members' expectations about themselves and others, and this interaction pattern may be continued throughout the groups' life until something disrupts the habit. Gersick and Hackman (1990) suggest that recomposition may be one factor that disrupts habitual routines; that is, recomposition may disrupt tacit coordination systems and prompt groups to engage in more explicit forms of planning, such as in-process planing.

Diversity

As more women, black and Hispanic people, physically challenged individuals, and former "retirees" enter the workforce, issues of diversity in groups and organizations are becoming increasingly important (Jackson, 1992). Because of the increased diversity, organizational teams and work groups are likely to be composed of

---

[4] Although Gersick and Hackman (1990) characterize habitual routines as automatic and scripted behavior that occurs without explicit deliberation, Pentland and Rueter (1994) noted that routines can require a great deal of cognitive effort and variety to accomplish a task successfully.

members with varying abilities, skills, expertise, knowledge, and personal attributes (personality and demographic variables). Such heterogeneity may facilitate the development of tacit coordination; that is, in diverse groups, it may be easy for members to form hypotheses about others' expertise based on salient social cues (e.g., gender, age, occupation). These hypotheses, whether right or wrong, provide the basis for tacitly coordinated behavior. Conversely, in homogeneous groups, differentiating cues are not so readily apparent, and members may need to discuss their special skills and interests in order to coordinate who will do what.

Whereas membership diversity may facilitate the emergence of differentiated behavioral expectations, other interpersonal dynamics associated with diversity may make tacit coordination more or less pervasive. For example, heterogeneity discourages the development of group cohesiveness and is associated with increased group dissociation and turnover compared to homogeneous groups (Jackson, 1992; Wagner, Pfeffer, & O'Reilly, 1984). Increase in conflict may diminish members' desires to coordinate cooperatively with others. They may stick with tacit means of coordination to avoid additional conflict in negotiating explicit assignments of responsibility. Also, conflict among members may induce them to think about the task and each others' areas of expertise more carefully (Nemeth, 1995), thereby promoting effective tacit coordination. Alternatively, conflict and turnover may prompt diverse groups to move toward in-process planning during the later phases of task completion. As mentioned earlier, turnover poses problems for groups that coordinate tacitly, in that the ex-member's expertise may not be known. The need to find a new member may spark discussion of what the ex-member's role was and what subtasks the new member will be expected to perform. In addition, if conflict grows, diverse groups may not care about evaluations associated with explicitly assigning task responsibilities to members. In summary, heterogeneous groups may be more or less likely than homogeneous groups to coordinate tacitly, depending on the visibility of members' expertise and the operation of conflict and turnover.

Temporal Factors

Time Pressure

Work groups often face time limits and deadlines that affect their task behavior and performance. Research investigating *social entrainment* has shown that work groups adjust their working pace to fit with the allotted time frame and continue to work at this pace after the time constraints or freedoms have been removed (Kelly & McGrath, 1985). Thus, groups that worked at a quick pace to meet a tight deadline continued to work swiftly on subsequent tasks when the deadline was removed, and groups that had ample time to complete their task developed a slow pace that continued on subsequent tasks with more stringent time limits. Although groups with more stringent deadlines worked swiftly, their performance quality suffered compared to groups with ample performance time. Moreover, they spent virtually no time evaluating proposed task ideas or engaging in nontask interpersonal behavior. McGrath (1990) maintained that time pressure induces groups to launch directly into executing the task instead of taking time to brainstorm and plan, whereas ample time allows groups to work on member support functions, such as defining members' roles and determining members' status. This reasoning suggests that a time deficit may require that members tacitly coordinate their actions to avoid using valuable task time to plan. When time is at a premium, tacit coordination may be less costly than explicitly coordinated action. Conversely, time surplus may facilitate in-process planning, because members have time to spare for such activity.

Temporal Milestones

A group's life may include natural breakpoints in the task (e.g., the end of a production period) or milestones that mark notable events (e.g., anniversary of the group's inception). Gersick and Hackman (1990) proposed that these milestones propel groups out of their habitual routines. Empirical evidence comes from a field study by Gersick (1988) examining naturally occurring task forces that each had a project to complete by a specified deadline. Despite the different tasks and time lines, each group developed a stable interaction pattern that lasted until the halfway point to the project deadline. This temporal midpoint marked a flurry of activity in which groups reevaluated their plans, dropped ineffective patterns, adopted new work perspectives, and made dramatic leaps in productivity. Teams apparently used temporal midpoints as markers against which to pace their activity toward the final stretch of production (Gersick, 1989). Because they only had half of their time left to complete the task, groups may have felt a sense that time was running out and therefore made changes in their task approach that would facilitate their timely task completion. Gersick and Hackman (1990) noted that this collective "midlife crisis" may only occur in groups with a clear goal, deadline, and the ability to make strategy changes. For these types of groups, milestones may encourage explicit coordination of behavior; that is, groups that have developed a tacitly coordinated interaction pattern may experience a crisis at their temporal midpoint, reevaluate their previous behavior, and explicitly plan how to approach the task as the deadline draws near.

Environmental Factors

Feedback

Once groups have made considerable progress toward task completion or have finished a project, they may receive feedback about their performance. Positive feedback is likely to reinforce behavioral patterns and strategies such that groups continue to do what they have always done. Thus, if tacit coordination developed, positive feedback likely will serve to perpetuate it. Conversely, negative feedback, or experiencing failure, would seem to propel groups out of routinized behavior. As

Weiss and Ilgen (1985) suggested for individuals, "either sudden, unexpected failure to reach stable goals or a re-evaluation or change of goals can result in the uncertainty necessary to reconsider the appropriateness of routines" (p. 60). Also, Tindale (1989) found that negative feedback led decision-making groups to change their decision strategies. However, Gersick and Hackman (1990) reported no evidence suggesting that failure initiates changes in habitual routines for groups. Instead, it seems that when groups fail, they adhere to existing interaction patterns more rigorously. In the face of failure, members work harder, but they tend not to reevaluate their performance strategies. Gersick and Hackman offered two explanations for why failure exacerbates the use of existing routines: escalation of commitment and social facilitation. The former line of work has shown that individuals (and probably groups) invest more of their resources into failing projects to try to recoup the losses already incurred (e.g., Staw, 1981), and the latter line of work demonstrates that failure elevates members' arousal, which increases the likelihood that habitual responses will be exhibited (Zajonc, 1965). In summary, some literature suggests that receiving negative feedback causes members to reevaluate and change their task strategy. Other literature suggests that if groups tacitly perpetuate interaction patterns and then experience failure, such feedback may actually reduce the likelihood that they will explicitly reconsider their task approach.

Goal Setting

Although many groups set goals for themselves (Weingart, 1992), goals are often set for groups by external sources, such as managers or community leaders. An abundance of research has shown that groups that are assigned challenging goals perform better than groups without explicit goals (Hinsz, 1995; Larson & Schaumann, 1993; Pritchard, Jones, Roth, Stuebing, & Ekeberg, 1988; Smith, Locke, & Barry, 1990; Weingart, 1992; Weingart & Weldon, 1991; Weldon, Jehn, & Pradhan, 1991). This effect has been demonstrated in ad hoc, laboratory, and naturally occurring groups.

Several researchers have claimed that group planning and strategy changes moderate the relationship between group goals and performance. Weldon et al. (1991) had three-person groups of management students build structures in one 15-minute session without a goal and two subsequent sessions with either a *low goal* (to construct one more structure than they had in the first session) or a *high goal* (to construct five more structures than they had in the first session). Results showed that group planning (i.e., discussion of what acts to perform, how to perform them, who should perform the acts) and strategy changes (i.e., change in acts performed by members across sessions) moderated the relationship between goal setting and quality of performance: Strategy change was associated with better performance. Similar results were obtained by Weingart and Weldon (1991) for small student groups working on a brainstorming task. Furthermore, Weingart (1992) demonstrated that small laboratory groups working on a structure-building task engaged in more in-process planning when a difficult goal was assigned than when an easy goal was assigned. Thus, challenging goals seem to increase the amount of planning that occurs as groups work, leading to improved group performance.

The existence of formal planning may reveal little regarding how much time was spent during planning or the quality of the planning (Pearce, Freeman, & Robinson, 1987). As such, Smith et al. (1990) examined how challenging group goals affect performance, quality of planning, and time spent planning. They operationalized high-quality organizational planning according to the following attributes identified by Lorange and Vancil (1977) and Steiner (1969):

> (1) a future orientation, (2) extensive interaction between organizational members, (3) a systematic and comprehensive analysis of the organization's strengths, weakness, opportunities, and threats, (4) a clear definition of the roles and functions of all members and departments, and finally, (5) the development and communication of action plans and the allocation of resources to actions plans. (p. 124)

Smith et al. (1990) observed business students in simulated organizations consisting of departments, divisions, and managers who met over seven sessions. Managers from each organization were given either a difficult goal or no goal for their organization's performance, and were either required before the simulation began to spend time planning or were not officially told to plan. Results showed that organizations with a difficult goal engaged in higher quality planning relative to those with no goal. Although the groups required to plan spent more time planning than those not instructed to plan, the actual amount of planning time was unrelated to performance. Time spent planning did, however, interact with the quality of planning, such that when planning quality was high, more time spent planning was associated with higher performance, but when planning was of poor quality, more time spent planning was associated with poorer performance. Thus, planning quality moderates the relationship between time spent planning and performance.

It is not clear why challenging goals evoke the need for in-process planning and improve the quality of planning. It is possible that difficult goals increase the coordination demand, which, as discussed earlier, elevates the need for explicit planning. Also, difficult goals focus attention on the need to match member abilities and task demands, and thereby encourage groups to develop explicit plans for allocating effort. Although no research has examined how group goals influence the relative use of tacit and explicit means of coordination, we suspect that specific and challenging group goals may facilitate explicit forms of planning.

Intervention

The setting of group goals, if done by an outsider to the group, can represent an intervention that facilitates effective planning. Gersick and Hackman (1990) suggested that interventions from outsiders may break groups out of their habitual routines. Of course, the type of intervention probably determines its effect on the group. Two interventions—planning encouragement and group training—are likely to have different effects on coordination mode.

Smith et al. (1990) found that setting aside a time period to plan increased the amount of planning in simulated organizations. Similar results were obtained by Shure, Rogers, Larsen, and Tassone (1962), who had five-person groups work on a problem-solving task across 20 trials. The task required that members pool their different information in order to reach a correct solution, and this pooling was only possible by passing notes among members. Groups were assigned to one of three planning conditions: (1) The *separate planning period condition* allowed members an extra 2 minutes before their task time began to plan, (2) the *cotemporal planning condition* did not provide an extra interval for groups to plan (thus, planning would have to occur during task time), and (3) the *no-planning period condition* allowed a 2-minute pretask period, but members could not communicate with one another either during the pretask period or during task time. Results showed that groups with a separate planning period performed better, eliminated redundant and ineffective messages over time, and were more organized than groups in the other two conditions. Thus, providing a separate planning period appeared to help groups coordinate before work began, so that they did not have to sacrifice valuable work time to plan. When groups needed to use task time to plan, they seemed to forego the planning in order to cope with immediate task pressure. It is important to note that a planning period likely aided performance effectiveness in this study, because the group task required considerable coordination (i.e., members held different information and could not speak to each other). When coordination demands are high, explicit planning is likely to be beneficial.

Group training may also be used as an intervention to improve team performance. As discussed earlier, group members trained together perform better than group members trained individually, presumably due to the development of transactive memory systems (Liang et al., 1995; Moreland et al., 1996). Although their research provides little evidence regarding whether transactive systems developed tacitly or explicitly, it does suggest that allowing members to learn the task collectively allows them to develop expectations and knowledge about their own and others' skills and abilities. As Rouse et al. (1992) proposed, the shared knowledge and expectations about members' likely behavior that arises from team training helps groups to better orchestrate their actions later on. Thus, when the purpose of group training is to give members experience working on the task and with each other, it may facilitate the development of tacit coordination.

Work Context

Much of the research presented herein examined coordination processes in laboratory or classroom groups and simulated organizations. There is reason to believe that such groups differ qualitatively from naturally occurring organizational groups (Jackson, 1992; Worchel, 1994; Worchel, Coutant-Sassic, & Grossman, 1992).

Laboratory groups usually are composed of strangers, given problems to work on that have correct answers, and work during a limited amount of time with their dissolution planned. Natural groups generally are composed of acquaintances or coworkers who come together voluntarily, find and define their own problems with solutions that cannot be objectively verified, and expect to work together across several meetings for an unspecified time period. Moreover, organizational teams work in an environment that is rich with instructions regarding members' responsibilities, work rules, and standard operating procedures.

In this respect, preplans are probably more likely to be used in natural groups than in laboratory groups. Also, because interventions, such as goal setting, are often implemented in organizations, natural teams may be more likely to engage in-process planning as well. However, the experience of working together provides natural groups with a rich array of knowledge about how others will approach the task. As discussed earlier, natural dyads possess highly differentiated transactive memory systems (Wegner et al., 1991). Thus, natural groups may be especially prone to rely on tacit coordination, particularly later in a group's life, after knowledge about other members, the task, and the organization has accumulated.

Likewise, tacit forms of coordination may be especially likely in ad hoc laboratory groups where the environment and history of the group are so vacuous that members must form hypotheses about others and the task in order to function collectively. In this case, tacit coordination may fail given that members know so little about one another and have so few cues to predict what others will do. Members probably would benefit from in-process planning in order to establish members' special skills. Indeed, task demands, such as a changing task or high task interdependence, may promote in-process planning and effective performance despite members' zero-history. However, given the limited time and impossibility of future meetings, tacit coordination may be particularly prevalent in laboratory groups.

Thus, despite their differences, natural and laboratory groups may exhibit similar coordination patterns. Moreover, the processes seen in laboratory groups may represent newly formed groups in natural settings who share many of the same qualities of lab groups (e.g., strangers, no history). Clearly, both laboratory and natural groups need to be studied to understand the basic processes involved in group coordination and to understand how such processes are implemented in work settings.

Implications and Conclusions

The theory and research presented in this chapter suggest several conclusions regarding how group members coordinate their activities. First, groups may avoid in-process planning unless the task is highly uncertain, variable, and complex. Group member turnover and difficult group goals enhance task complexity and thus would be expected to lead to in-process planning. Despite the apparent benefit of in-process planning for groups working on a highly interdependent task, members tend not to discuss strategy. However, situational factors such as having ample time to complete the task, reaching a breakpoint in the group's life, and receiving an intervention that encourages planning, may facilitate in-process planning despite groups' tendencies to avoid this mode of coordination.

Second, in-process planning may occur rarely without inducement because of the natural tendency to coordinate tacitly and task demands that make communication difficult while performing (e.g., in jazz bands). Group members use their knowledge about each other and the task to implicitly determine how to synchronize their actions. Assumptions about others and the task can be made either before interaction or while working together. Because tacit coordination is a time-saver relative to in-process planning, high time pressure may ensure that groups coordinate tacitly. Moreover, heterogeneous groups, with visible cues from which to form expectations, may be prone to use tacit coordination. Group training may promote tacit coordination by facilitating the development of task and member knowledge during interaction. At least under some conditions, negative feedback may intensify the reliance on habitual routines, such as tacit coordination.

Third, groups use preplans to the extent that they are available in the work environment and the group is not faced with conditions that make in-process planning likely (e.g., difficult goal, turnover). Natural groups may use preplans to the extent that they work in rich contexts that supply explicit job descriptions, schedules, and policies. Moreover, groups that have trouble discussing strategy (e.g., large groups) or work on easy tasks (e.g., low task uncertainty) may be prone to use preplans. Although preplans may be made explicit early in a group's history, the automatic execution of preplans probably turns quickly into tacit coordination as members act based on extracted knowledge about how the group operates.

The supporting literature thus far suggests some implications for improving the performance effectiveness of work groups in organizational settings. And, because many questions regarding group coordination are left unanswered, numerous implications exist for fruitful avenues of research.

Implications for Practice

Improving the quality, effectiveness, and efficiency of group performance are goals of organizational managers and group leaders. The research and theory presented in this chapter suggest that facilitating the successful coordination of group members may be a key ingredient to improving group performance. From this literature, we draw four implications for avoiding coordination losses in work groups.

First, one mode of coordination does not seem to be best in and of itself. Instead, the optimal means of coordination likely depends on several factors associated with the collective task, group composition, temporal markers and limits, and environmental constraints. Tacit means of coordination may be best suited for teams whose heterogeneous expertise is easily identifiable through social cues, and who work under considerable time pressure on a task that is simple, stable, and requires low or moderate interdependence among members. Moreover, tacit coordination likely will be effective when members share similar mental models for how expertise is distributed among members and what coordination demands are required for the task. Furthermore, interventions that encourage planning or assigning task strategies actually may diminish effectiveness when coordination systems have developed tacitly (e.g., Wegner et al., 1991). Planning appears to worsen performance when groups work on simple tasks that require little coordination (Argote, 1982; Hackman et al., 1976). In these cases, planning is unnecessary and detracts from time that could be spent working on the task. Thus, in-process planning should be encouraged when naturally developed tacit systems seem ineffective or when several operating factors (e.g., high task uncertainty and interdependence, challenging group goal, recomposition, time surplus) make explicit planning beneficial. In summary, modes of coordination that match the task and situational demands will promote effective group performance.

Second, if an intervention is necessary to improve the coordination of a group, introducing group goals, training programs, or planning periods may be beneficial. Such interventions may be needed when it is apparent that a group is experiencing coordination difficulty, as evidenced by continued failure, production inefficiency, or member dissatisfaction. In this case, the intervention should be introduced at a time when the group is experiencing a natural breakpoint, such as the end of a production period or midway through task completion. Groups may be open to change at breakpoints, thereby enhancing the chances that the intervention will "take." If coordination by tacit means is expected to be difficult for a new group (e.g., the group is expected to work on a highly interdependent or challenging task), interventions may be introduced at the group's inception. Given that group routines form early (Gersick & Hackman, 1990), starting members off with proficient coordination habits likely will serve them well during later stages of the group's life.

Third, preplans that are clear, specific, and congruent with members' skills and expertise may facilitate effective team performance. Clearly explicated job descriptions, coordination rules (i.e., who should do what, where, and how), and schedules (e.g., when subtasks are to be performed by members) may aid groups under conditions where in-process coordination is difficult, such as when group size is large. When the coordination is less demanding, unambiguous information regarding members' roles may facilitate the development of effective tacit coordination systems. For example, job descriptions may suggest members' expertise, thereby helping members form assumptions regarding others' likely task actions. In this way, the establishment of effective preplans may facilitate a form of tacit and/or explicit coordination that promotes the success of many groups. However, when groups work on a highly uncertain or variable task, or experience member recomposition, the need for in-process planning may increase, making preplans less effective.

Finally, the elimination of coordination barriers may improve group performance. As Larson and Schaumann (1993) found, when highly interdependent groups were allowed to preplan their work, performance was improved with a difficult goal relative to a "do your best" goal, whereas similar groups that were not permitted to preplan their work showed no performance improvements in response to a difficult goal. Other results have shown that the productivity of work groups can suffer when members have to communicate via a computer medium while working on highly interdependent or time-limited tasks (Farmer & Hyatt, 1994; Straus & McGrath, 1994). Also, a large group size may serve as a coordination barrier by making communication difficult (Van de Ven et al., 1976). If the coordination demands for a group are high (e.g., high task uncertainty or interdependence, difficult goal), then making in-process or preplanning difficult, by narrowing or eliminating communication channels, will invariably hurt group productivity.

Implications for Research

We hope that the ideas introduced in this chapter will help to stimulate more research investigating coordination processes in task-performing groups. Several relations between moderating factors, mode of coordination, and performance consequences have been suggested. However, many of the ideas presented herein have not yet been tested empirically. Because there is an unlimited number of questions to answer regarding group coordination, we merely will suggest some that seem particularly interesting.

First, a better understanding is needed of how the four modes of coordination operate either sequentially or simultaneously, depending on the moderating factors. Most studies examined only one mode of coordination (e.g., Wittenbaum et al., 1996) or compared the frequency of using preplans versus in-process planning without identifying where these coordination modes fell along the explicitness continuum (e.g., Argote, 1982; Ven de Ven et al., 1976). As such, no study to date has compared the relative use of tacit and explicit forms of coordination. When do teams break out of tacit coordination and use an explicit mode? Do groups generally move from tacit to explicit means of coordination, or does the movement go both ways? It is possible that they may co-occur under certain conditions. For example, when two moderators are at odds with one another (e.g., assigned group goal and time pressure), groups may use a combination of both tacit and explicit coordination.

Second, additional research is needed exploring the social and performance consequences of using different modes of coordination. Are social relations among members more congenial in groups that use tacit coordination? Or is cohesiveness facilitated through the use of coordination modes that are appropriate for a given situation? Uncovering when groups use different modes may yield insights into the consequences. For example, a group with an assigned goal may use tacit instead of, or in addition to, in-process planning if a time limit is imposed. This outcome might suggest that tacit coordination functions as a coordination time-saver. Understanding the relation between coordination mode and performance may aid the development of intervention techniques designed to improve team effectiveness.

Third, a better understanding of the process of tacit coordination is needed. Thus far, the process has not been studied extensively in interacting groups or in natural groups. Questions may address how well members' preinteraction hypotheses serve the group during interaction, how the group responds to failed performance, and whether members seem aware of the implicit strategies that they are using. Tacit coordination may not be a highly deliberate process, making it difficult for members to detect inefficient strategies (Wittenbaum et al., 1996).

Because group coordination is a key factor influencing group performance effectiveness, understanding the processes involved in how members attempt to synchronize their actions likely will suggest practical implications for improving group performance. We hope that this chapter sparks the interest of researchers who will put their efforts to this end.

Acknowledgment

Preparation of this chapter was supported by National Science Foundation Grant SBR-9410584 awarded to G. Stasser and a fellowship awarded to G. M. Wittenbaum from the National Science Foundation (DIR-9113599) to the Mershon Center Research Training Group on the Role of Cognition in Collective Political Decision Making at Ohio State University. Correspondence concerning this chapter should be addressed to G. M. Wittenbaum, Department of Communication, Michigan State University, East Lansing, MI 48824.

References

Argote, L. (1982). Input uncertainty and organizational coordination in hospital emergency units. *Administrative Science Quarterly, 27*, 420–434.

Argote, L. (1993). Group and organizational learning curves: Individual, system, and environmental components. *British Journal of Social Psychology, 32*, 31–51.

Argote, L., Insko, C. A., Yovetich, N., & Romero, A. A. (1995). Group learning curves: The effects of turnover and task complexity on group performance. *Journal of Applied Social Psychology, 24*, 512–529.

Bastien, D. T., & Hostager, T. J. (1988). Jazz as a process of organizational innovation. *Communication Research, 15*, 582–602.

Berger, J., Fisek, M. H., Norman, R. Z., & Zelditch, M., Jr. (1977). *Status characteristics and social interaction.* New York: Elsevier.

Bettenhausen, K., & Murnighan, J. K. (1985). The emergence of norms in competitive decision-making groups. *Administrative Science Quarterly, 30*, 350–372.

Bray, R. M., Kerr, N. L., & Atkin, R. S. (1978). The effect of group size, problem difficulty, and sex on group performance. *Journal of Personality and Social Psychology, 36*, 1224–1240.

Eisenberg, E. M. (1990). Jamming: Transcendence through organizing. *Communication Research, 17*, 139–164.

Farmer, S. M., & Hyatt, C. W. (1994). Effects of task language demands and task complexity on computer-mediated work groups. *Small Group Research, 25*, 331–366.

Gersick, C. J. G. (1988). Time and transition in work teams: Toward a new model of group development. *Academy of Management Journal, 41*, 9–41.

Gersick, C. J. G. (1989). Marking time: Predictable transitions in task groups. *Academy of Management Journal, 32*, 274–309.

Gersick, C. J. G., & Hackman, J. R. (1990). Habitual routines in task-performing groups. *Organizational Behavior and Human Decision Processes, 47*, 65–97.

Gooding. R. Z., & Wagner, J. A. (1985). A meta-analytic review of the relationship between size and performance: The productivity and efficiency of organizations and their subunits. *Administrative Science Quarterly, 30*, 462–481.

Hackman, J. R., Brousseau, K. R., Weiss, J. A. (1976). The interaction of task design and group performance strategies in determining group effectiveness. *Organizational Behavior and Human Performance, 16,* 350–365.

Hackman, J. R., & Morris, C. G. (1975). Group tasks, group interaction process, and group performance effectiveness: A review and proposed integration. In L. Berkowitz (Ed.), *Advances in experimental social psychology* (Vol. 8, pp. 45–99). New York: Academic Press.

Hinsz, V. B. (1995). Goal setting by groups performing an additive task: A comparison with individual goal setting. *Journal of Applied Social Psychology, 25,* 965–990.

Insko, C. A., Gilmore, R., Moehle, D., Lipsitz, A., Drenan, S., & Thibaut, J. W. (1982). Seniority in the generational transition of laboratory groups: The effects of social familiarity and task experience. *Journal of Experimental Social Psychology, 18,* 557–580.

Jackson, S. E. (1992). Team composition in organizational settings: Issues in managing an increasingly diverse work force. In S. Worchel, W. Wood, & J. A. Simpson (Eds.), *Group process and productivity* (pp. 138–173). Newbury Park, CA: Sage.

Kelly, J., & McGrath, J. E. (1985). Effects of time limits and task types on task performance and interaction of four-person groups. *Journal of Personality and Social Psychology, 49,* 395–407.

Kerr, N. L. (1983). Motivation losses in small groups: A social dilemma analysis. *Journal of Personality and Social Psychology, 45,* 819–828.

Kerr, N. L. (1989). Illusions of efficacy: The effects of group size on perceived efficacy in social dilemmas. *Journal of Experimental Social Psychology, 25,* 287–313.

Kerr, N. L., & Bruun, S. E. (1983). The dispensability of member effort and group motivation losses: Free-rider effects. *Journal of Personality and Social Psychology, 44,* 78–94.

Larson, J. R., Jr., & Christensen, C. (1993). Groups as problem-solving units: Toward a new meaning of social cognition. *British Journal of Social Psychology, 32,* 5–30.

Larson, J. R., Jr., & Schaumann, L. J. (1993). Group goals, group coordination, and group member motivation. *Human Performance, 6,* 49–69.

Levine, J. M., & Moreland, R. L. (1991). Culture and socialization in work groups. In L. Resnick, J. M. Levine, & S. D. Teasley (Eds.), *Perspectives on socially shared cognition* (pp. 257–279). Washington, DC: American Psychological Association.

Liang, D. W., Moreland, R. L., & Argote L. (1995). Group versus individual training and group performance: The mediating role of transactive memory. *Personality and Social Psychology Bulletin, 21,* 384–393.

Lorange, P., & Vancil, R. V. (1977). *Strategic planning systems.* Englewood Cliffs, NJ: Prentice-Hall.

McGrath, J. E. (1990). Time matters in groups. In J. Galegher, R. E. Kraut, & C. Egido (Eds.), *Intellectual teamwork: Social and technological foundations of cooperative work* (pp. 23–61). Hillsdale, NJ: Erlbaum.

McGrath, J. E., & Rotchford, N. L. (1983). Time and behavior in organizations. *Research in Organizational Behavior, 5,* 57–101.

Moreland, R. L., Argote, L., & Krishnan, R. (1996). Socially shared cognition at work: Transactive memory and group performance. In J. L. Nye & A. M. Brower (Eds.), *What's social about social cognition? Social cognition research in small groups* (pp. 57–84). Newbury Park, CA: Sage.

Moreland, R. L., & Levine, J. M. (1989). Newcomers and oldtimers in small groups. In P. B. Paulus (Ed.), *Psychology of group influence* (2nd ed., pp. 143–186). Hillsdale, NJ: Erlbaum.

Moreland, R. L., & Levine, J. M. (1992). The composition of small groups. In E. J. Lawler, B. Markovsky, C. Ridgeway, & H. A. Walker (Eds.), *Advances in group processes* (Vol. 9, pp. 237–280). Greenwich, CT: JAI Press.

Murnighan, J. K., & Conlon, D. E. (1991). The dynamics of intense work groups: A study of British string quartets. *Administrative Science Quarterly, 36,* 165–186.

Nemeth, C. J. (1995). Dissent as driving cognition, attitudes, and judgments. *Social Cognition, 13,* 273–291.

Pearce, J. A., Freeman, E. B., & Robinson, R. B. (1987). The tenuous link between formal strategic planning and financial performance. *Academy of Management Review, 12,* 658–675.

Pentland, B. T., & Rueter, H. H. (1994). Organizational routines as grammars of action. *Administrative Science Quarterly, 39,* 484–510.

Pritchard, R. D., Jones, S. D., Roth, P. L., Stuebing, K. K., & Ekeberg, S. E. (1988). Effects of group feedback, goal setting, and incentives on organizational productivity. *Journal of Applied Psychology Monograph, 73*, 337–358.

Rose, J. (1994). Communication challenges and role functions of performing groups. *Small Group Research, 25*, 411–432.

Rouse, W. B., Cannon-Bowers, J. A., & Salas, E. (1992). The role of mental models in team performance in complex systems. *IEEE Transactions on Systems, Man, and Cybernetics, 22*, 1296–1308.

Shure, G. H., Rogers, M. S., Larsen, E. M., & Tassone, J. (1962). Group planning and task effectiveness. *Sociometry, 25*, 263–282.

Smith, K. G., Locke, E. A., & Barry, D. (1990). Goal setting, planning, and organizational performance: An experimental simulation. *Organizational Behavior and Human Decision Processes, 46*, 118–134.

Staw, M. M. (1981). The escalation of commitment to a course of action. *Academy of Management Reveiw, 6*, 577–587.

Steiner, G. A. (1969). *Top management planning*. New York: Macmillan.

Steiner, I. D. (1972). *Group process and productivity*. New York: Academic Press.

Straus, S. G., & McGrath, J. E. (1994). Does medium matter? The interaction of task type and technology on group performance and member reactions. *Journal of Applied Psychology, 79*, 87–97.

Tindale, R. S. (1989). Group versus individual information processing: The effects of outcome feedback on decision making. *Organizational Behavior and Human Decision Processes, 44*, 454–473.

Torrance, E. P. (1954). Some consequences of power differences on decision making in permanent and temporary three-man groups. *Research Studies, State College of Washington, 22*, 130–140.

Van de Ven, A. H., Delbecq, A. L., & Koenig, R., Jr. (1976). Determinants of coordination modes within organizations. *American Sociological Review, 41*, 322–338.

Vaughan, S. I., & Stasser, G. (1996, May). *Imported and emergent self-knowledge as a guide for tacit coordination in teams*. Paper presented at the meeting of the Midwestern Psychological Association, Chicago, IL.

Wagner, W. G., Pfeffer, J., & O'Reilly, C. C. (1984). Organizational demography and turnover in top management groups. *Administrative Science Quarterly, 29*, 74–92.

Wegner, D. M. (1987). Transactive memory: A contemporary analysis of the group mind. In B. Mullen & G. R. Goethals (Eds.), *Theories of group behavior* (pp. 185–208). New York: Springer-Verlag.

Wegner, D. M. (1995). A computer network model of human transactive memory. *Social Cognition, 13*, 319–339.

Wegner, D. M., Erber, R., & Raymond, P. (1991). Transactive memory in close relationships. *Journal of Personality and Social Psychology, 61*, 923–929.

Weingart, L. R. (1992). Impact of group goals, task component complexity, effort, and planning on group performance. *Journal of Applied Psychology, 77*, 682–693.

Weingart, L. R., & Weldon, E. (1991). Processes that mediate the relationship between a group goal and group member performance. *Human Performance, 4*, 33–54.

Weiss, H. M., & Ilgen, D. R. (1985). Routinized behavior in organizations. *Journal of Behavioral Economics, 14*, 57–67.

Weldon, E., Jehn, K. A., & Pradhan, P. (1991). Processes that mediate the relationship between a group goal and improved group performance. *Journal of Personality and Social Psychology, 61*, 555–569.

Weldon, E., & Weingart, L. R. (1993). Group goals and group performance. *British Journal of Social Psychology, 32*, 307–334.

Wittenbaum, G. M., Stasser, G., & Merry, C. J. (1996). Tacit coordination in anticipation of small group task completion. *Journal of Experimental Social Psychology, 32*, 129–152.

Worchel, S. (1994). You can go home again: Returning group research to the group context with an eye on developmental issues. *Small Group Research, 25*, 205–223.

Worchel, S., Coutant-Sassic, D., & Grossman, M. (1992). A developmental approach to group dynamics: A model and illustrative research. In S. Worchel, W. Wood, & J. Simpson (Eds.), *Group process and productivity* (pp. 181–202). Newbury Park, CA: Sage.

Zajonc, R. B. (1965). Social facilitation. *Science, 149*, 269–274.

10

Groups, Technology, and Time

Use of Computers for Collaborative Work

Joseph E. McGrath and Jennifer L. Berdahl

Much has been written, both in the popular press and in more technical literature, about the widespread and still rapidly increasing use of computers (and other electronic technology such as videophones) in our society. Such presentations often offer a litany of ways in which computers can and have been used in attempts to facilitate collaborative work. Much of the early writing on these matters involved more hype than hypothesis and certainly more claims than empirical evidence supporting those claims. Rarer still were detailed statements of the ways in which such putative facilitating effects might be contingent on a myriad of member, group, task, and contextual factors.

More recently, there has been an outpouring of empirical research in this domain, so that there is now both a sizable body of research literature on how computers facilitate collaborative work and several relatively comprehensive and sophisticated integrations of that evidence (Egido, 1990; Hesse, Werner, & Altman, 1990; Hollingshead & McGrath, 1995; Kraemer & King, 1988; Kraemer & Pinsonneault, 1990; McGrath & Hollingshead, 1994; McLeod, 1991; Williams, 1977). From that research literature and those integrations of it, we can begin to piece together a relatively complex, though still incomplete, picture of the state of our knowledge on these matters. That picture contains some useful substantive generalizations, but it also contains some rather serious methodological and conceptual limitations.

This chapter begins with a brief sketch of the main ways in which computers and other electronic technology can and have been used to support collaborative work in groups, along with some of the main claims and findings about such systems, and some of the methodological and conceptual limitations of those findings. Then we

Joseph E. McGrath and Jennifer L. Berdahl • Department of Psychology, University of Illinois, Urbana–Champaign, Illinois 61820.

Theory and Research on Small Groups, edited by R. Scott Tindale et al. Plenum Press, New York, 1998.

describe two relatively large longitudinal studies we have conducted to explore the development, interaction, and task performance of continuing work groups with and without computer technology, and we present a very brief sketch of some of the main findings from those studies. We conclude the chapter with a discussion of some of the implications of those findings, both for groups using computers and for groups in general.

Groups Using Electronic Technology for Collaborative Work

This section presents a brief interpretive summary of some of the main empirical findings regarding collaborative work in groups using computers. It begins by considering different ways in which groups can make use of computers, then examines effects of such computer uses on group task performance.

Three Functions of Computer Use in Groups

To start with, groups use computers and other electronic technology in at least three different capacities. Adapting the distinctions used by McGrath & Hollingshead (1993, 1994), they are as follows:

1. *Computers as Information Systems (INFO)*: Computers can provide a means for greatly enhancing the amount and quality of information available (during a meeting) to one or more group members. Such a use is often at an individual-member level and may, but need not, impact upon the collaboration among group members.

2. *Computers as Task Performance Structuring Systems (PERF)*: Computers can provide a means for structuring the group's task and its performance of that task. Such systems are often referred to as group decision support systems (GDSS; e.g., DeSanctis & Poole, 1989; Valacich, Jessup, Dennis, & Nunamaker, 1992). They usually require the use of a group facilitator to operate the electronic system and to ensure the group's proper use of it, and they usually require the use of a common screen on which the communications sent by all members appear. This, in turn, requires that all members be able to view that screen.

3. *Computers as Communication Systems (COMM)*: Computers can provide a means for within-group communication. One of the most interesting aspects of such systems is that certain kinds of groups can be created with COMM that could not exist without electronic (or equivalent) mediation. First, some COMM, such as a computer conference system or a telephone conference system, make it possible for groups to "meet" *at a distance*—when members are not all in the same place. In principle, groups can use such forms of COMM to communicate simultaneously (i.e., synchronously) when members are in adjacent rooms, on different floors, in different buildings, or even in different cities, countries, or continents (McGrath & Hollingshead, 1993). Second, certain forms of COMM (e.g., E-mail, electronic bulletin boards) make it possible for groups to "meet" *asynchronously*—when members are

not only in different *places* but also are acting at different *times*. These kinds of systems offer especially exciting potential for new forms of groups and thereby have great potential for modifying our conceptions of what it means to be a group or to be doing a task collaboratively. In the subsequent discussion, we will deal with synchronous and asynchronous communications systems separately.

Group Task-Performance Effectiveness

The possibilities of both gains and losses in group task-performance effectiveness differ dramatically for these different uses of computers in groups. Consider some of the effects such electronic technology might have on group task performance:

Information Systems

If a group's task is sensitive to accessibility of large amounts of information, then the availability of an INFO that permits one or more members to access vast amounts of information more or less instantaneously would greatly increase that group's potential for effective performance. At the same time, such a system would put that group at risk for information overload, unless the information access system provides means for combining and integrating information as it is acquired and disseminated within the group. In that case, the group's effectiveness would depend on the quality and biases of that information-integration system. Such systems also make it possible for individual group members who control the operation of the electronic technology to acquire disproportionate information/expert power within the group's structure, and to use that power to control how information relevant to the group's task is distributed, withheld, or misrepresented.

Performance-Structuring Systems

If the group's task is to carry out rather complex cognitive activities (generating ideas, choosing among alternatives, comparatively evaluating possibilities) and requires extensive coordination of information and meanings among members of the group, then such a group may profitably make use of a performance structuring system. There are a number of such systems, usually referred to in the literature as GDSS or GSS. Some are manual and some are electronic. Earlier manual systems for helping groups perform specific kinds of tasks include such renowned systems as brainstorming, Delphi, Nominal Group Technique (NGT), and the like (see McGrath, 1984, for a review). More recent, computer-based systems include Arizona's Group-Systems (e.g., Dennis, George, Jessup, Nunamaker, & Vogel, 1988), Minnesota's Software Assisted Meeting Management (SAMM) system (e.g., Poole & DeSanctis, 1990), and others. All of these systems structure the group's task performance by systematically structuring the content and form of information to be used, the sequence of steps by which the task must be carried out, and/or the form and content in which the group must formulate its output. Most of them use a facilitator—a person trained in the use of the hardware and software of the system, who guides group activities on the task. Such a performance structuring system may improve the speed and quality of the group's task performance, provided the structure imposed by a PERF (i.e., GDSS) is in fact appropriate for solution of the group's tasks, and provided the group facilitator makes effective use of it. There is some evidence (Watson, DeSanctis, & Poole, 1988) that a manual (i.e., nonelectronic) version of such task-structuring modules can improve group task performance as much or more than the electronic version; hence, the improvement apparently comes from the task/ performance structuring more than from the electronic mediation aspects of it.

Communication Systems: The Synchronous Case

When computers are used primarily as a within-group, synchronous communication system (COMM), they offer both advantages and costs. One of the main and most obvious advantages is that they permit groups to "meet" even when members are in widely dispersed locations. The potential advantages of a COMM are paid for by a dramatic reduction in media richness of the communications that can take place with them. Compared to meeting face-to-face, computer conference groups must rely on communications via text and graphics, without benefit of the rich array of nonverbal and paraverbal information that helps the flow of meaning in ordinary face-to-face groups (Daft & Lengel, 1986; McGrath & Hollingshead, 1994; Williams, 1977). If the group's task requires extensive communication among group members on a problem for which no task structuring algorithm exists, then the effectiveness of a group operating with a COMM (such as a computer conference system) will depend on the extent to which the particular task(s) the group is doing require a relatively rich communication medium (Daft & Lengel, 1986; McGrath & Hollingshead, 1994). If all of the group's tasks merely require exchange of information, or if they entail exchange and use of specific alphanumeric or graphic information (as in solving simple intellective problems), then the relatively limited set of modalities that a computer conference permits may aid, or at least not hinder, group task performance. In contrast, if some of the group's tasks require exchange of attitudes, values, intentions, and commitments, and resolution of differences among members, the lack of media richness may lead to poorer task performance for groups using the COMM. This will be especially the case for groups whose members have had little previous history with one another (for a review, see McGrath & Hollingshead, 1994).

In addition to being a less rich medium, communication by means of a synchronous computer-mediated communication system takes more time than communication of an equivalent face-to-face message (i.e., it takes longer to type than it does to talk). At the same time, communication of a message in a face-to-face group takes *everyone's* time—only one group member can be speaking at any given time, lest there be chaos—whereas multiple members can compose and send messages at the same time in a computer-mediated group. These two counteracting factors could, in principle, tend to even out the relative amounts of participation in groups in the two media. But this is not, in fact, the case; face-to-face groups tend to have much more communication for any given group size and period of time. We will discuss this difference later when we examine results we have obtained in our recent studies.

Communication Systems: The Asynchronous Case

If the group's task and working conditions require that group members communicate with one another when group members are not engaged in task activities at the same times, then availability of an asynchronous COMM (e.g., electronic bulletin boards or E-mail, or, alternatively, voice mail or fax) may enable the group to work effectively on a task during a particular time frame, when otherwise they would not be able to meet at all. As for the synchronous case, the effectiveness of that work will be influenced by the media richness requirements of the task and by the frequency and fluency with which group members use the communication system. They will also be affected by the temporal complexity of the information exchange process. For example, the asynchronous system may allow for a more efficient use of individual time (each participates at times of his or her own choosing) and a more timely set of opportunities for input (each only makes contributions when he or she has something to say). At the same time, asynchronous systems can create perturbations in the temporal flow of messages between members that do not arise in synchronous communication systems. For example, member A may read and react to member B's messages, and B may react in turn to A's message, before member C ever reads the original message. As a consequence, the flow of conversation in such asynchronous COMM systems can be turbulent.

Group Interaction Process

There is a lot more to learn about groups than just the effectiveness of their performance on tasks. A number of researchers have studied the interaction processes by which groups go about their work when communicating via computers (compared to communicating face-to-face), and have examined some aspects of group structure and development, as well as longer-term consequences for group members. Especially notable in this regard is work by Poole, DeSanctis, and colleagues (DeSanctis & Poole, 1989; Poole & DeSanctis, 1989, 1990; Poole, Holmes, & DeSanctis, 1991; Watson et al., 1988; Zigurs, Poole & DeSanctis, 1988), by Kiesler, Sproull, and colleagues (Finholt, Sproull, & Kiesler, 1990; Kiesler, Siegal, & McGuire, 1984; Siegal, Dubrovsky, Kiesler, & McGuire, 1986; Sproull & Kiesler, 1986), by Jessup, Valecich, and colleagues (Connolly, Jessup, & Valacich, 1990; Dennis et al., 1988; Jessup & Valacich, 1993; Valacich et al., 1992), and by McGrath, Hollingshead, and colleagues (Hollingshead & McGrath, 1995; Hollingshead, McGrath, & O'Connor, 1993; Lebie, Rhoades, & McGrath, 1996; McGrath & Hollingshead, 1994; Straus & McGrath, 1994).

For example, researchers have noted the potential anonymity of members in such groups and the potential for group members to perceive and treat one another impersonally. They have credited those factors both with the oft-reported increase in the relative equality of participation among group members (compared to face-to-face groups) and with the occasionally noted outbreak of highly emotional and negative communications (called "flaming" in this literature; see Kiesler et al., 1984). Certain conceptual and methodological aspects of these and other features of group inter- action for face-to-face and computer groups are discussed in the next part of this section.

Some Conceptual and Methodological Issues

The body of research regarding the use of computers in groups contains a number of rather serious methodological limitations and faces several problems of interpretation (Hollingshead & McGrath, 1995; McGrath & Hollingshead, 1994; McLeod, 1991). One major limitation of the body of empirical evidence on groups using computers is the extent to which each group of researchers has worked with (1) different kinds of computer systems (various PERFs, and a variety of both syn- chronous and asynchronous COMMs), (2) different kinds of group participants (college undergraduates, MBA students, company middle managers, etc.), (3) differ- ent kinds of tasks, and (4) different patterns of dependent variables (see Hollingshead & McGrath, 1995, and McGrath & Hollingshead, 1994, for fuller discussions of this issue). The problem is not that the body of research explores a range of populations, systems, and conditions, and a variety of dependent variable effects—such variation could be an advantage, increasing robustness of findings and the generality of their application. The problem is that the systems, tasks, subject populations, and depen- dent variables seldom overlap across studies. It is as if researchers in lab A studied population X with technology Y and dependent variable set Z, while researchers in lab B studied population J with technology K and dependent variable set L, and so on. This leaves no basis for establishing whether, how, and how much any given set of findings is contingent on the particular set of member, group, task, and technology conditions, and the particular dependent variables selected for that study. It also makes it difficult to get an holistic view of the effects of computers on group development, interaction, and task performance.

Another major limiting condition—one by no means restricted to this substan- tive area—is that a very large proportion of the research is based on very short-term studies, often of people new to the use of computers, or of that particular computer system. Little of that work explores effects of experience over time, and virtually none of it explores effects of change in members, tasks, technology, or context. Ignoring effects of such factors *over time* may have had major consequences for how results have been interpreted. These issues are emphasized later in this chapter.

At an even more basic level, there are questions about the direct comparability of both interaction and task performance for groups communicating only via computers and those communicating face-to-face. The two media are different in fundamental ways. Each offers some possibilities for communication that the other does not, and each imposes some restrictions that the other does not. So they cannot always be compared meaningfully by making quantitative comparisons one variable at a time. Some of the channels by which humans communicate with one another—the para-verbal and nonverbal modalities, for example—are simply not available in communications via computer systems that transmit text and graphics only. But the individuals who are acting in those computer-mediated groups still need to fulfill the same functions as do their face-to-face peers (task performance, member support, and group well-being), and must do so by using the available channels (i.e., text and graphics). The same modalities, therefore, are not the same when groups have different communication systems.

Researchers, however, often overlook such qualitative differences as they attempt to compare groups using the different media. For example, many studies, in pursuit of both coding convenience and comparability of information, ignore the nonverbal and paraverbal aspects of face-to-face communication and, instead, compare written text from a log of computer transactions with a written text that is a transcription of the words spoken in face-to-face groups. Such comparisons can be systematically misleading, as illustrated later.

Consider, for example, how group members communicate agreement and disagreement to one another in computer-mediated and face-to-face groups. Human beings interacting face-to-face often use nonverbal means to indicate agreement (e.g., nodding, smiling), and disagreement (e.g., head shaking, grimacing), rather than always stating agreement and disagreement in so many words. In computer-mediated groups, however, agreements and disagreements must be stated in typed words (or graphics), rather than transmitted in nods or facial expressions. Hence, any simple count of number of agreements from text transcripts of both face-to-face and computer-mediated group sessions would be misleading. If members of the two kinds of groups actually agreed and disagreed equally often, there is likely to be more of both agreements and disagreements in the written words of the computer groups than in the (typed transcript of) spoken words of the face-to-face groups.

At the same time, face-to-face groups sometimes use verbalizations (such as "uh-huh") to express agreement, but frequently use such verbalizations simply to express understanding and attention, that is, as back-channel communication. So some "uh-huhs" in face-to-face communication are agreements, and some are not. In computer groups, similar nonword utterances seldom appear, and when they do, they are not back-channel messages but are either answers to direct questions or expressions of agreement.

As a consequence, a research study that simply counts number of agreements and disagreements from transcriptions of group interaction, comparing face-to-face and computer groups that actually had the same amounts of agreement and disagreement among members, would be likely to both over- and underestimate agreements in face-to-face groups, and to underestimate disagreements in those groups, relative to comparable interaction periods for computer groups. If those results are simply interpreted as more agreement in face-to-face groups, or more disagreement in computer-mediated groups, that research study will not just be wrong, but it will be systematically misleading.

The interpretations regarding more equal rates of participation by group members offer a good case in point to illustrate some of the methodological and conceptual pitfalls that make interpretation of results in this area hazardous. Some researchers have concluded that COMMs offer a democratizing influence, encouraging more communication by low-status members who, in face-to-face meetings, are inhibited in their participation.

Given the research evidence on which they are based, these claims and implications are problematic on two grounds. First, in most of those studies, there has been no attempt to determine whether it was actually low-status members who provided any increased participation that did occur. (Berdahl & Craig, 1996, addressed this latter question directly with respect to group members who belong to marginalized social categories based on gender in one of the longitudinal studies to be described later).

Second, most of the evidence regarding participation rates is presented in terms of *variations in proportions* of total group communication among group members. Such an index masks the fact that the total *volume* of communication acts is virtually always much lower (often, orders of magnitude lower) in groups meeting via COMMs than in face-to-face meetings of groups of comparable sizes, with comparable tasks, for comparable periods of time (see, e.g., Lebie et al., 1996). This dramatic reduction probably occurs in part because people can talk faster than they can type, and in part because many such studies compare people using computers, often for the first time, with people meeting face-to-face, which they have done all their lives. (We will comment later about the importance of studying groups over extended periods of time). This lower-variation-in-proportions measure most often reflects not so much an increase in participation by the lower-participating members, as rather a dramatic decrease in participation by all members, especially the higher-participating members— hardly a hallmark of democratization in the usual sense!

Concluding Comments

The body of research literature about groups using computers is still far from adequate for a full understanding of the value of such technology, and major questions need to be raised about the interpretation of what we already "know" about them because of a number of methodological and conceptual issues such as those noted here. Part of the problem arises because, although some of that research has been done by researchers with a sophisticated appreciation of both group theory and behavioral science research methodology (e.g., cited work by Kiesler, Sproull, and colleagues, and by Poole, DeSanctis, and colleagues), much of it has been done by researchers with great expertise in computer hardware and software but with limited appreciation of group theory and research. In our judgment, both the effective interpretation of existing evidence and the effective design of future research studies can be enhanced greatly if research on groups using computers is done from a relatively comprehensive theoretical perspective about the nature of groups and their interaction and performance.

We have based our studies of groups using electronic communication systems on a theoretical formulation regarding groups in general. That work is developed, and expressed, in a number of publications (Argote & McGrath, 1993; Arrow & McGrath, 1993, 1995; McGrath, 1984, 1989, 1991; McGrath, Berdahl, & Arrow, 1996; McGrath & Gruenfeld, 1993; McGrath & O'Connor, 1996). One crucial feature of that formulation is that it places considerable emphasis on the complex, adaptive, and dynamic nature of groups. Not only does the study of groups involve a complex set of factors having to do with membership, tasks, technology, and context, in the static case; it also involves the effects of both experience over time under relatively stable conditions and experience over time under changing conditions. We are in the process of integrating our prior theoretical work into a new theoretical formulation that stresses the complexity, adaptability, and dynamic aspects of groups (McGrath, Arrow, & Berdahl, 1998). That group-theoretic perspective has guided our empirical work, which will be discussed in the next section.

Descriptions of Two Longitudinal Studies of Groups and Technology

JEMCO-1

In the spring of 1992, we converted an advanced undergraduate class on the social psychology of organizations into a setting that combined research and instructional objectives. The class had approximately 80 students, who were placed into three- and four-person groups, with 11 groups meeting face-to-face (FTF) and 11 groups meeting via synchronous computer-mediated communication (CMC). Those groups worked on assigned tasks relevant to the course content for 2 hours each week during a 14-week semester. Their success in the course depended, in part, on their interdependent activities in these groups.

In this longitudinal experiment (referred to as JEMCO-1), we examined a number of questions about the impact of electronic technology and of changes in small work groups over time. Most studies of groups with electronic technology have been done with ad hoc groups that exist only for one session or have extremely time-limited group lives. (But, again, most studies of groups that *don't* use electronic technology also have been done with ad hoc groups that exist only for one session or have extremely time-limited group lives!) In those one-shot studies of ad hoc groups, certain performance disadvantages are often reported for CMC groups. We expected those disadvantages to diminish over time as groups gained experience with the new communication technology.

In order to study effects of changes in technology, membership, and tasks, we switched all groups to the other communication medium for 2 weeks in the middle of the semester, switched one member of each group for 2 weeks late in the semester, and used tasks of each of five types (cf. McGrath, 1984), distributed over weeks, with some tasks of each type early and late in the group's life.

Each week, we collected four panels of data from which dependent variables were derived: (1) individual and group task performance on that week's project; (2) a record of the group's interaction (videotapes of the FTF groups and logs of all messages of the CMC groups); (3) participant responses on a standard questionnaire about various features of the task, the group, the technology, and the context; and (4) an individual essay, followed by a group essay, relating that week's project to the ideas and materials of the course. These individual and group essays were scored to provide a major part of the participants' course grades. They were also scored for integrative complexity (Gruenfeld & Hollingshead, 1993; Tetlock, 1983), that is, the extent to which the essay reflected an integrated conception of multiple ideas and perspectives.

JEMCO-2

We ran a quasi replication of JEMCO-1 in the spring of 1994 (which we will refer to here as JEMCO-2). There were several modifications in design for JEMCO-2. First, we had more participants (about 119 at the outset) and, hence could form more three- and four-person groups. Second, within lab sections, we assigned individuals to groups randomly within sex to create groups of particular sex compositions. Third, after 7 weeks, we switched all participants to the other communication medium and *recomposed groups* for the remaining 7 weeks, assuring that individuals were not group mates in both halves of the study. This dual manipulation at the halfway point of the semester provided more groups but of a shorter duration (about 60 total groups for 7 weeks each). It also provided within-participant comparisons for interaction and performance within a FTF versus a CMC group.

Other differences for JEMCO-2 included a 1-week (rather than 2-week) temporary member switch (in week 5 of the first half of the study), a different array of group tasks reflecting a different mix of task types, and an improved feature of the software (which will be discussed later) that aided CMC groups as they collaborated on their weekly group essays.

Some Key Findings about Technology from the JEMCO Studies

There was a fundamental and all-encompassing question explored in both of these longitudinal studies: How do *group process*, *task performance* and *participant reactions* vary as a function of the group's *membership composition*, its *communication technology*, and the *task types* on which the group is working; and how do these relations *change over time*?

Analyses of data from those studies dealt with a broad set of independent and dependent variables. On the independent-variable side, we were particularly interested in effects of (1) technology differences and technology change, (2) task differences, (3) membership composition and change, and (4) interactions of those facets with one another and over time. On the dependent-variable side, we were particularly interested in (1) effectiveness of group performance, both on the weekly project and on the weekly group essays; (2) patterns of interaction; and (3) group development, including the leadership and influence structures that emerged, and the tone and intensity of interpersonal relationships within the group (e.g., positive affect, experience of conflict).

We had the opportunity to publish many of the findings of JEMCO-1 together in a single place: The August 1993 issue of *Small Group Research* (Vol. 21, No. 3) is a special issue of that journal consisting of six articles reporting various aspects of JEMCO-1 (Arrow & McGrath, 1993; Gruenfeld & Hollingshead, 1993; Hollingshead et al., 1993; McGrath, 1993; McGrath, Arrow, Gruenfeld, Hollingshead, & O'Connor, 1993; O'Connor, Gruenfeld, & McGrath, 1993). Likewise, in March 1996, we had the opportunity to publish many of the findings of JEMCO-2 as a special double issue of *Computer Supported Cooperative Work* (Vol. 4, Nos. 2 & 3), consisting of seven articles (Arrow et al., 1996; Berdahl & Craig, 1996; Bouas & Arrow, 1996; Cummings, Schlosser, & Arrow, 1996; Lebie et al., 1996; McGrath & Arrow, 1996; Rhoades & O'Connor, 1996). We will not present here the detailed evidence that is reported in those two journal issues. Instead, we will present only selected findings from those studies to help document the main points we wish to make in our final section, which offers a discussion and interpretation of those findings and other information from the research literature.

In this section, we will note briefly some of the main findings obtained thus far in our analyses of the JEMCO-1 and JEMCO-2 studies. Results are organized by dependent variables. We will focus our discussion on differences between CMC and FTF groups over time and discuss membership and task effects only when they involve interactions with technology and/or time. We, of course, discuss only results that meet conventional criteria of statistical significance unless otherwise noted. Furthermore, there is space to present results in only minimal detail. Readers are encouraged to consult the cited papers for further detail.

Performance on the Groups' Weekly Projects

In JEMCO-1, FTF groups performed better on group projects than CMC groups in the first 2 weeks, but by the third week, that difference had disappeared (see Hollingshead et al., 1993). Groups in the two media continued to have equal levels of performance on the weekly projects throughout the remainder of the 14 weeks, except for the weeks involving two specific experimental events. First, when all groups were switched to the other medium (weeks 7 and 8), the new CMC groups (who up to that point had been FTF groups) performed much poorer than the new FTF groups (who up that point had been CMC groups). When groups were returned to their regular communication medium in week 9, there again was no difference between groups of the two media conditions. Second, when one member of each group was switched to a different group within the same communication medium condition (weeks 11 and 12), CMC groups again showed lower levels of performance on the weekly projects than did FTF groups. That difference began to disappear in the second week of the member switch, and disappeared altogether when members were restored to their regular groups in week 13.

These findings together suggest that the performance difference between CMC and FTF groups in initial sessions was due more to the *newness of the medium* than to specific features of the computer-mediated communication system used in this study, or to the newness of the group. It is as if the unfamiliar communication medium places a burden or handicap on the CMC groups. That handicap can be overcome with a relatively small amount of experience (two weekly sessions), but those groups remain vulnerable to task-performance decrements if additional events (such as changes in membership) occur to perturb the group's development, interaction, and performance.

Performance on the Groups' Weekly Essays

Individual and group task performance on the weekly essays, and the relation between the two, provide an especially interesting test of effects of the communication medium, for three reasons: First, although the weekly projects discussed earlier involved a variety of task types (see Hollingshead et al., 1993; McGrath, 1993), the group's weekly essay was the same task every week. Second, quality of performance on both the individual and group essays each week contributed substantially to the participants' grades in the course, whereas performance on the weekly projects did not affect course grades. Hence, we assume that members and groups were highly motivated to do well on those weekly essays, whereas they may or may not have been highly motivated to do well on their weekly workshop projects.

Third, as noted earlier, in JEMCO-2 we introduced an important software feature that CMC groups used for essay composition that had not been available for essays in JEMCO-1, and that was not available to JEMCO-2 groups for weekly projects. We called that feature a "product box." It represents a potential advantage for group collaboration and is described below.

In both JEMCO-1 and JEMCO-2, the FTF groups sat around a table with a single sheet of paper on which to write their group essays. Usually, one member wrote the essay; they could, but infrequently did, take turns writing. Other members gave information to the essay writer (the "scribe") orally, as the scribe composed the essay.

The CMC groups in JEMCO-1 had to designate someone to write the essay, which had to be handwritten off-line. Other group members could give the essay writer information only via typed text on the computer screen.

In contrast, the CMC groups in JEMCO-2 composed their group essays on-line, in a part of the screen we called the product box. All members could still give the text writer information by typing text on the part of the screen we called the "message box," but they could also see the text as it was composed and edited in the product box. Only one person at a time could compose and edit in the product box, but any member could ask for editorial control. Thus, in JEMCO-1, collaboration was harder for CMC groups than for FTF groups. In JEMCO-2, however, it was actually easier for CMC groups to coauthor and coedit the group essay using the product box than it was for FTF groups, who still had to get the essay handwritten on a single sheet of paper while sitting around a table.

The effects of this change in software were dramatic. In JEMCO-1, scores on the group essays of the CMC and FTF groups did not differ across all 14 weeks. In JEMCO-2, FTF groups and CMC groups also had comparable group essay scores on the first group essay. Thereafter, the CMC groups had higher scores than FTF groups on group essays for 12 of the remaining 13 essays, with the other being a tie. CMC groups had significantly higher essay scores than FTF groups overall.

When we compare the group essay scores with the individual essay scores of group members, the collaborative advantage of the product box is even clearer. To put the matter in the terms characteristically used in the group research literature: On the essays for the first half of JEMCO-2, the FTF groups did "as well as or better than the average of their individual members" on 50% of the group essays, whereas CMC groups did "as well as or better than the average of their individual members" on 59% of their group essays. Those numbers are even more striking if the first essays (done while CMC groups were still learning how to use this new technology) are excluded. For groups during the second half of JEMCO-2—when individuals were all switched to a different medium, and new groups were composed—results essentially replicate those noted earlier. For the second-half groups, FTF groups had group essay scores as high as or higher than average individual essay scores 35% of the time; CMC groups did that 49% of the time. These differences were significant for each half of the study and for the two halves combined.

The product box also seemed to have effects on the integrative complexity of the group essays. In JEMCO-1, CMC groups had lower integrative complexity scores on their group essays than did members of FTF groups (Gruenfeld & Hollingshead, 1993). Integrative complexity increased over time for groups in both media, but the increase was especially notable for FTF groups. In JEMCO-2, the levels of integrative complexity of the group essays of CMC groups exceeded those in FTF groups (Cummings et al., 1996).

These findings—assuming they prove robust in further empirical tests—appear to be solid evidence of a facilitative effect on *collaborative work* that derives from a *feature of the technology itself*, as distinct from features of the user (such as experience/practice with the system or affective response regarding the use of the technology). Note also that it is a feature of the CMC system as a PERF (i.e., as a GDSS), rather than as a COMM (i.e., GCSS).

Interaction Processes

Besides these effects on performance on both the weekly projects and the weekly essays, in JEMCO-2 we also examined differences between communication media in the groups' interaction processes during the composition of the group essays in the first half of the study, weeks 2-7. Lebie et al. (1996) reported that FTF groups produced much more communication than did CMC groups, generating more than two-and-a-half times as many messages per minute. Groups in the two media also differed in the pattern of their interaction activity, and in how those patterns changed over time. CMC groups spent much less time than did FTF groups on several categories of activity relating to the interactive composition of the group essays (e.g., "reading aloud while composing"). At the same time, they spent more time than FTF groups on the mechanics of the essay-production process. Both of those results seem to reflect differences inherent in the two media. FTF groups also engaged in much higher levels of off-task behavior, mostly interpersonal communications, and this difference increased sharply in the latter weeks of groups' lives. This was also reported for groups' task interactions by Berdahl (1996), who analyzed group members' reports of amounts of task activity and social activity of self and others. CMC groups began with and continued to have higher levels of task activity and lower levels of social activity than FTF groups.

Together, these findings suggest that the CMC groups had to work harder to complete their tasks than did the FTF groups, even with the product box assisting their collaborative work considerably, and that the CMC system provided little opportunity and little time for those groups to engage in group-building interpersonal communications, even after a number of weeks of experience with the medium.

Conflict, Affect, and Interpersonal Relations

In JEMCO-1, we examined positive affect within groups (cohesiveness; Arrow & McGrath, 1993) and the experience and consequences of within-group conflict (see O'Connor et al., 1993). Over all weeks, members of CMC groups had lower positive affect toward their groups than did members of FTF groups. This suggests that the computer medium did have important effects on within-group affect, and these effects persisted even after considerable experience with the medium. This may be related to the idea, suggested earlier, that even after the CMC groups had overcome their task-performance deficit, they continued to carry a burden or handicap that made them vulnerable to subsequent perturbing events (e.g., membership changes). That handicap seems to be focused on intragroup affect and interpersonal relations.

Although groups in the two communication media did not differ in experienced conflict overall, when groups *changed communication medium*, members had higher levels of experienced conflict. At the same time, a *change in membership* produced decreased levels of experienced conflict. Overall, experienced conflict seemed to have three main sources: (1) Groups had higher levels of experienced conflict in initial meetings of, or changes to, a new/unfamiliar communication medium (i.e., CMC groups); (2) groups had lower levels of experienced conflict (and higher levels of positive affect) when there was a guest member in the group; and (3) groups had higher levels of experienced conflict when working on mixed-motive (negotiation) tasks than when working on collaborative tasks (Arrow & McGrath, 1993). Aspects of the group's history also played a part; groups with a history of much experienced conflict were better able to handle the conflict-producing mixed-motive tasks than were groups with a history of little previous group conflict. High levels of experienced conflict, in turn, were associated with lower levels of performance on the group's weekly projects, and with lower levels of positive affect toward the group.

In JEMCO-2, we examined how positive and negative affect influenced other aspects of groups (see Rhoades & O'Connor, 1996). In FTF groups, both positive and negative affect were important determinants of level of group cohesiveness, amount of participation, and amount of information processing, and the latter was in turn associated with individual and group performance on the weekly essays. In CMC groups, on the other hand, although both positive and negative affect were important determinants of group cohesiveness, neither affected amount of participation, only negative affect was related to amount of information processing, and neither positive nor negative affect was related to performance on the weekly essays.

In JEMCO-2, we also examined the development of group identity in CMC and FTF groups (Bouas & Arrow, 1996). Group identity was consistently lower for CMC groups, and this effect was even stronger for the reconstituted CMC groups of the second half of that study. Yet group identity was virtually unaffected by temporary membership changes in the CMC groups, whereas it was significantly affected by them in FTF groups. Furthermore, group identity started relatively high and steadily declined for both FTF and CMC groups in the first half of the study, whereas in the reconstituted groups of the second half, the patterns over time were more complex and differed for CMC and FTF groups.

Participation and Influence Structures

In JEMCO-2, we examined how the sex composition of the group interacted with both technology and time to shape the patterns of participation and influence that emerged in those groups (Berdahl, 1996; Berdahl & Craig, 1996). Results of these studies contradicted conventional wisdom about these matters. Contrary to the prevalent belief in the literature on computer-supported collaborative work, namely, that CMC groups are more egalitarian than FTF groups, Berdahl and Craig reported that participation was perceived as *more* centralized (i.e., less egalitarian) in CMC groups than in FTF groups in the groups' initial meeting. Those differences disappeared in later meetings; FTF and CMC groups were perceived as equally centralized for the remaining meetings.

The studies also examined the effects of sex composition alone and in combination with communication medium, to test predictions made by various theories of gender for the effects of these independent variables on social and task leadership (Berdahl, 1996) and participation and influence structures (Berdahl & Craig, 1996). These, also, did not fit conventional wisdom. Berdahl (1996) reported that across sex compositions and communication media, men and women engaged in similar levels of *task leadership* on the weekly projects. With respect to *social leadership*, however, women engaged in higher levels of social leadership than men in FTF groups, whereas men engaged in more social leadership than women in CMC groups.

Berdahl and Craig (1996) reported that solo males in majority-female CMC groups were perceived as having more influence than their female groupmates, whereas males in majority-male CMC groups were perceived as having less influence than their solo female groupmate. In other words, in the CMC groups, where status characteristics such as gender are presumed to be *less* salient, the solos of both genders were perceived as having greater influence than the members of the majority gender in that group. In FTF groups, on the other hand, where gender is expected to be highly salient, the ratio of male-to-female influence did not differ significantly in either majority-male or majority-female groups.

Some Implications

From these and other results of our work so far, as well as from our examination of the existing research literature, we can extract a number of very important themes about groups, technology, and time. Three themes in particular summarize much of what we have learned regarding groups using computer technology.

Theme 1: Technology Is Ubiquitous: It Both Drives and Constrains Group Action

We define *technology* (as a cultural anthropologist might) as a selected and organized set of tools, rules, procedures, and resources by which some social unit (an individual or a group) carries out the tasks of some project(s) intended to attain some purpose(s). We mean to include both the "hardware" and the "software" of it.

In that definition, *all* groups have a technology—including ordinary, everyday face-to-face groups. We usually don't think about face-to-face groups as having a technology. The technology of face-to-face groups is ordinarily invisible, that is, until we contrast such groups with those using tools/rules/procedures/resources that are more salient for us as a special technology (e.g., computer-mediated groups). This lesson was made clear to us when we carried out the media-switch manipulation in JEMCO-1. We took groups that had developed as computer groups for about 6 weeks and put them in the face-to-face condition for 2 weeks (and vice versa for the face-to-face groups). Member reactions to that change made it clear that we needed to re-think our interpretation of what was happening. For instance, groups previously in the computer-mediated condition spent time in the face-to-face condition learning each other's first names and otherwise getting acquainted on an interpersonal level. It was not the case—as we had been in the habit of thinking—that one set of groups had "had" a technology, and the other was now going to "get" a technology. Rather, both sets of groups were *changing technologies*, and every technology both affords a certain pattern of opportunities and imposes a certain pattern of constraints for the group.

So the lesson about technology has an important corollary: *Any technology poses both opportunities and constraints for a group, and all group activity is both driven and constrained by that group's technology* (and by other facets as well).

Theme 2: Most Effects Involving Technology Are Interaction Effects

One of the most pervasive features of the results of our experimental simulation studies is the observation that there are very few main effects of technology but lots of interactions between technology and other features of the situation, namely, features of tasks, features of membership and group structure, and especially effects of continuity and change over time. We can state those interactions more generally as propositions about groups, with and without computers—propositions needing further test.

Task–Technology Fit

When you study groups doing any one thing, the effects of the group's task can remain invisible. But when you begin to study groups doing more than one kind of thing, you quickly see that group task performance (as well as other aspects of group activity) depends, intricately, on what task(s) the group is doing. The literature regarding both computer-mediated and face-to-face work groups suggests that groups need a good fit between task and technology. A couple of earlier studies in our program (McGrath & Hollingshead, 1994; Straus & McGrath, 1994) dealt with that question, as have Daft and Lengel (1986; Trevino, Lengel, & Draft, 1987) and others. But the task–technology fit we found turns out to be more complex than reflected in either Daft's or our own earlier formulations. To put it simply: *The fit between task and technology is dynamic, not static. It changes over time* (see McGrath & Hollingshead, 1994). As groups gain experience with a stable set of components (i.e., members, projects, and technology), they can do any given task with a less rich communication system, and as changes occur in any of the group's components (e.g., a change in membership) they may need a richer communications medium to do any given task (McGrath & Hollingshead, 1994). Hence, it is really a three-way interaction: of task, technology, and time, or experience. Furthermore, when groups are studied over time, variations in task are inevitably confounded with variations in group experience and history.

Task–Technology–Membership Fit

Effective group performance also requires a good fit between that task–technology complex and features of the group's membership composition and group structure. It is obvious that group members must have, among them, all the abilities needed to do the group's tasks and the motivation to do them. They also must have a structure and division of labor that delivers those abilities to task components as needed and a communication system that provides links among members who need to coordinate their separate task activites. In truth, social psychologists have spent considerable effort on these matters over the years and have not made a lot of empirical progress. Maybe this is because membership factors (as with tasks and technology) turn out to be dynamic rather than static in their effects. In any case, *the "good fit" required for effective performance is a complex, dynamic fit of members, tasks, and technology over time.*

Theme 3: Groups Are Dynamic Systems That Change over Time

The overall problem being explored here is very complex even in the static case. Our framework implies that research on these matters must take into account key variables from each of at least four major panels of input factors: (1) member and group factors (composition and structure); (2) task factors; (3) technology factors; and (4) features of the embedding context(s). Things get much more complicated when we study these matters over time.

Time plays two very crucial, and quite different, roles in regard to the development and behavior of groups: (1) Time is a vehicle for the *accrual of experience*, which brings about changes within the group's pattern of activities; and (2) time is a vehicle for the *impact of change*—in membership, tasks, technology, and context. These two temporal facets, experience and change, have dramatically different effects. Furthermore, they interact.

Time Operates as a Vehicle for the Accrual of Experience

Experience derives from continuity of a given social unit: with respect to its membership composition and structure; with respect to type, difficulty, and other features of its tasks; with respect to features of its technology; and with respect to features of the physical, temporal, sociocultural, and organizational contexts within which that social unit is operating.

When a group gets to do the same kind of task over and over again, we speak of practice and learning, and we generally anticipate improvements in performance (that is, an increase in probability of certain desired responses and a decrease in probability of errors). We would expect the same kind of improvement to derive from practice with a given technology, and from practice with the same teammates. In JEMCO-1, we found such improvement over time for integrative complexity of both individual and group essays.

To put the matter more generally: *Experience produces systematic routinizing effects* on all aspects of the group–task–technology–context fit. That is to say, as work groups continue with the same membership and structure, doing tasks of a given type with a given technology while operating in given physical, temporal, sociocultural, and organizational contexts, they tend to transform what they have been doing into what Gersick and Hackman (1990) call "habitual routines."

Effects of experience are vital in our studies of technology. A very large portion of past research, purporting to compare work groups using computer technology to groups working without computer technology, have used ad hoc groups that had little or no previous experience *as a group* with that computer technology. This can lead to generalizations that are based on static conditions only. For example, most one-session studies of groups using electronic technology have found that *CMC groups take much longer to do specific tasks than do FTF groups*. Whereas some of that increased time is doubtless due to the limiting condition that it takes longer to type than it does to talk, even for very fast typists, much of it is likely due to CMC groups' lack of practice with their available technology—individually, and as a group—compared to groups using the FTF technology that they have been using all of their lives.

Analyses from JEMCO-1 bear this out: Differences in speed and quality of task performance were substantial and significant at the outset but diminished as groups gained experience with an initially new technology. Results from JEMCO-2 offer an even more dramatic example. FTF groups had higher scores on both individual and group essays on the first essay, but by the second essay, CMC groups not only caught up but had higher scores on both individual and group essays, and retained that superiority through the rest of their lifespan.

As evidence of this kind accumulates from longitudinal studies, we may have to *reinterpret* many seemingly robust, substantive findings from earlier one-shot studies of ad hoc groups, with and without electronic enhancements. To put the matter in another way: *For both CMC groups and FTF groups, we may have built a body of evidence that is statically robust but ephemeral over time—a body of temporal Type-1 errors.*

Time Operates as a Vehicle for Change

As a general proposition, we expect change arising from the group's relation to its embedding systems (rather than from internal developmental events) to produce reverberations throughout the system, perturbing all aspects of the member–task–technology–context fit. When work groups encounter changes in membership or structure, in task type or difficulty, in essential technology, and/or in context, then, by definition, their patterns of performance (their habitual routines) tend to be modified. These modifications are likely to affect the group's ongoing interaction process, the quality and speed of their work, task outcomes, and members' reactions to the experience. Some of these effects are likely to be for the better, and some for the worse.

Change in the different facets of the system (i.e., in membership composition and group structure, in tasks, technology, and context) seem to have different degrees and kinds of effects. In JEMCO-1, there seemed to be a hierarchy of importance of changes. In order of increasing importance were changes in tasks, changes in technology, and changes in membership. We changed task types on our groups frequently, with little apparent reaction from them, and with few systematic effects on interaction or performance—perhaps because they came to expect different tasks each week. If anything, groups appeared to enjoy the variety, as proponents of task and skill variety suggest (e.g., Hackman & Oldham, 1976).

In contrast, media changes attracted much reaction by participants and produced systematic differences in interaction process and task performance when those changes occurred. The groups assigned to the computer condition at the outset were very vocal, mostly in opposition to it. But those groups came to terms with the medium quickly and generated task products comparable to those of FTF groups. Members of those groups found ways to express the advantages of the CMC condition in their descriptive essays. When it came time for the experimental manipulations of media, those assigned to FTF groups at the outset were extremely vocal in their objections to our reassignment of them to the CMC condition, even for 2 weeks, and their task performance reflected the negative impact that the new technology had on them. The CMC groups were not particularly bothered by their experimental reassignment to the FTF condition in those weeks—after all, as individuals, they were already very familiar with the FTF technology into which they were being moved. In fact, they used the 2-week media switch to get more interpersonally acquainted with one another.

Membership changes seemed to produce the most impact on group process and, to some degree, on group outcomes. Both member-initiated absences and experimenter-initiated member switches, especially following long periods of membership stability, seemed to have *positive* effects on both group process and task performance (Arrow & McGrath, 1993). Some of those effects interact with technology.

What we are learning about dynamics, therefore, is that time carries two separate sets of effects—effects of *experience* (given continuity), and effects of *change*—and that experience and change often have contrasting but interacting effects. To put it simply, *Experience routinizes; change perturbs. Both routinizing and perturbing can have positive and negative effects. Furthermore, it matters greatly when the change occurs in the group's history.*

Concluding Comments: Implications for Groups Using Computers

We can summarize the main implications of these studies for our understanding of groups using computers by making the following main points:

1. The computer technology used in this study, and perhaps any kind of new technology, imposes some kind of performance handicap—perhaps more because it is new (i.e., a change) than because of the specific technology.
2. Such a task performance handicap can be overcome, and sometimes even reversed, with practice and experience. But improved performance may come at a cost in intragroup process—for example, in the level of positive affect,

conflict, and cohesiveness—because of the time and logistical demands of the technology.

3. Membership change can have positive consequences for group process, and for some kinds of group task performance, depending on the centrality of the lost and gained members, the source of the impetus for the change, and the group's past history of membership stability and change. Positive effects may be especially likely for groups using computers, and for groups that have not experienced much membership change previously. So membership change may help offset the process burden of new/changed technology.

At the same time, specific features of any given technology may lead to major losses—or gains—in group effectiveness that do not diminish and may even increase over time. The introduction of the product box for the collaborative production of group essays in JEMCO-2 is a case in point. After the initial week's use, the computer groups working with the product box did not suffer the process losses (i.e., group essay scores below "best member" essay scores) characteristic of both face-to-face and computer groups in JEMCO-1 (and widely reported in past group research literature). The computer groups in the first half of JEMCO-2 actually showed process gains in a number of cases; that is, group essay scores that were not only better than the score of the group's average member, but also better than the score of the group's best member.

So, research on these matters must take great care to distinguish between two kinds of effects. On the one hand, there are effects of any new or changed technology *just because it is new for that group*, and these are likely to be attenuated over time. On the other hand, there are specific effects on process and performance of important group functions that arise from specific features of that technology, and these may persist or even increase over time.

Research in this domain must also take care to analyze the relation between operational levels and conceptual levels of variables separately for different media. It is easy for researchers to fall prey to the obvious assumption that a given variable will be manifested in the same way (and therefore be measurable by the same set of operations) in all cases. But different media provide different opportunities and constraints for intermember actions, so variables such as relative participation and amount of disagreement must be measured in ways that are valid for each medium. This point is related to the idea, from cultural anthropology, that systems have both emic and etic aspects, and that the former need to be assessed in terms appropriate to the system.

Future research also needs to address the problem of nonoverlapping bodies of research information (Hollingshead & McGrath, 1995). This can be done if groups of researchers take care to incorporate into their studies the same kinds of technological systems, populations, tasks, and especially dependent variable measures as do other leading researchers in the field, so that the body of findings resulting from all of the work in this domain can meaningfully be woven together into a single, integrated tapestry of research information.

The most important lesson from our work so far, though, is not about technology, or tasks, or membership effects per se. Rather, it is about the interactions of these facets of work groups, and especially about their operation over time. Above all, therefore, future research in this domain needs to focus attention on effects of member, technology, and task factors over time, under conditions of both continuity and change of the group as a system.

Acknowledgments
    The work discussed in this chapter was heavily collaborative. It took place within a large, ongoing research program that has extended over a number of years. We wish to acknowledge the important contributions of our collaborating colleagues: Holly Arrow, Kelly Bouas, Deborah Gruenfeld, Andrea Hollingshead, Bettina Johnson, Linda Lebie, Joselito Lualhati, Kathleen O'Connor, Jon Rhoades, and Ann Schlosser. We also wish to express appreciation to several dozen undergraduate research assistants who provided invaluable project support in data collection and processing.
    Research on which this chapter is based was supported in part under NSF grants IRI 89-05640, IRI 91-07040, and IRI 93-10099 (J. E. McGrath, Principal Investigator).

References

Argote, L., & McGrath, J. E. (1993). Group processes in organizations: Continuity and change. In C. L. Cooper & I. T. Robertson (Eds.), *International review of industrial and organizational psychology* (pp. 333–389). New York: Wiley.

Arrow, H., Berdahl, J. L., Bouas, K. S., Craig, K., Cummings, A., Lebie, L., McGrath, J. E., O'Connor, K. M., Rhoades, J. A., & Schlosser, A. (1996). Time, technology, and groups: An integration. *Computer Supported Collaborative Work*, *4*(2 & 3), 253–261.

Arrow, H., & McGrath, J. E. (1993). Membership matters: How member change and continuity affect small group structure, process, and performance. *Small Group Research*, *24*(3), 334–361.

Arrow, H., & McGrath, J. E. (1995). Membership dynamics in groups at work: A theoretical perspective. In B. Staw & L. Cummings (Eds.), *Research in organizational behavior*, *17*, (pp. 373–411). New York: JAI Press.

Berdahl, J. L. (1996). *Gender and leadership in work groups over time: A test of five alternative models.* Unpublished master's thesis, University of Illinois, Urbana–Champaign.

Berdahl, J. L., & Craig, K. (1996). Equality of participation and influence in groups: The effects of communication medium and sex composition. *Computer Supported Cooperative Work*, *4*(2 & 3), 179–202.

Bouas, K., & Arrow, H. (1996). The development of group identity in computer-mediated and face-to-face groups with membership change. *Computer Supported Cooperative Work*, *4*(2 & 3), 153–178.

Connolly, T., Jessup, L. M., & Valacich, J. (1990). Idea generation using GDSS: Effects of anonymity and evaluative tone. *Management Science*, *36*, 689–703.

Cummings, A., Schlosser, A., & Arrow, H. (1996). Developing complex group products: Idea coordination in computer-mediated and face-to-face groups. *Computer Supported Cooperative Work*, *4*(2 & 3), 229–251.

Daft, R. L., & Lengel, R. (1986). Organizational information requirements, media richness, and structural design. *Management Science*, *32*(5), 554–571.

Dennis, A. R., George, J. F., Jessup, L. M., Nunamaker, J. F., & Vogel, D. R. (1988). Information technology to support electronic meetings. *MIS Quarterly, 12*(4), 591–624.

DeSanctis, G., & Poole, M. S. (1989). *Computer-supported meetings: A brief overview of the GDSS Research Project.* Minneapolis: University of Minnesota Press.

Egido, C. (1990). Teleconferencing as a technology to support cooperative work: Its possibilities and limitations. In J. Galegher, R. Kraut, & C. Egido (Eds.), *Intellectual teamwork: Social and technological foundations of cooperative work* (pp. 351–371). Hillsdale, NJ: Erlbaum.

Finholt, T., Sproull, L., & Kiesler, S. (1990). Communication and performance in ad hoc groups. In J. Galegher, R. Kraut, & C. Egido (Eds.), *Intellectual teamwork: Social and technological foundations of cooperative work.* Hillsdale, NJ: Erlbaum.

Gersick, C. J. G., & Hackman, J. R. (1990). Habitual routines in task-performing groups. *Organizational Behavior and Human Decision Processes, 47*, 65–97.

Gruenfeld, D. H & Hollingshead, A. B. (1993). Sociocognition in work groups: The evolution of group integrative complexity and its relation to task performance. *Small Group Research, 24*(3), 383–405.

Hackman, J. R., & Oldham, G. R. (1976). Motivation through the design of work: Test of a theory. *Organizational Behavior and Human Performance, 16*, 250–279.

Hesse, B. W., Werner, C. M., & Altman, I. (1990). Temporal aspects of computer-mediated communication. *Computers in Human Behavior, 4*, 147–165.

Hollingshead, A. B., & McGrath, J. E. (1995). The whole is less than the sum of its parts: A critical review of research on computer-assisted groups. In R. A. Guzzo & E. Salas (Eds.), *Team decisions and team performance in organizations* (pp. 46–78). San Francisco, CA: Jossey-Bass.

Hollingshead, A. B., McGrath, J. E., & O'Connor, K. M. (1993). Group task performance and communication technology: A longitudinal study of computer mediated vs face-to-face work groups. *Small Group Research, 24*(3), 307–333.

Jessup, L. M., & Valacich, J. S. (Eds.) (1993). *Group support systems: New perspectives.* New York: Macmillan.

Kiesler, S., Siegal, J., & McGuire, T. (1984). Social psychological aspects of computer-mediated communication. *American Psychologist, 39*, 1123–1134.

Kraemer, K. L., & King, J. (1988). Computer-based systems for cooperative work and group decision making. *Computing Surveys, 20*, 115–146.

Kraemer, K. L., & Pinsonneault, A. (1990). Technology and groups: Assessment of the empirical research. In J. Galegher, R. Kraut, & C. Egido (Eds.), *Intellectual teamwork: Social and technological foundations of cooperative work* (pp. 375–405). Hillsdale, NJ: Erlbaum.

Lebie, L., Rhoades, J. A., & McGrath, J. E. (1996). Interaction process in computer-mediated and face-to-face groups. *Computer Supported Cooperative Work, 4*(2 & 3), 127–152.

McGrath, J. E. (1984). *Groups: Interaction and performance.* Englewood Cliffs, NJ: Prentice-Hall

McGrath, J. E. (1989). Time matters in groups. In J. Galegher, R. E. Kraut, & C. Egido (Eds.), *Intellectual teamwork: Social and technological foundations of cooperative work* (pp. 23–61). Hillsdale, NJ: Erlbaum.

McGrath, J. E. (1991). Time, interaction, and performance (TIP): A theory of groups. *Small Group Research, 22*(2), 147–174.

McGrath, J. E. (1993). Introduction: The JEMCO workshop: Description of a longitudinal study. *Small Group Research, 24*(3), 285–306.

McGrath, J. E., & Arrow, H. (1996). Introduction: The JEMCO-2 study of time, technology and groups. *Computer Supported Cooperative Work, 4*(2 & 3), 107–126.

McGrath, J. E., Arrow, H., & Berdahl, J. L. (1998). *Groups as complex systems.* Newbury Park, CA: Sage Publications.

McGrath, J. E., Arrow, H., Gruenfeld, D. H, Hollingshead, A. B., & O'Connor, K. M. (1993). Groups, tasks, and technology: The effects of experience and change. *Small Group Research, 24*(3), 406–420.

McGrath, J. E., Berdahl, J. L., & Arrow, H. (1996). Traits, expectations, culture and clout: The dynamics of diversity in work groups. In S. E. Jackson & M. M. Ruderman (Eds.), *Diversity in work teams: Research paradigms for a changing workplace* (pp. 17–46). Washington DC: American Psychological Association.

McGrath, J. E., & Gruenfeld, D. H (1993). Toward a dynamic and systemic theory of groups: An integration of six temporally enriched perspectives. In M. M. Chemers & R. Ayman (Eds.), *Leadership theory and research: Perspectives and directions* (pp. 217–243). NY: Academic Press.

McGrath, J. E., & Hollingshead, A. B. (1993). Putting the "group" back in group support systems: Some theoretical issues about dynamic processes in groups with technological enhancements. In L. M. Jessup & J. E. Valacich (Eds.), *Group support systems: New perspectives* (pp. 78–96). New York: Macmillan.

McGrath, J. E., & Hollingshead, A. B. (1994). *Groups interacting with technology: Ideas, issues, evidence, and an agenda.* Newbury Park, CA: Sage Publications.

McGrath, J. E., & O'Connor, K. M. (1996). Temporal issues in work groups. In M. West (Ed.), *Handbook of workgroup psychology* (pp. 25–52). London: Wiley.

McLeod, P. (1991, February). *What we know, what we don't know, and what we think we know about GDSS: Results of a meta-analysis.* Paper presented at the Human Computer Interaction Consortium Workshop, University of Michigan, Ann Arbor, MI.

O'Connor, K. M., Gruenfeld, D. H, & McGrath, J. E. (1993). The experience and effects of conflict in continuing work groups. *Small Group Research, 24*(3), 362–382.

Poole, M. S., & DeSanctis, G. (1989). Use of group decision support systems as an appropriation process. *Proceedings of the 22nd Annual Hawaii International Conference on System Sciences, 4,* 149–157.

Poole, M. S., & DeSanctis, G. (1990). Understanding the use of decision support systems: The theory of adaptive structuration. In J. Fulk & C. Steinfield (Eds.), *Organizations and communication technology* (pp. 175–195). Newbury Park, CA: Sage Publications.

Poole, M. S., Holmes, M., & DeSanctis, G. (1991). Conflict management in a computer-supported meeting environment. *Management Science, 37,* 926–953.

Rhoades, J. A., & O'Connor, K. M. (1996). Affect in computer-mediated and face-to-face work groups: The construction and testing of a general model. *Computer Supported Cooperative Work, 4*(2 & 3), 203–228.

Siegal, J., Dubrovsky, V., Kiesler, S., & McGuire, T. (1986). Group processes in computer-mediated communication. *Organizational Behavior and Human Decision Processes, 37,* 157–187.

Sproull, L., & Kiesler, S. (1986). Reducing social context cues: Electronic mail in organization communication. *Management Science, 32,* 1492–1512.

Straus, S. G., & McGrath, J. E. (1994). Does the medium matter? The interaction of task type and technology on group performance and member reactions. *Journal of Applied Psychology, 79,* 87–97.

Tetlock, P. E. (1983). Cognitive style and political ideology. *Journal of Personality and Social Psychology, 45,* 118–126.

Trevino, L., Lengel, R., & Daft, R. (1987). Media symbolism, media richness and media choice in organizations: A symbolic interactionist perspective. *Communication Research, 14*(5), 553–575.

Valacich, J. S., Jessup, L. M., Dennis, A., & Nunamaker, J. F., Jr. (1992). A conceptual framework of anonymity in group support systems. *Group Decision and Negotiation, 1,* 211–241.

Watson, R., DeSanctis, G., & Poole, M. S. (1988, September). Using a GDSS to facilitate group consensus: Some intended and unintended consequences. *MIS Quarterly,* 463–478.

Williams, E. (1977). Experimental comparisons of face-to-face and mediated communication: A review. *Psychological Bulletin, 84,* 963–976.

Zigurs, I., Poole, M. S., & DeSanctis, G. (1988, December). A study of influence in computer-mediated group decision making. *MIS Quarterly,* 625–644.

11

Tapping the Power of Teams

Ernest J. Savoie

Teams, it seems, are de rigueur. According to a bevy of surveys, we can find them in all kinds and sizes of organizations—public, private, and nonprofit. As we look, we find teams doing all kinds of work, from manual to professional, all the way to the "thinking work" that goes on in the boardroom. Indeed, every self-respecting organization boasts of its executive team, though some would consider that an oxymoron in today's swap-the-top climate.

My discussion is in three parts. Part 1 reviews the reported extent of the use of teams and employee involvement in American organizations. Part 2 reviews the Ford experience. Ford has a reputation for best practices in these areas and is frequently benchmarked. Although Ford is not a microcosm of other organizations, some of its experiences may be instructive for others. Part 3 offers some broad observations about the future uses of teams.

Part 1: Looking Over the Landscape

Despite decades of experimentation and advocacy for forms of employee involvement, the panorama of teams that now characterizes organizational life is a phenomenon of the 1990s. According to the report *America's Choice: High Skills or Low Wages!* (Commission on the Skills of the American Workforce, 1989), only about 5% of U.S. workplaces had team-type arrangements in the early 1980s. Spurred on in part by the rapid spread of total quality management programs, the picture started changing by the second half of the 1980s. A 1994 Bureau of the Census survey conducted for the National Center on the Educational Quality of the Workforce

Ernest J. Savoie • College of Urban, Labor, and Metropolitan Affairs, Wayne State University, Detroit, Michigan 48202.

Theory and Research on Small Groups, edited by R. Scott Tindale et al. Plenum Press, New York, 1998.

(EQW; 1995) says that 54% of workers meet regularly in problem-solving groups similar to quality circles, and that 13% are in self-managed teams.

Most surveys of the usage of teams and of employee involvement are based on self-reporting by firms. The Commission on the Future of Worker–Management Relations (1994), chaired by former Secretary of Labor John Dunlop, sponsored a study of employee involvement in American firms as reported by employees. Princeton Survey Research Associates conducted the survey in the fall of 1994, using a representative sample of 2,400 employees in privately owned firms with more than 25 workers. The results confirm the wide diffusion of employee involvement. Fifty-two percent of the employees indicated that some form of employee participation program operates in their workplace. Thirty-two percent stated that they are personally part of self-directed work teams, total quality management, quality circles, or other forms of employee involvement.

The macrofactors fueling the expansion of forms of employee involvement, total quality management, and organizational transformation (reengineering, restructuring, reinventing, or whatever) are well known (Kochan, Katz & McKersie, 1986; Kochan, Cutcher-Gershenfeld, & MacDuffie, 1989; Bluestone & Harrison, 1988). They include powerful economic forces associated with global competitiveness, fast changes in information technology affecting how and where work is done, government regulation and deregulation of markets, and pronounced demographic shifts in the composition of the workforce. Although each industry and each organization faces its own conditions and its own imperatives, the cumulative forces buffeting the American economy show no sign of abating as we head into the first decade of the next century.

The expansion of involvement-type initiatives has created a thriving industry on teams, team formation, team building, teamwork, team spirit, and team rejuvenation. I have looked at many of the manuals, exercises, and training materials used by internal and external consultants and trainers in this area. Much of it builds on earlier work on the nature of groups and group interaction by psychologists, sociologists, and to a lesser extent, anthropologists. In many instances, we see a shameless (and sometimes mindless) replication of theory and speculation that goes as far back as the 1950s, when organizational development was emerging as a distinct field of inquiry. Today, teaming is part of the managerial lexicon, albeit more for competitive reasons than because of conversion to an academic catechism. Be that as it may, academics, consultants, and trainers have been part of it. So, if ubiquity is a measure of success, these advocates may properly bask in the sunshine of victory along with others. While they did not invent teams or groups, they did analyze, theorize, adapt, interpret, codify, expand, and espouse.

There is a wide variation in how organizations, consultants, and individuals define teams. Some people believe the self-managed team is an ultimate form and would like to reserve the word *team* for this archetype. (The classic self-directed, autonomous, or self-managed team in a manufacturing environment consists of 6–20 people organized around a variety of complementary tasks or skills, with a clear and relatively self-contained output; job rotation; pay for learning; no immediate or direct supervision; and some latitude with respect to scheduling, quality, and job assign-ment.) Other people aver that any small group is a team, and they do not like going beyond a self-imposed limit of 15–20 members. Still others, however, refuse to be bound by any limits and are quick to call any aggregation, whatever its size, a team (especially if they can call it "my team," or "our team"). Individuals, too, while acknowledging their tie to an immediate work group, do not hesitate to identify themselves as members of a plant or office team, a division team, a marketing or other functional team, or the company team. Although it in necessary to define a team when implementing specific team-building interventions, we need not for our purposes try to force-fit a concept of teams. To do so would be to miss the rich reality of the vast array and kinds of teams and of employee involvement in American workplaces.

Part 2: The Ford Experience

In the second part of this chapter, I will review selected portions of my experi-ence with employee involvement and teams during my more than 15 years working in this area at Ford. The discussion is neither a full history nor a case study. That would require too much space and too much detail. It would also be seen, most likely, as incomplete or as inaccurate from many others' points of view or experiences (unless, of course, such a document were assembled by a team!).

Ford is a very large organization employing some 350,000 people all over the world. It is the second biggest automotive company globally. In the United States, Ford is counted as the second or third largest industrial company, depending on how you measure such things (e.g., production, sales, employment, capital, returns). Many Ford operations, if separately incorporated, would be Fortune 500 companies on their own. Ford is in many different industries such as autos, trucks, automotive compo-nents, and financial services. My focus will be on U.S. automotive operations, where more than 140,000 people work in some 100 key locations around the country.

I will deal mostly with the national Ford picture, which was my assignment while at Ford. The view from operations would, in many cases, be quite different. The national task was to develop and provide an enabling framework. But the key reality for involvement and for teams was local. The local people had to shape their particular initiatives, find the resources, and deliver. Although I will refer to certain dates, I will not present a strict chronology. Many developments overlapped. In some cases, developments are best explained as though they occurred in an orderly sequence, separate from others. In reality, they did not.

Antecedents of Employee Involvement

Ford and union commitment to employee involvement (EI) began in earnest in late 1979 with the issuance of a Company Policy on Employee Involvement and a negotiated Letter of Understanding with the United Auto Workers (UAW), which represents more than 95% of Ford's hourly automotive workers. But as in most such developments, there was a prehistory.

During the 1960s and 1970s, Ford was a fairly typical, successful American company, organized along hierarchical lines for work design, with many specialty functions, and was considered to have what was then state-of-the-art management practices and style. Everything worked pretty much within boundaries. If I did the very best in my job and in my function, and if you did the very best in yours, Company performance would obviously be maximized.

The job of human resources (variously called industrial relations, personnel, labor relations) was primarily twofold: (1) to establish and maintain appropriate systems to support the prevailing forms of work organization (classifications, pay grades, performance rating, succession planning), and (2) to play a lead role in shaping pay, benefits, and other accoutrements of corporate welfare being created by the prodding of a powerful union in the protective environment of an expanding economy and of mostly domestic, semioligopoly competition.

Job security was not a burning issue. Despite recurring temporary layoffs due to cynical downturns, most production workers could expect to work for their lifetime and attain middle-class income and retirement. When temporary layoffs occurred, workers could count on a system of income benefits to tide them over. Layoffs among white-collar workers and management ranks were unknown.

But there were areas of concern, and a forward-looking management had to keep its eyes open for new developments. Quality and productivity could be improved. Assembly line workers, with monotonous jobs, were absent too often, processed too many grievances, were prone to strike, and did shoddy work. The media joined the workers in singing the blue-collar blues. Frederick Herzberg and other behavioral scientists were popularizing job enrichment or job enlargement as a way to motivate employees, improve work life, and improve product and service quality. Herzberg worked with AT&T, Cummins Engine, and the U.S. Air Force (Lawler, 1986).

At Ford, there was a brief flirtation with job enrichment in a few locations. In one instance, warehouse workers were given expanded duties. Previously, a picker would select parts, a packer would pack them, and a checker would check them. Using the job enrichment approach, these functions were combined so that one person would do all three, with a new classification—picker–packer–checker (not too imaginative!)—and at a slightly higher rate of pay. But, the changes were too minor to be sustained. The job was still quite routine, and some workers felt that instead of being hounded on one count, they could now be hounded on three. There was little accompanying change in management style. The gains in quality or productivity were considered by management to be minor. Warehousing was not considered a mainstream automotive operation, and manufacturing managers, believing that job enrichment could not easily be applied to assembly line work, felt there were few lessons for them. At the corporate level, there were no passionate champions in management or in the union. The warehouse experiment did not live up to expectations, and job enrichment at Ford did not take hold. This is not to say that forms of job enlargement and job redesign did not continue in some fashion. They did, and they do to this day. But, for some of the reasons just cited, job enrichment did not gain momentum, become a "cause," or serve as a rallying point for widespread organizational change.

During the 1960s and 1970s, Ford looked also at fledgling developments in what was called sociotechnical systems (STS) and semiautonomous work teams. Ford managers traveled to Sweden, where Volvo had introduced semiautonomous, or self-managing, work teams to increase worker satisfaction and to improve product quality and productivity. (Ford's conclusion: Volvo had introduced autonomous teams because of an outrageous absentee problem due to a tight labor market and excessive government employee sickness benefits.) Ford managers looked at the work of Eric Trist and Einar Thorsrud in England and Scandinavia. They evaluated what are now considered classic work-team and plant-redesign initiatives that were being undertaken in a handful of American companies. On both sides of the ocean, these were always "special cases," not suited to large assembly and manufacturing plants and to a taut labor–management relationship.

Closer to home, Ford watched what Rensis Likert and General Motors were doing at new plants with work-redesign and self-managing teams, but dismissed much of it as a GM "southern strategy" to avoid UAW representation of GM's new facilities. Ford saw mostly labor–management tension and a failing GM long-term strategy. At the same time, in traditionally structured plants, GM and the UAW agreed to undertake a joint quality-of-work-life (QWL) initiative to improve work conditions, product quality, and worker satisfaction. Ford followed the GM–UAW settlement with a similar pledge to explore developing a QWL program. Ford and the UAW met on the subject only one time, in 1973. They failed to reach an agreement on what QWL meant, or could be, and the negotiated UAW–Ford Letter of Understanding became inoperative. In the ensuing years, Ford kept assessing the GM–UAW QWL program and found it interesting but complicated, unfocused, and hard to quantify. A GM and a UAW observer (Weekly & Wilber, 1995, p. 91), reflected on the GM–UAW QWL experience, this way: "Efforts were isolated and lacked a systems approach. They were often very narrowly focused. Lessons learned from one program did not migrate to others; organizational learning did not take place."

Yet Ford was keeping its ear to the ground. It hired young Ph.D. organizational development (OD) specialists and seeded them in selected locations doing team-building and small organizational-improvement projects involving groups. Some plants with poor performance faced mounting pressures to improve and began experimenting with work-structure changes and problem-solving groups. At Ford headquarters, a small group of OD people, not sure of what was expected from them, was housed impatiently in a Personnel Research Department. OD did not have a clear charter, and the mainstream industrial relations community viewed OD as trendy, or as a useful insurance policy.

Though management was keeping an eye on the future, there wasn't enough pain (or vision?) during this period to induce massive, orchestrated change. The tested forms of management and hierarchy were working well enough. It was sufficient to do what had always been done. There was no widespread shared understanding of possible external threats and no deep dialogue with employees or their unions. Surely, the system would respond. It always had. Management was concerned but not threatened.

But what was mostly discomfort would soon become clear-and-present danger. The oil embargoes, causing long lines at the gas pumps, favored high-gas-mileage cars and shifted Japanese penetration of the U.S. auto market into high gear. Levin (1995, p. 186) reiterates statistics that were causing anguish in management and in union circles: "Between 1970 and 1980, Japanese vehicle exports to the United States surged six-fold ... to more than 2.4 million, or 21.4 percent of U.S. sales." Along with getting better gasoline mileage, American consumers began discovering superior Japanese product quality.

Teams of Ford people were dispatched to Japan to discover the source of Japanese success. A study team of Ford labor relations, industrial engineers, and quality experts concluded that one those sources was Japanese quality circles—an arrangement in which shop floor workers were given the opportunity and the time (often on their own time) to solve production and quality problems and pursue continuous improvement of work processes. Four Ford plants started such problem-solving groups in 1978 and 1979 in some of their operations with the support or tacit acquiescence of their local unions. These experiments soon proved themselves useful and provided the impetus to negotiate national support in 1979 for what would be called UAW–Ford employee involvement.

The Launch Years, 1979–1982

As it would turn out, the timing of the UAW–Ford agreement to introduce employee involvement could not have been more fortuitous. Disaster struck in 1980–1981 with a severe recession that compounded the effect of foreign competition. Plants had to be closed. Permanent layoffs took place. The blue-collar workforce was reduced by 100,000 people, a full 50%. For the first time, white-collar and managerial employees were laid off or went into retirement earlier than planned. The balance sheet ran red. Losses mounted, investment money shriveled up, future product programs were canceled, cash flow fell to a danger point, and creditors were edgy.

To many, employee involvement (EI) could not have been launched at a worse time. Morale sagged. There were few resources. There was no end point in sight. It would have been easy to walk away from employee involvement or relegate it to the sidelines. Instead, EI moved to center stage. Motivated leaders put the focus on quality improvement. Everyone could see that quality was connected to sales, customer satisfaction, a healthy bottom line, and job security. Later, "Quality Is Job One" would be recognized globally as a Ford rallying cry.

Clearly, the whole company had to do something to improve. The union and the workers had to be part of the improvement. The promise of EI had to be tapped (EI was "our" word; we did not like "quality control circles"—too Japanese, and we didn't like "QWL—too GM-ish and too vague). A new UAW vice-president and a new Ford labor relations vice-president headed the UAW–Ford National EI Committee. EI became their main agenda. Soon there were local EI committees in all Ford U.S. operations. The committees established voluntary problem-solving groups as their key improvement strategy. In practice, the EI groups looked a lot like quality circles. Senior management joined the fray, visiting plants, sponsoring conferences, and listening to worker presentations. There was a parade of jointly approved consultants, a new cadre of union and company facilitators, and internal OD people and trainers were now sought to help guide and build the EI process. Operating management took on the task of providing presence, ownership, resources, and support. Within 2 years, EI was firmly established at Ford.

The results were impressive. Within 6 months to a year after EI would be introduced into a department, productivity, quality, and employee commitment would increase, sometimes dramatically. Success stories were shared. Efforts expanded beyond the shop floor to include supporting service personnel. White-collar organizations experimented with their own forms of EI.

While EI was growing on the shop floor, some senior and operating management groups were immersing themselves in the Deming approach to quality improvement, which went beyond immediate problem solving to highlighting the role of processes, systems, statistical control, measurement, and management by fact (see Saskin & Kiser, 1991, for a short, readable account of Deming's quality management method). Statistical process control charts, Pareto charts, fishbone diagrams, flowcharts, and the plan/do/check/act cycle became part of Ford EI training and of Ford quality improvement projects. Later, process analysis would become an essential quality tool for white-collar and management groups.

Unfortunately, it is impossible to chronicle the Ford EI story in this space. EI problem-solving groups are frequently referred to as parallel organizations, or off-line teams, because employees leave the assembly line to join with others in problem identification and resolution (while doing so, other employees may replace them on their jobs in order to keep the line going). The pros and cons of this voluntary "quality circle" approach, the resources and investment needed, and the issues involved have been well-documented (e.g., see Ed Lawler's discussion of quality circles in his book, *High-Involvement Management*). Ford's experience is not too dissimilar. A major exception is that, unlike the quality circle movement, the Ford brand of EI persisted and did not fade away.

This formative period of Ford EI, 1979–1982, made three major contributions that continue to this day. EI changed management–worker interaction, improved union–management relations, and gave the parties confidence that they could handle major change by working together.

First, EI changed management–worker interaction, from mostly management control to greater employee participation: from "tell and do," to "ask, listen, accept or explain, and do"; from only necessary information, to wide and deep sharing of information; from "perform to standards," to "continuously improve"; from "my way," to "our way." This legacy of employee participation and empowerment, embodied in many forms and nurtured by company policy, union agreement, and management practice, continues to this day. Ford EI is alive and well after 15 years, a demonstration of unusual staying power for this type of initiative.

One of the hallmarks of early EI at Ford is that the basic problem-solving approach that was adopted was easy to understand and to diffuse, both within a location and from location to location. Managers, union leaders, workers, and support personnel could identify the UAW–Ford EI system and replicate it. The national agreement and the national joint committee provided a supporting platform, as well as active encouragement. An important element was the agreement that management would not dictate which projects employees worked on.

Some of the Ford EI focus has changed as problems have changed. There is increased recognition that teams need to be formed and re-formed as problems are solved, or as new ones surface. Another internally significant change is that EI facilitators were renamed employee resource counselors to recognize that they assist in a variety of initiatives that are like EI, but that have different program names (e.g., continuous improvement teams, preventive maintenance teams, variability reduction teams, Q-1 certification teams, total quality excellence teams, and learning teams). Employee resource counselors do more training and broader training than before.

EI had an important effect on Ford management style. It led to the formulation of participative management as the counterpart of worker EI (two faces of the same coin). As expressed by an operating executive vice-president, "We need to do with management what we are doing on the factory floor." EI contributed to the establishment of an Executive Education Center whose mission is to support continuous change, innovation, and the practice of employee empowerment. EI led to the reeducation of Ford middle management and Ford first-line supervisory management.

The second major contribution of Ford EI is that it helped improve labor–management relationships. For some 40 years, an adversarial or arms-length atmosphere was characteristic of auto industry collective bargaining, going all the way back to management resistance to unionization and to the UAW sit-down strikes of the 1930s. It is impossible to have teams, of whatever type, in such an atmosphere. As Ford and the UAW leaders deepened their EI efforts, they learned about each other, and they learned they could work together for mutual benefit in other arenas. Today, Ford–UAW joint programs are widely recognized for their excellence, and Ford locations are visited and studied by other companies and unions. Ford has experienced only two local strikes (related to sourcing matters) in the past 20 years, and no national strike. Ford's labor relations represents a competitive advantage that was nourished by EI.

The third major contribution of EI is that it gave management, the UAW, and employees the confidence that they could handle drastic change, that they could maneuver roller-coaster ups and downs, and that they could launch change initiatives of their own without waiting for a crisis to occur. Such confidence will be a critical mind-set for survival and success in a future of swift and unrelenting change.

Expansion

For Ford, 1982 was a watershed year. The cash squeeze was still on, and the future was clouded at best. In a dramatic early negotiation, the UAW made a vital contribution to Ford's turnaround by granting a substantial degree of direct labor-cost relief: Cost-of-living increases were deferred, there would be no annual wage increases, and a 7-day individual holiday plan (not national holidays) was discontinued. The Company agreed to a moratorium on plant closings, additional layoff and severance benefits, profit sharing, and a pledge to work jointly to retrain laid-off workers with resources provided by a 5-cent-per-hour contribution to a joint fund. Without the prior positive experience with EI, the negotiators are convinced that such a settlement could not have been reached.

The new training program was especially important and was established in much the same way as EI, with national and local committees and dedicated personnel. A special innovation was the construction of a physical National Training Center, with full joint governance by management and the UAW. Later, each Ford location would have its own training center. One of the first undertakings of the National Center was to plan and oversee the retraining and placement of some 50,000 laid-off workers who had little prospect of returning to Ford because of plant closings and other facility actions that had to be taken to address issues of industry and company overcapacity. The Center worked in partnership with state agencies, the U.S. Department of Labor, and Ford local unions and managements. After laid-off workers had been trained or placed, the National Center's efforts turned to the education and development of active workers to enhance the skills they would need for the future. National and local negotiated funds provide the finances for the Center's activities and for a broad array of joint initiatives developed in four subsequent negotiations, including major efforts in information sharing, health and safety, quality, and employee support services and child care. Many of these efforts, which collectively are called UAW–Ford joint programs, involve the use of task forces similar to those that characterize EI. To a large degree, these joint programs owe their existence to union and company success in implementing EI. UAW–Ford joint programs are widely recognized for their excellence, and the notion of joint training centers and of negotiated training funds has been adopted by companies and unions in the steel, communications, agricultural implement, and aerospace industries.

While EI voluntary problem-solving groups continued to operate and while the new joint programs were being created, some managers and union leaders believed that the benefits flowing from employee participation could be enhanced by instituting "full-time teams" in certain work areas in lieu of the voluntary groups that meet only 1 or 2 hours per week. They began installing self-directed teams on the shop floor, usually in manufacturing operations, where machining functions were performed that required considerable worker skills and commitment in order to obtain optimal machine utilization and product quality. Such teams, usually small (6–15 workers) were a "natural work unit," with a number of jobs to be performed, and generally were set up with pay for learning the different jobs. There was usually a team leader, often elected by the members, job rotation, no immediate supervisor, and the team had responsibility not only for its productivity and quality, but also for some aspects of scheduling, budgeting, inventory, and tool procurement. Forming these teams required special local union agreement because traditional work assignments and classifications were being reshaped. Also, although workers might choose to belong or not to belong to a self-directed group, once they chose to belong, their participation in the group's activities was mandatory. These self-directed teams are sometimes called "on-line" teams, because they constitute an intact work group as contrasted with the voluntary "off-line" EI groups who leave their regular work in order to problem-solve, and who may not meet as a full work unit.

Where they are appropriate for the kind of technology used and for the kind of work performed, and when they are properly installed and managed, self-directed teams do, indeed, perform very well. In some cases, efficiency, quality, and continuous improvement are enhanced to such a degree that fewer workers are needed for the same levels of output. Redundant workers must be reassigned to other positions, not always an easy matter. Managing such displacement is a critical ingredient in being able to perpetuate self-directed teams. People cannot be expected to willingly work their way out of their jobs.

Although some of these self-directed teams succeeded, other dropped by the wayside. Sponsors underestimated the amount of change and training involved, or expected too much, too fast. In my experience, training for on-line groups must be three or four times greater than the training for off-line groups. In some cases (e.g., assembly), the work is such that the skill differences involved may not be major enough to constitute real learning experiences or to justify pay differences.

But interest in self-directed, self-managed, on-line, semiautonomous teams continues to this day. Eight Ford plants have substantial numbers of employees working in such teams and plan to continue or expand their use of them. One plant is a showcase for Work in America Institute, which sponsors regular learning tours of the facility. Plants using such teams have learned that they still must have some off-line groups to handle interteam transactions and broader process, technological, and system issues that can be handled only from a plantwide view (e.g., the allocation of space for machinery, plant air quality, or the overall plant budget). Also, in some cases, it is necessary to coordinate contacts with suppliers, contractors, or customers in order to prevent potential duplication, confusion, or contradiction.

At one time, many people felt that they should move to the "ideal" of the self-directed team. In addition to the benefits to be derived from sustained teamwork, it was thought that there could be considerable savings in reduced direct supervision. Experience, however, revealed that the cost of the training and of the time needed for self-directed teams to operate successfully can be excessive versus the results obtained. Experience taught that it is difficult to install such teams in existing plants, where they run into human resistance to change and into imbalances when part of a facility operates with teams and the other part does not. It is much easier to install self-directed teams in new plants or in new operations, because people accept "that's the way work is done around here," and there is no prior work system that must be replaced. Another problem that sometimes surfaces is that some teams may turn to optimizing their own world, to the detriment of other teams or of the whole. A study of two Ford plants by an outside consultant (Abt, 1993) concluded that a well-run, traditional plant using employee task forces and voluntary groups was just as productive as a self-managed plant, had similar high quality, and a similar degree of employee commitment. The study concluded that rather than a special organizational structure, the critical ingredients for high performance are wide and deep employee participation (regardless of type), aligned goals and systems, management style, extensive training, labor–management joint ownership of the effort, and deep information sharing and feedback.

At the same time as Ford plants sought to improve, so did Ford offices. Rallying points were process improvement, program management, total quality excellence, and reengineering. Task forces were assembled, and cross-functional teams were formed, including, in some cases, having vendors and dealers as team members. Each new car, truck, or major component program is encapsulated in a team structure (sometimes fairly large, ranging from 150 to 700 people), is nurtured by team concepts, and has a team name. In order to enhance communication, give clear ownership of goals, and speed up decision making, there is a move to co-locate teams, so that they are together spatially. With the fuller globalization of the Company, there are cross-border teams, facilitated by videoconferencing, fax, E-mail, computers, and ever-proliferating, better, and cheaper information technology.

The above types of "office" teams—I will call them *knowledge-work teams* (KWTs)—have important differences compared to the better-known on-line or off-line *small-group teams* (SGTs). In SGTs, the work is fairly self-contained, is usually repeated and expected to continue, and membership is relatively stable. In KWTs, the work is broader, takes place over a longer period of time, and requires many more skills and competencies.

KWTs often have subteams or subgroups. KWTs must frequently procure internal or external resources in order to achieve their results. KWTs can be on-line or off-line (when off-line, they are usually labeled task forces or committees). Generally, KWTs are not expected to be permanent. They can be quickly recast when projects are completed, when unanticipated requirements pop up, or when new or different work must be done.

The Ford Lincoln Continental is one of Ford's top-of-the-line automobiles. The 1995 model Continental was developed by a KWT (Senge et al., 1994). There were 300 people working full time on the project for some 30 months. Most of these people did not work directly for the Program Manager. Their home base was in other organizations, such as finance, engineering, assembly, automotive components, or market planning. The Program Manager had little leverage over their future promotions. This cross-functional product development team faced tight timing and budget restrictions, yet was expected to make significant and costly improvements. They had to work hard at creating better styles of interacting and communicating. The team met with consultants such as Peter Senge, Fred Kofman, Bill Isaacs, Dan Kim, and Chris Argyris. The team established a learning lab and, with their consultants, developed training for all team members, with a heavy emphasis on building relationships, sharing knowledge, and being open in communicating even if the message was unpleasant. "A supplier would tell us that in the past he hadn't owned up to the fact that he was two weeks late because he did not want to tell us it was our purchasing department's fault. Now that we had shown the suppliers that they could talk freely, without repercussions, we would find things out." (Senge, p. 558) Team leaders felt there were dramatic results in quality improvement and time savings directly tied to better coordination between functions and to a direct focus on improving teamwork. Once the 1995 model went into production, Team Continental would be disbanded, and its people and its learnings would be dispersed throughout Ford.

The distinction between SGTs and knowledge-work teams is not between blue-collar work and white-collar work. Rather, the distinction is between fairly repetitive and bounded work versus larger and less bounded process and systems work. Some white-collar work may be fairly narrow in scope or depth (e.g., in insurance, banking, or in benefits or warranty processing) and lends itself to SGTs. Some blue-collar work (e.g., skilled trades) may be "plantwide" and may lend itself to KWTs. KWTs have the characteristics of what Mintzberg (1981) calls "adhocracies" (forming and re-forming, compared to more stable hierarchies). Mintzberg speculates that as much as one-fifth of future work may be done in "adhocracy" formats.

The expansion of the number and types of teams and of group work brings with it many challenges. One is the sheer magnitude of the effort needed to coordinate and align all this activity. There is a large potential for contradictions, overlaps, and unintended consequences. Another challenge is how to manage entirely different types of teams, especially tailoring motivational, reward, and measurement systems appropriately—all the while, maintaining a sense of stability and of belonging to the larger organization. Still another challenge is how to use team power without stifling individual initiative and innovation. Teams are not effective without effective leaders, and an imperative underlying all the above challenges is providing and enhancing the leadership to make team organizations successful.

Ford is reformulating many of its team and leadership initiatives to support its globalization strategy and has selected employee empowerment as the fundamental driver for carrying out all its business strategies. Along with employee empowerment comes change in job responsibilities and in how work is performed. Managing the human element of change is frequently overlooked in trying to make change happen. How well Ford links empowerment to its past initiatives, and how well it shapes and extends empowerment will be an important ingredient in the Company's future performance.

Part 3: Observations

The following observations are in addition to the challenges just noted for organizations as they deal with extensive and widely varying teamwork needs. My observations are offered to assist in program development and for future research.

1. The variety, sizes, shapes, and uses of teams will continue to proliferate in organizations. This will be spurred on by economic need, ideology, organizational learning, experience, imitation, and perceived performance. I will call an organization that uses a wide variety of team structures and approaches a proliferated team organization or a "proli-team organization."

- Managing a proli-team organization requires leadership of a higher and different order to handle the competing interests that are sure to arise, to keep the organization aligned with respect to goals and timetables, and to influence outside partners and suppliers whose cooperation is essential but who may have priorities or needs of their own. Leadership selection and leadership development for proli-team management will be critical at all levels of the organization. It is Job One for organizational success.

2.   Experts on classic off-line or on-line SGTs will need to continue deepening their efforts and their knowledge, because such teams will continue to be used.

- More attention must be focused in SGT environments on interteam relations, on tying to broader systems and processes, and on not optimizing team performance to the detriment of total organizational performance.
- More duties will be given to such teams, for example, integrating the work of part-time or contract workers. Some team duties may be taken away, for example, because of technology or product changes, and may be given to other teams or to facilities that do not use teams. Teams must be prepared for such eventualities, not only technically but also psychologically.
- As people retire or move to other jobs, new team members are likely to be different in gender, race, age, nationality, or culture because of demographic changes in the composition of the workforce. Past team building will have to be refiltered and new aspects added.

3.   New insights and new codifications are needed to enhance the operation of the KWTs.

- The use of KWTs is evolving rapidly, and better practices are in different stages of evolution. Focusing on practices that must be created may be as important as spreading practices that are known.
- These teams inevitably deal with system issues beyond their control and must be assisted when this happens. They must be prepared to accept frustration due to system constraints as an element of the broader, less boundaried work they do.
- Team-building and team-reinforcement methods must be developed that are more appropriate to KWTs. Small-group consultants must not simply re-package, retitle, and remarket themselves. *Caveat emptor.*
- KWTs are subject to tension, ambiguity, and undue stress. They should be offered assistance to handle these factors.
- Even more than the SGTs, these teams must deal with workforce diversity; with the presence of contingent, supplemental, and part-time workers; and with purchasing human services. Are supplemental workers part of the team? How should they be treated relative to information, meetings, and recognition? Might second-tier workers become second-class workers?
- Improvements in information technology are spurring on the development of global product development and engineering KWTs, often with people located in different parts of the world. Handling the cross-cultural implications of

global teams will be important if such teams are to be effective. In some cases, there will be tensions because of differences in pay and career opportunity for members from different countries who are on the same team, but who are compensated on their country's pay system. This will put pressure on human resource policies and reward systems.

4.   Labor unions will have to grapple with the challenges ahead for both SGTs and KWTs. A major need for unions is stability of arrangements, so they can assure members fair treatment and protection of rights. How do unions do this while handling frequent, unexpected, cumulative, and contradictory change, without political breakdown?

- Unions must educate themselves and their members on the changes ahead and what such changes may mean for the world of work. Unions must evaluate the different nature and needs of KWTs.
- Union leaders must fashion approaches to handling change that are acceptable to workers but that do not hurt workers in the long run (which might be quite short) by setting up impediments to competitiveness.
- Managements, if they want to reap the full promise of teams, must work with unions and workers to facilitate the acceptance of change, while recognizing union and worker needs for stability and fair treatment.
- When initiating change where there are unions, managements must take into account timing, intensity, past history, and the likely impact of the change on workers and on union leadership in order to gain acceptance for the change. For an employee-improvement initiative to be long-lasting, managements and unions must be equals in the governing of the initiative.
- Unions and managements must both emphasize training and skills development, and provide resources and leadership.

5.   Organizations, to be consistently high-performing, need competent, committed people who trust in the goodwill of their organizations and of their leadership.

- It is not enough for organizations to concentrate on factors that directly affect the performance of teams. Leaders must pay attention to the overall organizational climate, because this also affects team spirit and team performance.
- Leaders must build a supportive, overall organizational environment that fosters a sense of belonging, community, self-esteem, hope, growth, and trust. This higher-order requirement has been ignored or abrogated in too many instances, sometimes out of necessity, but too often because of indifference or ignorance. How to build, or rebuild, a psychological contract with employees that is suited to a volatile world is a matter of much debate and genuine concern.

Summary and Conclusions

The use of teams and of forms of employee involvement has mushroomed in American enterprises in the past 15 years. Teams, today, come in many sizes and shapes and do many kinds of work. There is a growing emphasis on KWTs, where work is more varied, has broader boundaries, and often requires the participation of many specialities. When properly structured and led, team approaches are seen to enhance productivity, quality, service, employee commitment, continuous improvement, and innovation. Ford Motor Company's experience with teams, employee involvement, and joint union–management initiatives, while unique in some particulars, is not atypical of what has occurred in American industry, and there are many insights to be garnered from the Ford story. One hallmark of the Ford approach has been its ability to develop, tolerate, and manage many different kinds of team- and employee-involvement configurations. Ford has been able to provide necessary national direction and support, and allow local tailoring to suit the technology, capability, and history of individual work units.

There are many challenges ahead, not only for Ford but also for all enterprises that seek to obtain the benefits of teamwork and employee involvement, while avoiding some of the pitfalls. The number, variety, size, shape, and uses of teams will continue to proliferate in organizations as they seek to improve bottom-line performance. This proliferation will be fueled not only by economic need but also by the possibilities afforded by information technology. More attention will have to be given to interteam relations and to optimizing total system performance as well as work-unit performance. Team training will have to be freshened, and new dimensions added, especially to handle knowledge work, to stimulate wider organizational learning, and to address the changing demographic composition of the workforce that will affect the dynamics of group interaction.

Human resource systems, especially pay and career ladders, will be challenged to accommodate the potentially conflicting need for team rewards versus individual rewards.

In unionized environments, both unions and managements must learn how to deal with intense and frequent change, while recognizing the need for stability and fair treatment.

Leaders must be developed who can handle complexity and contradiction, yet pursue a broader vision. Leaders must build a supportive overall organizational climate favorable to sustaining teamwork and employee involvement.

Clearly, there is a rich agenda for program development, for management and union innovation, and for research. Although we must beware that more may not always be better, for teams, no endgame is in sight.

References

Bluestone, B., & Harrison, B. (1988). *De-industrialization of America: Plant closings, community abandonment, and the dismantling of basic industry.* New York: Basic Books.

Commission on the Future of Worker–Management Relations. (1994, December) *Report and recommendations.* Appendix A: The worker representation and participation survey. Washington, DC: U.S. Department of Labor and U.S. Department of Commerce.

Commission on the Skills of the American Workforce. (1989). *America's choice: High skills or low wages!* Rochester, NY: National Center on Education and the Economy.

Educational Quality of the Workforce. (1995). *The EQW National Employer Survey: First findings.* Philadelphia, PA: National Center on the Educational Quality of the Workforce.

Kochan, T., Cutcher-Gershenfeld, J., & MacDuffie, J. P. (1989). *Employee participation, work redesign, and new technology: Implications for public policy in the 1990s*. Report prepared for U.S. Department of Labor Commission on Workforce Quality and Labor Market Efficiency, Washington, DC.

Kochan, T., Katz, H. C., & McKersie, R. B. (1986). *The transformation of American industrial relations*. New York: Basic Books.

Mintzberg, Henry (1981). "Organization Design: Fashion or Fit?" *Harvard Business Review*. 81106 (January–February): pp. 103–116.

Saskin, Marshall, and Kenneth J. Kiser (1991). *Total quality management*. Seabrook, MD: Ducochon Press.

Senge, Peter M., Charlotte Roberts, Richard B. Ross, Bryan J. Smith, & Art Kleiner (1994). *The fifth discipline fieldbook*. New York: Doubleday.

Weekly, Thomas L., & Jay C. Wilber. 1995. "United Auto Workers and General Motors Quality Network: General Motors Quality Management Process for Customer Satisfaction." In Edward Cohen-Rosenthal (ed.). *Unions, management, and quality* (pp. 87–128). Irwin and the Association for Quality Participation.

Zornitsky, Jeffrey J., Laurie J. Bassi, Ingrid Gould Ellen, & Jane Kulik (1993). *Thinking outside the lines: High performance companies in manufacturing and services*. Cambridge, MA: Abt Associates (Study sponsored by the U.S. Department of Labor).

12

Why Teams Don't Work

J. Richard Hackman

A few years ago, Paul Osterman, an economist at MIT, did a careful national survey of innovative work practices in U.S. manufacturing firms. He found that more than half the companies surveyed were using teams—and that some 40% of these companies reported having more than half the organization working in teams (Osterman, 1994). How well do all these teams perform? To judge from books and articles written for a managerial audience, the answer is clear: Teams markedly outperform individuals, and self-managing (or self-regulating, or self-directed, or empowered) teams do best of all.

Here are some reports from the field, cited by Osburn, Moran, Musselwhite, and Zenger (1990) in *Self-Directed Work Teams: The New American Challenge*. At Xerox, the authors report,

> Plants using work teams are 30 percent more productive than conventionally organized plants. Procter & Gamble gets 30 to 40 percent higher productivity at its 18 team-based plants.... Tektronix Inc. reports that one self-directed work team now turns out as many products in 3 days as it once took an entire assembly line to produce in 14 days.... Federal Express cut service glitches such as incorrect bills and lost packages by 13 percent.... Shenandoah Life processes 50 percent more applications and customer service requests using work teams, with 10 percent fewer people. (pp. 5–6)

Heady stuff, that, and it is reinforced by back-cover blurbs. Tom Peters: "Self-directed work teams are the cornerstone of improved competitiveness ..." Bob Waterman: "*Self-Directed Work Teams* seems too good to be true: dramatic improvement in productivity and a happier, more committed, more flexible work force. Yet ... they do just what they promise for the likes of P&G, GE, and Ford."

It makes sense. Teams bring more resources, and more diverse resources, to bear

J. Richard Hackman • Department of Psychology, Harvard University, Cambridge, Massachusetts 02138.

Theory and Research on Small Groups, edited by R. Scott Tindale et al. Plenum Press, New York, 1998.

on a task than could any single performer. Moreover, teams offer flexibility in the use of those resources—the capability to quickly redeploy member talents and energies and to keep the work going even when some members are unavailable. Teams composed of people from different units can transcend traditional functional and organizational barriers and get members pulling together toward collective objectives. And, of course, teams offer the potential for synergy, that wonderful state when a group "clicks" and members achieve something together that no one of them could possibly have accomplished alone. These are major benefits, worthy of the attention of the leaders of any purposive enterprise. No wonder Osterman found teams to be so popular.

But there is a puzzle here. Research evidence about team performance shows that teams usually do less well—not better—than the sum of their members' individual contributions. I first encountered this bleak fact as a beginning doctoral student at the University of Illinois. In a course on group dynamics, Ivan Steiner put on the board his now well-known equation: $AP = PP - PL$; that is, the *actual* productivity of a group equals its *potential* productivity (what the team is theoretically capable of, given the resources brought by members) minus what he called *process losses* such as coordination and motivational problems (Steiner, 1972). I was surprised that there was no term for process *gains*, the synergistic benefits that can emerge when people work together. The model, I thought, should really read: $AP = PP - PL + PG$.

It turns out that there is no empirical justification for that extra term. When interacting teams are compared to "nominal" groups (i.e., groups that never meet, whose output is constructed by combining the separate contributions of those who would have been members), nominal groups usually win. And when Steiner's models miss the mark in empirical studies, the problem usually is that groups fail to achieve even the relatively modest performance targets specified by those models.

At least for groups in the experimental laboratory. Maybe the laboratory context is so constraining that groups do not have the elbow room to show what they can do. Maybe the real advantages of groups are only to be found in organizational practice. I came up short on this hypothesis as well, this time at the hands of Bill Hicks, an editor at Jossey-Bass. My colleagues and I had completed an intensive study of some 33 different work groups of all different kinds—athletic teams, industrial production workers, top management teams, prison guards, airline crews, economic analysts, and more. We pulled our findings together in a book that I proposed be titled *Groups That Work*, a catchy phrase with what I thought to be a clever pun. Bill sat me down and said he'd be happy to publish the book, but not with that title: There were just too many groups in our study that barely worked at all. I went back to the manuscript and found that he was right. Probably 4 of our 33 groups were actually effective teams. The rest had problems so severe that our analysis was mainly about what had gone wrong with them. So the book was published with a parenthetical phrase after my clever title: *Groups That Work (And Those That Don't)*. Anyone who actually reads through it will discover, as Bill did, that most of our groups lie within the parentheses.[1]

---

[1]Moreover, the preface of the book offers a cautionary note about team effectiveness, based on the experience of the authors who wrote it. The book took 9 years to be completed, mainly because our own team suffered a near-total collapse midway through the project.

Other in-depth studies of real groups performing real work provide additional reasons for concern—such as Irving Janis's (1982) well-known demonstration that even highly cohesive groups composed of well-qualified, well-motivated people some-times fall into a pattern of "groupthink" that can yield disastrous policy recommenda-tions.

What, then, are we to make of all the team successes reported in the managerial literature? It is possible, of course, that the published claims are exaggerated, as writers have sought to catch the wave of enthusiasm about teams—to sell books, to build consulting practices, to market training programs, to become team gurus. That is not a sufficient explanation. Indeed, I trust the accuracy of the numbers about productivity and service gains that are reported in the popular books about teams. My concern, instead, is whether those numbers really mean what they seem to mean.

Consider first the attributions that are made about the *causes* of team successes. After teams have been implemented in an organizational unit, its performance typically is compared to that of a conventional unit (or, perhaps, to the same one before teams were installed). Such comparisons are fraught with interpretive ambi-guities, because there invariably are many differences between the units compared—in technologies, labor markets, senior managers, and so on. It almost never is the case that the *only* change is that work previously done by individuals is now performed by teams. Was it the teams that generated the improvements, or was it one of the other differences between the units? It is not possible to know for sure.[2]

Questions also can be raised about the *staying power* of any performance improvements obtained when teams are installed. The implementation of any new management program, be it self-managing teams or anything else, invariably involves intense scrutiny of the unit where the changes will occur. Taking a close look at any work unit that has been operating for a while almost always surfaces some inefficien-cies and poor work procedures. These incidental problems are corrected as part of the change process—it would be foolish not to. But in making those corrections, an interpretive ambiguity is introduced. Was it the team design that resulted in the improvements found, or was it that a shoddy work system was shaped up? Virtually any intervention that is not itself destructive has a better-than-even chance of generat-ing short-term improvements, simply because of the value of intently inspecting a work system. This, in addition to any benefits from the well-known "Hawthorne effect" (Roethlisberger & Dickson, 1939). The question, then, is whether short-term improvements associated with the introduction of teams are sustained over time as the newness wears off and inefficiencies begin to creep back into the system. Again, it is not possible to know for sure—at least not without an appropriate longitudinal research design.

---

[2]The solution to this problem, of course, is to conduct experimental research on the impact of team designs for work, because true experiments allow unambiguous inferences to be drawn about the causes of any effects obtained. Unfortunately, experiments are rarely a viable option for comparing team and traditional work designs in organizations. For one thing, the level of experimenter control required in such studies (i.e., to randomly assign people to teams and teams to experimental conditions) would not be tolerated by most managers who have work to get out. And even if an organization were found in which managers would relinquish such control to experimenters, there would be serious questions about the gener-alizability of findings obtained in such an unusual place (Hackman, 1985).

So what is going on here? How can we reconcile the amazing reports from the field about the benefits of teams with the gloomy picture that has emerged from scholarly research on group performance? Do teams generate the benefits for their organizations that are claimed for them, or do they not?[3]

My observations of teams in organizations suggest that teams tend to clump at *both* ends of the effectiveness continuum. Teams that go sour often do so in multiple ways—clients are dissatisfied with a team's work, members become frustrated and disillusioned, and the team becomes ever weaker as a performing unit. Such teams are easily outperformed by smoothly functioning traditional units. On the other hand, teams that function well can indeed achieve a level of synergy and agility that never could be preprogrammed by organization planners or enforced by external managers. Members of such teams respond to their clients and to each other quickly and creatively, generating both superb performance and ever-increasing personal and collective capability. Teams, then, are somewhat akin to audio amplifiers: Whatever passes through the device—be it signal or noise—comes out louder.

To ask whether organizational performance improves when teams are used to accomplish work is to ask a question that has no general answer. A more tractable question, and the one explored in the remainder of this chapter, is what differentiates those teams that go into orbit and achieve real synergy from those that crash and burn. As we will see, the answer to this second question has much more to do with how teams are structured and supported than with any inherent virtues or liabilities of teams as performing units.

Mistakes Managers Make

In the course of several research projects, my colleagues and I have identified a number of mistakes that designers and leaders of work groups sometimes make. What follows is a summary of the six most pernicious of these mistakes, along with the actions that those who create and lead work teams in organizations can take to avoid them.[4]

Mistake 1: Use a Team for Work That Is Better Done by Individuals

There are some tasks that only a team can do, such as performing a string quartet or carrying out a multiparty negotiation. There are other tasks, however, that are inimical to team work. One such task is creative writing. Not many great novels,

---

[3]There is a large and diverse published literature on the performance of self-managing teams. Here is a "starter set" of illustrative and informative pieces: Cohen and Ledford (1994), Cordery, Mueller, and Smith (1991), Gunn (1984), Jackson, Mullarkey, and Parker (1994), Poza and Marcus (1980), Wall, Kemp, Jackson, and Clegg (1986), and Walton (1980).

[4]Some of the material in the next section is adapted from Hackman (1990).

symphonic scores, or epic poems have been written by teams. Such tasks involve bringing to the surface, organizing, and expressing thoughts and ideas that are but partially formed in one's mind (or, in some cases, that lie deep in one's unconscious), and they are inherently better suited for individual than for collective performance. Even committee reports—mundane products compared to novels, poems, and musical scores—invariably turn out better when written by one talented individual on behalf of a group than by the group as a whole working in lockstep.

The same is true for executive leadership. For all the attention being given to top management teams these days, my reading of the management literature is that successful organizations almost always are led by a single, talented and courageous human being. Among the many executive functions that are better accomplished by an exceptional individual than by an interacting team is the articulation of a challenging and inspiring collective direction. Here, for example, is a mission statement copied from a poster in a company cafeteria: "Our mission is to provide quality products and services that meet the needs of individuals and businesses, allowing us to prosper and provide a fair return to our stockholders." Although I do not know how that particular statement was prepared, I would be willing to wager that it was hammered out by a committee over many long meetings. The most engaging and powerful statements of corporate vision, by contrast, invariably are the product of a single intelligence, set forth by a leader willing to take the risk of establishing collective purposes that lie just beyond what others believe to be the limits of the organization's capability.

Beyond creative writing and executive leadership, there are many other kinds of tasks that are better done by individuals than by teams. It is a mistake—a common one and often a fatal one—to use a team for work that requires the exercise of powers that reside within and are best expressed by individual human beings.

Mistake 2: Call the Performing Unit a Team but Really Manage Members as Individuals

To reap the benefits of teamwork, one must actually build a team. Real teams are bounded social systems whose members are interdependent for a shared purpose, and who interact as a unit with other individuals and groups in achieving that purpose (Alderfer, 1977). Teams can be small or large, face-to-face or electronically connected, and temporary or permanent. Only if a group is so large, loosely connected, or short-lived that members cannot operate as an intact social system does the entity cease to be a team.

Managers sometimes attempt to capture the benefits of teamwork by simply declaring that some set of people (often everyone who reports to the same supervisor) is now a team and that members should henceforth behave accordingly. Real teams cannot be created that way. Instead, explicit action must be taken to establish and affirm the team's boundaries, to define the task for which members are collectively responsible, and to give the team the autonomy members need to manage both their own team processes and their relations with external entities such as clients and coworkers.

Creating and launching real teams is not something that can be accomplished casually, as is illustrated by research on airline cockpit crews. It is team functioning, rather than mechanical problems or the technical proficiency of individual pilots, that is at the root of most airline accidents (Helmreich & Foushee, 1993). Crews are especially vulnerable when they are just starting out: the National Transportation Safety Board (NTSB) found that 73% of the accidents in its database occurred on the crew's first day of flying together, and 44% of those accidents happened on the crew's very first flight (National Transportation Safety Board, 1994, pp. 40–41). Other research has shown that experienced crews, even when fatigued, perform significantly better than do rested crews whose members have not worked together (Foushee, Lauber, Baetge, & Acomb, 1986), and that a competent preflight briefing by the captain can help reduce a crew's exposure to the liabilities of newness (Ginnett, 1993).

This substantial body of research has clear policy implications. Crews should be kept intact over time, preflight briefings should be standard practice, and captains should be trained in the skills needed to conduct briefings that get crews off to a good start (Hackman, 1993). Yet in most airlines, crew composition is constantly changing because of the long-standing practice, enforced by labor contracts, of assigning pilots to trips, positions, and aircraft as individuals—usually on the basis of a seniority bidding system. Virtually all U.S. airlines now do require that crew briefings be held. Yet captains receive little training in how to conduct a good one, some briefings are quite cursory (e.g., "Let's get the social hour over real quick so we can get on out to the airplane"), and schedules can get so hectic that crew members may not even have time for proper introductions, let alone a briefing, before they start to fly together.

Creating and launching real teams is a significant challenge in organizations such as airlines that have deeply rooted policies and practices that are oriented primarily toward individuals rather than teams. To try to capture the benefits of teamwork in such organizations, managers sometimes opt for a mixed model in which some parts of the work and the reward system are structured for individual performance, whereas other parts require teamwork and provide team-based rewards. Research has shown that such compromises rarely work well. Mixed models send contradictory signals to members, engender confusion about who is responsible and accountable for what portions of the work, and generally underperform both individual and real-team models (Wageman, 1995). If the performing unit is to be a team, then it should be a *real* team—and it should be managed as such.

Mistake 3: Fall Off the Authority Balance Beam

The exercise of authority creates anxiety, especially when one must balance between assigning a team authority for some parts of the work and withholding it for other parts. Because both managers and team members tend to be uncomfortable in such situations, they may implicitly collude to "clarify" who is really in charge of the work. Sometimes the result is the assignment of virtually all authority to the team—which can result in anarchy or in a team heading off in an inappropriate direction. Other times, managers retain all authority for themselves, dictating work procedures in detail to team members and, in the process, losing many of the advantages that can accrue from team work.

To maintain an appropriate balance of authority between managers and teams requires that anxieties be managed rather than minimized. Moreover, it is insufficient merely to decide how much authority a team should have. Equally important are the domains of authority that are assigned to teams and retained by managers. Our research suggests that team effectiveness is enhanced when managers are unapologetic and insistent about exercising their own legitimate authority about *direction*, the end states the team is to pursue. Authority about the *means* by which those ends are accomplished, however, should rest squarely with the team itself.[5]

Contrary to traditional wisdom about participative management, to authoritatively set a clear, engaging direction for a team is to empower, not depower, it. Having clear direction helps align team efforts with the objectives of the parent organization, provides members with a criterion to use in choosing among various means for pursuing those objectives, and fosters the motivational engagement of team members. When direction is absent or unclear, members may wallow in uncertainty about what they should be doing and may even have difficulty generating the motivation to do much of anything.

Few design choices are more consequential for the long-term well-being of teams than those that address the partitioning of authority between managers and teams. It takes skill to accomplish this well, and it is a skill that has emotional and behavioral as well as cognitive components. Just knowing the rules for partitioning authority is insufficient; one also needs some practice in applying those rules in situations where anxieties, including one's own, are likely to be high.[6] Especially challenging are the early stages of a group's life (when well-meaning managers may be tempted to give away too much authority) and when the going gets rough (when the temptation is to take authority back too soon). The management of authority relations with task-performing groups is much like walking a balance beam, and our evidence suggests that it takes a good measure of knowledge, skill, and perseverance to keep from falling off.

---

[5] As used here, the terms *manager* and *team* refer to conventional organizational arrangements in which some individuals ("managers") are authorized to structure work for performance by other organization members. Teams that have been given the authority to monitor and manage their own work processes are therefore called "self-managing." In some circumstances, teams also have the authority to set their own direction. Examples include physicians in a small-group practice, a professional string quartet, and a mom-and-pop grocery store. These kinds of teams are referred to as "self-governing" (Hackman, 1986).

[6] Given that newly minted MBAs increasingly find themselves working in or leading task-performing teams immediately after graduation, it is unfortunate that few MBA programs provide their students with practice and feedback in developing such skills.

Mistake 4: Dismantle Existing Organizational Structures So That Teams Will Be Fully "Empowered" to Accomplish the Work

Traditionally designed organizations often are plagued by constraining structures that have been built up over the years to monitor and control employee behavior. When teams are used to perform work, such structures tend to be viewed as unnecessary bureaucratic impediments to group functioning. Thus, just as some managers mistakenly attempt to empower groups by relinquishing all authority to them, so do some attempt to cut through bureaucratic obstacles to team functioning by dismantling all the structures that they can. The assumption, apparently, is that removing structures will release the pent-up power of groups and make it possible for members to work together creatively and effectively.

Managers who hold this view often wind up providing teams with less structure than they actually need. Tasks are defined only in vague, general terms. Lots of people may be involved in the work, but the actual membership of the team is unclear. Norms of conduct are kept deliberately fuzzy. In the words of one manager, "The team will work out the details."

If anything, the opposite is true: Groups with appropriate structures tend to develop healthy internal processes, whereas groups with insufficient or inappropriate structures tend to be plagued with process problems.[7] Because managers and members of troubled groups often perceive, wrongly, that their performance problems are due mainly to interpersonal difficulties, they may turn to process-focused coaching as a remedy. But process consultation is unlikely to be helpful in such cases, precisely because the difficulties are structurally rooted. It is a near impossibility for members to learn how to interact well within a flawed or underspecified team structure.

Our research suggests that an enabling structure for a work team has three components. First is a well-designed team task, one that engages and sustains member motivation. Such tasks are whole and meaningful pieces of work that stretch members' skills, that provide ample autonomy for doing what needs to be done to accomplish the work, and that generate direct and trustworthy feedback about results. Second is a well-composed group. Such groups are as small as possible, have clear boundaries, include members with adequate task and interpersonal skills, and have a good mix of members—people who are neither so similar to one another that they are like peas in a pod nor so different that they are unable to work together. Third is clear and explicit specification of the basic norms of conduct for team behavior, the handful of "must do" and "must never do" behaviors that allow members to pursue their objectives without having to continuously discuss what kinds of behaviors are and are not acceptable. Although groups invariably develop their own norms over time, it is important to establish at the outset that members are expected to continuously monitor

---

[7]This point is reinforced in a quite different context by an essay written by Jo Freeman (1973) for her sisters in the feminist movement in the 1970s. The message of the essay is neatly captured by its title: "The Tyranny of Structurelessness."

their environment and to revise their performance strategy as needed when their work situation changes.

The key question about structure, then, is not *how much* of it a team has. Rather, it is about the *kind* of structure that is provided: Does it enable and support collective work, or does it make teamwork more difficult and frustrating than it need be?

Mistake 5: Specify Challenging Team Objectives, but Skimp on Organizational Supports

Even if a work team has clear, engaging direction and an enabling structure, its performance can go sour—or fall well below the group's potential—if it has insufficient organizational support. Teams in what Richard Walton (1985) calls "high commitment" organizations can fall victim to this mistake when they are given challenging objectives but not the resources to achieve them. Such teams often start out with great enthusiasm but then become disillusioned as they encounter frustration after frustration in trying to obtain the organizational supports they need to accomplish the work.

If the full potential of work teams is to be realized, organizational structures and systems must actively support competent teamwork. Key supports include (1) a reward system that recognizes and reinforces excellent team performance (not just individual contributions); (2) an educational system that provides teams, at their initiative, any training or technical consultation that may be needed to supplement members' own knowledge and expertise; (3) an information system that provides teams the data and forecasts members' need to proactively manage their work; and (4) the mundane material resources—equipment, tools, space, money, staff, or whatever—that the work requires.

It is no small undertaking to provide these supports to teams, especially in organizations that already have been tuned to support work performed by individuals. Existing performance appraisal systems, for example, may be state-of-the-art for measuring individual contributions but wholly inappropriate for assessing and rewarding work done by teams. Corporate compensation policy may make no provision for team bonuses and, indeed, may explicitly prohibit them. Human resource departments may be primed to identify individuals' training needs and to provide first-rate courses to fill those needs, but training in team skills may not be available at all. Information and control systems may provide senior managers with data that help them monitor and control overall organizational performance, but teams may not be able to get the information they need to autonomously manage their own work processes.

To align existing organizational systems with the needs of task-performing teams usually requires managers to exercise power and influence both upward and laterally in the organization, and may involve difficult negotiations across functional boundaries. For these reasons, providing contextual supports for teams can be a significant challenge for managers whose experience and expertise has mainly involved supporting and controlling work performed by individuals. That challenge is worth taking on, however, because an unsupportive organizational context can undermine even teams that are otherwise quite well directed and well structured. It is especially shattering for a team to fail merely because the organizational supports it needs cannot be obtained.

Mistake 6: Assume That Members Already Have All the Skills They Need to Work Well as a Team

Once a team has been formed and given its task, managers sometimes assume their work is done. A strict hands-off stance, however, can limit a team's effectiveness when members are not already skilled and experienced in teamwork—a not uncommon state of affairs in cultures where individualism is a dominant value.

It can be helpful, therefore, for leaders and managers to provide some coaching to individuals in honing their team skills and to the team as a whole in developing good group performance practices. There is no one best way to provide such help, nor is there any one best coaching style. Like teaching a class, coaching a group is done best when the leader exploits his or her own personality and style to get the lesson across.

Still, some things are known about the types of interventions that are helpful to teams and, importantly, about the times when different interventions are most likely to "take." All social systems, including task-performing teams, go through discernible stages or phases over time (Bales & Strodtbeck, 1951; Tuckman, 1965). Moreover, different task and interpersonal issues become salient for groups at those different times. The issues that are on members' minds when they first meet, for example, are quite different from those that command their attention as they are finishing up the work. Effective coaching interventions address issues that are naturally alive for the group at the particular time when they are made. Those that ask members to consider matters that are not salient for them at the time may do little other than distract the team from getting on with its work.

Recent research has identified three times in the life of a task-performing group when members are likely to be especially open to coaching interventions: (1) the beginning, when a group is just starting its work; (2) the midpoint, when half the work has been done and/or half the allotted time has passed; and (3) the end, when a piece of work has been finished.

There is much on a group's plate when members first come together to perform a piece of work—establishing the boundary that distinguishes members from nonmembers, starting to differentiate roles among members, developing initial norms about how members will work together, and engaging with (and, inevitably, redefining) the group task. Members' decisions about such matters, whether made explicitly or implicitly, establish a track for the group on which members stay for a considerable time (Gersick, 1988; Ginnett, 1993). A coaching intervention that helps a group have a good "launch" can significantly enhance members' engagement with each other, their commitment to the team, and their motivation to perform the work as well as they can. The payoff of a good launch can be substantial when, later in the team's life, members encounter thorny task or interpersonal challenges.

A second window for coaching interventions opens around the midpoint of the group's work. Research has shown that a group tends to stay on its initial track until about half of its allotted time has elapsed, at which point members experience a major upheaval that can result in a significant change in how they operate (Gersick, 1988). At such times (or at other natural breakpoints or low-workload periods), coaching interventions that encourage members to reflect on their work thus far and the challenges they next will face can be quite helpful to them in revising and improving their task-performance strategies.

The third special opportunity for coaching occurs at the end of a performance period—when the work is finished or a significant subtask has been accomplished. It is well established that people do not learn well when they brim with anxieties, including those that have to do with getting a piece of work finished on time and well. Because such anxieties dissipate once the work is finished, postperformance periods offer an especially good time for coaching interventions aimed at helping members capture and internalize the lessons that can be learned from their work experiences.

Although I am uneasy about the applicability of examples from athletic teams to work teams in organizations (both their tasks and their contexts are so different that generalization from one to the other must be done with caution), the behavior of good athletic coaches does illustrate the different coaching functions that can be performèd at different times in the life of a group. In the locker room before the game, coaches tend to focus on matters of *motivation*, establishing that the contest about to begin will be quite challenging but that the team has a real chance to win if members play hard and well. Halftime, back in the locker room, is a time for *consultation*, revising the game strategy for the second half of play based on how things have gone thus far. The next day, when the team has gathered to review the game films, is the time when coaches focus on *education*, helping to build individual and team proficiency in preparation for the team's next contest.[8]

There are, of course, many things that coaches can do at times other than those just discussed. They can, for example, be continuously alert for opportunities to recognize and reinforce competent team self-management, they can help the group obtain outside assistance or resources, and they can provide a generally supportive

---

[8]These three coaching functions reinforce the contributions of the structural and contextual features previously discussed. The motivational function reinforces the motivational benefits of a well-designed group task and of an organizational reward system that recognizes and rewards team excellence. The consultative function reinforces group norms that support team self-management and the group's use of data provided by the organizational information system. The educational function helps the group take advantage of both good composition (i.e., members who have an appropriate mix of task-relevant skills) and of organizational systems that provide teams with any needed training or technical consultation.

and encouraging context for teamwork. Still, these three times in the life of a group—the beginning, midpoint, and end—offer openings for coaching interventions that may be especially welcomed by group members and helpful to them.

No matter how well-designed, well-timed, and well-executed coaching interventions are, they are unlikely to be of much help if a team's overall performance situation is poor. If members are unclear about what they are supposed to accomplish, if the team or its task are badly designed, or if the surrounding organization places obstacle after obstacle in the team's path, then a leader would be well advised to focus first on solving these more fundamental problems. It is nearly impossible to coach a team to greatness in a performance situation that undermines rather than supports teamwork (Wageman, 1996).

A favorable performance situation, on the other hand, yields a double benefit: Teams are likely to have less need for coaching interventions (because they encounter fewer problems that lie beyond their own capabilities), and the coaching that they do receive is likely to be more helpful to them (because they are not preoccupied with more basic, structurally rooted difficulties). Over time, such teams may become skilled at coaching themselves and perhaps even enter into a self-fueling spiral of ever-increasing team capability and performance effectiveness—just the kind of pattern that is described in all the popular books that tout the benefits of organizational work teams.

Why It Doesn't Happen

Imagine a team whose leaders have made none of the six mistakes described in the preceding section. The following facts would be true for that team:

1. The task is one that is fully appropriate for performance by a team.
2. The team is an intact performing unit whose members perceive themselves as a team and that others deal with as such.
3. The team has a clear, authoritative, and engaging direction for its work.
4. The structure of the team—its task, composition, and core norms of conduct—promotes rather than impedes competent teamwork.
5. The organizational context provides support and reinforcement for excellence through policies and systems that are specifically tuned to the needs of work teams.
6. Ample, expert coaching is available to the team at those times when members most need it and are ready to receive it.

All of the evidence that my colleagues and I have been able to obtain suggests that a team for which these six conditions hold would be likely to perform very well. It is, however, much easier to create these conditions for some types of teams, and in some kinds of organizations, than in others.

Consider, for example, a product development team in an entrepreneurial organization. The product development process lends itself to teamwork because it requires coordinated contributions from several different specialties. Product development teams generally have a clear and engaging direction, and perform whole pieces of work for which they are relatively autonomous and about which they receive direct feedback (i.e., the product is created and works, or it isn't and doesn't). There are no built-in obstacles to composing the team well or to establishing task-appropriate norms of conduct. Such teams typically have access to the information and technical assistance they need for their work, and substantial rewards and recognition commonly are bestowed upon successful product development teams. With ample material resources and a little coaching to help in navigating the rough spots, there is no reason why most product development teams cannot be primed for good performance.

Start-up organizations, such as new plants or offices, also provide favorable settings for establishing the conditions that support team effectiveness. So long as those who design the new organizational unit are relatively free of structural or policy constraints imposed by a parent organization they should be able to design a team-based unit in which the six facts listed earlier are true.[9]

Yet most of the teams my colleagues and I have studied fall far short of meeting these six conditions. Why should this be so? The conditions themselves are not subtle, complex, or difficult to understand. Indeed, they are just the kinds of things that an alert manager surely could learn from experience. Are there more fundamental obstacles on the road to successfully structuring, supporting, and leading teams?

I have observed two such obstacles, one more commonly found in organizations that aspire to cooperative or democratic ideals, the other more characteristic of teams in established business corporations and public agencies.

The Co-Op Obstacle

It has always bothered me that we in the United States, who cherish the principles of political democracy, so infrequently apply those principles to the workplace. Some years ago, therefore, I took a close look at worker cooperatives, organizations whose charters explicitly embrace democracy and where all important matters are decided by membership vote. Some of the co-ops I examined were so small that the whole organization operated as a single work team; others were larger enterprises that had many teams within them.

I found a number of successful work teams in cooperative organizations, but also a surprisingly large number of failures. The reasons for the failures are instructive.

---

[9]It is not happenstance that some of the most successful team-based organizational start-ups have been located far from corporate headquarters. A remote location provides a measure of freedom from potentially constraining corporate systems and policies that is unavailable to units within sight of corporate offices. Indeed, a number of highly successful team-based start-ups have gotten into trouble when corporate managers eventually discovered that the start-up organization was ignoring or violating corporate policy in the interest of creating a favorable environment for teamwork. For the same reason, attempts to diffuse the lessons learned from remotely sited, team-based units back to headquarters facilities often are unsuccessful.

Too often, co-op members debated endlessly about their values, purposes, and collective directions—while competitors who had a more focused business strategy took their customers away. Collaboration and teamwork were so highly valued that virtually all tasks were done by teams, even those that would have been better performed by individuals. Equity and equality were such dominant values that members found it difficult to delegate real authority to any of their number. To maximize the choices of member-owners, team composition often was based solely on personal preference rather than on an analysis of the mix of skills that the work actually required. And, finally, I found members of many co-ops quite reluctant to establish and enforce use of organizational structures and systems that could have supported teams in their work.

The democratic ideals of co-ops are wholly consistent with the use of self-managing teams to perform work. It is ironic, therefore, that in cooperative organizations, those ideals so frequently get in the way of creating the very conditions that promote team effectiveness.

The "co-op mistake" also is occasionally seen in other organizations, including businesses and public agencies, where ideological considerations come to dominate decision making about organizational structures and practices. I had the good fortune to observe and document many of the innovative organizational practices that founder Don Burr and his colleagues developed at People Express Airlines in the 1980s. That company turned out to experience some of the same kinds of issues in structuring and supporting its many self-managing teams as do worker cooperatives, and for some of the same reasons.

Part of Burr's vision for People Express was to create a nonbureaucratic organization in which the inherent power of individuals and teams, locked up or suppressed in traditionally structured firms, could be unleashed in the service of customers, colleagues, and shareholders. To accomplish this, Burr and his senior management colleagues formulated a set of precepts that served as the guiding vision for the enterprise, they created self-managing teams throughout the company, and they made sure that every organization member was supported by leaders who had been well trained in the People Express precepts.

In its early years, when organization size was less than 1,000, People Express was a remarkable success—one of the fastest growing firms in the history of American business. Coordination among individuals and teams happened naturally in real time in the halls of the company offices at Newark airport, on airfield ramps, and in airplanes. Customers queued up to get seats on People Express, the company was the darling of Wall Street, and social scientists (including this one) wrote articles that described the company's innovative organizational form and probed the reasons for its success (Hackman, 1984).

As People Express grew, it became increasingly difficult for members to coordinate in halls and airplanes, and operational problems became frequent and severe enough that many backers of the organization suggested that the time had come to beef up the organization, to install structures and systems to support its self-managing workforce. To do so, however, would have been a retreat from the values on which People Express had been founded—namely, the transcending power of vision and leadership to unleash and direct the energies of organization members.

Values prevailed. Rather than installing the structures and systems that his backers advocated, Burr and his colleagues redoubled their efforts to ensure that all members of the organization deeply understood the company's vision and added even more trained leaders to coach and teach organization members. In a time of trouble, the founders reaffirmed the principles that had been responsible for their early success and behaved more vigorously than ever in accord with them.

It did not work. As People Express continued to grow, and as other airlines developed strategies for competing with it in the marketplace, financial and operational results deteriorated further. Eventually, disillusionment set in for some organization members and, finally, the operation itself cratered. At that point, it was only a matter of time until the company was acquired by a competitor and People Express ceased to exist.

In both the worker cooperatives and People Express Airlines, ideological currents ran strong and deep. And in both cases, perversely, those strong collective values made it nearly impossible for leaders to install the structural and contextual features that are among the key conditions for team effectiveness. These organizations, and many like them, attest to the fact that visionary direction and abundant coaching, by themselves, are insufficient to ensure the success of work teams in organizations.

The Corporate Obstacle

Many existing businesses and public agencies have in place organizational structures, systems, and policies that have been tuned over the years to control and support work performed by *individual* employees. Managers are understandably reluctant to overturn well-established organizational features just to see whether work teams actually generate the benefits claimed for them. Veteran managers have, after all, weathered quite a number of organizational innovations that had their origins in the behavioral sciences—management by objectives, job enrichment, T-groups, zero defects, quality of worklife, gain sharing, and a multitude of others. And, no doubt, there will be more to come after work teams have had their day and passed on.

There are two different strategies that managers use to implement work teams without upsetting the corporate applecart. One is to try to capture the benefits of teamwork by relying mainly on rhetoric and training. Members are told that they are now in teams, team leaders are appointed, and everyone is sent off to get training in good team processes. It is easy to implement teams this way—neither organizational structures nor managers' own behaviors need change. But such teams are more ephemeral than real, and mere changes in appearances rarely yield measurable improvements in organizational outcomes.

The second strategy is to form real teams—intact, performing units whose members share responsibility for some product or service—but to lay them atop existing organizational structures and systems. The rationale, as one manager told me, is to see how well they perform before making other organizational changes that could be hard to reverse. With this strategy, one typically sees encouraging results early in the lives of the new teams, followed by a gradual diminution of both team performance and member commitment as the teams encounter obstacles rooted in long-standing and team-unfriendly organizational arrangements. That pattern is inevitable, I believe, when one seeks to obtain the benefits of work teams on the cheap, without providing them the organizational supports that they need to prosper over the long term.

In the foreword to *Self-Directed Work Teams* (Osburn et al., 1990), David Hanna, then-manager of organization development at Proctor & Gamble, identifies skepticism as the largest single roadblock to team success: "Beware of skepticism!" he warns. "Doubt your doubts.... Self-directed teams really do work" (pp. vii–viii). Indeed they can—but not without providing them the direction, structure, contextual supports, and coaching that makes excellent teamwork possible. And those supports turn out to be harder to arrange in established corporations and public agencies than is usually acknowledged either by managers who form teams or social scientists who study them.

Roots of the Obstacles

The co-op obstacle and the corporate obstacle are two sides of essentially the same coin. In both cases, there is an unwillingness or inability to establish the set of conditions that enable teams to perform well. For co-ops, the reluctance stems from an ideologically based preference for vision and leadership over hierarchy, structure, and bureaucracy. For corporations, the problem is the unfriendliness to teams of those organizational structures and systems that already exist—and with which managers are reluctant to meddle.

The reason why these obstacles are so pervasive and hard to circumvent is that both their co-op and corporate versions reflect what sociologists call "institutional" forces (DiMaggio & Powell, 1983; Zucker, 1977). Institutional forces result in organizations situated in similar environments becoming increasingly similar and persistent over time.[10] They specify a set of "right answers" for organizational design

---

[10]Specifically, DiMaggio and Powell (1983) identify three processes that foster similarities across organizations and the temporal persistence of organizational features. Mimetic or imitative processes involve organizations turning to others of the same general type, especially those that are viewed as successful, as guides for how their own enterprise should be structured. Normative processes involve the cross-organization diffusion of socially defined "correct" ways of operating. It is not so much a question of how things actually are done in other enterprises, but what infused values and community expectations specify about how they *should* be done. Coercive processes involve agents with legitimate authority (such as government representatives) specifying how certain things must be done.

and management, and they are notoriously difficult to redirect—even in the face of resolute managerial action or significant environmental shocks (Allmendinger & Hackman, 1996).

Countering institutional forces is not management as usual. Nor do such forces yield gracefully to planned organizational change programs of the flipchart and to-do-list variety. As will be seen next, creating organizational conditions that support work teams is, more often than not, something of a revolutionary act.

What It Takes

The conditions that foster team effectiveness are simple and seemingly straight-forward to put in place. A real team with work that lends itself to teamwork. A clear and engaging direction. A group structure—task, composition, and norms—that promotes competent teamwork. Team-friendly reward, educational, and information systems. And some coaching to help team members take advantage of their favorable performance circumstances.

Yet to install these simple conditions is also to determine the answers to four fundamental questions about how an enterprise operates:

1. *Who decides*? Who has the right to make decisions about how the work will be carried out, and to determine how problems that develop will be resolved?
2. *Who is responsible*? Where do responsibility and accountability for perfor-mance outcomes ultimately reside?
3. *Who gains*? How are monetary rewards allocated among the individuals and groups that helped generate them?
4. *Who learns*? How are opportunities for learning, growth, and career advance-ment distributed among organization members?

The answers to these four questions express some of the core values of any enterprise, and it can be maddeningly hard to change them. For one thing, to change the answers to the four questions is almost certain to threaten the turf and personal interests of currently powerful organizational actors. These individuals are therefore likely to find lots of good reasons why it would be ill-advised or excessively risky to alter standard ways of operating.

Moreover, the answers to the four questions are, in established organizations, supported by deeply rooted institutional structures: the authority structure ("Who decides?"), the work structure ("Who is responsible?"), the reward structure ("Who gains?"), and the opportunity structure ("Who learns?"). These structures not only give an organization much of its identity, but they also promote predictability and continuity over time. Predictability and continuity are much to be valued during times of business as usual. But when circumstances change and innovations such as work teams are called for, these deep structures can be among the strongest impediments to getting teams in place and working well.

Indeed, it may be that fundamental change can be accomplished in an established organization only when it has become destabilized for some other reason—for example, the departure of a senior manager, the rapid growth or dissolution of an organizational unit, financial disaster, or the introduction of a new technology that requires abandonment of standard ways of operating. Fundamental change cannot be accomplished either as an "add-on" (as managers in some corporations appear to wish) or as a one-step transition to utopia (as members of some cooperative enterprises appear to wish).

Creating organizational conditions that actively support work teams, therefore, is in many organizations more a revolutionary than evolutionary undertaking. And people get hurt in revolutions—especially those who lead them, and even when they are successful.

Consider the experience of Pete Townsend (not his real name), a production manager at a semiconductor plant where David Abramis and I conducted some research several years ago (Abramis, 1990). Pete had started out as a production worker at the plant. Although he had no formal training in semiconductor manufacturing (indeed, he was studying at night for his high school diploma), he thought he had a better idea about how to make semiconductors. Over time, he promulgated what turned out to be something of a revolution in using self-managing teams to manufacture memory chips.

Pete began to experiment with his idea shortly after being prompted to manage one of the plant's production units (called a "fab"). He converted serial production lines, the standard work design in semiconductor manufacturing, into small teams, each with major responsibility for one part of the chip. Team members learned each others' jobs, took on increasing responsibility for quality control, and were encour-aged to do whatever needed to be done within the bounds of their limited authority to increase yield (i.e., the proportion of usable chips relative to the total number of starts).

Initial results were encouraging. Yields increased, production workers seemed pleased with their new responsibilities, and managers of other fabs began to take an interest in what Pete was doing. Then Pete called me up one day and said, "I think you ought to come out for a visit. There have been some interesting developments at the plant." Whenever Pete called, I would come, as I was fascinated by what this home-taught manager was up to. It just happened that the corporate vice president for human resources was visiting the plant the same day that I was. And it just happened that we three found ourselves having coffee in Pete's conference room, talking over what he was learning from his team experiment. As if scripted, I asked, "So how are the teams going?" "Big problems," he responded. "Yields are great, but team members are noticing that *somebody* is making more money now than they used to—and it isn't them." I reacted as Pete no doubt knew I would. "This is serious. Unless you provide them some kind of rewards and recognition based on team performance, the whole thing could crater." "Can't do it," he responded. "All I have to work with is an end-of-year bonus pool, and I can only use it to reward outstanding *individual* performers. Doing that could undermine the teams."

The conversation followed the course that Pete no doubt had anticipated when he arranged for the vice president and me to visit on the same day. By the end of the meeting, he had obtained from the vice president an exception to corporate compensation policy that enabled him to offer his teams performance-contingent financial rewards. Over the next year, Pete did the same kind of thing with the plant's director of maintenance (so that all teams would have their own maintenance support persons who would get to know their particular equipment, and from whom they could learn how to perform basic maintenance tasks on their own) and with the director of engineering (so that engineers would consult with team leaders to arrange times for process tests that would not disrupt regular production work). Given that the corporation took its compensation policy quite seriously, and that both maintenance and engineering personnel stood much higher in the plant status hierarchy than did hired-off-the-street production workers, the special arrangements Pete negotiated were extraordinary political accomplishments.

The production teams continued to perform well, although their rate of improvement slowed considerably. And Pete still kept them on a relatively short leash, retaining unto himself decision-making authority about those matters he considered most important. Abramis and I finished up our research, which showed that although there was much to admire in what Pete had created, the teams were not really self-managing. And then, prompted by an economic downturn in the semiconductor industry, Pete finally decided to go all the way. The production teams, he declared, would now be called "asset management teams," and they would be given authority to manage all of their resources in pursing collective objectives.

The transition to asset management teams was difficult, as transitions always are when decision-making authority and accountability for outcomes are altered. But eventually the changes "took," and performance measures for Pete's fab reached new highs. Indeed, his unit was more profitable than any comparable unit in the company, and he began receiving visitors not just from headquarters but also from managers at other high-technology manufacturing firms. By all measures, Pete had achieved a great success with his work teams.

Not long thereafter, I received another telephone call from him. "Probably you ought to come out for another visit," he said. "This time to say good-bye. They've decided that some changes need to be made in my area, and the main change is going to be me." It turned out that the human resources department recently had completed its annual employee attitude survey, and the job satisfaction of people in Pete's area had dropped from previous levels. That was the reason given to Pete for his termination. It was the only time in my many years of organizational research that I have heard of someone whose production numbers are at the top of the scale being fired because of a dip in scores on an attitude survey.

Pete went too far. Drawing both on his intuitive understanding of what it takes to make a great team and on his considerable political skill, he had succeeded in putting in place almost all of the conditions that are needed to foster work-team effectiveness. His work was revolutionary, and it was more than his organization could tolerate.

People get hurt in revolutions. Especially those who lead them. Even when they are successful.[11]

Thinking Differently about Teams

Because creating and supporting work teams in organizations often requires the redirection of strong institutional forces, the activity is more appropriately viewed as revolutionary than as management-as-usual. Let me conclude this chapter by suggesting that both research on teams and competent leadership of them also require unconventionality in how one *thinks about* teams and the factors that affect their performance.

Scholars and organizational actors construe influences on work-team performance differently. We scholars want to know specifically what causes the performance outcomes that obtain. To find this out, we deconstruct the performance situation, first conceptually, and then empirically—perhaps in a laboratory experiment that isolates the suspected causal factors or using structural equation modeling with survey data. We want to rule out as many alternative explanations for the focal phenomenon as we can. We want to pin down the *true* causal agent.

Organizational actors, on the other hand, are not much interested in teasing out the relative influence of various possible causes of performance. Instead, they are prepared to draw upon all resources at their disposal to overdetermine outcomes in the direction they prefer. They welcome rather than shun both the confounding of variables (which is the bane of research that seeks to make unambiguous attributions about causality) and redundant causes (which is a sign, in scientific work, that concepts have not yet been specified clearly enough).

Although the preferences of scientists and practitioners do differ, they are not mutually exclusive. There is no a priori reason why one cannot generate models of social-system phenomena that are, at the same time, conceptually sound, capable of guiding constructive action, and amenable to empirical assessment and correction. The model of team performance described in this chapter was generated in that spirit. Rather than specify the main causes of group productivity (or provide a long list of all possible causes), I have proposed a small set of conditions that, when present, increase the chances—but by no means guarantee—that a group will develop into an effective performing unit.

To think about the conditions within which groups chart their own courses is very different from conventional scholarly models (in which the attempt is to link causes tightly to effects) as well as from action strategies that derive from those models (in which practitioners attempt to manage team processes more or less continuously in real time). As a metaphor, consider two alternative strategies that could be used by a

---

[11]Pete spent several months in a corporate outplacement center looking for work, and eventually accepted a position as production manager at a box manufacturing plant in Mexico. Some months later, he moved back to the United States and shortly thereafter suffered a fatal heart attack.

pilot landing an aircraft. One strategy is to "fly the airplane down," continuously adjusting heading, sink rate, and airspeed with the objective of arriving at the runway threshold just above stall speed, ready to flare the aircraft and touch down smoothly. A second strategy is to get the aircraft stabilized on approach while still far from the field, making small corrections as needed to heading, power, or aircraft configuration to keep the plane "in the groove." It is well known among pilots that the safer strategy is the second one; indeed, when a pilot finds that he or she is in the first situation, the prudent action is to go around and try the approach again.[12]

To be stabilized on approach is to have the basic conditions established such that the natural course of events leads to the desired outcome—in this case, a good landing. The same way of thinking applies in many other domains of human endeavor. Consider, for example, constantly tinkering with a nation's interest rates, money supply, and tax policies versus getting fundamentally sound economic conditions in place and letting the economy run itself. Or micromanaging the development of a child versus creating a good family context that promotes healthy, autonomous development by the family's youngest member. Or managing a physical injury such as a moderately serious burn with surgery and multiple drugs versus fostering the general health of the patient and letting the body heal itself. Or trying to foster creativity by telling someone to "Be creative" and giving the person lots of creativity exercises versus providing a relaxing and resource-rich setting and letting the creative response appear when it will.

In all of these instances, the better strategy is to devote the first and greater portion of one's energies to establishing conditions that lead naturally to the desired outcomes and the lesser portion to on-line process management. The same considerations apply to the design and management of social systems, very much including work teams in organizations.

The implications for leaders and members of work teams are clear. Their first priority should be to get in place the basic conditions that foster team effectiveness. In this chapter, I have attempted to summarize what is known about those conditions, and I have pointed out that establishing and sustaining them is a far-from-routine undertaking in many existing organizations. Once the basic conditions are in place,

---

[12]Because I wanted to make sure that the technical details of this example were correct, I asked Jack Maher, a Delta Airlines captain, to review it. His response amplifies the point of the example: "The first strategy is typical of pilots who are new to an airplane. They tend to overcontrol because they are behind the airplane, see change too late, and make aggressive control inputs that are usually excessive. They cognitively tunnel on the control instruments and have a very limited ability to sense and process environmental cues. New pilots also tend to be procedure bound, which for them is safer. But if a pilot flies like that all the time, we know immediately he or she is weak, flying is a struggle, and the pilot is not having fun. The second strategy is where we like to be. In sports psychology it is called optimum flow, such as in basketball when you become one with the game. Although I joke about it with other pilots, I hum to myself during approach and landing to facilitate the state of flow. The nice result is that in this state I can see more of the environment and expand my cognitive ability to plan adaptive responses to future events. For example, in bad weather I envision the picture I expect to see when we break out of the clouds, I can see where a missed approach would take me, and if I lose an engine I know how I can modify the miss to get more performance out of the airplane and avoid terrain and obstacles."

then leaders and members can "manage at the margins," making small adjustments and corrections as needed to smooth a group's progress toward its objectives. As Wageman (1996) has pointed out, dealing with emergent team problems and opportunities is manyfold easier—and far more likely to be successful—if conditions favorable to team performance are already in place.

The challenge for social scientists is to take more seriously than we have heretofore the implications of thinking about social systems in terms of conditions rather than causes.[13] Moreover, we need to find ways to study the evolution of social systems that do not destroy or caricature systemic phenomena in order to make them amenable to study using conventional cause–effect conceptual models and research methodologies.

Both scholars and practitioners compromise their own espoused objectives when they hold constant conditions that may be among the most substantial influences on their phenomena of interest. Yet we regularly do this: Researchers do it to achieve experimental control, and practitioners do it to preserve established organizational structures and systems. Until both scholars and practitioners accept the risks of revolution and break out of traditional ways of construing and leading social systems, chapters such as this one will continue to be about why teams don't work rather than why they do.

References

Abramis, D. J. (1990). Semiconductor manufacturing team. In J. R. Hackman (Ed.), *Groups that work (and those that don't)*. San Francisco: Jossey-Bass.

Alderfer, C. P. (1977). Group and intergroup relations. In J. R. Hackman & J. L. Suttle (Eds.), *Improving life at work*. Santa Monica, CA: Goodyear.

Allmendinger, J., & Hackman, J. R. (1996). Organizations in changing environments: The case of East German symphony orchestras. *Administrative Science Quarterly, 41*, 337–369.

Bales, R. F., & Strodtbeck, F. L. (1951). Phases in group problem solving. *Journal of Abnormal and Social Psychology, 46*, 485–495.

Cohen, S. G., & Ledford, G. E., Jr. (1994). The effectiveness of self-managing teams: A quasi-experiment. *Human Relations, 47*, 13–43.

Cordery, J. L., Mueller, W. S., & Smith, L. M. (1991). Attitudinal and behavioral effects of autonomous group working: A longitudinal field study. *Academy of Management Journal, 34*, 464–476.

DiMaggio, P. J., & Powell, W. W. (1983). The iron cage revisited: Institutional isomorphism and collective rationality in organizational fields. *American Sociological Review, 48*, 147–160.

Foushee, H. C., Lauber, J. K., Baetge, M. M., & Acomb, D. B. (1986). *Crew factors in flight operations: III. The operational significance of exposure to short-haul air transport operations* (Technical Memorandum No. 88342). Moffett Field, CA: NASA–Ames Research Center.

Freeman, J. (1973). The tyranny of structurelessness. In A. Koedt, E. Levine, & A. Rapone (Eds.), *Radical feminism*. New York: Quadrangle Books.

---

[13] Among possible leads for pursuing this possibility is the principle of "equifinality" set forth by systems theorists such as Daniel Katz and Robert Kahn (1978, p. 30), and the theory of multiple possibilities proposed by Leona Tyler (1983). Whereas equifinality alerts us to the fact that the same outcome can occur in response to many causes, multiple possibility theory posits that the same cause can generate a variety of outcomes. Taken together, the two notions offer an intriguing alternative to standard stimulus–response models in which situational causes are tightly linked to behavioral effects.

Gersick, C. J. G. (1988). Time and transition in work teams: Toward a new model of group development. *Academy of Management Journal, 31*, 9–41.

Ginnett, R. C. (1993). Crews as groups: Their formation and their leadership. In E. L. Wiener, B. G. Kanki, & R. L. Helmreich (Eds.), *Cockpit resource management*. Orlando, FL: Academic Press.

Gunn, C. E. (1984). *Workers' self-management in the United States*. Ithaca, NY: Cornell University Press.

Hackman, J. R. (1984). The transition that hasn't happened. In J. R. Kimberly & R. E. Quinn (Eds.), *New futures: The challenge of managing corporate cultures*. Homewood, IL: Dow Jones–Irwin.

Hackman, J. R. (1985). Doing research that makes a difference. In E. E. Lawler, A. M. Mohrman, S. A. Mohrman, G. E. Ledford, & T. G. Cummings (Eds.), *Doing research that is useful for theory and practice*. San Francisco: Jossey-Bass.

Hackman, J. R. (1986). The psychology of self-management in organizations. In M.S. Pallack & R. O. Perloff (Eds.), *Psychology and work: Productivity, change, and employment*. Washington, DC: American Psychological Association.

Hackman, J. R. (Ed.). (1990). *Groups that work (and those that don't)*. San Francisco: Jossey-Bass.

Hackman, J. R. (1993). Teams, leaders, and organizations: New directions for crew-oriented flight training. In E. L. Wiener, B. G. Kanki, & R. L. Helmreich (Eds.), *Cockpit resource management*. Orlando, FL: Academic Press.

Helmreich, R. L., & Foushee, H. C. (1993). Why crew resource management? Empirical and theoretical bases of human factors training in aviation. In E. L. Wiener, B. G. Kanki, & R. L. Helmreich (Eds.), *Cockpit resource management*. Orlando, FL: Academic Press.

Jackson, P. R., Mullarkey, S., & Parker, S. (1994, January). *The implementation of high-involvement work teams: A four-phase longitudinal study*. Paper presented at the Occupational Psychology Conference of the British Psychological Society, Birmingham, UK.

Janis, I. L. (1982). *Groupthink* (2nd ed.) Boston: Houghton Mifflin.

Katz, D., & Kahn, R. L. (1978). *The social psychology of organizations*. New York: Wiley.

National Transportation Safety Board. (1994). *A review of flightcrew-involved, major accidents of U.S. air carriers, 1978 through 1990*. Washington, DC: Author.

Osburn, J. D., Moran, L., Musselwhite, E., & Zenger, J. H. (1990). *Self-directed work teams: The new American challenge*. Homewood, IL: Business One Irwin.

Osterman, P. (1994). How common is workplace transformation and who adopts it? *Industrial and Labor Relations Review, 47*, 172–188.

Poza, E. J., & Marcus, M. L. (1980, Winter). Success story: The team approach to work restructuring. *Organizational Dynamics*, 3–25.

Roethlisberger, F. J., & Dickson, W. J. (1939). *Management and the worker*. Cambridge, MA: Harvard University Press.

Steiner, I. D. (1972). *Group process and productivity*. New York: Academic Press.

Tuckman, B. W. (1965). Developmental sequence in small groups. *Psychological Bulletin, 63*, 384–399.

Tyler, L. E. (1983). *Thinking creatively: A new approach to psychology and individual lives*. San Francisco: Jossey-Bass.

Wageman, R. (1995). Interdependence and group effectiveness. *Administrative Science Quarterly, 40*, 145–180.

Wageman, R. (1996). *A field study of leadership of self-managing teams: The effects of design choices and coaching*. Unpublished manuscript, Graduate School of Business, Columbia University, New York.

Wall, T. D., Kemp, N. J., Jackson, P. R., & Clegg, C. W. (1986). Outcomes of autonomous work groups: A long-term field experiment. *Academy of Management Journal, 29*, 280–304.

Walton, R. E. (1980). Establishing and maintaining high commitment work systems. In J. R. Kimberly & R. H. Miles (Eds.), *The organizational life cycle*. San Francisco: Jossey-Bass.

Walton, R. E. (1985). From control to commitment: Transformation of workforce management strategies in the United States. In K. B. Clark, R. H. Hayes, & C. Lorenz (Eds.), *The uneasy alliance: Managing the productivity–technology dilemma*. Boston: Harvard Business School Press.

Zucker, L. G. (1977). The role of institutionalization in cultural persistence. *American Sociological Review, 42*, 726–743.

Index

St. Louis Community College
at Meramec
Library